# Adventurous
# Use of the Sea

Design and composition by Claire MacMaster
barefoot art graphic design

Printed by Printworks Global Ltd., London & Hong Kong

First Edition

# *Adventurous Use of the Sea*

Formidable Stories of a
Century of Sailing from the
Cruising Club of America

TIM MURPHY

*Editor, Sheila McCurdy*

# Contents

# A BRIEF HISTORY OF THE CRUISING CLUB OF AMERICA

The Cruising Club of America was born of the desire of a group of dedicated cruising sailors to form a club in North America similar to the Royal Cruising Club in Britain. Foremost in their objectives was the promotion of ocean voyaging in small yachts, the sharing of information regarding destinations, the development of suitable cruising yacht designs and the celebration of the accomplishments of oceangoing sailors. In 1922 thirty-four Charter Members formally launched the Cruising Club, outlining rules for membership and participation, electing officers, and adopting the signal of the Club, the blue wave on a white field that has been flown proudly by the membership for 100 years. In its earliest pronouncements the Cruising Club proclaimed:

> *"Let us refuse stoutly to accumulate an on-shore contingent: let the membership in the Club be a mark of achievement. This policy will give us a standing at home and abroad such as no American yacht club has ever had. Besides, it will make the Club burgee a bit of bunting that all afloat will respect, and that sea lovers everywhere will strive to possess. Thus, we shall become an active force influencing others to make adventurous use of the sea."*

And true to that sentiment, the CCA has remained a club without a clubhouse and invites into its membership only truly qualified bluewater yachtsmen and women who are considered good shipmates. Over the many decades of the club's existence there have occurred, and sometimes even raged, debates concerning the compatibility of cruising and racing in our activities. But the actions of the Club speak for themselves and the CCA has, since 1926 served alongside the Royal Bermuda Yacht Club in sponsoring the Newport Bermuda Race and, consistent with its original objectives, has fostered the development of rating rules and safety guidance to ensure the healthy support of ocean racing.

Since its founding, the Cruising Club has grown to a membership totaling over 1400. Members yachts total over 1000 in number and average 41.3 feet in length. Its activities are organized around eleven Stations and three Posts stretching from Bermuda to the Pacific Northwest, from Southern California to Nova Scotia. While a large portion of the membership has traditionally clustered on the East coast, vibrant activity has extended to the Great Lakes and the West coast as well. Cruises, both regional and club-wide have always been part to the calendar and in early years targeted sites near New York and Boston only to expand to the Caribbean in later decades. More recent cruises have ranged as broadly as to New Zealand, the Ionian Sea, the Baltic and Thailand. The original objectives of the Club are carried out through the publication of Cruising Guides which share important destinations, the celebration of members' accomplishments and writing with the annual publication of *Voyages,* the continuing advancement of safety-at-sea education for members and the wider community, and the presentation of Awards such as the Blue Water Medal, Far Horizon Award and Young Voyagers Award which are recognized around the world as honoring important bluewater passages. The Club's continuous leadership in yacht racing rating rules development since the 1920's has produced safer and faster yachts and helped to make both racing and cruising more widely embraced.

The history of the Cruising Club of America is packed with fascinating characters, some famous and others less so, who have extended the range of cruising in small vessels to the world over. Members have served in war with great distinction. They have added to our knowledge of the environment of the sea. The Club has welcomed women into its ranks since 1994 and the contribution of female members has been immeasurable. Sailors young and old, on yachts powered by sail and motor, on seas throughout the world have added to the lore of the CCA.

Some years ago the yachting author and past CCA Historian John Rousmaniere compiled an excellent history of the Club in an article written for *Nautical Quarterly.* A summary was published more recently in the Cruising Club's semi-annual news publication *The Gam* and can be found on the CCA website. It makes great reading and provides the flavor for the Club and its activities.

And so, the Cruising Club has successfully navigated its first century and stands poised to continue to foster "Adventurous Use of the Sea."

Douglas Adkins
Historian

# FOREWORD BY THE COMMODORE

In this the 100th year of the existence of the Cruising Club of America, we celebrate its wonderful history, the fabric of which is woven by sailors and their yachts over the years. "Adventurous Use of the Sea" is a phrase that harkens back to the intrepid founders of the CCA in 1922. It is still the touchstone for membership in this unique yachting club that has no clubhouse. The CCA thrives on the energy of its 1,400+ members who sail far and wide across the seas of the world. Tim Murphy, in this book, vividly captures the essence of the CCA with stories of past and present members, their love of the sea and their bonds of friendship. The Brief History of the CCA, by present Historian Doug Adkins, preceding this page, serves as context for these great stories.

This September, 2022, in Newport, Rhode Island, will be a proper Centennial Celebration of the CCA, bringing hundreds of members together to conduct the business of the Club and, more importantly, to talk about shared experiences on the ocean to learn from each other and revel in the rich history of the CCA. The 11 Stations and 3 Posts serve as the regional geocenters of the Club and generally have their activities at a leading yacht club in their area. There are monthly luncheons with speakers often detailing unique sea stories and local organized "gams" or cruises that get everyone out on local waters. There are over 1,000 yachts in the CCA fleet, both sail and power, that seek adventure on the sea. Cruises over the years have included Scotland, Ireland, Turkey, Greece, New Zealand, Grenada, Nova Scotia, Newfoundland, British Columbia, Bermuda, the Azores and more.

The Club has, as one if its main activities, the sponsoring of Safety at Sea seminars that are designed to help sailors engage in proper preparation of yacht and crew for going to sea. These seminars are often held in the lead up to the Newport Bermuda Race. The Bermuda Race, now beginning its second century, is co-hosted by the Royal Bermuda Yacht Club and the CCA. Run every other year in even numbered years, it offers a unique offshore racing experience and because of the Gulfstream and its attendant weather systems, it is considered one of the top offshore races in the world. The story of the yacht *Dorade* is detailed in these pages, and offers us a serious example of a unique yacht, now in its 10th decade of life and its storied racing heritage in the Bermuda Race, as well as transatlantic and transpacific yacht races.

I would be remiss in not mentioning the close relationship of Mystic Seaport to the CCA, which houses the CCA archives. The CCA burgee has flown over the Mystic Seaport for decades and CCA members have been and continue to

*Adventurous Use of the Sea*

be closely involved in Mystic activities. Another charitable outreach by the CCA is the Bonnell Cove Foundation, a 501c3 organization that provides grants to worthy maritime causes including junior sailing.

This book is the product of the hard work of Tim Murphy as the author as well as its editor, Sheila McCurdy, a past commodore of the CCA and well respected lecturer at Safety at Sea seminars. The CCA is grateful for the tremendous effort that has gone into this book and hopefully you as the reader will enjoy these stories and be inspired by the sailors profiled in these pages.

Fair Winds to All,

Christopher L. Otorowski
Commodore
Cruising Club of America

# Ocean Sailing for the Fun of the Thing

*By gathering into a group all who are fond of off-shore work, we sow the wilderness of the sea with a host of acquaintances, for whose houseflags we shall always be expectantly watching. And we convert the winter into a season of sport, wherein those who have been afloat swap their summer's experiences with each other, and share them with their unfortunate shorebound club-fellows.*
—Henry Wise Wood, 1923

I am not a member of the Cruising Club of America, the celebrated group of passionate ocean voyagers founded in 1922, and this is no insider's clubhouse tour. (The CCA is proud to report that it has no clubhouse.) Rather, this book is an appreciation of some adventuresome sailing pioneers from a club that's full of them, men and women who built the boats and roamed the oceans and planted the seeds for a thriving community of cruising sailors in America and beyond. In the broad sense, I am a lifelong member of that club.

You may be a sailor, or maybe not. No matter. Open this book to any chapter heading and tuck into a ripping-good sea story about people from all walks of life—people with and without substantial means, people who did and did not grow up sailing, people who shared a deep curiosity about life, the ocean, and the intricacies of boat design. Or read the whole book from beginning to end, and another story will emerge running through and alongside all the others. The larger story is a hundred years of disagreements, refinements, dissents, and high-stakes bets that ultimately lead to the fleet of boats we know today—also, to a sumptuous profusion of ways to use them. Maybe you'll see something you'd like to try.

On re-reading a draft manuscript of this book, I noticed that I'd repeated the same Homeric phrase in several of the chapters: something about a person or a boat "that launched a thousand ships." The finished version of the book omits that repetition, but the point is real and—in this age of boats mass-produced from fiberglass-reinforced plastic—accurate. CCA founder Bill Nutting, a marine journalist at the time, was drinking with a buddy in the Prohibition winter of 1923 when he came across the lines for a 47-foot Colin Archer North Sea lifeboat. Fascinated, he reduced them to 32 feet, the smallest size that he thought would still permit sitting headroom under the side decks in the main saloon. What started as one man's spirited flight of fancy became the *Eric* design attributed to William Atkin, which five decades later became the Westsail 32 of which some 833 were built and sold, or 1,100 if you count the subsequent modifications. Carleton Mitchell, a Navy photographer during

World War II, spent years doodling and dreaming of the boat that would correct the faults of his John Alden-designed ketch or his Phil Rhodes-designed yawl. The result, the Olin Stephens-designed *Finisterre,* won three consecutive Bermuda Races and starred in a series of mid-1960s *National Geographic* magazine features that extolled Caribbean sailing. Within just a couple of seasons, beamy centerboard sailboats proliferated, and so did a brand-new Caribbean bareboat charter industry. In 2007 *The Wall Street Journal* profiled Minnesota hog farmer, Roger Swanson, and the crew of *Cloud Nine* as they became the first American yacht to transit the Northwest Passage in a single season. Before then, yachts in ones and twos attempted the passage and often failed or spent several seasons trying; since then, in a warming climate, hundreds of yachts have transited in *Cloud Nine's* unencumbered wake. Cal 40 designer Bill Lapworth also created the 24-foot fiberglass sloop, *Dove,* that 16-year-old Robin Lee Graham singlehanded most of the way around the world in the late 1960s, inspiring a generation of new voyagers who followed his travels in *National Geographic.* Doug Fryer's realization that he wouldn't be able to retrieve a hypothermic person gone overboard in Puget Sound led to the Lifesling that's so ubiquitous on today's boats. And the example of Irving and Exy Johnson and their seven circumnavigations aboard a schooner and a brigantine, both named *Yankee,* rippled out to multiple tens of thousands of students introduced to the sea. The subjects in these chapters, by and large, had an outsized influence on the people and boats we meet on the water today.

People and boats. Boats and people. Throughout these stories, boats are main characters, too. What *Dorade* did, *Belvedere* could never do, yet both were exemplary purpose-built boats destined for the yachting history books. *Cloud Nine* was perfect because she accommodated so many people; *Nereida* was perfect because she accommodated so few. The first two *Yankees* needed bigness to accomplish the Johnsons' mission of educating young people on back-to-back circumnavigations from 1932 through 1958; the third *Yankee* needed relative smallness to fulfill their evolving goals through the 1970s. In this succession of stories, you'll notice that relationships between sailors and boats can run as deep as those between lovers, and sometimes deeper.

A wonderful thing happens when you ask two or more people about what happened, and when. Never mind how or why. As often as not, two tellings of the same event contradict each other with a perfectly pitched counterpoise. It's the same for published documents. On one page of *The Track of the Typhoon*, Bill Nutting tells us that in October 1920 he was having his first design discussion with Casey Baldwin in Nova Scotia for the boat that would take them on their future transatlantic voyage; on a subsequent page he tells us that in November 1920, *Typhoon* was beating her way across New York Harbor, with two transatlantic voyages, plus the boat's designing and building, all behind her. One sailor recalls a Northwest Passage transit as ice-free, as a historic change in Arctic navigation; another crewmember says the passage wasn't ice-free but that the boat simply had better reporting equipment that year. "And if you want to believe Dad's lobster stories," says Alex Kuhner, "that's on you."

For my part, I've aimed to fix clear factual errors in the source material where possible, but to let different voices ring out in their vigorous diversity where the room for interpretation permits.

This book isn't a comprehensive history of the CCA, and there are far more great sea stories out there than there was room to tell within these covers. Cruising Club members and sailorly insiders can read this book as they'd watch the Academy Awards, finding the CCA equivalent of Oscar snubs aplenty. For the subjects that are featured here, the chapters avoid lifetime-achievement hagiographies. Some stories don't even depict the subject's greatest accomplishment. Instead they might focus on a learning curve, early steps that brought mere mortals *toward* their eternal seats in the pantheon of bluewater sailors, steps the rest of us might imagine we ourselves could emulate.

Back in 1922 the Cruising Club of America members first gathered together and tried some brash experiments with a single aim: to promote ocean sailing for the fun of the thing. Race to Bermuda? One of the club's charter members, Herb Stone, editor of *Yachting* magazine and an energetic ocean-sailing cheerleader, set this objective: "To encourage the designing, building, and sailing of small seaworthy yachts, to make popular cruising upon deep water, and to develop in the amateur sailor a love of true seamanship, and to give opportunity to become proficient in the art of navigation." As simple as that premise sounds, you'll see running through these pages spirited tensions without end—between pure adventure and safety, between pure cruising and racing, between individuals and community, even between definitions of who gets to play. A hundred years later, none of these tensions has been *solved*. But they did set off an epidemic, inspiring a heap of ways to go voyaging and do it well.

Many of the subjects in the following chapters are wonderful raconteurs in their own right. Treat this book as a syllabus, a reading list that you can follow in as many directions as there are compass points. The semester—or the lifetime—you spend with these bold and restless souls can't help but stir something in yours.

So get comfy and settle in for some good tales. But as you do, heed just one last word of caution.

The risk of infection is high.

—Tim Murphy, 2022
Gloucester, Massachusetts

Casey Baldwin, James Dorsett, and William Washburn Nutting (left to right)
take their ease at anchor following their renowned 1920 Atlantic crossing from Baddeck,
Nova Scotia to Cowes, Isle of Wight in an impressive 22 days aboard the 45-foot *Typhoon*.
Yes, small boats could cross oceans. Getting home would be harder.

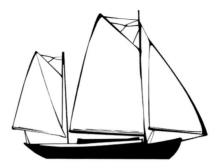

# Bill Nutting and Friends:
# A New Spirit of Cruising Is Born

*Apart from the question of the risk involved, which is a matter of personal opinion,*
*I feel that what American yachting needs is less common sense,*
*less restrictions, less slide rules, and more sailing.*
*Is "Safety First" going to become our national motto?*
—William Washburn Nutting
*The Track of the Typhoon,* 1921

Alexander Graham Bell was alive and well and summering at Baddeck, Nova Scotia, in 1913 when a lone American sailor aboard a 28-foot cutter turned up in late August—a rare event in that time and place. At 66 years old, Bell had long before invented the telephone, founded the American Telephone and Telegraph Company, and served as the second president of the National Geographic Society. It was now aeronautics and waterborne hydroplanes that held his attention, and in 1919 his Hydrodome number 4 hydrofoil would go on to set a world speed record of more than 70 mph across the water. Bell had built a laboratory and boatyard at his Beinn Bhreagh estate, and for some five years he'd been conducting experiments with engineer Frederick W. "Casey" Baldwin. Baldwin, for his part, flew an airplane of his own design in March 1908, making him the first British subject and probably the third person after the two Wright brothers ever to take flight.

The lone voyager who sailed into their cove was William Washburn Nutting. From the moment he landed, Bill Nutting found this band of vigorous thinkers as congenial as he could have hoped. An illustrator and journalist by trade, Nutting had set off from New York aboard *Nereis* earlier that summer with a sporting spirit but scant experience of open-ocean sailing or navigation. By the time Nutting arrived in Baddeck, he'd amassed a good summer's worth of adventure. Approaching Nantucket, between Horseshoe

Bill Nutting at Purdue University. "He can do a little of everything and is particular how he does it," read his yearbook caption. "He dabbles a little in music, literature, art and athletics, and has a propensity for ladies of the Roycroftie type. Twenty years will see him globetrotting in Red Autos and Air Ships."

and Tuckernuck Shoals, he stood up to hail the crew of the Cross Rip Lightship just as *Nereis* jibed, her boom sending him into the swift and chilly tides. Only outrageous fortune saved him from drowning, as he watched his unmanned vessel sailing away. Instead, he was able to grab a loose line, and haul himself back aboard to safety. This was not the last time that dumb luck would account for the survival of someone gone overboard from one of Nutting's boats. Nor would all of Nutting's sailing adventures end without calamity.

In Baddeck Nutting and Baldwin hit it off particularly well, their friendship built on boozy late-night debates about the contradictory virtues of the perfect ocean-going yacht.

The outbreak of World War I interrupted Nutting's plans to return the next summer. During a reporting trip to Europe in 1915–16 he was briefly imprisoned in Russia as a spy. When the United States entered the war, Nutting was commissioned as a lieutenant in the U.S. Naval Reserves to instruct the U.S. Merchant Marine in the use of anti-submarine devices. This experience gave him the source material to write *Cinderellas of the Fleet* about the Navy's ingenious 110-foot sub chasers and introduced him to several of the 36 men who in 1922 would join him in founding the Cruising Club of America.

### *Typhoon* Crosses the Atlantic

After the war Nutting made his way back to Baddeck to pick up his conversation with Baldwin. It was from these dialogues that the William Atkin-designed ketch *Typhoon* was born—and a voyage that would shape generations of ocean cruising sailors to come.

> It would be hard to say just when the "Typhoon" had its beginning. Possibly it was one night in [October 1919] in the snug cabin of the "Elsie," way down at the other end of Nova Scotia. "Casey" Baldwin and

I, not to mention Johnny Walker, had sailed up the Bras d'Or Lake after ducks and at nightfall had anchored in a little cove several miles from Baddeck. It had been a year since Baldwin had trod the gay white way [piloting HD-4 to its world speed record] and six since "Nereis" and I had plowed out the great Bras d'Or Passage bound for Newfoundland… There were many things to talk about.

"Casey" and I did most of the talking, while Johnny, faithful fellow, just sort of stood by and furnished the inspiration.

Finally we got down to the inevitable subject of boats and more particularly of cruising boats, for, after all, what sort of a boat can hold a candle to a cruiser for the great big gobs of enjoyment that it returns on the investment?

Baldwin was a racing man; he favored a light thoroughbred like *Elsie*, designed by George Owen under Nat Herreshoff's Universal Rule. She was 56 feet on deck and 36 feet on the waterline, and built at Bell Laboratories for Gilbert Grosvenor, the *National Geographic* president and editor. Casey was "all for a big boat—as big a one as possible without going beyond the strength of one man in the matter of the mainsail and the ground tackle, which are really limiting factors."

Nutting disagreed vigorously. He had singlehanded for hundreds of miles aboard *Nereis* on his first trip to the Canadian Maritimes. "I think a singlehander should be as small as possible without sacrificing full headroom—say, 28 to 30 feet on deck." Still, in the course of the conversation he conceded that singlehanding wasn't the most desirable way to cruise, and so their talk turned to the best boat for deep-sea cruising in general. The compromise they struck was "a 40-footer, fisherman style, ketch rigged with an auxiliary motor"—which grew to 45 feet on deck by the time Baldwin and yacht designer William Atkin got through with her.

Later on, Atkin was critical of his creation. "Too full aft, too fine forward," he wrote of *Typhoon* in 1924. "The result of these unbalanced ends is that in rough water the bow jumps too much; and this is hard not only on the gear, but on the crew, as well."

Yet Nutting remained enamored of *Typhoon*'s design. "I like a broad stern," he wrote as she was being built. "And remember the *Spray*, with a stern as broad as one of Will Rogers' jokes. Don't let them tell you that a broad stern won't run before a sea. It will rise up and over the sea instead of splitting it, and while this very fact may cause the bow to root if too fine, I feel that the tremendous reserve buoyancy of the forward sections above the waterline will prevent this in our case."

On July 17, 1920, Nutting and Baldwin set off for England, together with

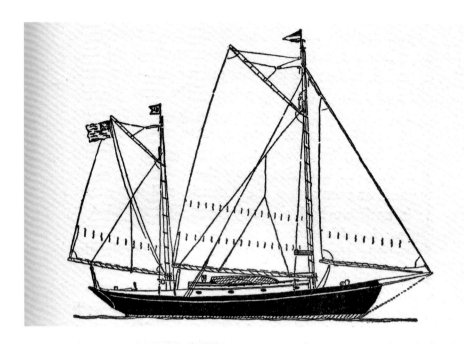

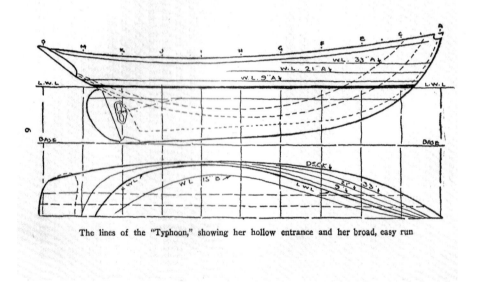

The lines of the "Typhoon," showing her hollow entrance and her broad, easy run

Top: *Typhoon*, was conceived by Bill Nutting and Casey Baldwin,
and designed by William Atkin to cross oceans and be sailed easily by a crew of three or four.

Above: Accommodations below were simple and a bit cramped.
The only theoretical disagreement was whether the fine bow and broad stern
made the boat hard to handle in a seaway.

Jim Dorsett, a young engineer who'd been working on the record-breaking Hydro-dome at Bell's laboratory. It was to be a more momentous and dangerous set of voyages than any of the young men could have anticipated.

Feeling he needed some rationale to explain the voyage, Nutting set himself the goal of arriving in Cowes by August 10 to cover the Harmsworth Trophy Races for *Motor Boat* magazine—just 24 days to cross the Atlantic in an untested vessel. "We'll not only have to cut out such alluring prospects as a party at the Royal Cork Yacht Club and possibly even a very important call at St Pierre, Miquelon," wrote Nutting on learning that *Typhoon*'s launch date would be pushed into early July, "but also we shall have to drive her for all she is worth across the intervening two thousand odd miles of North Atlantic."

That said, ship and crew quickly settled into their routines. Nutting described life at sea after they'd sailed for a week eastbound from Cape Race, the south-eastern tip of Newfoundland:

> Scene: Cabin of the "Typhoon," at an angle varying from ten to twenty-five degrees from the horizontal, looking aft.
>
> In right foreground, unoccupied pipe berth folded against sheathing; farther aft, transom on which reclines blanketed form of J. D. in attitude like cartoonist's conception of "a morning after"; still farther aft, galley with drain board and range covered with pots, pans and dishes in artistic disarray.
>
> Seated at table endeavoring to write, with remnants of dinner sliding hither and yon, W. W. N., cursing softly as coffee slips to loo'ard and is lost in blanketed form of J. D..
>
> Up-stage, well-nourished form of F. W. B. struggling to maintain vertical position, ever and anon coming up sharply on one side or the other as ship rolls, tripping over boots and wet oilskins and skidding dangerously on oil-soaked floor, all the while endeavoring, with all the helplessness of a thoroughgoing engineer, to keep the home fire burning in the Shipmate range.
>
> Farther up-stage, companionway steps, beneath which may be seen the shrouded figure of a motor with pressure gauge on air tank reading zero, and out the hatch above, the light of a lantern reflected on the wet mizzenmast and deserted wheel. The ship is sailing herself.

In that first week, *Typhoon* made 1,037 nautical miles, averaging nearly 150 miles per day. "Never to our knowledge has a small craft of her type made a better run," wrote Nutting. By then they'd mastered the art of living under

*"It was a roaring, wild, wonderful night, the sky pitch black,*
*the sea a driving stampede of weird, unearthly lights.*
*The countless crests of breaking waves made luminous patches*
*in the blackness as though lit by some ghostly light from beneath*
*the sea, and the tops, whipped off by the wind,*
*cut the sky with horizontal streaks of a more brilliant light,*
*like the sparks from a prairie fire.*
*Never have I seen such phosphorescence."*

constant motion, a condition Nutting deemed "strenuous beyond the dreams of a landsman."

Three days out, they encountered their first full gale. When it came, the list of items Nutting & Co. hadn't gotten to before setting off was still long. "We should have had the sea anchor ready and the line rove through the bull nose on the end of the bowsprit so that we could have thrown it over from the cockpit," Nutting wrote. But now it was too late to risk sending someone out to the end of the sprit. "The only thing to do was to stick it out in the cockpit and take a chance that the jib and mizzen would stand the punishment."

Through that first blow and all the days that followed across the Atlantic, Nutting's spirit never dipped below full enthusiasm. He described his first midnight watch as the gale built: "It was a roaring, wild, wonderful night, the sky pitch black, the sea a driving stampede of weird, unearthly lights. The countless crests of breaking waves made luminous patches in the blackness as though lit by some ghostly light from beneath the sea, and the tops, whipped off by the wind, cut the sky with horizontal streaks of a more brilliant light, like the sparks from a prairie fire. Never have I seen such phosphorescence."

In Casey Baldwin, Nutting had found his ideal shipmate. "Now and then I looked out the companionway to see how things were going," wrote Nutting of his sleepless off-watch in that first gale. "Casey, drenched and grinning, was in his element. The wind was still increasing, but there was no trace of concern in his voice as he shouted back a 'cheerio' through the racket. He was enjoying himself as only the man at the wheel can at such a time.

"His expert seamanship and his cool judgment and iron nerve and his never failing humor, all of these make him the best man on the water that I have ever known," wrote Nutting.

*Typhoon*'s skipper was no less pleased with his vessel, despite the ribbing he'd

Casey Baldwin was the perfect shipmate for Bill Nutting. He was an adventurous engineer and consummate seaman. He was equally at home at the helm of rudimentary aircraft, experimental hydroplanes, or a sturdy ketch.

taken from the old salts. As the wind came aft, they furled the mizzen and sailed under jib alone. "*Typhoon* ran beautifully with none of the predicted rooting; the fine bow and broad stern seemed to work in perfect harmony," wrote Nutting. Securing the main boom in its crutch, all hands went below to sleep while the vessel sailed herself.

The second week of *Typhoon*'s passage was easier than the first. During several days of northwesterlies, they attained multiple day's runs of more than 170 miles. On the evening of August 6, *Typhoon* made landfall. It was with all the trepidation familiar to new celestial-navigators that they approached the craggy, tide-swept English coast. "Our afternoon longitude put us almost on the meridian of Bishops Rock, but night came on without picking it up," wrote Nutting. "And then at 9:25, just as we were beginning to fear that the drubbing had been too much for the little Waltham clock, we caught the glow of the light, still down below the horizon. It was just where it should have been—about three points off the port bow—and again we were very much surprised and not a little elated. Our trans-Atlantic run had been made in 15 days, 9 hours and 25 minutes from Cape Race, and we know of no other small craft that has done it in better time."

From Baddeck to Cowes, they logged a total of 2,777 nautical miles in 22 days, 1 hour and 22 minutes. They arrived at their destination with a day and a half to spare.

At Cowes *Typhoon* made a good impression, and Nutting spent a memorably

Casey Baldwin was in his element when challenges mounted
and problems needed solving—"the best man on the water
I have ever known," said Nutting.

sociable August of 1920. There he met General John Seeley, the Lord Lieutenant
of Hampshire who brought regards from King George V, a sailor himself. And
the Earl of Dunraven came aboard *Typhoon*; he'd owned the three *Valkyries* that
between 1887 and 1895 tried to wrest the America's Cup from the New York
Yacht Club. Thomas Ratsey, dean of yacht sailmakers on both sides of the Atlantic,
became a good friend. On learning that *Typhoon* carried no trysail, Ratsey gave
Nutting the one from his own *Dolly Varden*—the proverbial shirt off his back,
and a gift that would prove invaluable later in the Gulf Stream when the gales
of November came blowing. Perhaps most consequentially, Nutting met Claud
Worth.

"Before leaving England," Nutting wrote, "there is one institution we must
mention because I hope that some time there will be such a one in our country. This
is the Royal Cruising Club whose membership included many of the real cruising
yachtsmen of England. My friend, Mr. [Claud] Worth, the vice-commodore, told

*Typhoon* at Cowes. Seventy years after the schooner America raised the eyebrows
of English yachtsmen in that famous race around the Isle of Wight, news spread of another
American yacht and her crew who had expanded the horizons of ocean sailing.
Officials and famous sailors came to meet the sociable crew.

me many interesting things about the activities of this organization and presented
me with a number of the charts which it publishes. These charts cover much of
the English coast. They are conveniently arranged in small sheets of a scale about
that of our own 1/80,000 scale U.S. Coast Survey charts and they contain all the
information required by a small boat, much of which is not shown on the regular
Admiralty charts. At the outbreak of the war the data compiled by the Royal
Cruising Club was of inestimable value to the Admiralty which, I believe, co-op-
erates with the Club to some extent in the work of preparing the charts. Why can't
some such club be started on this side of the Atlantic?"

*Typhoon*'s reputation spread throughout the British Isles. A year later, Nutting's
future shipmate Arthur Hildebrand, cruising down the English coast, fell into

Claud Worth (center) of the Royal Cruising Club invited Nutting aboard *Tern II*.
Their conversation reinforced Nutting's notion about bringing his ocean sailing
friends together in an organized club in the U.S.

conversation with a Liverpool pilot. "He told me he admired American yachting, saying that we had better boats, and did more real offshore cruising than they themselves did. He was judging by the *Typhoon*, and the *Lloyd W. Berry*, and the *Diablesse*." The latter two boats were owned by Roger Griswold and Frits Fenger, respectively, men who would become early CCA members.

Closer to home, *Typhoon*'s reputation had spread up the Hamble River to a band of Sea Scouts sailing and rowing open whaleboats. They were led by a 21-year-old named Uffa Fox who occasionally guided his "nippers" across the English Channel and up the rivers of France for their holiday outings (with or without their parents' knowledge or consent). When *Typhoon* lost her mate— Casey Baldwin was called to the Admiralty in London, then home to complete a project at Bell's laboratory—the Scouts appeared in the nick of time, just before Nutting and Dorsett were obliged to set off for New York decidedly shorthanded.

"When it came to Baldwin's leaving, it was just plain hell," wrote Nutting.

England's Sea Scouts, led by 21-year-old Uffa Fox, visit *Typhoon* at Cowes.
Fox and 18-year-old Charles Hookey would sign on for the westbound transatlantic crossing.

"I tried to pound the typewriter that morning while he packed, and when old faithful Harry Speed rowed him away to the Southampton steamer, there seemed no joy in the world at all. Judging from Casey's face, on which the characteristic grin was struggling hard to stay put, he, too, was having a hard time of it." Casey Baldwin would go on to become a charter CCA member. In the 1930s he represented Victoria in the Nova Scotia legislature and led the effort to create the Cape Breton Highlands National Park. "Later I became well-acquainted with Casey Baldwin," wrote Olin Stephens in his autobiography, "and found him to be every inch the hero I expected."

Aboard *Typhoon*, the Sea Scouts took the sting out of Casey's departure. "I had seen and admired these youngsters in the Hamble River the day before," wrote Nutting, "and as they luffed their long, rakish whaleboat alongside *Typhoon* with all the snap and skill of an American Coast Guard crew, I had an idea. They, too, had one, for it seems that there were all sorts of stories afloat about the plans of the *Typhoon*."

Their scout master—the very Uffa Fox who would grow up to become the yacht designer and author of almost cult-like renown—offered to sign on, there and then, for the transatlantic voyage. And if Nutting desired a fourth hand, Fox recommended a strapping 6-foot 2-inch scout of 18 named Charles Hookey. All parties came to a quick agreement. Overriding the disapproval of Fox's father toward the entire project, the scouts rowed 14 miles across the Southampton Water and up the Hamble River to a moored boat where Fox's gear was stashed, then back again to *Typhoon*.

"They were back in three hours," wrote Nutting, "and at last things looked bright again."

### *Typhoon's* Homeward Track

*Typhoon's* first brief stop after England was at Roscoff Harbor on France's Brittany coast in September 1920, followed by longer stops in El Ferrol and La Coruña, Spain. On the eastbound crossing to England, Nutting had left all the sextant navigation to Baldwin; now, here in the Bay of Biscay, Nutting was getting his first real experience of it. "For this reason I decided to lay a course for Cape Ortegal, which is the northernmost point of Spain, rather than for Finisterre, which is somewhat farther [west]. This would permit of a bad landfall without much possibility of missing the coast of Spain entirely."

Nutting reported that *Typhoon's* run across the Bay of Biscay was uneventful. "The notorious bay certainly did not live up to its bad reputation."

(The same could not be said for Nutting's future fellow CCA members Roger Griswold, Harold Peters, and Gordon C. Prince aboard the schooner *Lloyd W. Berry* later that season. "They must have been a hard-bitten group of men," wrote Jack Parkinson in *Nowhere Is Too Far*, "for it was December 22nd when they set out on their return trip. Held up by bad weather for three weeks in Plymouth, they touched at Brest and then laid a course south across the Bay of Biscay. Here they met one of the Bay's winter gales, which have been feared by sailors for centuries and have caused the loss of many a ship. One can only admire their seamanship. They alternately hove to, ran, and hove to again, using oil. At one point they were forced to chop away the standing bulwarks with axes to clear the decks of water.")

*Typhoon* took 17 days to cross the 850 miles from La Coruña to Santa Maria in the Azores—a day and a half longer than their roughly 2,000-mile passage from Newfoundland to England. Might they have made a better passage with Casey Baldwin still aboard? In light of future events, some of Nutting's friends thought so. As it was, Nutting had reckoned eight or nine days, and provisioned accordingly. En route, they ran out of kerosene and candles and most of their food. For much of the earlier leg to England, Dorsett had been prone to seasickness, but while he'd now gained his sealegs, Fox and Hookey were "down and out from the swell" as they left the Spanish coast. Through it all, Uffa Fox remained cheerful and stood his watches. "He is the only man I have ever known who could actually sing while seasick," wrote Nutting.

*En route, they ran out of kerosene and candles and most of their*
*food. For much of the earlier leg to England,*
*Dorsett had been prone to seasickness, but while he'd now gained*
*his sealegs, Fox and Hookey were "down and out from the swell"*
*as they left the Spanish coast. Through it all,*
*Uffa Fox remained cheerful and stood his watches.*
*"He is the only man I have ever known who could actually*
*sing while seasick," wrote Nutting.*

Calm days produced log entries like this one from September 25: "Noon—Log 389.1 miles. Latitude 40° 47′ 57″. Day's run 2.6 nautical miles, the worst yet."

Or September 26: "An exasperating day. Saw nothing to break the monotony but a barrel covered a foot thick with sea growth."

Or September 27: "Fine, sunny day, but flat calm."

When the breeze did come up, it was hard and on the nose. September 28: "Just before dark decided that we had better heave-to rather than fight it out under jib and mizzen all night. Crew sick and skipper in need of rest. Got out Thomas Ratsey's trisail and Fox and I bent it on with some difficulty, Fox gamely sticking to the job between sick spells at the rail. Doused jib and I had my first sousing on the bowsprit. She rose to a tremendous height and then fell and I thought the whole bow would go under, but she fetched up with the stick awash and all I got was a splashing and a boot full of water."

Any breeze that came seldom lasted long. September 30: "We were becalmed for a while this morning from eight to ten and poor old Fox at the wheel said: 'They were the worst two hours I ever spent in all my bloody life.' These long swells with practically no wind are the worst thing we have to contend with."

Finally, on the afternoon of October 2 came the call, "Land Ho!" But with the wind on the nose, they prepared themselves for an all-nighter of hard beating. It was probably a blessing that *Typhoon*'s crew didn't know what Aeolus actually had in store for them.

October 3: "This has been an exciting day, the most exciting one thus far, and I suppose we should be discouraged if we allowed ourselves to indulge in such feelings. Here we are hove-to again under Tom Ratsey's trisail in a howling gale that has left us with a broken mizzenmast, all messed up below, and thoroughly tired out."

Why so exhausted? With San Miguel visible 10 miles to windward, *Typhoon* bashed into it all through the night under jib and mizzen. At dawn, having gained only five miles toward their goal, they tried adding a double-reefed main to finish the job. "Once, in trying to tack, we missed stays and received a knockdown that nearly buried the companionway and we were forced finally to take off the mainsail entirely. She was easier under shortened rig, but the wicked seas and the wind, now a full gale, made it impossible to come about."

From here they could clearly see the green hills of San Miguel and smell the smoky land "that was like that of a Harris tweed on a rainy day." But try what they would, they couldn't make the approach. As Nutting and Fox were securing the jib on the bowsprit, *Typhoon* was hit by a "staggering sea" that sent Fox over the lifeline; he caught hold of a shroud before the boat pulled away. Meanwhile, a flying block walloped Dorsett in the head, and Hookey injured himself falling down the companionway. "Lying out on the bowsprit, I got the gaskets around the jib to save it, as the bowsprit and in fact the entire bow was going under every time we dove into the steep ones," wrote Nutting. "The forestay seemed to have loosened up and every moment I thought the mainmast was going too, but we rigged up a back stay and nothing carried away. That experience on the bowsprit was the most convincing argument for a knockabout rig that I have ever encountered."

Three days of hard struggle after that Harris-tweed whiff of land, Nutting's noon fix now put San Miguel 48 miles distant. From that first land-ho, *Typhoon's* crew would endure a full five days—alternately becalmed in long nauseating swells and hove-to in the teeth of gales, and Fox again nearly washed overboard in a big sea, this time from inside the cockpit coaming—before they finally set foot on shore.

"As we touched the shingle a dozen willing hands grabbed the little tender, carried her far up the beach, and then welcomed us most heartily in perfectly good old slangy American," wrote Nutting. "Out of the noise and confusion that ensued we gathered that we had made the town of San Laurenco on Santa Maria and that most of the inhabitants had served their time in the shoe factories of Massachusetts."

After a brief stay, *Typhoon's* crew sailed 55 miles to the larger port of Ponta Delgada on San Miguel, where for 10 days they recuperated and socialized and reprovisioned for their final leg home. The crew of an American freighter used their cargo boom to lift out *Typhoon's* broken mizzen mast and make repairs. And here they picked up a fifth crew, a former Army flier and now an admiralty lawyer from Boston named Manson Dillaway.

It was the next leg of the voyage that would cause the biggest stir back in

Charles Hookey, Manson Dillaway, Uffa Fox and Jim Dorsett
were the crew with Bill Nutting when *Typhoon* left Ponta Delgada, Azores,
in mid-October for a nearly disastrous passage to New York.

New York.

As *Typhoon* set off, Ponta Delgada gave them a raucous sendoff. "Every ship in the place, regardless of nationality, broke out her siren and blew salute after salute, which we returned with our foghorn and with many dips of the ensign. It was a tribute from big ships that plow the Seven Seas, to a tiny craft that played their game for fun—a tribute that blurred the eyes of her crew and brought strange lumps into their throats as she rounded the breakwater, met the heave of the open sea and squared away into the path of the moon."

But it was already October 19, late in the season to flirt with the 40th parallel in the North Atlantic Ocean. At first, all was peace and sweetness aboard *Typhoon*. "After the excitement was over," wrote Nutting, "it was a relief to sit at the wheel and feel the little ship alive again after her period of inactivity. For hours I stayed on deck enjoying the poetry of it alone in the moonlight—the easy rhythmic motion as she lifted to the seas and dipped into the hollows—the regular swish, swish of the bow wave—the occasional dash of spray. It was one of those nights when one loses all sense of time and worry and feels in harmony with the scheme of bigger things."

By November 16, 28 days out of Ponta Delgada and now well into the Gulf Stream, all sense of peace was a distant memory. For three days they'd been battling gales but making disappointing progress—300 miles for 72 hours of heavy going. That morning they were overtaken by a squall from the southeast. "At 6:00 the lacing on the main gaff carried away and ten minutes later, during a severe rain squall, the wind backed to E NE and increased in intensity. I drove her for a while with now and then a sea coming clear over me, filling cockpit and thundering on the cabin trunk."

Nutting worried that with the wind this strong they might lose the jib entirely. They'd already lost use of their mainsail and a spinnaker whose tack had exploded.

Midafternoon there came "a tremendous crash which gave us the impression we had been run down." Nutting describes "the moment everything was blotted out by hot, dense steam caused by solid water coming down the Liverpool head and into the Shipmate range. As the steam cleared, I remember feeling greatly surprised that the weather side of the cabin and even the port lights were still intact." *Typhoon* had broached, causing the first of two knockdowns in two days, with both mastheads under water. Nutting silently thanked Casey Baldwin, who'd insisted on adding a 3,000-pound lead shoe to the keel, while Nutting himself had argued for inside ballast, fisherman-style, to speed up the building time. Casey's lead shoe had proven "sufficient to right the ship," wrote Nutting. "She had come back slowly but she had come back."

If the gales of the recent days had been impressive, November 17 showed *Typhoon's* crew something new. "After we finished lashing the tender," wrote Uffa Fox in his personal log, "I undressed in cockpit and stood up in the rain and bathed with real soap. W. W. N. was amused and said, 'Well, you intend to go to your Maker clean anyway.' Heaviest wind we have had, also sea."

That afternoon the wind came around to the southwest. "We could see that we were in for something even worse than the northeaster of the day before," Nutting wrote. "A new and bigger sea had made up over the remains of the old one, causing a confused condition that was worse than anything we had yet encountered. The wind, unlike the steady blow of Tuesday, came in a succession of hard punches, howling and cold and carrying with it the tops of seas that stung like bird shot."

To slow the boat and regain some control, they put two lines overboard to create drag through the water, one with a heavy iron bucket lashed to the bitter end. Now Nutting worried about losing the trysail. He sent Dorsett, Fox, and Hookey forward to launch a sea anchor, like a parachute in the water, then furl

*Eventually he turned on his back with the line over his shoulder.*
*Now Jim Dorsett was planing over the surface of the Atlantic*
*Ocean in a full gale. Meanwhile, the three men on deck hauled*
*away on the line. "As we drew him close under the counter,"*
*wrote Nutting, "he looked up with a half-choked grin and said,*
*'Well, Skipper, here I am.'*
*I think it was the most beautiful display of downright courage*
*that I have ever seen and it would have brought*
*the tears had we time for any such emotion."*

the trysail as he brought *Typhoon* head to wind. With Fox forward and Dorsett on the side deck, *Typhoon* took an exceptionally large sea over the port quarter that washed the sou'wester hat off Nutting's head at the helm and left Fox clinging to the mainmast with his arms and legs, and up to his shoulders in green sea. Dorsett, on his way to being washed overboard, grabbed hold of the mizzen rigging. "That was a hell of a big one, Skipper," he called to Nutting, as he made his way forward to join Fox.

And then *Typhoon* broached broadside to the waves for the second time. "I remember going down under tons of solid water, with a last impression of Dillaway's face framed in the porthole as he pumped out the oily bilge water to form a 'slick,' " wrote Nutting. "There was no sense of direction or time, only a terrible helplessness and a feeling that possibly at last the cruise was over."

This time Dorsett did go overboard. In his first moments of clarity, Nutting instinctively looked off to leeward and saw the man's head 75 feet off. He recalled Jim's father on the dock at Baddeck, asking Nutting to look out for his son, as the influenza had taken everyone else in his life. He knew there was no hope of maneuvering *Typhoon* in those conditions. As Nutting considered going overboard after Dorsett—never mind that he was wearing heavy sea boots and a long oilskin coat—he saw Dorsett making toward one of the lines they'd streamed aft. He hoped it was the one with the bucket attached.

Alas, it was not. Dorsett took hold of the line, but *Typhoon* was moving too fast for him to keep a grip without being pulled under. Eventually he turned on his back with the line over his shoulder. Now Jim Dorsett was planing over the surface of the Atlantic Ocean in a full gale. Meanwhile, the three men on deck hauled away on the line. "As we drew him close under the counter," wrote Nutting, "he looked up with a half-choked grin and said, 'Well, Skipper, here I

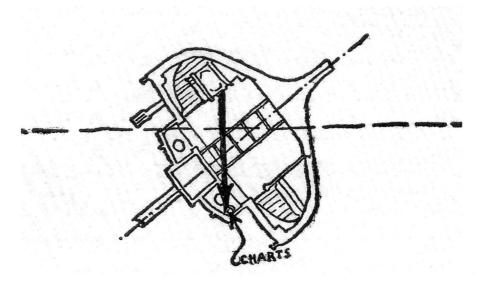

In the Gulf Stream in November, *Typhoon* took a 120-degree roll,
from which she only slowly recovered. Nutting silently thanked Casey Baldwin
for insisting on a 3,000-pound lead shoe appended to the keel.

am.' I think it was the most beautiful display of downright courage that I have ever seen and it would have brought the tears had we time for any such emotion."

A survey of the damage below revealed what had occurred. Across the saloon settee were scattered ashes from the bottom of the Shipmate stove, and sticking to the high side of the cabin trunk were the remains of food from the sink. *Typhoon* had been knocked head over heels, all the way down to 120 degrees from vertical. As they learned, Fox, too, had gone overboard. But when the mainmast came down on his head, he had the presence of mind to grab hold and refuse to let go; *Typhoon* eventually righted herself, and Fox was unceremoniously deposited back on deck. Still more impressive, he had the presence of mind to strike the trysail to slow *Typhoon's* boatspeed as Dorsett struggled to grip his line.

Through all these tribulations, Fox was impressed with the growth he witnessed in his young charge, Charles Hookey. Often seasick and sullen at the beginning of the passage, "Charles has altered wonderfully since the gale off San Miguel and now is the busiest man on the ship," wrote Fox. The nipper was receiving an incomparable education, as he himself relates of *Typhoon's* second knockdown:

> I looked to windward and saw a very large wave coming and grabbed
> the mizzenmast with my left arm. I heard the wave hit, being blinded with
> water. I was not surprised to see her knocked down, having experienced

*"As I think back on it now it was a wonderful picture—the dimly-lighted cabin, the wreckage, the songs punctuated by the crashing blows from breaking seas and through it all the constant humming of the steel shrouds sounding through the fabric of the boat like the drone note on a bagpipe. Then we all turned in and slept soundly."*

somewhat the same thing the day before when I was at the wheel. Then I thought all was up. When she came up I saw Jim about 50 yards away, and I thought all was up with him. It was lucky we had the ropes astern, one of which he got. I pulled in on both ropes for all I was worth, not knowing which one he had hold of. It took us about ten minutes to get him to the ship, having about as much as we could do to get him aboard having oilskins and seaboots on. I have never been so pleased as when we got Jim aboard safely. I helped put the sea anchor over, which parted, and then we all went down in the cabin leaving her to look after herself. It was a great experience, which I would not have missed for the world.

With their sea anchor gone and half their sail inventory blown out, *Typhoon's* crew pulled the companionway closed, braced themselves, and cooked up what remained of their scant provisions. "A bottle of Domecq cognac from Spain, which I was saving for some sufferer from the constitutional amendment, was broken out and we sang everything we could think of out of sheer joy at having Dorsett back again. As I think back on it now it was a wonderful picture—the dimly-lighted cabin, the wreckage, the songs punctuated by the crashing blows from breaking seas and through it all the constant humming of the steel shrouds sounding through the fabric of the boat like the drone note on a bagpipe. Then we all turned in and slept soundly."

Three days later, *Typhoon* was sailing through the Verrazano Narrows toward home.

### Ocean Sailing for the Fun of the Thing: A New Epidemic

Bill Nutting's *Typhoon* voyage quickly attained notoriety. Ripples from it traveled in several directions at once, and some of them still run through sailors today.

In the immediate aftermath of *Typhoon's* homecoming came a front-page story in the November 23, 1920, edition of the *New York Tribune*, followed by an editorial

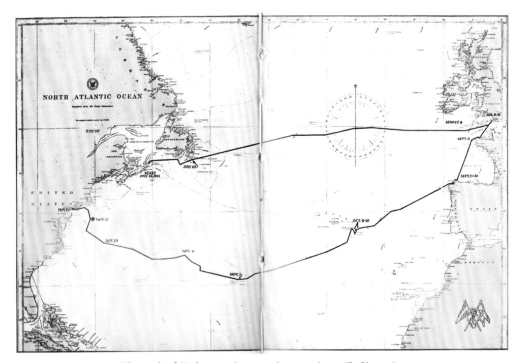

The track of *Typhoon*, and soon to become the stuff of legends:
"Since her launching in July she had completed a cruise of seven thousand-odd miles
that had taken her twice across the North Atlantic."

aimed at discouraging other would-be voyagers from the unsafe practice of setting off to sea in small boats with shorthanded crews. The "bully" news story gratified Nutting, but the *Tribune's* editorial inflamed the proselytizing zealot in him.

"Shades of Steven Brodie!" I thought, when I read the harrowing accounts of our cruise the following morning and I felt myself losing standing as an amateur sailor and skidding into a class with Steve and the immortal who went over Niagara Falls in a barrel.

Not that there was any serious motive behind the cruise of the "Typhoon." We were not trying to demonstrate anything; we were not conducting an advertising campaign; we hadn't lost a bet. Nor were we subsidized by anybody who had—or was. I had the little vessel built according to Atkin's and my own ideas of what a seagoing yacht should be and we sailed her across the Atlantic and back again for the fun of the thing. We feel that the sport of picking your way across great stretches of water, by your own (newly acquired) skill with the sextant, pitting your wits against the big, more or less honest forces of nature, feeling your way with leadline through fog and darkness into strange places which the travelers of trodden paths never experience, chumming with the people of the sea—these things, we believe, are worth the time, the cost, the energy—yes, and even the risk and hardship that are bound to be a part of such an undertaking. We did it for the fun of the thing and we believe that no further explanation is necessary.

Many people who seem not to realize that size is the least important element in the seaworthiness of a vessel, felt that in looping the Atlantic in so small a boat we had taken too great a chance. Now, apart from the question of the risk involved, which is largely a matter of personal opinion, I feel that what American yachting needs is less common sense, less restrictions, less slide rules and more sailing.

And is "Safety First" going to become our national motto?

I think it is reasonable to say that a country is only as big as its sports. In this day when life is so very easy and safe-and-sane and highly-special-ized and steam-heated, we need, more than ever we needed before, sports that are big and raw and—yes, dangerous. Not that we recommend taking chances with the "roaring forties" in the middle of November or crossing the Atlantic on the fiftieth parallel at any time of the year. This sort of yachting, I suppose, will never be popular. But I do hope that if there is any result from this book on the "Typhoon" it will be to inspire a confidence in the possibilities of the small yacht and instill in the young-sters an interest in the sea and a desire to explore our wonderful coast line in their own little ships.

Bill Nutting wasn't the first sailor to cross an ocean in a small shorthanded boat for the adventure—although it must be said there were only a few who'd done it before him. Alfred "Centennial" Johnson is credited with the first solo west-to-east transatlantic passage; in 1876 he sailed a 20-foot decked dory from Gloucester, Massachusetts, to Liverpool, England, in 66 days. "I made that trip because I was a damned fool, just as they say I was," Johnson said years later. Joshua Slocum accomplished his well-publicized solo circumnavigation aboard the 36-foot 9-inch gaff-rigged sloop *Spray* between April 1895 and June 1898. Slocum's book *Sailing Alone Around the World* was a popular best-seller of its time. He and *Spray* were prominently featured at the 1901 Pan American Exposition in Buffalo, New York, and on the strength of his fame Slocum socialized with the likes of Mark Twain and with President Theodore Roosevelt at the White House. Howard Blackburn made two solo transatlantic voyages, one 62-day passage from Massachusetts to England in 1899, and another 39-day passage aboard the 25-foot Friendship-type sloop *Great Republic* to Lisbon in 1901—a transatlantic record that stood unbeaten for nearly four decades, and all the more remarkable given that Blackburn had lost all his fingers and most of his toes in January 1883 to frostbite in a fishing dory off Newfoundland. (In 1928 Blackburn was inducted as an honorary Cruising Club member, alongside Captain Nathanael Herreshoff, the "Wizard of Bristol," Rhode Island; and Commodore Ralph Munroe, founder of the Biscayne Bay Yacht Club in Coconut Grove, Florida.) The German-Canadian sailor J. C. Voss wrote the popular *Venturesome Voyages of Captain Voss* about his round-the-world travels begun in 1901 aboard *Tilikum*, a dugout canoe with the remarkable dimensions of 38 feet of length overall, including figurehead, and *five feet six inches of beam*. In 1905 *Tilikum* and her skipper were one of the most popular exhibits at the great Exhibition at Earl's Court, London. And in 1911 Thomas Fleming Day, founder of *Rudder* magazine, crossed the Atlantic in a 32-foot yawl named *Sea Bird* with two crew; before Nutting, Tom Day fervently advocated for amateur ocean sailing, spearheading ocean races from New York to Marblehead, Massachusetts, in 1904; to Hampton Roads, Virginia, in 1905; and to Bermuda between 1906 and 1910.

Yet for some reason, in the early 1920s Nutting's advocacy for a particular spirit of ocean cruising caught fire in a way that had never happened before. It wasn't for his seamanship that Nutting's legacy still matters today; it was for some other attribute. Malcolm Gladwell, in his 2000 book *The Tipping Point*, explores the ingredients of "epidemics," the sociological trends that take off and flourish, while others fizzle and die. Bill Nutting—with the founding of the Cruising Club of America and his promotion of ocean sailing purely for the fun of the thing—caught the imagination of a confident country looking forward to taking on recreational adventures.

Nutting's published writings and conversations with influential people espoused the big, raw, even dangerous sport of ocean sailing that contrasted heroically with a sense that life had gotten too easy after World War I and the advent of modern conveniences. William Washburn Nutting was a person with the rare gifts of conveying and convincing others to join him in his grand ambitions. When the yacht designer, Olin Stephens, wrote his autobiography late in life, he recalled reading *The Track of the Typhoon* as a teenager, and the indelible effect it had on him.

A close look at the roster of early CCA members illustrates just how thoroughly Bill Nutting embodied the function of a network hub. During the nineteen teens, Nutting held an informal salon from his editorial post in Manhattan. George Bonnell, Sydney Breese, Bayard Rodman, Kenneth Stephens, W. P. Stephens—all these men "were in the habit of dropping in at the *Motor Boat* offices to talk boats," Nutting wrote. During his stint in the U.S. Navy and while interviewing

*Nutting moved about one hundred fathoms of chain in the forepeak and produced a couple of bottles of Spanish brandy (those were prohibition days), and the assembled company settled themselves in the cabin, which was covered with fuel oil and still a shambles from the two knockdowns in the Gulf Stream. He then proposed for the first time the founding of the Cruising Club of America.*

the sub-chaser crews for his book *Cinderellas of the Fleet,* Nutting came to know Herbert L. Stone, Alf Loomis, George Wallace, Sandy Moffat, Charles Cobb, Evans R. Dick, Samuel Wetherill, Maclear Jacoby, and Walter Wheeler Jr. From his voyages to Nova Scotia, Nutting drew in F. W. "Casey" Baldwin, Gilbert Grosvenor, and Aemilius Jarvis. Perhaps his most important connection was with the Englishman Claud Worth, vice-commodore of England's Royal Cruising Club, founded in 1880. It was Worth who planted in Nutting's mind the seed to start an American club on the RCC model.

In *Nowhere Is Too Far: The Annals of the CCA,* Jack Parkinson describes Nutting's homecoming reunion with his American mates, an anecdote that may be read as the Club's origin story.

Late in the evening [of November 20, 1920] the *Typhoon* crept into Gravesend Bay and anchored off the old Atlantic Yacht Club.

Among the early files of the Cruising Club is an account written by W. P. Stephens of Nutting's arrival in New York. The day after *Typhoon's* voyage ended he moved up the Bay and anchored off Bay Ridge, seeking a lee from a strong northeaster. It was his intention to proceed through the East River to New Rochelle, his ultimate destination, the following day. But by that time the newspapers had the story and, what with interviews and greeting old friends, it was not until nearly twilight of a dull November afternoon that he got underway. As W. P. Stephens puts it, "With that procrastination and utter disregard of both tide and time which was so characteristic, much of the day was wasted."

With several friends aboard (Cruising Club members to be), they began to buck a foul tide through the East River, with no power and *Dolly Varden's* trysail replacing the blown-out mainsail. By 10 p.m. they realized the attempt was hopeless and pulled into the old New York Yacht

Club slip at East 23rd Street. Nutting moved about one hundred fathoms of chain in the forepeak and produced a couple of bottles of Spanish brandy (those were prohibition days), and the assembled company settled themselves in the cabin, which was covered with fuel oil and still a shambles from the two knockdowns in the Gulf Stream. He then proposed for the first time the founding of the Cruising Club of America.

It was a little more than a year later, after many gatherings at Beefsteak John's in Greenwich Village, that the Cruising Club of America was informally ratified at the home of Syd Breese on West 57th Street in February 1922 and more formally affirmed among a larger gathering at the Harvard Club in March. By May the Club's burgee was commissioned, a nine-man board of directors appointed, and William Washburn Nutting elected the Club's first commodore.

*Typhoon's* cabin, in a pristine state—when not turned upside down mid-ocean—where in November 1920 Nutting first proposed the founding of the Cruising Club of America after arriving back in New York.

With the North Atlantic behind her, *Typhoon* worked her way through Hell Gate on the East River, using the few sails she had left including the storm trysail gifted by Thomas Ratsey before leaving Cowes. Several future members of the Cruising Club of America had joined Nutting for the final leg of his adventure.

Leiv Eiriksson at Reykj[...]

Nutting did not build the Colin Archer adaptation that he had envisioned.
He found *Liev Eiriksson* laid up in Norway and bought her—a boat
"that out Archered-Archer. She was broader of beam, shallower of body,
fuller in every line, and she had no outside ballast whatsoever."

2

# A Thousand Years Behind: The Vanishing Track of *Liev Eiriksson*

He was a charming character and good company, a good sailor in some ways,
but foolhardy and had too much courage.
—George Bonnell

I take the liberty of bringing the jeopardy of these men to your personal attention
in full confidence that you will not permit these American citizens
to lose their lives in waters so near our coast through government inaction.
—Henry Wise Wood
To U.S. President Calvin Coolidge

They had originally intended to start at about nine o'clock in the morning
but their number of friends at Julianehaab was so great and the leave-taking with
each one took so long, that it was three o'clock in the afternoon before they were
ready to leave. We then gave them three cheers and they set out on the voyage,
which was to be their last.
—A. C. Rasmussen
Governor of the Royal Danish Colony Godthaab, Greenland

Bill Nutting did not rest on the laurels of his first transatlantic voyage. Not long after he published *The Track of the Typhoon*, he rekindled an infatuation with a yacht type that had taken hold of his soul on the banks of a Copenhagen canal in 1915—a type that marked a stark contrast from *Typhoon*.

By the winter of 1923, Nutting had met Arthur Hildebrand (left), a man whose flights of enthusiasm matched his own. Hildebrand had recently returned from a year of cruising from Scotland to the Greek islands. He is also remembered for designing the Blue Water Medal for the brand new Cruising Club of America.

## Flirtations with the *Redningskoiter*

In those early years of the 20th century, American yachts tended to fall into one of two categories: fishermen or racers. The fishermen types had developed over 200 years of hard-earned experience bringing back cod and halibut, summer and winter, from the North Atlantic. Experience over time refined the designs for a reasonable balance among payload, safety, and speed. Meanwhile, shorthanded and even singlehanded fishing crews were sailing smaller Friendship sloops to their catch closer inshore. *Great Republic,* the 25-foot yacht that Howard Blackburn sailed from Gloucester to Lisbon in 39 days, was a modified Friendship sloop; William Atkin owned this boat at the time when he was designing *Typhoon,* and he applied some of what he'd learned from her. John Alden's *Malabars* of the 1920s illustrate the high point of fishermen-type yachts.

By contrast, the racing boats of those years, the "raters," emphasized minimal wetted surface. With no obligation to remain at sea through any weather, racers

*"There was the cockpit full of water and our empty water kegs floating about with the last of our salt beef. Charles looked exactly like Robinson Crusoe on his raft just leaving the wreck. He looked so funny that I laughed like hell which made W. W. N. wild as he had just discovered his pajamas all covered with fuel oil. Then we had a heated argument, the skipper and I (raised voices but could not wave our arms as we had to hold on to either end of the table) about boats' sterns."*

were more lightly built than fishermen, and their hull forms were defined by handicapping rules. In 1902, Nathanael Herreshoff devised the Universal Rule with three parameters: length, sail area, and displacement. This rule produced "letter boats," ranging in size from S-Class (0 to 17 feet) to J-Class (65 to 76 feet). Rated length broadly referred to waterline length but in practice changed almost seasonally, according to the whims of New York Yacht Club committees. As the rule encouraged pronounced overhangs—meaning that the boat's resting waterline length was far shorter than its overall length—it spawned boats that were always much longer than their rated length. *Elsie*, owned by Gilbert Grosvenor, editor of the *National Geographic* magazine, so beloved by Casey Baldwin, was a modified P-class yacht (rating 25–31 feet) that stretched to 56 feet overall. Meanwhile, the International Rule produced "Metre boats." Devised in 1907 under the auspices of the British-based Yacht Racing Association (now Royal Yachting Association), this rule comprised such parameters as waterline length, beam, sail area, freeboard, and others. In Nutting's day, the Six Meter and Eight Meter classes were popular on Long Island Sound. Designer Olin Stephens' legendary 1929 creation, *Dorade*, was a modified Meter boat.

For *Typhoon*, Nutting commissioned a fisherman type, but that's not exactly what designer William Atkin returned. "She is not really so much of a fisherman as you thought—below the waterline," wrote Nutting. "Note the slightly hollow waterlines and sections at the bow, which correspond somewhat to Herreshoff's racing practice. Baldwin spoofed me a bit for holding out for a fisherman and then sending him the designs of a 'rater.'"

Nutting took no end of guff for his professed love of a "broad stern." Uffa Fox, who would become a renowned yacht designer in his own right, captured one moment in his journal after *Typhoon's* first of two knockdowns in the Gulf Stream: "There was the cockpit full of water and our empty water kegs floating about with the last of our salt beef. Charles looked exactly like Robinson Crusoe on his raft just leaving the wreck. He looked so funny that I laughed like hell which made W. W. N. wild as he had just discovered his pajamas all covered with fuel oil. Then we had a heated argument, the skipper and I (raised voices but could not wave our arms as we had to hold on to either end of the table) about boats' sterns. I believe in a double ender and the skipper in a broad stern. *Typhoon* is a wonderful boat but I think she'd be more wonderful if she had a stern like a Scotch fishing nabbie."

Sometime after the end of the *Typhoon* voyage, Nutting's tastes crash-jibed in another direction entirely. Starting in 1923 he was smitten by the *redningskoiter*, traditional Norwegian lifeboats he'd seen seven years earlier on a reporting trip through Scandinavia during the war. American yachtsmen of the time had perhaps heard of these craft, but few had ever seen one. To Nutting's mind, these double-enders were brought to perfection by the Scottish-Norwegian yacht designer Colin Archer (1832–1921).

"Although strange to an eye accustomed to the racing yacht type, which is now practically international and has few local characteristics no matter where you find it, or to the fisherman type as we know it in America," wrote Nutting, "these boats held a fascination for me that grew with the acquaintance, and I resolved that one day I should own one and try it out."

With their broad beam carried both forward and aft for so much of their length, Nutting didn't expect the *redningskoite* to be fast. "But I figured that a type that has survived the test of centuries in a country that depends so largely on its boats, must have other virtues." Nutting appreciated "that symmetry which Mr. Archer must have felt essential to the 'best boat for the worst weather.'" This last line would become familiar to every sailor in the 1970s.

In the winter of 1923, Nutting was poring over a copy of E. Keble Chatterton's *Fore and Aft Craft* with his friend Arthur Hildebrand, who'd recently returned from a cruise from Scotland to Greece and published *Blue Water* about that trip. One particular drawing in Chatterton's book rekindled a glow in Nutting's heart.

"We came upon that design by Colin Archer of a Norwegian auxiliary lifeboat, or *redningskoite*, and this brought back my old resolution. The lines in Mr. Chatterton's book scale to about 47 feet overall. After a few rough measurements we decided that if the boat were reduced to 32 feet overall, we could get headroom under a trunk of reasonable height and sitting headroom under the side decks, and so, for convenience, we had the design photostated 16 inches overall, or to a scale of one-half inch to the foot. With these lines to work from, I spent a couple of evenings making a skeleton model." He took his drawings and model to his old mate, yacht designer William Atkin, to clean up the lines. They named

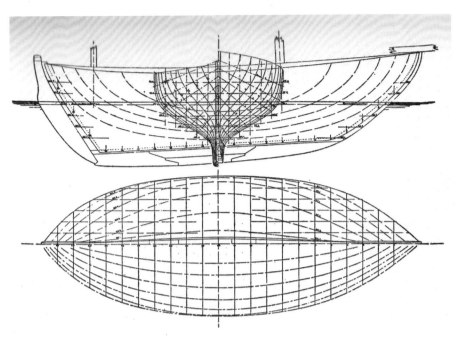

In Chatterton's *Fore and Aft Craft*, Nutting found drawings for a 47-foot Colin Archer-designed Norwegian rescue boat. The double-ended and round-bottomed shape was a distinct departure from *Typhoon*. Nutting was not one to repeat himself on adventures.

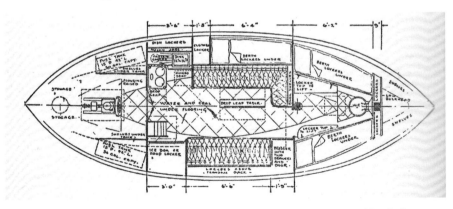

Nutting reduced Colin Archer's lines to 32 feet, the smallest size that would still allow sitting headroom under the side decks. "Like two ends without any ship between them," quipped one fellow CCA member.

the design *Eric*, for the Viking explorer Eric the Red.

"It is more than too bad that Mr. Nutting should not have lived to see the popularity of his child," Atkin wrote many years later, "for some 175 sets of blueprints of the 32-footer were sold by the designer within three years after the plans appeared in *Motor Boat*; and many more have been sold since."

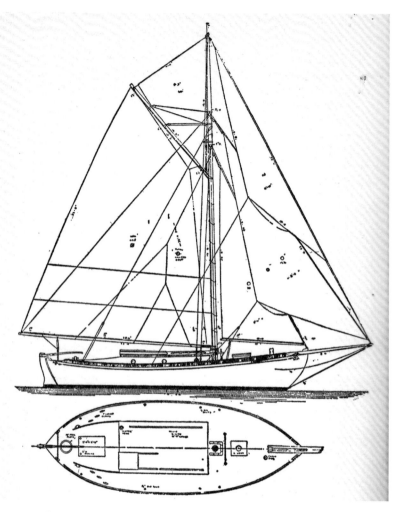

"Without doubt *Eric* will be a remarkable sea boat," wrote Atkin.
"She will carry on endlessly and comfortably, but she will not be fast."
Many an owner of the derivative Westsail 32 chose that same happy combination.

Today we might say it's too bad that neither Nutting nor Atkin survived to see the popularity of their child. *Suhaili*, the boat Sir Robin Knox-Johnston sailed in the first-ever solo nonstop circumnavigation in 1968–69, was an *Eric* built in Bombay of Indian teak. (Her 312-day passage time now looks quaint alongside François Gabart's 43-day record set in 2017.) In 1969 yacht designer W. I. B. Crealock adapted *Eric* for fiberglass construction; two years later, Lynne and Snider Vick acquired the molds and named her the Westsail 32. Lynne reprised the line, "the best boat for the worst weather" in her marketing copy. When *Time* magazine highlighted the cruising lifestyle in a June 1973 Modern Living feature, it devoted two pages, with photos, to the Westsail. A pull-out quote in large type

Young Robin Knox-Johnston sailed his small ketch, *Suhaili*, to a legendary victory in the first non-stop circumnavigation in 1969. The ketch closely followed the design made by William Atkin for *Eric*, drawn for Nutting in 1923.

read: "With her teak decks, hefty fiberglass hull, and her sea-kindly lines, this Westsail cruiser is a happy combination of blue water traditions and modern building techniques. She can take her crew anywhere in the world."

In those countercultural times of the mid-1970s, the *Time* story lit a roman candle, and Westsail orders jumped to more than 100 units per year. At every boat show for the next several seasons, the lines of people waiting to climb aboard a Westsail were among the longest. Meanwhile, other designers and builders created knockoffs, many of them built in Taiwan. By the time Westsail International went out of business in 1979, some 833 Westsail 32s had been launched, for a total of 1,100 Westsails ranging from 28 to 43 feet. CCA member and CBS news anchor Walter Cronkite owned one.

While the Westsail fan club has all but forgotten Bill Nutting's role in bringing the *redningskoite* to America, Atkin never did. "*Eric*, as you all know, is not my child," Atkin wrote. "When Bill Nutting and Arthur Hildebrand first became interested in this vessel somehow I was away and therefore missed the preliminary talks which culminated in this miniature of one of the finest of the late Colin Archer's designs. The cabin plan has remained very like his first draft, and as I see the thing this is most remarkable. Nutting alone is responsible for the layout and looking at it from every angle it is excellent."

When Nutting and Atkin drew *Eric*, neither of them had ever sailed a boat of

> *"We had saved our lives by a good half minute, and I shall never forget the forced cheer with which 'Hilly' tried to comfort our profound depression. It was, after all, his first shipwreck, and his mind balanced the hideous fact that we had lost our ship against the thrill of a great adventure."*

this type. "Without doubt *Eric* will be a remarkable sea boat," wrote Atkin. "She will carry on endlessly and comfortably, but she will not be fast. For her length there is too much displacement to expect much speed."

Till now, all their talk about the boat's behavior remained idle speculation. Nutting knew this, and he was driven to try one for himself.

## They Skelped Across the Skaggerack

Arthur Hildebrand was a man whose flights of enthusiasm were equal to Nutting's own. Harrison "Hal" Smith remembered Hildebrand from age 14: "He had already given himself over body and soul to the sea on which he was to adventure so ill prepared and to which he was to give his life. 'Hilly's' schoolbooks were scribbled over with the profiles of schooners, brigs, yachts of all shapes and sizes, in harbor or at sea. But I was destined to be drawn into the circle of his charm, for even then he could talk when the mood seized him as no one else I knew could talk."

At age 17, conspiring "against the peace of our families," Hilly and Hal and another boy chartered a boat from a Maine fisherman and cruised the coast, continually bailing out "that part of the Atlantic Ocean which flowed in through her seams, for she absorbed water like a sponge," remembered Smith. Next summer, they did it again, this time in a "sturdy sloop called the *Bonny Doone*." Goaded by Hildebrand, they ventured way downeast, well up into the Bay of Fundy. And there, as Smith wrote, "we had sunk her, as we deserved to, on a reef off a miserable place called Briar Island. We had saved our lives by a good half minute, and I shall never forget the forced cheer with which 'Hilly' tried to comfort our profound depression. It was, after all, his first shipwreck, and his mind balanced the hideous fact that we had lost our ship against the thrill of a great adventure."

Nutting and Hildebrand had found each other, and they were both itching for another great adventure. At first they planned to build an *Eric* to sail from the U.S. East Coast. But then they met Magnus Konow, "one of Norway's best amateur helmsmen," according to Nutting. Konow said there were plenty of converted *redningskoiter* in Norway, already built. "Why not come and get one?"

The two men resolved to do just that. "Of course we would sail her back across the Atlantic," wrote Nutting, "and what more suitable route than the track of the dragonship? Here was a route untraveled by any ship, so far as we know—certainly by no small one—since it was first sailed. This was the route for the ship we hoped to find."

Through that winter of 1924 their friends were alarmed by the plans they heard. Hal Smith described his own grave misgivings: "'Hilly' had met 'Bill' Nutting, an amateur yachtsman who had crossed the Atlantic in his own boat and had twice almost lost her by holding on too long in a gale. 'Bill' had become enamored with the type of boat they build in Norway, a shallow-draft sloop which from 'Hilly's' sketches filled us with apprehension. One night we dined in New York and 'Hilly' talked as he had never talked before. My friend is mad, I thought, when he described the gap of eight hundred miles across the stormiest waters in the world, when he pointed out with a forefinger trembling with eagerness that grim and terrible shore, the coast of Greenland, when he described the icebergs they would meet beyond Cape Fear."

At a CCA dinner Nutting displayed the lines of his beloved *redningskoite*; one of his table mates quipped that it looked like "two ends without any ship between them."

Undaunted by such reactions, Nutting and Hildebrand carried on to Norway. The boat they found on the beach in Lyngor was no Colin Archer design, but they bought her anyway. She'd been built two years earlier of oak and pine as a ketch-rigged auxiliary fisherman, then converted into a cutter-rigged cruising boat. By Nutting's own measurements (differing from the builder's), she was 42 feet 6 inches on deck, 36 feet 10 inches on the waterline, 15 feet 6 inches across the beam, and drew 6 feet. After all their indoor fussing with the tweaky adjustments for *Eric's* lines-on-paper, Nutting and Hildebrand had now committed themselves to an actual boat. "If full waterlines were treason we could only make the best of it," wrote Nutting. "Here was a boat that out-Archered Archer. She was broader of beam; she was shallower of body; she was fuller in every line, and she had no outside ballast whatsoever." Having *still* never sailed such a craft, in their weaker moments the two men despaired of growing old before this boat ever made headway against the Westerlies of the North Atlantic.

*Liev Eiriksson* (or sometimes *Leiv*) was the name they gave their Nordic craft. "Spell it Lief Erikson, as the moderns do, if you like," wrote Nutting, "but remember that he was a man who felt a fair wind behind him and saw unknown open water to the Westward and drove that long dragon-ship of his over the endless gray seas of a dim, hard, empty ocean to the shores of a whole new continent—the first white man to touch America. We named our ship after him."

Together with an American illustrator named John Todahl and a Dane named Bjarne Fleischer, they sea-trialed *Liev Eiriksson* in the inland waters between Norway and Denmark, then set off for Iceland by way of the Shetland and Faroe islands.

After 1,500 miles under sail and power, Nutting reported back to Herb Stone at *Yachting* on the boat's performance. "We have run dead before it without ever tripping our boom; we have driven to windward in a full gale and confused sea without shipping solid water; we have ghosted along over unrippled fjords when seemingly the only wind was that produced by our own motion; we have rolled the white nights through on glassy swells of the sort that form the heaving floors of hell; and we have done it all with a greater degree of comfort than we would have thought possible—with less wear and tear on gear and with a higher degree of efficiency than we would have dared to hope for in our theorizing days."

Nutting sent these lines from Reykjavik in the first week of August 1924. The same week, Hildebrand wrote a long letter home to his CCA mates. As these were the last communications received from either man, and as no member of the *Liev Eiriksson* expedition survived to publish the saga of their voyage, here is Hildebrand's letter in full.

> On board "Leiv Eiriksson"
> Reykjavik Harbor
> August 8, 1924.
> Martin S. Kattenhorn,
> Commodore, The Cruising Club of America
> Sir:
> The expedition, sailing under your flag, in command of William Washburn Nutting, with intent to cross the Western Ocean over the route of the late Cap'n Leiv Eiriksson to Iceland, Greenland and Vinland the Good, and with the subsidiary object of investigating the ocean-ography, fauna, Flora, and Norse drinking customs of the region lying immediately adjacent to that route, begs to submit the following partial report of its progress:
> This is great stuff.
> We found the ship, Marty, and we fitted her out for sea, and a few others, spry lads, and bright as new paint; we took her up to Kristi-ania haven, by the Powers, and lay to a big mooring off the King's Own Yacht Club while we got stores and gear aboard—and, man, it's gear; we jammed her down the Swedish coast through the inside passages, where the rocks are that close together, a man couldn't ask for anything closer,

were he with his best girl; we skelped across the Skaggerack, where there's been big fights between frigates in the old days; we were back in Norway again, then, and we worked her all around the coast past the Naze to Bergen, inside when we could, stopping in at snug ports and taking life as it came, under canvas when the wind was fair, worming her along under power when we had a bad slant; we've been up great fjords and seen the glaciers rolling down into the sea like bad dreams on a black night of evil thoughts. We took her out across the North Sea, with a gale of wind rumbling off to loo'ard over the heaving brink of the world, as shut up safe and dry in the hold of her, by thunder, singing songs, we was that pleased with her, and eating good sea food out of kegs that dripped salt brine when we speared out the chunks of mutton. And, Marty man, there's spirits walking these seas—we picked up two Vikings—Viking seamen, by the Powers, that carried sail when they was alive, and was never afraid of wind or wave, all across the Western Ocean—bound West, they was, when we found them buried under big stones in the Shetland Isles, and we signed them on and took them aboard with us, man to man for the last Western voyage. They're aboard with us now; you'll meet them and shake hands with them—if only they had their hands left on—and "How do, Commodore?" they will pipe up, and "Pretty well, thank you," you will say, because these are your kind of men. We was four days at the Faroes, with a wicked sea swinging in across the roadstead, and the ship rolling crazy, like a pan on a blooming galley hook. It was there that we met up with whales—finbacks, sixty-nine feet long—twenty-six of them they'd shot and brought in while we were there, and we saw men wading knee-deep in purple blood. A great place, the whaling station at the Faroes, and you'd do well, Sir, to send the fleet. You'll maybe think we was sick of the wet weather by that time, seeing as how there was never a day without rain and fog, with a dripping wind sighing in over the sea, and us with our sails never dry except when we was under way, and not even then, to speak truth. Not us. We was away when the whales let us go, bound Northwest for Iceland; five days we fought light head winds and fog, and then we came out of it, clear of the weather of the damned Gulf Stream (saving your presence, Sir) and into clear bright days of wind and green seas with the sun shining on the snow on the tops of the mountains, that far away they looked no more than smooth white clouds. We put in on the beach, in a place where Ingoldfr landed in old times, ten hundred and fifty years ago, by thunder, and the worst coast for landing on, and the wickedest beach, that ever was in this world. I mind lads at home that would grow long white beards at the sight of the jumping breakers and the sand driving off the clouds like thick smoke, and us rowing in through the froth, carrying stuff to take pictures so we could convince those same lads later on when we come back. To sea again, we called in at Heimaey—which is "Home Island" in the language these people use, Sir—and spent three days of sunny summer weather that beats Lloyd's Harbor in the best of days, by the Powers, seeing as how you wouldn't be expecting to find it here, in 64 North, within spitting distance, in a manner of speaking, of the Polar Sea. Aye; and we beat up for that harbor in the tight teeth of a gale of wind, no less; force seven on the Beaufort Scale it was, with a mean sea to go with it; thirty five miles, by the Great Hook Block, in ten hours by the blessed clock. She's a ship, this one, and you can lay to it. And now we're in Reykjavik, with the Navy here, and planes flying in the air like you've maybe seen in pictures, Sir, and parties ashore, and such, and tomorrow, or the day after, when the wind serves, we are going to Greenland.

This is great stuff.

The foregoing, Sir, is a partial account of our operations to date and will, when occasion offers and circumstances permit, be supplement by further communications covering the events of our subsequent progress.

By direction,

Arthur S. Hildebrand

What happened to *Liev Eiriksson* and company?

On October 24, 1924, CCA Commodore Marty Kattenhorn sent his first overdue alarms to the U.S. Secretary of State and the U.S. Navy; the last messages anyone in New York had from *Liev Eiriksson* were those two early-August letters from Reykjavik. Only later would word come from others that the little cutter had landed at Julianehaab, Greenland, then departed on September 8 for Battle Harbour, Labrador.

Cruising Club members went to extraordinary lengths to find and help their friends. "It is feared that they are fast in the ice off the west coast of Greenland, or the coast of Labrador, or are ashore upon the Greenland coast or on the Labrador coast," wrote Kattenhorn in a published advertisement. "In either case they are in need of succor, and it is urged that the utmost endeavors be made to find and relieve these yachtsmen."

On October 31, CCA member Henry Wise Wood sent the following telegram to the President of the United States, Calvin Coolidge:

The crew of *Liev Eiriksson* were rife with enthusiasm for their passage,
but they departed late from Greenland as fearful fall gales were likely to set in.
Many tragic stories of the sea forget to mention the family and friends left behind.
Here is Nutting with his wife and daughter, before his final voyage.

THREE AMERICAN CITIZENS [...] WHO LEFT JULIAN-HABB GREENLAND ON SEPTEMBER EIGHTH FOR BATTLE HARBOR LABRADOR IN THE AMERICAN OWNED YACHT LIEF ERICSSON ON THEIR WAY TO THIS PORT ARE NOW FORTYTWO DAYS OVERDUE AND GRAVE FEARS ARE ENTERTAINED FOR THEIR SAFETY STOP THE CRUISING CLUB OF AMERICA OF WHICH I AM A MEMBER APPEALED TO THE NAVY DEPARTMENT ON OCTOBER TWENTYFOURTH FOR THE IMMEDIATE DISPATCH OF AN ICE PATROL BOAT TO SEARCH THE WATERS BETWEEN GREENLAND AND LABRADOR STOP WILL YOU PLEASE WIRE ME THAT PRACTICAL STEPS HAVE BEEN TAKEN BY THE DEPARTMENT TO SUCCOR THESE MEN UNQUOTE NO ANSWER HAS COME TO HAND STOP AS NO TIME IS TO BE LOST I TAKE THE LIBERTY OF BRINGING THE JEOPARDY OF THESE MEN TO YOUR PERSONAL ATTENTION IN FULL CONFIDENCE THAT YOU WILL NOT PERMIT THESE AMERICAN CITIZENS TO LOSE THEIR LIVES IN WATERS SO NEAR OUR COAST THROUGH GOVERNMENTAL INACTION STOP I RESPECTFULLY URGE THAT A VESSEL BE SENT AT ONCE FOR THEIR RELIEF

*"I think often of that night, for the vital issues of life rarely take form so instantaneously and so dramatically. But, as I have said, we let him go. Perhaps the War has something to do with it. It seems so important now that a man should live his life and fulfill his desire, whether it is to die comfortably in bed, or storming one of the Poles. After all, death is not so important, nor indeed so rare, and heroism is both."*

These efforts prompted the Navy to send the *USS Trenton* from New York in early November to search the waters from Greenland to Labrador. She found wreckage, but from the wrong yacht. Well into the spring of 1925 Kattenhorn continued to receive letters from Arthur Hildebrand's mother and others, bearing hopeful tidings from someone in Denmark, or from some Arctic outpost. But no trace of *Liev Eiriksson* or crew was ever found.

Much later, Hal Smith still remembered his distressing dinner with Hildebrand and Nutting in that New York winter of 1924. "Pat and I, 'Hilly's old shipmates, faced each other and one of us said, 'He'll never come back.' Should we have spoken to him? It was beyond our courage, and why it was I cannot explain. I think often of that night, for the vital issues of life rarely take form so instantaneously and so dramatically. But, as I have said, we let him go. Perhaps the War has something to do with it. It seems so important now that a man should live his life and fulfill his desire, whether it is to die comfortably in bed, or storming one of the Poles. After all, death is not so important, nor indeed so rare, and heroism is both."

A dozen years later, A. C. Rasmussen, governor of the Royal Danish Colony Godthaab in Greenland, recalled the enjoyable fortnight of August and September 1924 that he spent with *Liev Eiriksson's* crew. "Julianehaabe was filmed and photographed from one end to the other by Mr. Nutting and Mr. Hildebrand. There was a great deal of life in the Colony during those days and Mr. Nutting showed a live, vibrating activity, being here, there and all over with his apparatuses. Mr. Hildebrand was the more attentive—rather silent and quiet—observer."

By Rasmussen's telling, the latter-day Vikings narrowly missed a chance to walk in the footprints of their namesake. "The original intention was to have the *Liev Eiriksson* visit Brathalid, where the one, for whom the boat was named, had lived. But as a trip like that would require at least three days the idea was given up, although reluctantly, as Mr. Nutting would have liked to follow the route from where Liev Eiriksson had lived to the old Vineland, the same route that Liev Eiriksson himself had traveled about 900 years ago."

Rasmussen's recollection of Nutting's departure leaves no doubt that he was describing the same man—with that same "procrastination and utter disregard of both tide and time which was so characteristic"—that W. P. Stephens sketched at *Typhoon's* homecoming four years earlier.

"They had originally intended to start at about nine o'clock in the morning," wrote Rasmussen, "but their number of friends at Julianehaab was so great and the

The last photograph of "Bill" Nutting and his crew, taken as they were leaving Julianshaab, Greenland, on the voyage to Labrador. The little ship has not been heard of since. Left to right: William W. Nutting, Arthur Hildebrand, Bjarne Fleisher.

Bill Nutting, Arthur Hildebrand, and Bjarne Fleisher exhibit high spirits visiting the town of Julianehaab, Greenland, shortly before setting out for Battle Harbor, Labrador, some 600 miles to the southwest. This would be the the last photograph of the crew, which also included the artist John Olaf Todahl.

leave-taking with each one took so long, that it was three o'clock in the afternoon before they were ready to leave. Loaded with souvenirs from Greenland and tokens of remembrance from all of us the vessel put out from the bridge, where the Danish colony had gathered to see them off and the parting was as festive as it could be made under our primitive conditions. The 'Vikings' sang their gay songs at the parting. After it got out for some little distance it made a curve back and they filmed us where we stood on the bridge waving. We then gave them three cheers and they set out on the voyage, which was to be their last."

Bill Nutting was a man who left an impression long after he was gone. He was "a charming character and good company, a good sailor in some ways, but foolhardy and had too much courage," recalled charter CCA member George Bonnell. Rufus Bradford Burnham, Nutting's friend and colleague from the *Motor Boat* editorial staff, remembered him, too, adding one or two details. "Bill was a daring and often reckless sailor who took risks. He may have been swamped or drowned when all hands were asleep, or he may have had a fire on board as he was not too careful with matches around gasoline."

Whatever William Washburn Nutting was, he was that thing entirely.

The man who graduated from Purdue University with a B.S. in mechanical engineering left this impression on the yearbook staff in 1906: "If Bill hadn't been thrown among civilized surroundings and hadn't been held in check by his strong ambition and good sense, he might have been a counterpart to Jesse James or

Frank Merriwell. He can do a little of everything and is particular how he does it. He dabbles a little in music, literature, art and athletics, and has a propensity for ladies of the Roycroftie type. Twenty years will see him globetrotting in Red Autos and Air Ships."

Those undergraduate yearbook editors knew their man. Eighteen years later, in one of his last letters home, Bill Nutting, ever restless, closed with these words from Bergen, Norway, at the edge of the Arctic Circle:

"It is two o'clock in the morning. An hour ago, it was growing dark; it is growing light now—our latitude is sixty and we are bound northwest. We have been sitting in the cabin smoking Hal Smith's cigars; I have tried to think how I could present the true and accurate aspect of this ship, when the analogies and the comparisons with things at home are so remote and unsatisfactory; how I could convey a sense of our enthusiasm for her, and confidence in her, and her quality of complete security—like the log houses in the high windy valleys at the heads of the fjords. We shall sail this afternoon at six. There will be a heavy sea offshore, and wind, and driving gray rain.

"Next week, beyond the Faroes, or off Rifstangi, I shall sit down again in this cabin, in the midnight daylight, and write something of equipment and design and arrangements and rigging and behavior, and tell you something of what we are doing and how we are getting on, and from time to time I shall go to the hatch to see what sort of weather we are having and whether or not the seas are breaking aboard—and I will set that down, too.

"But right now—well, there is open water to the westward, and we are a thousand years behind."

John G. Alden loved sailing and did not let even a death-defying winter passage
discourage him from his chosen course. He poured everything he learned
in every step of his career into his next design, constantly improving,
and often winning against ever stiffening competition.

# A Great Boost to a Great Sport:
## *Malabar IV* and Beyond

The boat had made magnificent weather of it at all times,
and from then on I was very much in love with this type of boat,
a vessel that sails on her bottom, not on her beam ends.
—John G. Alden
of the fishing schooner *Fame*

"Gale" was John Alden's middle name, and it was a spate of North Atlantic gales in the winter of 1907 that shaped the man who crafted the boats that for a time marked the high water in twentieth-century American yacht design.

Descended nine generations down from that famous John Alden who

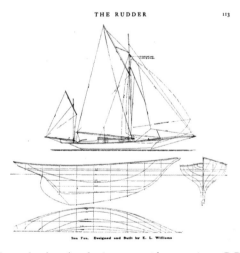

Alden's designer's eye developed early. As an unpaid apprentice to B.B. Crowninshield,
he scraped together enough cash to buy *Sea Fox*, a E.L. Williams design,
with which he won every race in a 1905 Marblehead regatta.

crewed aboard the *Mayflower* and jumped ship at the Plymouth Plantation, circa 1620—the one who in the Longfellow legend bested Miles Standish for the heart of Priscilla Mullens—John G. Alden spent the summers of his childhood near Sakonnet Point in Rhode Island. His first sailing memories, circa 1890, were of a flat-bottomed rowboat aboard which he'd voyage solo down the full length of Long Pond, flying an umbrella for a squaresail. His age was six years old. From that improvised rig, John graduated to catboats by age 10. Within a few years he outgrew those and so with several mates started a teenage yacht club. For $65 each, they bought a small fleet of 21-foot lapstrake knockabouts built near Dorchester Bay in Boston. The builder arranged to deliver the boats 60 miles to the boys in Sakonnet, but John made a separate arrangement. He had his boat shipped 180 miles to the Alden family home in Troy, New York. Why? So that the adolescent could sail it down the Hudson River, around Manhattan, through Hell Gate, and up Long Island Sound back to Rhode Island. He left with a dollar in his cruising kitty and for much of the three-week journey lived on bread and tomato sauce and canned frankfurters. Along the way he suffered crew desertions, lightning squalls, one capsize, and a full-blown chewing out by a rich man in Noroton who 25 years later commissioned him to build a schooner.

Sailing was not only in the boy's blood but also in his mind. During the America's Cup summer of 1895, the contenders for the U.S. defense joined a New York Yacht Club cruise from Huntington Bay to Martha's Vineyard and back, racing as they went. *Vigilant* had successfully defended the Cup in the previous 1893 match—the first of five Nathanael Herreshoff designs to do so. She was a centerboard sloop built of smooth Tobin bronze measuring 124' X 86' 2" X 26' 3" X 13' 6" with her board up, and flying more than 11,000 square feet of sail. Her uncommonly wide beam allowed her movable ballast of 70 Swedes to keep the yacht in optimal race trim, prompting a clause in the next challenge from the Earl of Dunraven that "yachts should be measured with all the weights on board, dead or alive." During the 1895 NYYC cruise *Vigilant* faced a bitter rival in *Defender*, a newer Herreshoff creation. Measuring 123' X 88" 6" X 23' X 19' and setting 12,600 square feet of sail, *Defender* was built of bronze, steel, and (for the first time in a yacht) aluminum. She proved the faster boat, but gear failures over the summer had forced her to exit several major races. Bad blood between the *Vigilant* and *Defender* afterguards ran all through that summer.

On August 2 the Goelet Cup took the NYYC fleet from Newport around Block Island and past West Island, where Sakonnet Point spectators could watch the mark-rounding from shore.

"A group of men formed a circle around John, who proceeded to give them complete details, such as overall length, waterline length, beam, draft, and sail area

*Next young John talked his way into an unpaid apprenticeship
in the office of B. B. Crowinshield, a designer famous
for his magnificent racing yachts but also for his Gloucester
fishing schooners. Within a year Alden worked his way
up to paid draftsman at $15 a week.*

of each of the yachts in the trial race," wrote Alden biographer Robert Carrick. "He also knew of the particular qualities of each boat, how she performed on or off the wind, and the special talents of each skipper."

Alden was 11 years old.

## Trial by Ice

In 1902 the aspiring yacht designer, age 18, flouted his parents' wish and avoided the Massachusetts Institute of Technology. Instead, he got himself hired as errand boy in the Boston yacht-design office founded by Edward Burgess, creator of America's Cup defenders *Puritan* (1885), *Mayflower* (1886), and *Volunteer* (1887)—then promptly fired when Edward's son, Starling Burgess, caught John Alden sketching his own ideas at vacant drafting tables and generally interfering with the firm's real business.

Next young John talked his way into an unpaid apprenticeship in the office of B. B. Crowinshield, a designer famous for his magnificent racing yachts but also for his Gloucester fishing schooners. Within a year Alden worked his way up to paid draftsman at $15 a week. Walking home along the Boston waterfront one evening, he came across *Sea Fox*, a 28-foot yawl with a clipper bow, a high-peaked gaff main, and a sprit-style mizzen. Designed and built by E. L. Williams a decade earlier, the boat featured a ballast ratio that was fully half of her displacement. "Her model and general design are a credit to any designer at any time," Alden wrote of *Sea Fox* forty years later. Faced with an unshakable infatuation and an asking price of $250, John worked nights and borrowed money and bought the boat. In his first season with *Sea Fox*, his funds were sufficient to paint half the boat buff color; the other half stayed green. Still, with a borrowed spinnaker, the yawl won every race in a three-day Eastern Yacht Club regatta in Marblehead, netting her skipper $87.50 in cash prizes—which he "promptly spent at the clubhouses."

B. B. Crowinshield owned, in addition to his design business, the controlling share of a fishing company. In December 1907 word came back from Nova Scotia that small pox had broken out aboard one of the company's schooners and that the ship was now held up in a Halifax quarantine. The 23-year-old draftsman

The B. B. Crowinshield-designed *Adventuress* was a cousin of the fishing schooner *Fame* that established Alden's new working theory after a winter voyage in 1907. "From then on, I was very much in love with this type of boat, a vessel that sails on her bottom, not on her beam ends."

offered to round up a crew and bring the schooner home to Boston. Into that service John Alden pressed his younger brother Langford and three college pals, boys who were only too eager for a taste of adventure over their Christmas holiday.

The fishing schooner *Fame*—125 feet overall, 96 feet on the waterline, 25-foot beam, 16-foot draft, two-masted and gaff-rigged—was normally manned by 23 professional crew. John hired Capt. Joshua Nickerson from Cape Cod, "who was over 60 at the time," and expected to gather delivery crew in Halifax after fumigating the ship. But *Fame's* former captain and crew, feeling bitter toward these newcomers, spread word round the docks that the schooner was cursed. A headline in the local paper ran, "Young American Millionaires Come to Take the *Fame* Home." Meanwhile, someone had put out the word that *Fame* had previously breached an arcane regulation that forbade U.S. fishing vessels from taking on bait or ice in Canada without a license. John and crew were tipped off to the news that a man would arrive on the next train to give witness to the illegal transaction, and furthermore that the captain of the revenue cutter planned to confiscate *Fame* at dawn. That's when the boys and their aging captain decided they could handle the ship themselves and resolved to slip out of Halifax Harbour in the middle of a blustery late-December night.

Their madcap escape had all the makings of a Douglas Fairbanks swashbuckler film. Here's how Langford Alden remembered the exit, some 60 years later:

So we very quietly, and without lights, got all the sails ready to hoist, brought all the chain of the anchor up on deck and arranged it so that it would not foul in running out, and took the top off the windlass so that we could knock the chain up over the top of it quickly. At the given signal, we hammered the chain off the windlass and hauled on the lower and upper jib.

There was a stiff wind blowing straight down the harbour, and the chain ran out so fast that sparks flew from the metal around the hawse-hole. In less than a minute, I would judge, we had payed off and were under way at a good speed. At the first sound, our neighbors [*Fame's* former crew—now murderously angry] were on deck and into their dories, pulling for our ship, and we lined the rail armed with boathooks and belaying pins, but we did not have to use them, as we gathered headway so quickly. The last we saw of them, they were pulling toward the revenue cutter.

We then turned to hoist the foresail, which was a longer job—and then the mainsail, which was very difficult, as we had the wind in back of us and blowing in the neighborhood of 40 knots. With our four lowers set, we then began to make real speed, probably logging over twelve.

We needed all we could get, however, for we soon could see the lights of the revenue cutter, and also the sparks coming out of her funnel. She gradually gained on us, and the ten miles of the harbour and the further distance to the three-mile limit which was then in force, seemed about a hundred. We had too great a start, however, and she finally caught up to us about five miles off shore. She came very close alongside, and her captain hailed us through a megaphone—

"You fellows are just now outside my jurisdiction, and I cannot stop you from going on, but I want to advise against it. You are in no shape as to crew to handle that craft in heavy weather, and there are storm warnings posted from here to Florida. I will have to seize the boat if you do come back, and hate to do it too, but that would be better than all of you going to call on Davy Jones."

There was a chorus from all of us, and much as he must have felt the advice was sound, Captain Joshua shouted back—

"I reckon as how a good Easterly ought to take us to Boston all the quicker, captain, so I guess we'll keep on. I've got a sound ship and willing crew that wouldn't man the sails to take her back to Halifax if I told them to, so I calculate as how I'll have to lay our course for Cape Sable and Cape Ann. Thanks for the advice, which I know is well meant."

"Well, boys, you've got the right stuff in you, and God be with you. So long."

And so they were off. For a while *Fame's* crew made good time of it, clearing all the buoys and headlands of the Nova Scotia coastline. Just one more good day's run, and they'd be inside the protection of Cape Ann. But the wind blew harder, then harder still. The boys tried to double-reef the frozen heavy canvas mainsail and made a hash of the job. The entire main split right along its reef points. Then the jib broke loose and exploded into pieces that weren't worth the saving. A bolt of adrenaline shot through John when in the poor visibility of a driving winter rain *Fame* passed a lobster pot close aboard. He immediately called for a sounding and got 35 fathoms; a second sounding gave 28.

"Tack!"

John Alden was surprised how deftly *Fame* under foresail came through the wind and onto starboard tack, which now carried them eastward, back out into the Atlantic. In that anxious moment, he believed the ship was closing precipitously on the New England coast. In retrospect, he reckoned they must have been crossing Cashes Ledge, still some 75 miles offshore. His snap judgment—erroneous—would prove consequential.

For three days, *Fame's* crew hove-to on starboard tack in a storm that veered from southeast to northwest. "It seemed now," said Langford, "that if you stuck your head up over the rail, you would have your eyebrows blown off. The Weather Bureau reported 88 knots at the Highland Light, which was fairly near to where we were. With only two sails and laying-to, we had our lee rail buried to the cabinhouse. There was nothing for us to do except just stay that way and wait for it to blow itself out."

Meanwhile, their food ran low; in the melee of Halifax, nobody had provisioned the ship. "It was a case of every man for himself," John recalled. Finally the wind abated enough to try sailing again. If they steered northwest, John figured, they'd surely find the continent eventually. He reckoned they were somewhere off Cape Cod. For another three days they sailed that way.

At a Cruising Club of America dinner in 1954, John recalled his first sight of land.

Later the wind hauled from northwest to southwest and we sighted a three-master, the *William E. Litchfield*, reefed and heading southeast. We

*"It seemed now," said Langford, "that if you stuck your head up over the rail, you would have your eyebrows blown off. The Weather Bureau reported 88 knots at the Highland Light, which was fairly near to where we were. With only two sails and laying-to, we had our lee rail buried to the cabinhouse. There was nothing for us to do except just stay that way and wait for it to blow itself out."*

asked him where we were and thought he said "Nauset Light, 6 ¼ miles northwest." The Captain and I were in the fore rigging and I soon saw land. I said to Captain Nickerson, "That doesn't look like Nauset, more like Chatham." The Captain yelled at the top of his lungs, "By God, put her about, boys. We are way down off the Jersey coast."

We tacked with the wet, torn mainsail and she came around and we headed east. On the way out we passed a black can buoy that made us very uncomfortable with our 16 feet of draft. However, we didn't hit and it got very rough and started to rain. We completely split the main and dropped it, running up the Jersey coast under fore and jumbo. We were very weak and dizzy from lack of food and we couldn't lift the mainsail off the stove pipe and as a result a bad hole was burned in it. The old Captain quite distinguished himself by recognizing Absecon lighthouse when he saw it. He hadn't been down that way for 20 years, so he said.

Northbound toward New York Harbor they raced with sheets eased and making good time. By nightfall they could see the loom of the Navesink Light. John thought they might make shelter behind Sandy Hook before a new gale came blasting out of the northwest, but that was asking too much. When the gale did come, they had no choice but to foot off away from New York Harbor and toward the Long Island beach. When they got too close, they jibed over and headed back for the Jersey shore. Several times they reached back and forth in temperatures falling now well below freezing and the wind building. In exasperation they resolved to set an anchor in open ocean. John remembered it this way:

We were icing up badly, and the dories which had been new when we left Halifax, were badly smashed by seas coming aboard. We had one 700-pound anchor left [in their hasty exodus they'd jettisoned *Fame's* primary anchor in Halifax] and some 300 fathoms of 3½-inch-diameter brand new manila cable leading directly from the hawsepipe to the hold. We should first have taken a turn around the bitts, which we did not do, but were afraid of the anchor which we had on the rail. It was blowing around 60 miles an hour and very cold. It was nearly 3 a.m. when the anchor got away from us and the boat started to go astern at a high rate of speed. We did not have a turn around the bitts and we were unable to overhaul enough of the new cable to get one.

We dropped the sails but the boat continued to go astern very fast and we had visions of losing our one remaining cable and anchor. There were kinks in the new cable and we tried jamming the cable in the kinks by inserting some large beams which we found in the hold, but they were snapped at once and it seemed as if we would surely lose our cable. However, one of the crew had more brains than the rest of us and he jammed the hawsepipe with some canvas so we were able to get a turn around the bitts, and to our great relief, *Fame* did not drag.

Through the next day and night they lay thus anchored in the New York shipping channel flying an upside-down ensign in the rigging as a sign of their distress. And although they were once nearly run down by a liner, no ship came to their aid. Finally on the second morning, a revenue cutter came alongside, and— after many pointed questions about where *Fame* had come from and why—towed ship and crew to a dock near Fulton Market. "Finally we went to the Murray Hill Hotel for dinner," recalled Langford. "We were ravenous, and I ate the biggest meal I ever had. As a matter of fact, I couldn't seem to get filled up for about six weeks after."

"On this trip my brother Langford lost 22 pounds and all of us lost from 10 to 12 pounds," said John. "We had been given up for lost and we were about 10 days out of Halifax."

## The Making of the Malabars

The *Fame* delivery left a permanent mark on everyone aboard. But the mark it left on John—a boat-mad boy weaned on the great racing yachts of the early 20th century—would leave a still deeper mark on that first crucial generation of recreational ocean sailors. In those seminal winter weeks of 1907–08 John G. Alden composed the working theory that would forever guide his long professional practice.

"The boat had made magnificent weather of it at all times," he later said of *Fame*, "and from then on I was very much in love with this type of boat, a vessel that sails on her bottom, not on her beam ends."

*The* Fame *delivery left a permanent mark on everybody aboard.*
*But the mark it left on John would leave a still deeper mark*
*on that first crucial generation of recreational ocean sailors.*
*In those couple of weeks Alden composed the working theory*
*that would forever guide his practice.*

A little more than a year later, John Alden married, left Crowinshield, and started his own yacht-design firm. In the 1910 Bermuda Race he crewed aboard Demarest Lloyd's schooner *Shiyessa*, a race they narrowly lost to Harold Vanderbilt's Herreshoff-designed *Vagrant*. John's nascent design practice endured lean years, but he picked up a smattering of plum commissions. In the January 1913 edition of *Yachting* he published a design for what he called "The Ideal Two-Man Cruiser." If readers of that issue were paying attention, they would have seen the first manifesto from the man who within the decade would come to dominate American yacht design. Of his ideal craft, John Alden wrote this:

"She should not be confused with many of the so-called 'cruising yawls,' with long overhangs and all-outside ballast, which sail 'on their ear' in anything over a 15-knot breeze and would pound themselves open in a summer gale on Georges. The midship section shows a generous submerged area, with bilges sufficiently hard to insure the boat's sailing on her bottom instead of on her side, as all who have attempted to cruise in a racing machine know to their sorrow. Then the generous freeboard and easy sheer, combined with good buoyancy and easy entrance forward, will produce the type of vessel which alone is fit to go to sea—that is, one that will ride the seas easily and be relatively dry, and, at the same time, will be able to go to windward through a head sea and wind."

John Alden didn't invent these precepts out of thin air. Instead, his *Fame* delivery led him to a cultural well of boatbuilding and design experience that had been refined over 200 years by raw trial and error in New England, the successes scored by record fresh-fish profits at market, and the failures paid in the lives lost among the hundreds of New Englanders who set off for the shallow North Atlantic banks and never returned. Statistics show that a young man from Gloucester in 1863 had a better chance of survival joining the Union Army and fighting at Antietam than shipping out on a fishing schooner.

The creators of the fishing schooners were modelers, not designers with pencil and paper, as we know them. The builders used trial and error to identify improvements and eliminate failures. Before the 1880s, "there was no general knowledge on the part of modelers or builders of the difference between initial

For the century beginning around 1720, Chebacco boats exemplified standard American fishing boats. With good fishing close inshore, the boats maximized beam to provide ample payload. Only around 1850, with the advent of railroads and ice houses, did American fishing boats evolve into the great schooners—fast and weatherly—that John Alden would emulate as he set the state of the art in 1920s oceangoing yacht design.

stability, the first resistance of a vessel to the heeling power of the wind, and the range of stability, the ultimate point to which a vessel may be forced before capsizing," wrote yachting historian and CCA honorary charter member W. P. Stephens. New England shipbuilders mostly repeated the shapes and structures that had already worked, beginning with the two-masted bluff-bowed Chebacco boats around 1720. These were seldom longer than 40 feet, of ample size and performance for two men and a boy to fish in inshore waters.

"The fishing schooners need not have been of extremely large capacity for their dimensions," wrote yacht-design historian Howard Chapelle (a draftsman in John Alden's design office) of those 18th-century craft. "Before the Revolution the New England fishermen did not need to fish the eastern Grand Banks and most of the colonial offshore fishing was on the banks in the Gulf of Maine, or on the banks between Cape Cod and the Bay of Fundy, relatively close to home." With little need to be either fast or weatherly, these vessels were bluff-bowed, with their full beam carried well into the forward sections.

But as demand increased and fishing moved out to Georges and Grand

Banks, these hull forms proved deficient. "The inability of the 1830 bankers to work to windward in heavy weather was the cause of many losses of vessels and lives," wrote Chapelle. "If they went adrift when anchored on the windward side of the Georges, for example, or were embayed in Chaleur Bay on the north shore of Prince Edward Island, for another example, many could not work clear in a gale and were soon in breaking seas on the shoals. Here they were out of control and were soon knocked down and swamped, or grounding, they broke up."

Like so many other technologies, American shipbuilding was an interplay between emerging ends and means. The greatest of all new *means* in this context was ice: new icehouses in Gloucester and Boston that preserved fresh food for transport. For 200 years, Americans had little choice but to take their fish dried, smoked, or salted. But once ice could deliver fish fresh to the dinner plate, consumers demanded it—and paid premium prices to get it. Meanwhile, other new means (canals, railroads) opened consumer markets far into the continent.

The first rail line came to Gloucester in 1846; the first icehouse, in 1848. In 1847 Andrew Story of Essex, Massachusetts, launched *Romp*—the American fishing schooner that changed everything. At 65 feet overall, with a 19-foot 9-inch beam and 7-foot 1-inch draft, *Romp*, the first so-called "sharpshooter" schooner, had "a straight keel of marked drag, moderately raking sternpost, with round tuck, upper-and-lower transoms, square stern, raking stem rabbet with a rather long, pointed cutwater fitted with headrails and billet," wrote Chapelle. "The midsection was formed with sharply rising, long straight floors, high, hard turn of the bilge, and some tumble home in the topside. The model was supposed to have some slight resemblance in lines to the Chesapeake Bay keel schooners, but wider and more powerful."

In *Romp's* first season, Gloucester crew refused to go out in her; she didn't look right. Yet here was the first example of what we today would recognize as a classic American fishing schooner: a vessel that could not only beat to windward safely but could also get back to port first to set the market price.

It's interesting to note that within two years of *Romp's* launch another similar experiment with irreversible results was happening 250 miles away in New York.

"Prior to 1849 the yachts of both America and England were modeled on the 'cod's head and mackerel tail' principle; the midship section, or point of greatest breadth, being about one-third of the length from the stem; the entrance thus being very round and full, while the two-thirds of after-body or run gave a long, clean delivery," wrote W. P. Stephens. "In 1849 George Steers modeled and built the pilot boat *Mary Taylor* with a long, hollow entrance and a relatively short run; in marked contrast with all his previous practice. Why he thus went contrary to all established ideas on both sides of the Atlantic is a question to which there is no answer."

This was the same George Steers who, one year later, would apply what he'd learned with the *Mary Taylor* to create the schooner *America*, setting off the America's Cup.

Over the next 80 years *Romp's* basic form would be tweaked and modified by degrees. It was only in the 1880s that the designing of fishing schooners—by the likes of Edward Burgess, Thomas McManus, and John Alden's employer B. B. Crowninshield—emerged as its own activity distinct from the earlier design-build modeling methods that had dominated for all those decades before. Still, with *Romp* the mold for an American original form was cast.

"Even if we disregard the somewhat apocryphal origin ascribed to the term 'schooner,' it must be admitted that this rig, fore-and-aft, two masted, is distinctly an American institution," wrote W. P. Stephens. "The schooner rig itself, and the form of hull best suited to carry it, attained their highest development on this side of the Atlantic."

This was the cultural well that John G. Alden was dipping into when he extolled the virtues of an oceangoing craft that "will ride the seas easily and be relatively dry, and, at the same time, will be able to go to windward through a head sea and wind."

The U.S. entry into World War I interrupted John's design practice for much of 1917, but it wasn't long after the Armistice before he emerged with the series of oceangoing yachts mellifluously named for a Cape Cod shoal (now known as Monomoy) that would forever be linked with his name. In a 1928 magazine article John Alden described the genesis of his *Malabars*:

> The first of my *Malabars* has the fisherman as the basis of her design. Let us first look at the true fisherman as exemplified in the Gloucestermen, which I have always admired and with a few of which I had something to do years ago. Simple in section, all her ballast inside, short ended, low sided for ease of handling dories, beamy to gain capacity, fast and able but never quite at her best until loaded, easy to build and therefore cheap—we find many qualities here desirable for a yachtsman.
>
> Let us also look at the *Lloyd W. Berry* [owners Roger Griswold and Harold Peters, early CCA members]—a 60-foot schooner designed or rather modeled by Charles A. Morse of Friendship sloop fame, and built by C. A. Morse and Son of Thomaston, Maine. [*Author's note:* The same property evolved into Lyman-Morse Boatbuilding, owned by the family of CCA member Cabot Lyman and managed by Drew Lyman.] She is a slightly modified fisherman and a fairly successful yacht.
>
> Recalling the ease with which the *Lloyd W. Berry* handled and how

Alden admired the *Lloyd W. Berry*, built by Charles A. Morse of Thomaston, Maine.
Visiting the yard in hopes of finding a fishing schooner he could convert, he walked away
with a handshake agreement: Morse would build a new boat of Alden's own design
on a cost-plus basis with no contract. The result was the first of the Malabars, pictured here.

well she sailed, my mind became fixed on the schooner rig and I wandered
Down East to Morse's yard hoping to find some small fisherman that
could be converted at small cost. As Mr. Morse put it, he was "too busy
to talk." I was halfway up the hill when I was hailed to "come back here."
The result was that I ordered a schooner from him, the 41½-foot overall
*Malabar I*. This had been far from my intentions, but, being the result, I
hastened back to my office to draw the plans.

John Alden designed *Malabar*, and Morse built her, as well as the next four
*Malabars*, on a cost-plus basis with no written contract. John intended *Malabar*
to be sailed shorthanded, even singlehanded. Her considerable sheer forward gave
way to a cutaway forefoot but then plenty of drag in the keel. A fine entry allowed
her to handily cut through a chop, while breadth in the quarter sections encouraged her to stand up to plenty of sail. Ease of handling? *Malabar I* could beat to
windward under her 284-square-foot foresail alone.

Alden sold *Malabar I* at the end of her first season and so set a pattern that
would repeat for the next decade and more: build a *Malabar* for himself over the

From his design office in Boston, Alden brought forth a string of classic boats, mostly schooners, that pleased clients, inspired copy-cats, and frustrated his professional competition.

winter; sail her in the summer; then sell her in the fall. "A season's intimate living with one boat," said John, "has shown me where to improve her or given me new lines to experiment with."

## The Right Boats for the Right Moment

While John Alden was experimenting with his first *Malabar*, William Washburn Nutting was returning from his transatlantic *Typhoon* adventures, and Roger Griswold and Harold Peters from theirs aboard *Lloyd W. Berry*. The sub-chaser commanders and lieutenants were returning home from their World War I commissions. Something new was in the water—a new spirit of oceangoing adventure that for the first time was larger than an individual Joshua Slocum or Howard Blackburn or Tom Day. The overflowing enthusiasm John felt toward ocean sailing was not his alone but was now shared by a growing cohort. When the Cruising Club of America was formalized in 1922, John G. Alden was among its charter members.

One of those sub-chaser commanders was Herbert L. Stone, the *Yachting* editor and another CCA charter member. Delivering *Malabar II* through a gale with John in 1922 set off Herb's own flights of enthusiasm. "For ease of handling," he wrote of *Malabar II*, "she has anything I have ever been on beaten, coming and going. She was hove-to in a strong southeaster some 15 hours between Thomaston and Cape Ann, and under reefed foresail she fore reached slightly all night, making very little leeway, so that the next morning when the wind slacked off so that she could be put on her course again, she had made only 5 miles leeway." *Two's* subsequent owner took her on a four-month Atlantic circle between April and July—and never once reefed. Lowering one or two sails was all she needed in heavy weather, and still she sailed balanced.

Sailing *Malabar II* inspired Herb L. Stone to reanimate the Bermuda Race in 1923.
"For ease of handling, she has anything I have ever been on beaten, coming and going."
Two's subsequent owner sailed her on a four-month Atlantic Circle and never once reefed.
Lowering one or two sails was all she needed in heavy weather, and still she sailed balanced.

Here was a vessel, Stone thought, that exemplified his aspirations for some event that would encourage a whole generation of oceangoing cruising sailors. In *Yachting's* January 1923 issue, Stone published the notice for a race to Bermuda, a course that had not been sailed for 13 years; the last one, in fact, had been the very race in which Alden crewed. Stone's initial race rules set out the following enduring goals: "To encourage the designing, building, and sailing of small seaworthy yachts, to make popular cruising upon deep water, and to develop in the amateur sailor a love of true seamanship, and to give opportunity to become proficient in the art of navigation."

He hoped his proposition would attract a half dozen boats. Nearly two dozen crossed the starting line. Remarkably, every boat that started also finished, more than 600 miles later in the Onion Patch, a nickname for Bermuda that derived from the island's most famous 19th century export. The modern Bermuda Race was reborn.

By that summer of 1923, John Alden had built his fourth *Malabar*. While the first three were similar in design and build, with only minor modifications

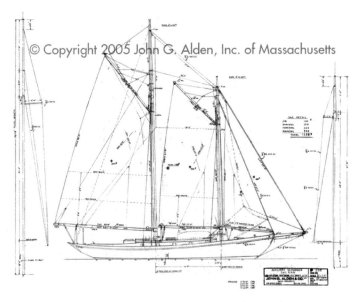

Design No. 205, *Malabar IV*, was a great leap forward for Alden,
an all-out racer with accommodations for a larger crew.
The sail area expanded, and she was the winner in every race she started in 1923.

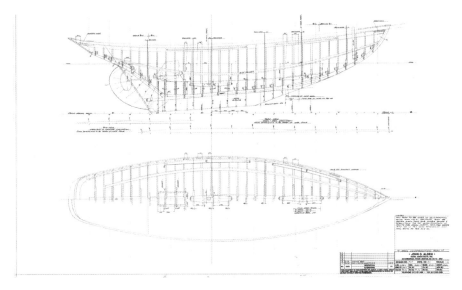

The construction details of *Malabar IV* show a strongly built boat
made to stand on her feet with a deep keel. Her internal
and external ballast was nearly half of the displacement.

*Malabar IV*, winner of the 1923 Bermuda Race. She represented the state of the art in ocean sailing yachts for the next decade until younger upstarts would try something new.

of a lengthened bow and diminished sheer, as well as a single unbroken cabin house, the *Four* was a complete departure. For one thing, John Alden had fallen overboard from the foredeck while singlehanding *Three* in Buzzards Bay. By luck, he was able to grab on to the shrouds and haul himself back aboard, but in subsequent man-overboard drills he was never again able to get himself back aboard. With his thirst for singlehanding slaked, he designed a purpose-built racer with provisions for crew and even a paid hand. *Four* measured 47 feet on deck, 35 feet 6 inches on the waterline, and 12 feet across the beam. He added ballast, particularly in the keel—49 percent of the yacht's total displacement, compared to 33 percent in the first *Malabar*. He put it to use with 1,220 square feet of sail area in the lowers, plus a main topsail.

It worked. *Malabar IV* won all eight races she started in 1923.

In *A Berth to Bermuda*, yachting historian John Rousmaniere reflected on her showing in that seminal moment in ocean sailing. "The overall winner had not been coddled. This was John Alden's 47-foot gaff-headed schooner *Malabar IV*, the first of his boats designed with racing in mind, with a cloud of sail that pushed her through the whole fleet in the light going after the start and carried her brilliantly to the finish. *Malabar* won the race on sheer power."

Marine journalist, William H. Taylor, reflected on Alden's influence in a

1962 article for the *Cruising Club News*: "If there was any doubt about who was designing smart seagoing sailing craft, that 1923 Bermuda Race dispelled it. It wasn't only that John Alden won it in *Malabar IV*, but "Malabars" took three of the first five places among 23 starters. *Malabar I*, renamed *Damaris* and owned by Dave Atwater, was fourth boat and the fifth, Jack Parkinson's *Mary Ann*, was practically a sister ship to *Malabar II*."

These were the kinds of results that would dominate ocean racing for the next decade and more, before such younger upstarts as Olin Stephens and Phillip Rhodes would introduce still faster ocean voyagers. Every Bermuda Race through the mid-1930s saw Alden yachts at or near the head of the fleet.

Olin Stephens, another boat-mad kid of 18 who would go on to become one of the most prominent yacht designers of the 20th century, sailed one of those races with John Alden.

> One way or another, I pressed Sam Wetherill, *Yachting* magazine's assistant editor, to get me a berth on the new *Malabar IX* for the Bermuda Race of 1928, and one way or another it worked, so I was invited. John Alden, Sam Wetherill, and their crew were certainly the most successful offshore racing sailors of their day. After 1928, John and I were competitors rather than members of the same crew, but I respected him greatly even though I preferred a rather different type of boat than his. He loved going to sea and he loved to race. Further, winning was good for his business, but he never let the urge to win overcome his judgment as to the nature of the proper seagoing yacht. I say this as one who has faced the same problem, and I feel sure that it was John's nature to think first of the sea. With his eye and his feeling for shape, he had the tools to apply his seagoing experience. It has been a pleasure to be reminded of the part John played in the development of offshore sailing and racing. He provided a great boost to a great sport.

Olin's younger brother, Rod Stephens, Jr., skippered *Dorade* to first in Class B
in the 1932 Bermuda Race. The crew had plenty of talent, and no doubt were helped
by the easily driven, narrow hull, and impeccable sails.

# 4

# Sailing with Olin:
# Aboard *Dorade*, Across Oceans and Decades

Why would you name your boat after a vent?
—passing sailor, to Matt Brooks

Just after dawn on a summer day—July 21, 1931—a signalman at England's southwestern-most promontory hoisted three blue-and-white flags: one with 16 squares; the second shaped like a swallow's tail; and the third featuring an equilateral cross. Their simple message: "You are first." The white yawl

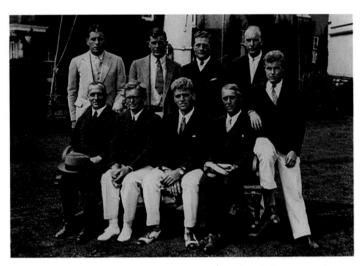

The youth of Olin and Rod, Jr. was evident as they posed with the crew, and two English welcomers, after the 1931 Transatlantic Race. Olin is seated second from the right, Rod, Jr. is third from the right. Their father, Rod Stephens, Sr., the fourth from the right, paid to have *Dorade* built, and he also raced the 3,000 miles from Newport, Rhode Island, to Plymouth, England.

below, 39 feet on her waterline, had just beaten nine other yachts, including two 70-footers, in the 1931 Transatlantic Race from Newport, Rhode Island—by two full days.

"The beginning of some history for the world of boating was made at that moment," wrote yacht designer Francis Kinney almost 50 years later.

This story begins two years before that transatlantic landfall, on still another summer day, when a 21-year-old college dropout in The Bronx sat drawing inked lines on linen. That was Olin Stephens drawing the lines of *Dorade*, based on his design work for the new hot class of racing boat, the International Six Meter. It was just weeks before the stock market crash that would precipitate the Great Depression.

Olin and his brother Rod, eighteen months younger, had been attracted to sailing and yacht racing during childhood summer vacations to Cape Cod, and from their home in Westchester County, New York. No generations of sailors had come before them in the Stephens family line; this enthusiasm was all their own. The boys' teenage years coincided with a new wave of enthusiasm in the United States for ocean sailing as a sport, marked by the founding of the Cruising Club of America in 1922 and the reintroduction, after more than a decade, of the Bermuda Race in 1923. Holding ocean races was the best way to develop skills in new sailors, reasoned *Yachting* editor, Herb Stone and his CCA cohorts, as well as to inspire quality in a new fleet of oceangoing sailboats.

For all their youth, the Stephens boys were keen observers, and as they approached adulthood, they received ever more invitations to race with, and against, the leading sailors of their time. Of their late teen years, Olin wrote,

Rod Stephens, Jr. was a keen observer and practitioner of all manner of seamanship skills. From an early age he understood ocean conditions, could get the most out of any boat and crew, and was as prepared as possible. He claimed he cruised at 95% of racing efficiency. From *Dorade's* cockpit, he calmly sizes up a following sea, mid-ocean.

*After that 1928 Bermuda Race John Alden offered
Olin Stephens a job in his design office. But instead of accepting
Alden's offer, Olin—bankrolled by his father and abetted
by his brother—embarked on a brash experiment
that would establish a new state of the art.*

"Rod and I were no longer shy in approaching the giants of sailing." The boys were 16 and 17 in May 1925 when Sherman Hoyt, the best round-the-buoys sailor of those days, gave them their first taste of sailing Six Meter yachts. "Six Meters were, and still are, one of the very finest sailboats to race," wrote Kinney in *You Are First*, his 1978 biography of the Stephens brothers. "Their performance is supreme. Their speed and responsiveness, the way they thrust to windward! These were sensations utterly foreign to Rod and Olin, who had known only the poor performance of their other boats."

In 1928 both boys crewed in the Bermuda Race aboard contenders designed by John Alden—Olin aboard *Malabar IX* with the master designer himself, and 18-year-old Rod aboard the Marconi-rigged schooner *Teal*. Alden's *Malabar IV* had won the 1923 Bermuda Race, and his *Malabar VII* had won in 1926. In fact, John Alden designed all but one of the five schooners that ever won Bermuda races. Throughout the 1920s, Alden's fisherman-type schooners competed with Nathanael Herreshoff's creations as the state of the art in American yacht design.

After that 1928 Bermuda Race John Alden offered Olin Stephens a job in his design office. But instead of accepting Alden's offer, Olin—bankrolled by his father and abetted by his brother—embarked on a brash experiment that would establish a new state of the art.

In his 1999 autobiography, *All This and Sailing, Too*, the much older Olin Stephens reflected on that 1929 season when he was creating his first ocean-going yacht—a design he named for the swift dolphinfish, or dorado. No detail from Olin's previous summer aboard *Malabar IX* seemed to escape his attention. "The popular fisherman-type had a combination of outside and inside ballast, and the ballast that was inside and higher contributed less to stability," Stephens wrote. "Frames in the Maine-built schooners were generally sawn and doubled to reinforce the necessary joints. But it seemed anyone who was serious about racing-yacht design could visualize a faster combination, and the key was in City Island construction."

*Anyone?* The young fellow who could visualize that faster combination would grow up to become the man the National Academy of Sciences deemed "the preeminent designer of sailing yachts" of the 20th century. Like many other great inventors, Olin Stephens looked at the things he saw around him—the materials, the techniques, the structures—and mixed them in ways they'd never been mixed before. Occasionally, Olin or Rod would add some entirely new detail. But mostly he mixed existing ingredients in entirely new ways.

With that in mind, it's worth examining the problems 21-year-old Olin identified, and the solutions he discovered as he set about creating *Dorade*. "Weights and lines routinely received my first consideration—weights having an importance above all," Stephens wrote. By the 1920s New England boatbuilders had amassed more than two centuries of experience sending sailboats and crews into the North Atlantic after cod and halibut, summer and winter, with the faster vessels fetching the top market prices. It was from this deep cultural well of assumptions and techniques that Alden's schooners were built. Meanwhile, a separate fleet of racing yachts was built lighter with the understanding that they'd remain inshore, safe from the ocean's worst rages. Olin saw a middle way between these boatbuilding cultures. His innovation for a new ocean racing boat was to blend the building techniques he saw around him on Long Island Sound—particularly at Henry B. Nevins Inc. on City Island—with scantlings aimed at offshore ocean conditions. Instead of sawing, doubling, and bolting pieces of oak to create the curves for a boat's frames, as the New England builders of fishing schooners did, the "City Island way" (following Nathanael Herreshoff's practice) was to steam-bend the oak. This way, the grain, and therefore the strength, followed the curve of the lumber.

Olin described it:

> The bent framing in particular was much lighter than the double-sawn fisherman-type framing made up of short sections overlapped to support the joints. By using wider frame spacing, part of this doubled weight could be saved, but only at the cost of heavier planking needed by the greater span between frames. Similar weight-saving was made in the decking where beams were placed at each frame, permitting relatively light deck planking. Most of *Dorade's* deck beams were spruce, lighter than the oak of the fisherman-type, and offsetting the closer spacing. Such savings permitted a higher ratio of ballast to displacement. All of this, except a little trimming ballast, was outside on the keel where its longer lever arm contributed more to stability than was possible with the combination of outside iron and whatever went inside on the more conventional boats.

*"In any design the most important factors of speed
seem to be long sailing lines and large sail area,
with moderate displacement and small wetted surface.
Then comes beauty, by which is meant clean, fair, pleasing lines.
Though per se beauty is not a factor of speed,
the easiest boats to look at seem to be the easiest to drive."*

To obtain seagoing strength, Olin specified 9-inch centers for *Dorade's* steam-bent 2-inch-square white-oak frames—more conservative than the Nevins convention of 11 ¾-inch centers, but still lighter than sawn-and-bolted pieces of oak. That closer spacing justified 1 ¼-inch planking of Honduras mahogany, following scantlings adopted under the race-boat convention of the Universal Rule but lighter than the traditional fisherman-type specs. His spruce deck beams were lighter than traditional oak, but he added strength by running them in unbroken lines athwartships, even across opening hatches. A low, almost flush, cabin house further contributed strength. For deck planking, he specified white pine: still grippy, but much lighter than traditional teak. How much lighter? Olin didn't know. He just knew it was lighter. For *Dorade's* cabin sole he replaced traditional teak and holly with a lighter cork material. Lead ballast (at roughly 700 pounds per cubic foot) replaced the schooner's traditional iron (500 pounds per cubic foot), and he placed virtually all of it in the keel, much lower in the boat. In detail after detail, Olin identified weights and either reduced them or moved them lower in the boat—and did so without any of the tank-testing or computational fluid dynamics or other quantitative tools that he and later generations of designers would eventually rely on. Olin would come to adopt and even pioneer some of those emerging scientific practices in yacht design—and despite his lack of formal mathematical training. But all of that came later. "With *Dorade*," Olin wrote, "the design work was strictly comparative and intuitive." What intuition! On his first try, Olin's decisions saved one-fifth of the weight of a similar boat built in the traditional New England method.

Now let's look at the *lines* that Olin drew. A page from *Yachting* magazine's January 1928 issue carries the first published words from Olin Stephens, then age 19, including these about his initial design of a Six Meter: "In any design the most important factors of speed seem to be long sailing lines and large sail area, with moderate displacement and small wetted surface. Then comes beauty, by which is meant clean, fair, pleasing lines. Though *per se* beauty is not a factor of speed, the easiest boats to look at seem to be the easiest to drive."

The boy who wrote those lines had already spent many a Sunday hanging around the City Island waterfront "to study, admire and photograph boats." In 1927, when the Seawanhaka Corinthian Yacht Club hosted the Scandinavian Gold Cup at Oyster Bay, New York, the competing international Six Meters were shipped from Europe to the Nevins yard for commissioning. All the while, Olin watched.

"I compared the contrasting designs and was impressed by the beauty of the boats designed and built in Scotland by William Fife, Jr. His signature was unmistakable in the clean, nicely balanced ends, the midsection with a little more beam and a firmer bilge than most, and his use of a touch of sheer more than the minimum required by the rule. His art did not stand in the way of performance." This was the same William Fife whose photographed sailboats caught Matt Brooks' eye at the yacht broker's office on a fateful day in May 2010.

With *Dorade's* lines as with her weight, Olin drew from examples he saw among the coastal racing fleet and applied them to his oceangoing boat. Compared to her offshore sisters, *Dorade* is, above all, a narrow sailboat. "I drew *Dorade's* lines in the same short period as those of two new Six Meters. *Dorade* had essentially the same beam-to-length ratio as they did." This sentence flows easily enough from Olin's pen, but among the old salts of 1930 it amounted to heresy. Alden's *Malabar X* and Bill Nutting's *Typhoon* came in with a waterline-length-to-beam ratio of 2.9; Nutting's beloved *redningskoite*, between 2.4 and 2.5. *Dorade's* 10-foot 3-inch beam on a 39-foot load waterline comes to 3.8. While greater beam allowed the fisherman-types to carry more sail and conferred good performance off the wind, *Dorade's* slender lines, together with her high ballast-to-displacement ratio, made her uncommonly weatherly among the seagoing craft of her day.

Olin and Rod were fortunate in one aspect of their lives that cannot be over-looked: a supportive and generous father. Roderick Stephens Sr. encouraged his sons' sailing interests from early on, buying the series of cruising and racing boats that gave them a chance to learn for themselves, even as their experience quickly outstripped his own. When Olin left the Massachusetts Institute of Technology partway through his freshman year, the gregarious Rod Sr. introduced him to potential employers, clients, and partners. Most consequentially, he had the will to believe in Olin's first great experiment, as well as the means—even in those early Depression days, having recently sold a coal-distribution company—to sponsor it. It was Rod Sr. who commissioned Minneford Yacht Yard on City Island to build *Dorade* for an agreed fee of $20,000, plus $8,000 for equipment and fit-out. That's $418,000 in 2020 currency. Rod Sr. owned *Dorade* for her first two seasons, then gifted the boat to the boys, giving them their start.

Until the 1930s, heavy gaff-rigged schooners, derived from fishing and other coasting vessels, dominated the ocean racing fleets. *Dorade* heralded a new design era of lighter hull construction, deeper keels with external ballast, and tall Marconi rigs for better close-hauled performance.

Dorade's debut season of 1930 turned heads but didn't yet rise to the stuff of legends. In that year's Bermuda Race, by his own admission, Olin botched the navigation, adding 10 miles and doubling the distance of the ultimate beat around Kitchen Shoals. In the final tally, *Dorade* lost to Alden's *Malabar X* and a smaller schooner called *Malay*. The top three boats in Class A that year were fisherman-types, as were the first and third finishers in *Dorade's* Class B.

Olin later recalled the last miles of that race:

> There was some compensation in the fact that we saw twelve larger boats ahead of us toward the finish and on the way passed them all, crossing the finish line ten seconds ahead of the leader.
>
> Looking back, that beat, as we ticked off one boat after another, is still a high point in my sailing experience because it confirmed all I had hoped for in *Dorade*—a real sea boat that could go to windward with the out-and-out racers.
>
> In the lee of the islands there was very little sea but there was just enough slop to hurt the schooners with their greater beam and less-efficient rigs. *Dorade's* narrow hull sliced through that chop, just loving it. Our tacks were long as we approached and became shorter as the lay lines grew closer. The breeze was moderate, maybe ten to twelve knots and just shifting enough to let us take advantage of the headers. We were racing every second; some of the others were cruising, but it took nothing away when we heard later how observers at St. David's had seen a tiny spot of white come in over the horizon, and how rapidly it grew. Their appreciation of our last few miles eased the disappointment of failure to win.

An editorial in *Boats* magazine recorded *Dorade's* performance and proclaimed that she would "alter the whole concept of the ocean racer and make profound changes in defiance of the sailing world of her time."

Olin and Rod, ever the keen observers, paid careful attention to which of their experiments had worked at sea and which didn't. They spent the winter of 1930–31 correcting flaws. And then they launched *Dorade* for the 1931 season that would become the stuff of legend—a season that would include the personal congratulations of Great Britain's King George V and culminate in the first-ever ticker-tape parade through downtown New York City in honor of a boatload of amateur yachtsmen.

At noon on July 4, 1931, *Dorade*, engineless through all of the six years that the Stephens family owned her, dropped her tow and fell off to the left side of the course in a fleet of 10 boats, each one racing across the North Atlantic Ocean and bound for Plymouth, England.

## How She Rolls

Despite all of his attention to weights, on her original launch day, *Dorade* came in 4,000 pounds heavier than Olin had calculated: closer to 38,000 pounds than 34,000 pounds. With her narrow beam, she sat significantly lower in the water, with an actual load waterline of 39 feet, instead of 37 feet 6 inches. But because

*Dorade* had her flaws, which Olin recognized early on, and would not repeat in later designs. The narrow beam, which was meant to reduce water drag on the hull and increase speed, made her very tender. She heeled excessively and rolled persistently downwind.

his lines for her hull were so fair, so balanced, so flowing, this mistake did not fundamentally harm the boat's sailing behavior. Rod simply repainted the waterline, and Olin adjusted her handicap rating.

More consequential was the sail area. *Dorade* was too tender. One of the first items on Olin and Rod's agenda before the 1931 Transatlantic Race was to reduce the rig—shorten the mast, shorten the boom, and remove the bowsprit altogether—bringing her sail area from 1,192 to 1,079 square feet. And that beam? It "was certainly too narrow," Olin later wrote. "As a result she heeled too easily and too far, losing drive from her rig and forcing her crew to live in a limited space and remain balanced at a high angle of heel." This flaw was more serious; the only solution was to design more boats. "Out of that fault came *Stormy Weather*," said Olin, "a boat with two feet more beam, faster, roomier, and more stable."

In the 2015 Rolex Fastnet Race, the contemporary owners of *Dorade* and *Stormy Weather* would have a chance to test whether what Olin believed was true.

These two boats—launched in 1930 and 1934—are still out there on the water, still ocean sailing, still racing competitively. It's worth the pause to let that sink in.

Sailors through the decades have agreed on one thing: *Dorade* rolls like no other craft they've ever known. Wave after wave, set after set, when sailing off the wind, *Dorade* rolls, dipping first her boom, next her whisker pole. Again and again, mile after mile, gunwale in, gunwale out.

"Have only one fault to find with *Dorade*," wrote Sherman Hoyt in his 1950 memoir. Erstwhile guru to the teenaged Stephens brothers, in 1933 Hoyt crewed under Rod, age 22, for *Dorade's* second transatlantic passage, this time to Norway. "Perhaps it is more an acquired vice than an intrinsic fault and whisper it softly among the ocean going crowd, but *Dorade* is a roller-maniac. At any time running free with or without provocation she is prone to indulge in orgies of rolling. Unreasonable, unrestrained, free wide and handsome she rolls with blissful abandon. Perhaps it is our deep loading, her narrow beam or the rather heavy mast, but my can she roll!"

A 9-by-4-inch notebook filled with penciled jottings from the summer of 1931 tells the whole story of *Dorade's* first transatlantic passage in delicious detail. We here in the 21$^{st}$ century have only to fill in the cycling sibilance of a thousand-mile seaway as it froths along the waterline, the creaking of spruce and oak and mahogany at work, and the propulsive acceleration in our guts as we race down the faces of those gray North Atlantic combers.

> *Sunday, July 12, 4 p.m.,* course E. x S. ½ S. Wind: W., moderate. 9.0 knots. Rolling quite a lot. (Because she is running before the wind.)
> *Monday, July 13, 6 a.m.* W., moderate (breeze). Hit 10.8 on the gauge. Spinnaker dropped. Called all hands. Hauled in safely. Halyard chafed through at head block. Rod to masthead, reeved double halyard.
> *4 p.m.* (Steering) E. x S. W.N.W., (still) fresh. 9.8 knots. Hit 10.85 twice. Grand sailing!
> *Tuesday, July 14, 2 p.m.* Wind: S.W., fresh. Best speed so far 11.4 knots for the Commodore! 11.35 for Rod. 11.3 for John.
> *Thursday, July 16, 12 noon.* S.W., fresh. Set new record of 11.7 knots!
> *2 p.m.,* course S.E. x E. ¾ E. S.W., fresh (breeze). 11.2 knots. (Boiling along!)
> *Saturday, July 18, 3 a.m.* S.W. x W., fresh (breeze). 11.1 knots. Doused light spinnaker and balloon jib. Set heavy spinnaker, storm jib, forestaysail.
> *6 a.m.* Blowing hard and rolling a lot.
> *7 a.m.* S.W. x W. fresh +. Breezing up. 11.2 knots.

*With that,* Dorade *won the triple crown*
*of ocean racing: the Transatlantic Race,*
*the Fastnet Race, and the TransPac Race.*

For five consecutive hours on one night of *Dorade's* 1931 transatlantic passage, her crew drove her consistently beyond 11 knots.

As a skipper and navigator, Olin had honed his skills since the 1930 Bermuda Race. An informal survey of the contestants for the 1931 Transatlantic Race hinted that most of them would pick a course far enough south to benefit from the boost of Gulf Stream current. Olin considered this. As youngsters, he and Rod had read *Track of the Typhoon*, which describes a more northerly eastbound route hugging Newfoundland's Cape Race, then advancing quickly toward 50 degrees north latitude. In spring of 1931, Olin wrote to Casey Baldwin, Nutting's partner for *Typhoon's* outbound passage, to learn more about those northern stretches of ocean. This route would more closely follow the great circle between Newport and Plymouth, reduce the total number of miles sailed, and, with any luck, put them in a zone of stronger westerlies. The downsides included fog, shoal water, and maybe icebergs.

"There was another consideration," Olin later wrote. "If most of the fleet, as I believed, were to take a southern route, and we went with them, we would be racing most of the fleet. Other things being equal this would be one chance in ten. If we went north the odds were one chance in two."

Olin went north, and the rest is history. *Dorade* beat that transatlantic fleet of mostly larger boats by two days and more. And lest anyone think this result was a fluke, she handily won that year's Fastnet Race. She won her class in the 1932 Bermuda Race. In 1933, Rod sailed her back to Europe and won the Fastnet again—after which, race committees on both sides of the Atlantic started revising their rating rules. Rod's 8,000-mile transatlantic summer of 1933 earned him the CCA's Blue Water Medal for that year. In 1936, the Stephens brothers sold *Dorade* to James Flood of San Francisco, a St. Francis Yacht Club member, who entered her in that year's Honolulu Race (now the TransPac). And how did *Dorade* perform under new ownership? She swept: First overall. First in class. First on elapsed time. First time ever. With that, *Dorade* won the triple crown of ocean racing: the Transatlantic Race, the Fastnet Race, and the TransPac Race. After eight decades and counting, no other yacht has ever matched that achievement.

Before we leave the Stephens family, there's one small matter we can't overlook, and that's the ventilation into the boat's cabin while at sea. *Dorade* was not

The "Dorade box" was an innovation of Rod's to solve the curse of breaking waves on deck being funneled through the ventilation scoops onto the crew living below. His hardware design moved the cowl vent from the deck to the top of a box with scuppers to let any water run out on deck. Under the box and offset from the vent, a raised collar around the hole in the deck allowed only air to pass below. Ocean sailing became drier, at least below.

born with Dorade vents. That invention, now so ubiquitous on seagoing boats, evolved in steps, and all credit for that one goes to Rod.

At first before we started across the Atlantic in April, 1933, she had cowl vents on high necks. The cowls were arranged to turn at the tops of these necks. Next I put in a low baffle just inside the mouth of the cowl with a scupper hole at the base of this plate. It didn't work very well as far as keeping water out. Then I got the idea of putting a box over the tube, which I cut off above the deck. Then the idea of having the cowl tube come into this box forward of the deck tube came to me. At that stage the box had screw-in cover plates for two holes, one above the downtake and one above the cowl tube's forward position. Later we simplified this scheme by eliminating the hole above the downtake.

## A Winning Restoration

Pam Rorke Levy and Matt Brooks knew some but not all of *Dorade's* history as they stood among a small group of folks in Newport on that day in September

Some people believe classic yachts should be treated like pampered pets.
Matt and Pam wanted *Dorade* to continue to race the oceans of the world.
Maintaining an octogenarian racing yacht in racing trim
is not for the faint of heart or wallet, and it is a labor of love.

2010 when they became her new owners. But there was one thing that Matt clearly did know.

"After the contract was signed," Matt recalled, "I said to the broker and to the various people that were in and around the boat that we planned to take her out in the ocean and repeat all of her earlier races." The responses from the assembled gathering were skeptical. "You'll ruin the boat." "You don't take things like this out in the ocean!"

From the time Olin and Rod sold her to James Flood in 1936, *Dorade* had passed through a dozen different hands, mostly on the Pacific coast. For a decade in the 1980s and 1990s she served as a sail-training vessel for teenagers at the Four Winds-Westward Ho camp on Orcas Island in Puget Sound. Beginning in 1996, Giuseppe Gazzoni-Frascara took her to the Italian Mediterranean coast and underwrote an extensive refit at Cantiere Navale dell'Argentario—inaugurating another new era.

"Classic-yacht restoration had been limited to a few, large, outlying projects," wrote Douglas Adkins in his book *Dorade: The History of an Ocean Racing Yacht*.

At the time, Elizabeth Meyer had restored the J-Class *Endeavour* and founded the International Yacht Restoration School in Newport, which initially focused on restoring 12-foot Beetle Cats. But the *Dorade* refit started something else. "In many ways, the restoration of *Dorade* changed all of that for a cadre of important boats in the medium size range. In 1930, *Dorade* and Olin Stephens achieved a breakthrough in the field of yacht design. Some 67 years later they created another breakthrough in the field of yacht restoration." When Gazzoni-Frascara completed his refit, the Sparkman & Stephens firm, from which Olin had retired in 1978, presented him with the "Rod Stephens Restoration Award for the Outstanding Restoration of *Dorade*, S&S Design #7, 1997."

*Dorade* raced again in Europe, but mainly in inshore regattas among classic-yacht classes. As later owners would discover, her 1996 refit was more cosmetic than structural. Ocean sailing, particularly ocean racing, was not in the picture—that is, not until September 2010. If Olin's original experiment was brash, so too was Matt Brooks' declaration that he'd see her compete again in the great ocean races where she first made her name.

"Edgar Cato had really saved the boat," said Pam, referring to *Dorade's* owner from 2006 to 2010. "He went in and replaced a lot of the frames in the middle of the boat that had never been addressed. That's not sexy work. That's invisible work. It means taking the whole boat apart, and he replaced the frames with like kind. It was a very expensive process. But he really set the boat up so that it could actually, eventually go back into the ocean."

And now, her 15th owners intended to prepare her to do just that.

Matt Brooks contacted Greg Stewart shortly after he purchased *Dorade*. "Matt had decided he wanted to retrace all the races," Stewart recalled, "and we were going to do a restoration on the boat. At that stage, she was more set up for inshore sailing. The first thing we needed was an engine. But when we got into things, the scope of work just magnified. It became new mast, new electrical system, new galley, new navigation station. We just really went through the whole boat."

Still, the refit posed one puzzle after another. Olin was a technological innovator, but he launched *Dorade* eight years before the invention of polyester—the essential component in today's composite boatbuilding resins—as well as the Dacron that long ago replaced cotton sails and manila rope. Which choices are within bounds for a restoration to original condition?

For the regattas that allow it, Matt did choose to fit *Dorade* with cutting-edge North 3Di sails, which are composed of 21st-century materials and technology. The winches are not self-tailing—and not powered, either. In 1930 *Dorade's* complement of 12 winches was one of her defining forward-looking features in an era when many of her competitors still managed sailing loads with block and tackle.

Matt and Pam and crew took *Dorade* "down under" for the 2017 Sydney Hobart Race,
winning second place within two rating rules. She is seen here
running past the basalt cliffs of Tasman Island.

During their first year of ownership, they watched the 2011 New England summer sailing season come and go. *Dorade's* planned nine-month refit stretched to thirteen. So in late fall of 2011, Matt and Pam had her shipped south for the Caribbean winter and spring sailing seasons.

As Team *Dorade* began notching ocean-racing victories, there were always two competitions at play in Matt's mind: *Dorade* versus the contemporary fleet, and *Dorade* versus her former self from those days in the early 1930s, when Olin and Rod were pushing her so hard. The log entries from *Dorade's* 2015 Transatlantic Race show that the Stephens brothers had never really left the cockpit. Team *Dorade* 2015 beat Team *Dorade* 1931 by more than a day, despite adding more than 200 ice-avoidance miles to the course. And just as in 1931, the crew enjoyed only a brief pause before it was time to tune up for the Fastnet—in which *Dorade* would meet her younger sister, *Stormy Weather*, and arguably her greatest rival.

The two boats had met in the 1934 Bermuda Race, the last major ocean race in which Olin skippered *Dorade*. The result? *Dorade* crossed the line more than

*Dorade* and *Stormy Weather*, Olin's 1934 beamier improvement on *Dorade's* design,
had a head-to-head contest in the 2015 Fastnet Race, rounding the famous "Rock"
with *Stormy Weather* leading by seconds halfway through the 600-mile race.
Neither of them were young, yet both were doing what they were designed to do.
*Dorade* finished ahead to earn second in class.

Opposite: The venerated Sparkman and Stephens *Dorade* showed her winning style
on the 2013 Transpac Race. Her owners, Matt Brooks and Pam Rorke Levy,
proved that the yawl, after 83 years, was still competitive; she finished first overall.
The 52-footer turned heads in 1931 when—with her 23-year-old designer Olin Stephens
skippering—she crossed the finish line two days ahead of the next boat
in the 1931 Transatlantic Race to England.

five hours ahead of *Stormy*. After that, with the exception of a few smaller regattas
on Long Island Sound, more than 60 years passed before the two boats met
each other again, on the European classic-yacht circuit. At the start of the 2015
Fastnet, the first real ocean test between these siblings since 1934, the rivalry was
still spicy.

 People from Rolex, the Fastnet Race sponsor, saw a story here. Shortly before
the race, they told Pam and Matt that they intended to film the event—and more

Olin Stephens kept pace with his famous designs.
He was out on the water watching boats
at the age of 100, just the summer before he died, in 2008.
His keen interest in advancing yacht design never faded.
And oh, what advances he made!

particularly that they wanted to put camera crews aboard both *Stormy Weather* and *Dorade* to witness this historic meeting firsthand. "And" writes Pam, "because I had been a filmmaker for 35 years, it made sense for me to go along."

In his book *Dorade*, Doug Adkins posited a theory on how this boat has been experienced by women and men. "She was always a man's boat. Not overly comfortable, with a cockpit that required creative seating, she delivered wet plunges to weather in a heavy sea and a dark and cramped interior. There had never been and never were to be feminine devotees of *Dorade*. She was beautiful and exciting to men, and generally seen as a rival for attention, adulation and resources by women."

Pam's experience with *Dorade* stands as a stark revision of this thesis. "Well, I love her," she said. "To me she's part of the family. She's like a really wise older sister. You are trusting her with your life, and there's a real feeling of that contract with her: that you're going to take care of her, and she's going to take care of you."

Olin, perhaps with some regret, had never made *Dorade* a part of his own family. "I am often asked about my boys and sailing and can only say that they missed something that was a great experience for me. It would have been difficult for me to give them what I had, largely because my sailing was all with clients and much of it was abroad. Undoubtedly more effort on my part could have given them greater opportunities, but despite the real joy of my own early days on the water my personal sailing became more and more a business."

Olin was 99 years old the last time he sailed *Dorade*. "He sailed with Cato in fall 2006, and then I think some in '07," said Stewart. "I remember 2008, I was steering *Dorade* for Edgar in the New York Yacht Club Spring Regatta in June, and Olin was out in a tender. Olin waved over and said, 'Hi Greg.' And that was the last time I ever saw him." Olin Stephens, age 100, died on September 13, 2008.

Through the years of Pam and Matt's relationship with *Dorade,* Pam has connected with Olin's family in New England. For the 2015 Transatlantic Race, she invited Sam Stephens and Olin Stephens IV, Olin's son and grandson, to come to Newport to watch the start. It was the first time either of them had ever been aboard *Dorade*.

Other yacht owners built a relationship with Olin while he lived and worked. Pam and Matt are the first of *Dorade's* owners who endeavor to maintain his legacy.

"Olin was a very humble person," Pam said. "I hope that what we're doing would make him proud."

Electa "Exy" and Irving Johnson were full partners from 1932
on a series of sailing vessels named *Yankee*. For 26 years they sailed with young paying crew,
circling the globe seven times, and writing articles and recording film for *National Geographic*.

# 5

# Irving Johnson: The Women and Men Aboard *Yankee*, Around and Around and Around the World

It is almost appalling when we consider that Irving Johnson skippered
the two *Yankees* seven times around the world. Certainly he is worthy to take his
place in history with Magellan and Sir Francis Drake
as one of the world's greatest sailors in sail.
— John Parkinson, Jr.
*Nowhere Is Too Far*


My father has been given a tremendous amount of credit for the voyages that he
did, but he couldn't have done it without my mother. They really worked as a pair.
—Robert Johnson


In January 1935, Irving Johnson landed at Cape Town, South Africa, halfway
through his first circumnavigation, when a message came in from his brother
back in Massachusetts.

"Girl Scout troops booked for *Yankee's* summer charters."

Irving brought this news back to his crew of mostly young men. More
than a dozen in number, they'd all been aboard the 92-foot 19th-century
North Sea pilot schooner since Gloucester. Fourteen months underway
had shown them what shipboard rigors any future crew would face. Don't
take this charter, they counseled. A crew of girls could never handle *Yankee*
under sail.

"The story goes," says Nancy Richardson, "that Irving marched up to the
Western Union office in Cape Town and was going to send a telegram and tell
his brother to find somebody else for the summer charters. But the telegram
cost something like $35. And this was in the 1930s. It would have cost that

much to hire the ship for a week. So Exy convinced Irving that it would be OK, and they should try it. And for all the summers until World War II, and then for a dozen more years on Brigantine *Yankee*, the charters were mostly all Girl Scout Mariners."

When Nancy Richardson first met Irving Johnson, she was a third-grader in Maplewood, New Jersey, circa 1949, still too young by several years to become a Girl Scout Mariner. Her mother had brought her to a film presentation Irving gave at the junior high school in her home town, a show that illuminated *Yankee's* world voyages to the South Seas, to Southeast Asia, to the African continent. Then and there, Nancy resolved to commit her life to discovering the world he opened to her. Decades later she went on to direct the Girl Scout Mariners nationally and take a leading role at the American Sail Training Association and the Los Angeles Maritime Institute. Today she holds a world record for logging sea miles aboard more than a hundred sail-training ships.

And who was the "Exy" in her anecdote?

She was Harriet Electa Search Johnson of Rochester, New York, by way of Smith College and Berkeley and Paris, also the wife and lifelong shipmate of Irving Johnson—and, perhaps too secretly, the key to the whole *Yankee* legend.

## The *Yankee* Legend

Women of the era generally accepted the secondary role to their partners, but that did not mean they were not fully competent and deserving recognition. It was said that Ginger Rogers was every bit the dancing equal of Fred Astaire, but, with a knowing wink, it was also said that she had to perform backwards and in high heels. Rogers was not shy about her achievements. She said, "You know, there's nothing damnable about being a strong woman. The world needs strong women. There are a lot of strong women you do not see who are guiding, helping, mothering strong men. They want to remain unseen. It's kind of nice to be able to play a strong woman who is seen."

There were several women who sailed the oceans with their husbands in the mid-20th century. The well-known voyaging couples Eric and Susan Hiscock and Miles and Beryl Smeeton were Blue Water Medalists for their passages in the 1950s. Less well know were William and Phyllis Crowe who set out from Hawaii in 1948 and caught up with their friends Irving and Exy Johnson in Samoa, during *Yankee's* Fourth World Voyage. At the completion of their circumnavigation, Phyllis Crowe became the first woman listed along with her husband in the awarding of the Blue Water Medal in 1950.

The Cruising Club of America, reflecting the era, welcomed Irving as a member in 1947, but chose not accept women members until 1994. It should be

*And the* Yankee *legend arguably owes* everything *to her.*
*"A lot of people don't realize how really important my mother*
*was to the whole thing being successful at all,"*
*said Robert Johnson. "It was a real partnership,*
*and they had complementary skills."*

added that the Johnsons did not receive the Blue Water Medal, because they were not considered amateurs. With or without recognition, Exy carried out her essential role of managing many aspects of their livelihood and family life. Virtually everything Irving did, Exy did, too—sometimes with a baby on her hip. And the *Yankee* legend arguably owes *everything* to her. "A lot of people don't realize how really important my mother was to the whole thing being successful at all," said Robert Johnson. "It was a real partnership, and they had complementary skills."

That partnership had its beginnings in 1931 aboard Warwick Tompkins' North Sea pilot schooner *Wander Bird*. "Gwen Tompkins was a college friend of mine," wrote Exy, "and on a visit aboard *Wander Bird* in Boston in the spring I had been completely fascinated by the life the Tompkinses led sailing their schooner more than half the year. My seagoing experience and knowledge were a perfect zero, and one weekend aboard even at anchor introduced me to things I never knew existed—ships under sail, long passages at sea, bunks, charts, swinging tables and incomprehensible sailing talk. But the ship herself somehow appealed to my absolute ignorance and wonder. I took the train back to Rochester, family, and job, determined that I must sail with the *Wander Bird* in the fall."

When Exy did eventually return to *Wander Bird* (by then in France) and resolved to sail aboard her (transatlantic to the US East Coast), the news set off alarm bells back at the Search residence. "That was entirely unsatisfactory for her parents," said Robert Johnson, speaking of his maternal grandparents. "Her mother sent her father to France with one ticket over and two tickets back to pick up their daughter. Well, he came over, and he and his daughter had a discussion, and he went back alone."

It was in Le Havre during that season of heightened feelings that Exy Search first met Irving Johnson, *Wander Bird's* 27-year-old mate.

"My seagoing equipment included a Siamese kitten," wrote Exy, "for in Paris they cost only a fraction of what they do in New York and I had always wanted one. The poor kitten, however, lasted only three days under sail. I believe this kitten did not help to give Irving a very favorable first impression of me, but that was not my aim in life till at least a couple of days later. In the meantime I found out what a nuisance long hair was on a schooner in dirty Channel weather and inquired for the ship's barber. The unanimous response was 'Irving,' and as he took a long time at the job and I watched carefully in the mirror, our acquaintance ripened. Beyond this point I shall only say that it was a perfect cruise for three months."

*Wander Bird* crossed the Atlantic from Europe by the southern route that's typical of fall crossings, then headed north to New England. "My father noticed that my mother enjoyed sailing even when it got cold," said Robert. "There was some snow, I believe. He thought that if she could enjoy sailing under those conditions, that was a very good sign."

Irving and Exy married in 1932, then applied some of what *Wander Bird* had taught them. For one thing, Warwick Tompkins took aboard paying passenger-crew to defray the schooner's costs. Irving, for his part, had saved the earnings from a string of crewing positions "in banks that didn't fail," according to Robert. With the Great Depression on in Europe as in the States, it was a buyer's market for old sailing ships.

The ship they found, similar to *Wander Bird*, was a 92-foot Dutch pilot schooner built at the end of the previous century for continuous North Sea service. The Johnsons named her *Yankee* of Gloucester, fitted her out for voyaging, and set about assembling an amateur crew to sail around the world. The model of living that they invented in that summer of 1933 was one they'd follow through the next three decades, interrupted only by World War II.

"Our plan," wrote Exy, "was to sail with a number of young people who would share the expenses of long cruises. Irving would be owner and skipper, and the crew, with the exception of a regular sea cook, would be amateurs. Everyone would help sail the ship, standing regular watches, four hours on and eight off. We knew this was possible because we knew our ship. If we got one of those North Sea pilot schooners, we could start right off on long cruises with green, amateur crews because the high bulwarks would keep them aboard, and they would not be too scared to handle sail anywhere on deck; the long keel would make for comfort at sea and livable conditions below, and the sail plan did not require Banks fishermen of many years standing to handle even in the worst weather. It was this conviction that the ship of our choosing could do what we asked of her that made us believe in the world cruise as a reality from the very first."

From their first year together, the Johnsons lived out their lives in three-year cycles: 18 months circumnavigating the world, then for the next 18 months weeklong summer charters and wintertime lectures to earn some money. Between 1933 and 1941, *Yankee* circumnavigated three times, providing the material for two books and the first of ten inspiring *National Geographic* features. Along the

The Schooner *Yankee*, ex-*Tegel*, was a 92-foot Dutch pilot schooner built at the end of the previous century for continuous North Sea service. With their young crew and growing family, the Johnsons circumnavigated three times aboard her between 1933 and 1941.

way, the Johnsons had two sons. "There were no children on the First World Voyage [1933–35]," said Robert Johnson. "My brother, Arthur, was ship's baby on the Second World Voyage [1936–38], and I was ship's baby on the Third World Voyage [1939–41]."

The outbreak of war compelled Irving and Exy to sell the first *Yankee*, known forever afterward as "Schooner *Yankee*." Shortly after the war, the Johnsons purchased a second North Sea pilot schooner of similar dimensions, which Irving converted to a brigantine rig for trade-wind voyaging with an amateur crew. Aboard this ship they reprised the rhythm of their earlier lives and circumnavigated four more times between 1947 and 1958. Their second ship came to be known as "Brigantine *Yankee*." In all, the Johnsons circumnavigated seven times between 1933 and 1958.

Robert does not recall the story about his father's initial reluctance to take Girl Scout Mariners aboard, as Nancy Richardson does. "I have never heard the story about possibly not chartering to the Girl Scouts, but that does not mean it is not true," he said. "Both the *Yankees* were very safe ships because of their high bulwarks and other reasons. On all the world cruises we left Gloucester with crews as green as the GS Mariners. The *Yankees* could be handled safely and with very few people, especially when near a shore with many possible harbors."

Here, Exy describes the crew composition at the outset of *Yankee's* Fourth World Voyage in November 1947:

Two young women had a great perch to take in Rapa Iti Island in French Polynesia, which is hard to get to even today. Exy wrote, "*Yankee*'s experience convinced us that women are an asset on long cruises. They make a ship homelike, prevent barrack-style conversation, please the eye and the camera."

Then it was the eve of sailing day and the crew and their families were together for the first time at a farewell dinner. Twenty-four people, who in a year and a half ahead would come to know each other as few people outside their own families ever would, were looking each other over hopefully, speculatively.

They looked good to us that night and we felt they would make a good crew. We believed that if we picked a group of young men around twenty [years old], girls somewhat older, and a few others of any age, and all were reasonably average human beings, we could make out together. In picking crew for a long cruise, we do not look for people of great sailing experience. The first mate must be chosen with care, of course, as one who has sailed and can take the Skipper's place in an emergency. Among the others there are sure to be some who have sailed enough to furnish a second and third mate to take charge of watches. But we look primarily for people who will be able to get along with each other.

We have always included some girls in the crew of the *Yankee*, the number depending on the cabin arrangements and the number of children we had at the time. In the new ship we had room for four girls in the two double cabins. Louise Stewart of Philadelphia planned to make only part of the cruise. She was one of the most attractive and talented girls who had ever sailed with us, having gone through Wellesley, had a part on Broadway, written a column for *Ladies' Home Journal* and become a captain in the Marines doing public relations work. Besides, Louise was extremely photogenic and we were always improving the salability of our pictures by getting Louise into them.

The three girls who went all the way around the world were the answer to anyone's objection to taking women to sea. They were good company and good sports; they put a great deal of interest into the cruise and got a tremendous amount out of it, both at sea and ashore. We would gladly keep them on *Yankee* forever.

Including young women among the crew was a choice Exy had advocated from the very beginning. "*Yankee's* experience convinced us that women are an asset on long cruises," she wrote. "They make a ship homelike, prevent barrack-style conversation, please the eye and the camera."

Not to say that *Yankee* was an experiment in proto-feminism. More accurately the Johnsons' example was a bridge between the Victorian norms of a generation before and the full gender equity that the following generation would so widely seek. "I realized, and I think the other girls came to realize, that we had to occupy a certain kind of position," Exy reflected in 1992. "It was kind of a case of staying out of the way of the boys, not getting in their hair, because it was a young man's cruise, really."

## He Was a Man's Man

Irving Johnson as a young man was steeped in the old-school romance of the sea, entirely intoxicated in the spirits of Rudyard Kipling and Jack London. Born in 1905, he trained his body relentlessly and took up boxing so as to hold his own in the rough-and-tumble fo'c'sle those stories had taught him to expect. "He stood on his head on the top of every telephone pole in Hockanum, Massachusetts," said Betsy Johnson, Robert's wife. Though his trained fists were never called upon to settle a shipboard dispute, Irving Johnson's oaken physique formed a solid part of the *Yankee* legend. Well into his sixth decade, the skipper would challenge young crew to do as he did, holding a shroud with

He was a man's man. To prepare for the rigors he imagined he'd face at sea, Irving "stood on his head on the top of every telephone pole in Hockanum, Massachusetts," said his daughter-in-law Betsy.

both hands and extending his body rigidly parallel to the deck. The ship's log records none who could match him.

"My father had an air of authority, whether on the ship or not," said Robert. "He never had discipline problems."

Before meeting Exy, Irving had shipped out with the merchant marine and accepted several yacht-crewing positions. In 1929 he joined the crew of the four-masted barque *Peking* out of Hamburg, one of the last sailing cargo ships. From the 16-millimeter footage he gathered and later edited into the famous film *Around Cape Horn*, scenes show Irving climbing hand-over-hand down the luff of a squaresail. He helped deliver Sir Thomas Lipton's J-Class *Shamrock V* trans-atlantic through a hurricane back to England after an America's Cup challenge in the fall of 1930, and crewed aboard George Roosevelt's *Mistress* in the 1931 Fastnet Race. In the 1932 Bermuda Race he sailed aboard the schooner *Twilight*, arriving eight hours behind Olin Stephens' Class-B winner *Dorade*.

By virtually any measure, Irving Johnson delivered the goods. In the summer of 1941, when U.S. involvement in wars on two fronts seemed imminent, Irving and Exy sold their beloved *Yankee*, and he joined the U.S. Navy—encouraged by his friend William J. Donovan, whose wife, Ruth, and two children had sailed long stretches with the Johnsons aboard *Yankee* in the seasons just before "Wild Bill" created the Office of Strategic Services, precursor of the CIA. Irving was already stationed in Honolulu when the sun rose on that infamous December day. (And so, by the way, was Exy. While virtually every American civilian dependent evacuated following the Japanese attack on Pearl Harbor, she successfully petitioned the Navy commandant for permission to remain in Honolulu to aid the war effort.)

"War caught me in Hawaii, advising the Navy on locations for new South Seas bases," Irving wrote of his time in the so-called "Survey Navy," an arm of the U.S. Navy Hydrographic Office. "In Pearl Harbor stood the *USS Sumner*, the Navy's special survey ship. *Sumner* got off to a fighting start December 7, 1941, when one of her three-inch guns exploded the first Japanese torpedoplane in mid-air. Destiny brought us together. Of all the Navy assignments available, none could have suited me better than duty as navigator with rank of Lieutenant Commander. I was eager to make charts."

And so he did. The state of play was that the U.S. Navy was operating in a region where its best charts were a century out of date, with consequences as harrowing as the Japanese guns. One of the few battleships in the Pacific in those early days of the war, *USS South Dakota*, tore out her bottom in 1942 on an unreported reef.

"In 1942 the *Sumner* was detailed to load Marines and take over the Wallis Islands," wrote Irving. "I was assigned to the party because, I believe, I was the only Navy man who had been to Wallis before the war. I remembered from my *Yankee* days that Uvéa, the main island in the Wallis group, was surrounded by a coral reef whose dangerous lagoon channel had already claimed several ships. For safety's sake, we entered the channel on a slack tide, which lasted barely 15 minutes. I took station in the crow's nest. There I looked deep into the clear water, just as I did from *Yankee's* square-sail yard a few years earlier. We were nervous lest an enemy shell end our survey before it began."

In the Navy, Irving eagerly took on new challenges. "As professional divers were not available, we accepted the job," he wrote. "We entered blasted hulls [of Japanese ships] in total darkness. Codes, messages, charts and other secrets were jimmied from compartments."

From Guadalcanal through Iwo Jima, Irving Johnson typically arrived alongside or even ahead of the Marines. "The survey of Iwo Jima proved the most thrilling, difficult, and dangerous of all," Irving wrote. "Our first job was to rush a survey for harbor development near the front line. *Sumner's* crew men worked under sniper fire in small boats and beside the Marines ashore. As bullets splashed nearby, they found it difficult to concentrate on sextant angles. The enemy poured volleys at us from caves in the hills, dragging their artillery back into the earth after firing a couple of rounds. Determination of Iwo Jima's exact position on the planet was a hard job, because the island, built of volcanic ashes, was so loose at the joints that it refused to stay still. We were trying to use an astrolabe, a delicate instrument employed for determining position by the stars. Gunfire and demolition blasts, shaking the entire island, made observations inaccurate within a hundred yards. Finally we were compelled to maroon our astrolabe party on a bare but solid patch of rock half a mile from Iwo Jima. There men built a five-ton concrete pillar to hold the instrument steady. Disregarding land-mass errors, they were able to locate a spot not much larger than a barrel head. Such extreme accuracy was needed for the sake of secret Loran navigational installations."

Following his Navy days, Irving would henceforth answer to Commander Johnson or *Captain*. "To former crewmates he was always referred to as *Skipper*," said Betsy Johnson.

## Around the World in Brigantine *Yankee*

Once the war had well and truly ended, the Johnsons straightway went looking for a ship. "We left New Orleans last June, Irving getting out of the Navy and the boys out of school the same day," Exy wrote to a friend in 1946. "We drove home and were only on hand a week or so when Irving sailed in the Bermuda Race on the schooner *Brilliant* (which didn't do any winning) and from Bermuda flew to England to buy the only boat in the world we wanted. There just aren't any others.

After World War II, Sterling Hayden found the Johnsons their new pilot schooner in England, this one a German war prize. For tradewind voyaging with an amateur crew, Irving converted this new *Yankee* to a brigantine rig. "I'm just trying to pick the best rig for the job," Irving told a skeptical crowd of sailors. "That's not going back; that's going ahead."

We have found the North Sea pilot boats have a combination of qualities that no others have, and this seems to be the only one afloat in good condition."

The new ship was similar in type to their previous ship. But while Schooner *Yankee* was built of wood in Holland in the 1890s, Brigantine *Yankee* was built of steel in Germany in 1912. Called *Duhnen*, she'd been used during the war by the German Luftwaffe. The British Royal Air Force had taken her as a war prize.

Aboard Brigantine *Yankee,* Exy and Irving and crew sailed four more times around the world between 1946 and 1958.

"Sterling Hayden, our mate on the Second World Cruise [1936–38], was in northern Europe at the end of the war and had a chance to look over the sailing ships still afloat," wrote Exy. "It was he who discovered the *Duhnen* and first told us about her." This was the same Sterling Hayden who served in the Office of Strategic Services in Yugoslavia, before becoming a Hollywood actor in such films as *The Asphalt Jungle* (1950), *Johnny Guitar* (1954), *The Killing* (1956), and who played the iconic General Jack D. Ripper in Stanley Kubrick's *Dr. Strangelove* (1964). Sailors know him for his books *Wanderer* (1963) and *Voyage* (1976). Irving described Sterling Hayden as the most natural sailor he'd ever met.

The *Duhnen* answered their wishes almost perfectly. "No other ship we saw combined such comfort, dryness, and size (96 feet), the qualities we needed most," wrote Exy. The one significant change Irving made to this new *Yankee* was to convert her rig from schooner to brigantine, a rig he designed himself—and a decision that some of his fellow sailors criticized as backward-looking. These were the post-war years when weatherly ocean-sailing yachts drawn by Olin Stephens and Philip Rhodes set the tastes, with their sleek lines, their tall Marconi mains, and their overlapping genoa headsails.

"I'm just trying to pick the best rig for the job," wrote Irving in a piece for *Yachting*. "That's not going back; that's going ahead."

In this case, the job to be done is to push a 96-foot strongly built, North Sea pilot boat around the world. The crew will be large, but all-amateur, and many of them will never have been to sea before. The schooner rig in the larger sizes was never designed for long ocean passages in the Trades. Its main use was in coastwise work. Long booms and gaffs combined with large sails cause the most trouble in a big schooner. They slat and chafe and are hard to control. Unintentional jibing is much more dangerous than getting caught aback with a square-rigger. A long main boom will hit the tops of the seas, and running wing and wing makes steering too difficult to be practicable.

The new *Yankee's* mainsail and its boom and gaff are small for the size of the ship yet the square rig forward will furnish plenty of sail for running. Jibing will not be eliminated but its danger will be far less and the mainsail will never need reefing. By the time it has to come in, the storm trysail will provide sufficient sail aft. It's surprising how well square sails work to windward if they are properly cut and the yards are braced around far enough. Notice that without any squaresail, there remains a complete staysail schooner rig.

Strange as it may seem, in the old *Yankee* we always figured anybody could furl the squaresail, but only the best men could tackle our gaff topsail. Those who know square rig realize that it's twice as easy (and safe) to furl sail on a yard as to grapple with a big gaff topsail. After all, the main loss of men on the old clippers was not from falling out of the rigging, but from getting washed overboard, and that's something we never have to worry about.

After the long war, getting back to sea in their new *Yankee* was a pleasure for the whole Johnson family.

"The ship sailing steadily along felt good to us," wrote Exy. "Her behavior brought back the familiar feelings that make sailing fascinating. There is the sensation of lying in a groove instead of a flat bunk as the ship heels over and the equally familiar jolt when you suddenly forsake that groove as the ship comes about and leans the other way. Your ear, only a foot from the blue ocean overside, grows used to the sound of seas roaring past."

Through repetition and careful attention, the Johnsons worked out the kinks

"Those who know square rig realize that it's twice as easy (and safe) to furl sail on a yard as to grapple with a big gaff topsail. After all, the main loss of men on the old clippers was not from falling out of the rigging, but from getting washed overboard, and that's something we never have to worry about." – Irving Johnson

of a model that sustained them through that astonishing record of seven circumnavigations. Among other things this experience taught them exactly how much each voyage would cost. A form letter addressed to prospective crew in 1950 lays out the arrangement:

> The expenses are divided evenly among all the group on board. The captain estimates that each full share on the Fifth World Voyage will amount to $4,860, or about $9 a day. [That's $53,817, or $99.16 per day in 2020 dollars.] This amount covers all expenses aboard the *Yankee* whether she is at sea or in port. If the total expense turns out to be more than that, Comdr. Johnson will pay the balance, as most crew members do not feel that they can obligate themselves for an unknown amount. If the expenses turn out to be less than the estimated amount, he will refund the balance divided equally among all the crew members. Comdr. Johnson and his wife will not receive any of this balance as he does not wish to profit from any overestimate that he might make. His living is made by lecturing between cruises and writing books and magazine articles.

Each new amateur crew inevitably suffered seasickness in those first few days after their November departure from New England, and they nearly always endured a proper cold dousing as they crossed into the Gulf Stream on their initial outbound leg. But once into the warmer Southern waters, newcomers would be introduced to the pleasures of life at sea.

"As the *Yankee* sailed steadily along in the warm blue seas of the Tropics," wrote Exy, "the skipper introduced the crew to his favorite sport, 'bos'n chairing.' A davit is swung out and the boatswain's chair hung from it on block and tackle. You climb in and someone on deck lowers away. Then you get a real ride, dragging through the water at the *Yankee's* side. At three knots, it is a languid, cooling bath; at five it is a brisk ride; at seven you whip though the water with every bit of energy absorbed in holding yourself upright; at nine only a few men try it, and everyone gathers at the rail to watch. Sometimes the rider is completely out of sight in a smother of foam; sometimes he is in mid-air for several seconds between the top of one wave and the next. It is a mad ride, and never a silent one. Whoops and shouts come from the boatswain's chair, often cut off abruptly just in time to avoid swallowing the next wave."

Again and again and again, *Yankee's* itinerary would visit some of the places on the planet most remote from urban civilization: the Galapagos Islands, Pitcairn Island, Borneo, Siam, Bali, Mozambique. Taken together, the Johnsons' books and superbly illustrated *National Geographic* articles provide some of the best available longitudinal studies of isolated cultures from the 1930s through the 1950s, particularly in Oceania.

## From Sail Training to Sea Education

Among the papers in the Irving and Exy Johnson Collection at Mystic Seaport Museum is an invoice from American Flag Company of New York for $6.54, dated September 30, 1950. It is for a Cruising Club of America pennant, 24 inches by 36 inches—the only club flag, according to Robert, that *Yankee* ever flew.

Although the Johnsons invented their own model for taking amateur crews to sea for their own reasons, the *Yankee* cruises exemplified one of the CCA's earliest core values. In its first year, the CCA launched what it called the Apprentice Plan. Under Sandy Moffat's direction, the members aimed to recruit young men to sail aboard their boats "in order that they might be taught seamanship and develop a love of the sea, thereby perpetuating the ideals of the Club."

It's hard to imagine that any single member did more than Irving Johnson to spread the values of the CCA Apprentice Plan. And it's equally hard to imagine that without Exy that exposure to the sea would also extend to young women. In the end, it's almost impossible to overstate the impact *Yankee* had on generations

*It's hard to imagine that any single member did more than Irving Johnson to spread the values of the CCA Apprentice Plan. And it's equally hard to imagine that without Exy that exposure to the sea would also extend to young women.*

of both men and women. For every young woman who actually sailed aboard *Yankee*, some innumerable multiple was inspired by the *National Geographic* articles and, as Nancy Richardson tells us, Irving's in-person presentations.

In an interview before the 2020 start of the Vendée Globe Race, solo circumnavigator Samantha Davies described the crucial role of models and mentors. "I never even imagined that I could cross an ocean. It was too scary and too far. I loved boats, and I kind of wanted to design them, but to be on one was just beyond my expectations or dreams. Yet without knowing it, the fact that Tracy Edwards had done what she'd done with *Maiden* and her crew [1988 Whitbread Round the World Race] connected something in my brain, or ticked a box that had never been ticked before. It made me and probably a lot of other women or girls realize that things were possible that weren't even imaginable at the time."

As Tracy Edwards influenced Sam Davies, so Exy Johnson influenced an earlier cohort of young women who would become voyagers. To be in a position to influence anyone beyond the deck of one boat or the walls of a single room, a person needs a medium through which to communicate—and Electa Search had already generated a handsome stack of press clippings before she ever met and married Irving. It was she who wrote the final drafts of the books and articles that lit the flame in so many people to take to the sea. With only rare exceptions, those writings referred to "the skipper" in the third person. The first-person "I" was almost always Exy. The sparkle on the page that ignited so many spirits, that was all hers.

As Robert Johnson said of his parents, "It was a real partnership, and they had complementary skills." While Exy could light up a page, Irving could light up a room.

In 1936 W. W. Norton & Co. published *Westward Bound in the Schooner Yankee*, by Captain and Mrs. Irving Johnson. One sailor inspired by the Johnsons' yarns was CCA member Drayton Cochrane, who commissioned the German builder Abeking & Rasmussen to build him a North Sea pilot schooner as much like *Yankee* as possible. He called his ship *Westward*. (Devotees of the Concordia class may recognize his name: "Drayton Cochrane was the person directly responsible for launching us into business with Abeking & Rasmussen," wrote Waldo

Howland in his memoir, *A Life in Boats.* "Between 1950 and 1966, without benefit of a single contract or disagreement, the German shipyard built for the account of Concordia Company some ninety-nine sister ships of *Java.*") For a transoceanic passage aboard *Westward* in 1961, her first season afloat, "Draytie" Cochrane earned a CCA John Parkinson Trophy.

From the initial building of *Westward,* the *Yankee* influence carried still farther. "Irving was very much the inspiration for Corwith Cramer, who started the Sea Education Association in 1970," said Seán Bercaw, longtime captain of the SEA school ships. "Cory had grown up seeing Irving's talks and decided, 'I want to do a program like that.'" To realize his dream, CCA member Cory Cramer created a board of directors and purchased the *Westward* as its first school ship. Irving and Exy and Robert Johnson all served on the board over SEA's five decades, as have many CCA members.

"The North Sea pilot schooner is not a coastal boat," said SEA president Peg Brandon, a CCA member and longtime SEA captain with some 20 years and 100,000 sea miles in her wake. "It's a serious platform, whether it's for cruising or oceanographic research. It's very seakindly and can stay on station and take students out to sea without beating them up. Cory Cramer found the suitable vessel with good seakeeping qualities in the *Westward,* which was Draytie Cochrane's vessel. And that was inspired by Irving and Exy Johnson's *Yankee.* So there's a thread all the way through."

For more than 30 years *Westward* introduced SEA students to the world above and below the ocean surface. When you add up the voyages aboard *Westward,* as well as the newer SEA ships *Corwith Cramer* and *Robert C. Seamans,* the number of young women and men of high school and college age who have stood watch under sail at sea exceeds 10,000, a number that still grows every semester.

As Cory Cramer developed SEA, he and his colleagues made some subtle but crucial adjustments to the model that Irving and Exy invented. "In January of 1972 they boarded their first group of students, which they called *apprentices,*" said Peg. "Certainly now they're called *students.* Being curious about the ocean as well as about sail training was always part of our mission, and I think that may be different from Irving and Exy Johnson. The first sampling of the air/sea interface with a net was barely a week into *Westward's* first SEA trip. In the early days at SEA there was no academic credit, but that came along pretty quickly—something that students can take home that can be measured by others."

Meanwhile, in Newport, Rhode Island, circa 1973, another organization was being formed to introduce young men and women to the challenges and rewards of ocean sailing. Originally called the American Sail Training Association (now Tall Ships America), it published the first comprehensive directory of sail-training ships

*As my* Young America *captain, Pete Vanadia, was fond of saying, "A misspent youth is a joy forever." And so it is—for me as for so many of those fortunate young men and women who sailed with the Johnsons and on the cruises they inspired.*

and programs. The creator of that first ASTA directory was Nancy Richardson, national director of the Girl Scout Mariners, the very third-grader who back in 1949 heard Irving speak in her home town. And to carry that thread of influence just a little further, I—Tim Murphy, the author of this book—read a 1981 article Richardson published in *Cruising World* that told of a sail-training program aboard the 130-foot brigantine *Young America*. The final paragraph alerted readers to a scholarship opportunity. At age 16, I wrote the letter that won that scholarship. It provided for a weeklong cruise in New England, after which I was invited to volunteer for two more weeks, which I stretched into *six consecutive months* of voyaging from Newport, Rhode Island, through the Chesapeake Bay, to Key West, Florida, completing my high-school junior year through correspondence courses.

As my *Young America* captain, Pete Vanadia, was fond of saying, "A misspent youth is a joy forever." And so it is—for me as for so many of those fortunate young men and women who sailed with the Johnsons and on the cruises they inspired. For, truly, Irving and Exy set ripples into motion that keep on rippling, far beyond the wake of their own *Yankee*.

### The Porpoise Watch

It's fashionable in the 21st century to speak of "intentional communities." The composition of *Yankee's* two dozen amateur crew certainly answered that description, even as it ran right through the Johnsons' nuclear family.

"I am delighted to be starting all over again," Exy wrote to a friend between the war and *Yankee's* Fourth World Cruise. "The only thing that really hurts is that we cannot take both boys all the time. I am not worried about their education, which can be had anywhere at any time, but 18 months on a schooner with older people is not the life for them, and they would be hard on the cruise, too. You know how everyone in a home feels the need of somewhere to send small boys off at times—a play room or a basement or just outdoors. Small boys have to have scope for the kind of thing that doesn't fit either the living room or a small bedroom. Well, you can see how it would be on the boat—no place, not even outdoors to go to. Besides they should be learning things from their own age group and not just from their elders."

Robert, the younger, stayed ashore with Irving's sister in Massachusetts when his parents set off on the Fourth World Cruise. "My aunt was a very nice person, motherly," said Robert. "But my preference was to be on the voyage all the time." When *Yankee* touched at the Philippines, Arthur and Robert swapped places. As the boys grew into their teens, they attended New England boarding schools when they weren't voyaging with *Yankee.*

"On the Fourth, Fifth, and Sixth Voyages, my mother taught me with the Calvert system," said Robert. "It's tough! It was always much easier when I was ashore."

Meanwhile, each *Yankee* crew took on its own character. "Like the nursery rhyme's old woman and her many children who live in a shoe, we are one big family, boys in the main cabin, girls in the two double cabins, and the Johnsons in the skipper's cabin across the stern."

The life of each cruise developed its own rhythm. "On some evenings everybody drifted aft as if by common impulse," wrote Exy, "and around the boy or girl at the helm the talk and song and laughter would swirl. Sometimes the subject was photography, or sports cars, or philosophy; we have even discussed Marcus Aurelius. Living in *Yankee* at sea is like living on a tiny island a thousand miles from nowhere. The people come together in warm, permanent friendships born of evenings on the afterdeck and perils shared in the rigors of a stormy pitch-black night."

Occasional log entries would read something like this: "Wind light. Lovely tropical evening. The porpoise watchers are not watching porpoises."

Porpoise watchers? The watchkeeper was writing in code.

"Often people would ask us whether we worried about shipboard romances," wrote Exy. "How could we? We did our own courting many years ago aboard the schooner *Wander Bird,* and we have never once regretted the outcome of our own porpoise watches on the bowsprit. Here, as one crewmate put it, was 'the only place where two people could speak of things not meant for 22 other pairs of ears.'"

Seán Bercaw, the SEA captain and educator, owes his life to *Yankee's* romantic spirit of the porpoise watch, as do his two sisters. Seán's father, Jay Bercaw, was *Yankee's* first mate for the Fifth World Voyage and half of the Sixth. Seán's mother, Gretchen, sailed aboard one of *Yankee's* summer charters. "My mother was a bit influential in that," said Robert Johnson. "When Jay was mate on *Yankee* for one summer, Gretchen was a Girl Scout Mariner leader. My mother managed to maroon them both on Block Island for a few hours, and my understanding is that was intentional."

"That's definitely true," confirms Gretchen. "Exy was a great lady, and because this was after the 1950–52 circumnavigation, she knew Jay well. Robert's brother, Arthur, really teased Jay about it, because he could see from the eye contact that there was something going on."

Robert Johnson reckons *Yankee* averaged one marriage per voyage. But marriages or no, the diaspora of *Yankee* crew spreads out across the oceans in circles that are widening still. Frederick L. Jackson, Jack Braidwood, and Bob Loomis each served as mates aboard a *Yankee* cruise on their way to becoming CCA members. Jay and Gretchen Bercaw—with their children Mary K, Katrina, and Sean—circumnavigated aboard their own 38-foot Sea Wolf ketch *Natasha* in the early 1970s and inspired CCA members, Scott and Kitty Kuhner, later on to do the same with their own kids. Julie Pyle sailed on the Sixth Cruise and met Rodney Nicholson when *Yankee* touched at Antigua; together they founded Nicholson Yacht Charters and pioneered the yacht charter business. Lydia Edes sailed on the Sixth World Cruise; her daughter, Lynne Shore, won the US Gold Medal in the 470 dinghy event at the 1988 Olympics in Seoul. The Johnsons prepared Art and Gloria Kimberly to sail their own brigantine, *Romance,* around the world over more than two decades, and the Kimberlys prepared Dan Moreland who is now leading his eighth circumnavigation with amateur crew aboard the barque *Picton Castle*.

After the Seventh World Cruise ended in 1959, Irving and Exy spent the next 18 years exploring Europe and North Africa aboard ketch *Yankee*, designed by Olin Stephens, producing two more books, plus many magazine articles and lecture films.

In 2002, the Los Angeles Maritime Institute, with direction from Nancy Richardson, launched a pair of 110-foot brigantines "charged with giving tens of thousands of young people the opportunity to experience self-discovery, life changing adventure and education found only on a tall ship at sea." Among other missions, the ships take today's Girl Scout Mariners to sea. The two ships are called the *Irving Johnson* and *Exy Johnson*. And although Irving had died in 1991, Exy and Robert were on hand for the naming.

*Yankee's* ripples ripple ever on. And it all started from a pair of adventuresome newlyweds in 1932, looking for their own way to go out and see the world.

"No life could be more simple," Exy wrote. "Almost childishly so. But it was a very satisfying existence. There was never any question of being bored. I don't think the word could ever be applied to sailors—passengers, yes—but not to anyone who had ships and the sea to deal with."

A Concordia yawl makes her way upwind under shortened sail, under jib and jigger, leaving a rocky shore neatly to leeward.

Pressed in his task by the mizzen staysail, the navigator takes a sight in the Gulf Stream, aboard *Malay*. As many as 15 sights a day revealed that the Concordia was well situated in the strong eastward flow of the Stream, taking her to a surprising victory, and into her place in history as the smallest boat to win the Bermuda Race.

# 6

# *Malay* and Her Sisters: How Concordia Owners Invented the Stock Racer-Cruiser

I freely called on the time and skill of many willing hands to help me carry out my
plan for the creation of a forty-foot boat which, in essence,
should sail on her bottom, not on her side, and, at that, approach the speed limit
to be met with off, or along, shore on our Atlantic seaboard.
All other details were subordinate to these cardinal qualifications.
—Llewellyn Howland Sr., on commissioning *Java*

A spirit moved upon the face of the waters, and it was very, very good. The spirit
is symbolized by the moon and star, and made real in the shape of the Concordia
yawl. When Waldo Howland, Llewellyn Howland, and Ray Hunt sat down to
create a simple, practical daysailer and coastwise cruiser, they could little have
suspected they would be giving life to one of the all-time classic yachts.
—Elizabeth Meyer, *Matinicus* owner

Instead of my owning her, she owned me.
—Dan Strohmeier, *Malay* owner

Ross Sherbrooke was another of those boat-mad kids, 18 years old and freshly
graduated from high school in June 1954, when he sailed to Newport, Rhode
Island, to watch the start of that year's Bermuda Race. Whenever Ross took
the boat, it was family policy to check in each day with his father to let him
know their whereabouts. He first tried to reach his father with the boat's
old-fashioned double-sideband radio, but failing that, he went ashore and
stood in line at the Ida Lewis Yacht Club payphones, "and, of course, called
collect to the old man." Ross let his dad know what a good sail they'd had
that day, then hung up the phone. That's when he felt a hand on his shoulder.

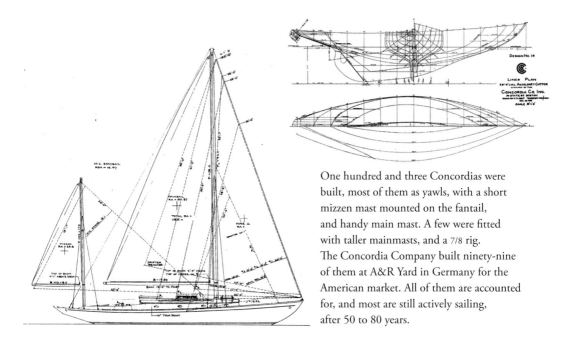

One hundred and three Concordias were
built, most of them as yawls, with a short
mizzen mast mounted on the fantail,
and handy main mast. A few were fitted
with taller mainmasts, and a 7/8 rig.
The Concordia Company built ninety-nine
of them at A&R Yard in Germany for the
American market. All of them are accounted
for, and most are still actively sailing,
after 50 to 80 years.

"Did you say your name was Ross Sherbrooke?"

The hand, as it turned out, belonged to Dan Strohmeier.

"Would you like to go to Bermuda?" he asked.

Dan Strohmeier owned *Malay*, the second Concordia yawl ever built. Dan
had never sailed to Bermuda before, never done much ocean racing either. "Until
January 1954," he wrote, "*Malay* was quite content to be a kennel dog, so to
speak, taking our family on pleasant cruises and on a few short races in which she
did not exert herself too strenuously. In January, however, something happened.
She suddenly became a bird dog, and instead of my owning her, she owned me."

In an essay published in 1958 for the 20th anniversary of the Concordia class,
Dan reflected on how he himself ended up in that 1954 Bermuda Race. "It all
happened when I slyly asked the superintendent of Jakobson's Shipyard, whither
*Malay* had gone to spend the winter, what my friend Jack Parkinson was doing
to his boat, a sister and boat-shed companion of *Malay*. Why, just a few items in
preparation for the 1954 Bermuda Race! That did it. If *Winnie of Bourne* would
go to Bermuda, so would *Malay*. Or was it because she was a namesake of my
father-in-law's schooner in which he won the race in 1930?"

Through acquaintances at Bethlehem Steel Fore River Shipyard, where Dan
built his career, Ross's name had been passed along as someone who'd make good
crew. As Dan later recalled, "Ross Sherbrooke came aboard as a last-minute
replacement for Ed Ferris, beached by shoreside entanglements, and immediately
proved his worth by injecting youth into an otherwise 'old man' crew and an
uncommon amount of experience as a top-notch small-boat racing skipper."

In the history of Bermuda Races, that 1954 event stands out as the first time that competitors had access to new data coming in from the Woods Hole Oceanographic Institution, indicating a meander in the flow of the Gulf Stream – an oxbow bend that promised a long lane to the southeast if you hit it right. After this information was presented at the Skippers' Meeting, Ross recalled the reaction among the gathered sailors. "All the old-timers, George Roosevelt and all those guys said, 'That's baloney. We've done it before, and we know the Gulf Stream.' But Dan thought, 'That's an interesting opportunity.'"

Dan Strohmeier remembers the race:

That night back on board we took another look at our strategy and made a decision born of meteorological ignorance that probably won the race for us. Those who sail the race are familiar with the great clockwise circulation of air around the Azores High, which produces the easterly trade winds in the latitudes of the West Indies and the prevailing southwesterlies of our latitudes. The Newport–Bermuda rhumb line, roughly SSE magnetic, cuts through the western part of this air circulation so that the wind at Newport is likely to be SW while that at Bermuda is more southerly. Thus the race is usually a thrash to windward, mostly on the starboard tack, with the wind drawing ahead as the island is approached. Because of this and the easterly set of the Gulf Stream, it is therefore sensible to gain a cushion to windward (westward) of the rhumb line early in the race. This is winter rocking-chair strategy. It all goes into a cocked hat if during the race an atmospheric whirlpool comes drifting along in that moving ocean of air. We studied the evening's weather data, made no sense out of it, and decided to ignore it.

The Gulf Stream prediction, however, had a genuine ring to it. Conditions permitting, we would enter it at 38° 20' N, 70° 00' W where the 2-to-4 knot current would swing to the SE, only slightly west of our current plan.

The flags flying from *Malay* were made of stiff little boards, to hold the code out for all to read. Dan was an engineer, and a tinkerer, and he loved the code flags, but didn't like the added windage of fluttering in the rigging.

With 77 boats entered, there had never been a larger Bermuda Race fleet than the one assembled in 1954. *Malay*, at 39 feet 10 inches long, was one of the smaller vessels, small even within Class D. That day, Saturday, June 19, was one of fine

Captain Dan Strohmeier making an adjustment to some small line,
in the middle of the Bermuda Race, aboard *Malay*.

weather, sunny and clear, but little wind. "Our three-week supply seemed to have
lost its margin," Dan recalled of his impression there among the nearly stalled
fleet off Castle Hill.

All day long after the midday gun they watched their competitors tack away
to the east in light air. "We gambled on a westerly and immediately after the start
stood over on the port tack to meet it. So did many other boats, but some of the
larger ones, well-endowed with Bermuda experience, kept on to the eastward
on starboard tack. All during that sluggish afternoon we watched our port-tack
companions, one by one, go over to starboard tack and disappear to the eastward.
If they were right, we were wrong. Still, there was nothing to suggest a shift of
wind to the east, so we held on and buoyed our spirits by cheering every time one
of our friends peeled off to eastward."

The break *Malay's* crew had been waiting for came after midnight Sunday,
with a sudden westerly shift.

"We tacked at once, set the mizzen staysail, and began to fly, still climbing to
the westward away from the rhumb line," Dan wrote. "The night was warm, the

Even in light air, the crew of *Malay* concentrates on keeping her going.

sea was smooth, and porpoises played under the bow by moonlight as we indicated over 7 knots in a freshening breeze. Did we dare believe we were making an end run around most of the fleet still in soft air to the eastward?"

Something else was pretty exciting. All morning long, while the sails hung limp and slatting, *Malay's* speed through the water approaching nil, her crew repeatedly shot sun sights. "We could not believe it at first, but as we plotted line after line of position there could be no doubt that the Woods Hole prediction was right—the first time this sort of thing had even been attempted. The Gulf Stream was actually carrying us SE at 3 to 4 knots! It was fun to be part of this milestone in oceanographic history."

Still, *Malay* stayed well west of the rhumb line, even as the rest of the fleet continued to place their bets on the more easterly course. Dan describes the winning tactics:

"For better or worse we left the southern edge of the Stream on port tack. For the second time in two days we would gamble on a westerly shift.

Monday night wind continued to rise but there was no shift. We

"All during the race thus far, clear skies and a third-quarter moon fulfilled
a navigator's dream. We averaged about 15 sights a day.
Sailing to windward most of the time, compass courses were taboo."

held on until about 0400 Tuesday morning when we decided we had
served the interest of westerly position long enough and had better get
down to the business of reducing the distance to Bermuda. So we tacked
but could not fetch the island. By 0800 it was breezing up and the lee
rail was well buried with white water occasionally above the tops of the
leeward cabin ports. We seemed to be overburdened and so reefed the
main, holding on to our genoa. However, speed fell off ¼ knot so the reef
was shaken, and all day we carried full sail in fairly heavy going. We could
not help thinking this was *Malay* weather, for we knew others would be
shortened down in this kind of breeze.

All day Tuesday and through Wednesday morning, *Malay* sailed on
starboard tack. As the breeze built, they reefed again, this time gaining
speed after the maneuver.

"By Wednesday afternoon when we had sagged 15 miles east of the
rhumb line we picked up Bermuda on the radio and received the first and
only wind forecast that made sense to us. We could expect a shift to the

Some considerable traffic can get in the way, going along the treacherous channel to Hamilton, after the finish the night before.

west. But when? If it came right away we could stay on starboard tack and eventually fetch the island. A hitch on the port tack might be wasted but we would get the westerly sooner. So we tacked and got a westerly shift within two hours. Again we went back to starboard tack, just fetching the island with 150 miles to go."

Ross Sherbrooke tells us what happened next.

We went into St. George, because it was the middle of the night, and going around through the treacherous channel to Hamilton was not appropriate, especially for a first-timer. I've done it in the dark since, but not the first time. Next morning we sailed around and came through Two Rock Passage to Hamilton. Of course, nobody knew what the score was. I don't think we had the spinnaker up, but we were sailing along because Danny always preferred to sail, which suits me fine. Most of the time, when we were coming alongside another boat, we'd generally sail up to raft up to them, make an egg-shell landing. Anyway, there was one of these bum boats sailed by a local captain with his captain's hat. And he came by with a bunch of college kids on the boat. And as they looked back, the ladies screamed the name of the boat. '*Malay!* The winner!' And that's the first we heard of it. Danny, who loved women, suggested, 'Come on over!' So they came alongside, and the girls got off the boat. And everybody stuck around, and we all had a drink, including me. And

The smallest yacht in Bermuda Race history had just collected the overall prize.
Dan wrote, "I confess to a lump in my throat as I looked at the same Bermuda ensign
in our starboard rigging that the schooner *Malay* flew 24 years before."

then within a half hour or so the Governor-General of Bermuda came out in his Admiral's barge. I think it was Lord Hood and Lady Hood. And after everyone had had plenty to drink—it must have been noon-time by then—we were relaxed, and the gin bottle was empty. Danny had a wonderful way of throwing up a gin bottle off the side of the boat and then whacking it with a winch handle as it came by. He did that, and there was a great cheer.

As the initial mirth of that landfall gave way to more sober reflections, Dan wrote, "I confess to a lump in my throat as I looked at the same Bermuda ensign in our starboard rigging that the schooner *Malay* flew 24 years before."

As for Lord Hood, he too cut a more refined figure before the distinguished crowd at the 1954 Bermuda Race trophy presentation—at which the smallest yacht in Bermuda Race history had just collected the overall prize. "Those who won will never know why, and those who lost will never lack for explanation." Strohmeier responded: "Couldn't agree more."

The winning crew of *Malay*, at the prize-giving ceremony at the Governor's Mansion, Bermuda, 1954. Dan Strohmeier holding the magnum, Bud Ferris, Pete Shumway, Orlin Donaldson, and Russ Knowles. Ross Sherbrooke was off partying on the island.

Many newspaper clippings of the 1954 Bermuda Race victory, showing the fervent attention paid by the media to sailboat racing in the 1950s.

The magnificent steel-hulled *Little Vigilant*, commissioned by Drayton Cochrane,
and the diminutive Concordia, *Misty*, side by side for an evening raft up and cocktails.
Both yachts were built in the fifties by Abeking & Rasmussen.

## Birth of the Concordia Class

The boat that won the 1954 Bermuda Race was hull #2 of a class of wooden sailboats that by 1966 would grow to 103 vessels—owing in no small part to *Malay's* outstanding Bermuda Race result, plus one or two other major wins over the next few seasons. Henry Sears won the 1955 New London–Annapolis Race aboard *Actaea*, Concordia hull #4. Ray Hunt's *Harrier*, Concordia #30, won it in 1957, after sweeping six races at Cowes Week in England on her way home from the builder, Abeking & Rasmussen in Germany. The growing class sparked a sort of social club of Concordia owners, including many CCA members, and an ever-deepening lore among sailors, which lives on today.

"It was the racing successes of the Concordia class that first caught the widespread attention of buyers, whether they were racing-minded or not," wrote Waldo Howland, who owned and ran the Concordia Company's boat business from 1932 through 1969. "But the first Concordia yawl was designed primarily as a daysailer and coastwise cruiser, and it is as an all-around family boat that the

Concordia Thirty-nine and Forty-one have seen their widest, longest, and most continuous use."

What became the Concordia class started as a single custom-made boat for a single owner. That boat was *Java*, conceived after the Hurricane of 1938 and launched before the hurricane of World War II. She was designed by a young man of as yet little renown, C. Raymond Hunt, a partner of Waldo's and the man who would become the father of the deep-vee powerboat hull, as well as the iconic Boston Whaler.

The client who commissioned her was Waldo's father: Llewellyn Howland Sr. of the village of Padanaram in South Dartmouth, Massachusetts. His recollections of the genesis of the Concordia yawl deserve reflection:

> I have been conscious of a faith that luck—good or bad—more often than not is in the nature of a paradox, not to be defined on the spur of the moment but only after the passage of time has crystallized it into its true shape and significance. And coeval with this point of view as to luck has run that insatiable, beggaring plague—a love of boats—that has imposed on me the burden of owning one or more 'sailing sirens' as a necessity. Consequently, year after year, I have bought boats—with a single exception—as I bought my shoes, in the ready-made market with the foreknowledge that while they might fit to a degree, they could not give me the comfort and satisfaction that a boat of my own design and built to my order might be expected to produce.
>
> Then—wonderful to relate!—the long succession of make-fits was brought to an end in the fall of 1938 when a hurricane roaring over our southern New England coast destroyed not only lives and property—my boat of the moment among hundreds of others.

Llewellyn Howland, lover of paradox, sparked one with his creation of this yawl, *Java*. From his custom-made dream a stock-boat legend was born. Shortly after Llewellyn's death in January 1957, CCA member, Jack Parkinson, and author of *Nowhere Is Too Far*, spoke for many fellow sailors when he concluded a story about a recent Baltic Sea cruise aboard Concordia #11, with these words: "I will end this tale with a bow to the *Winnie of Bourne*, who gave us all this fun. That old sailor and author, the late Llewellyn Howland, created a lot of pleasure for a lot of people when he dreamed up the Concordia yawl."

*Java* was built over 10 months and launched at Casey Boat Yard in Fairhaven, Massachusetts, in 1939. The next season, under Waldo Howland's direction, *Malay* (ex-*Jobisca*, ex-*Ina*) was built to the same design at George Lawley's yard in

The knotty pine paneling was used for the interiors on all the Concordias built by Abeking & Rasmussen. It was a locally sourced wood, easy to work into a stylish recessed panel, light-weight, and elegant when polished to a warm glow. The dual-purpose Concordia berths were folded up like Murphy-beds to port and starboard, when not needed.

Boston. After World War II, Waldo directed Casey to build two more: *Halcyon* in 1946, and *Actaea* in 1950. But as Waldo, Llewellyn Howland's son, began to feel the first pressure of a growing market for the design, he came up against supply constraints. CCA member Drayton Cochrane introduced Waldo to the yacht builders Abeking & Rasmussen in Lemwerder, Germany, and only after that could the true series-production of the Concordia class take off. For Howland, the key to the whole project, even before skilled craftsmanship, was finding a builder with a reliable supply of wood.

"Quality boatbuilding lumber—mahogany from Africa and South America, teak from India—is not acquired by picking up the telephone or writing a letter to the local sawmill," wrote Waldo, following a 1951 visit to Abeking & Rasmussen. "Finding the right trees, felling them, and assembling them as a full shipload could take many months of planning ahead. Once the logs reached Germany, they had already been partly seasoned. I was told that as a matter of convenience, logs were occasionally left in the brackish water until other space was available. During World War II, Abeking & Rasmussen hid many of the big logs in nearby shallows to save them for peacetime boatbuilding. Certainly it was a miracle that these logs survived the war in excellent condition and were ready for use in postwar yacht construction."

Together with the German boatbuilders, Waldo spec'd white oak for the Concordia's backbone (stem, keel, sternpost, deadwood, and horn timber), African mahogany for planking, and Indian teak for the cockpit floor and cabin sole. Concordia called for locust trim on deck and below, and while A & R had never worked with it before, they accommodated Waldo. As for knotty pine in the cabin interior, Waldo liked the polished German white pine as a replacement for American Eastern pine.

Satisfied with the supply chain, Waldo next examined the practices of A & R's craftsmen. Here again he was satisfied. Henry Rasmussen had visited the United States years earlier, with a stop at Nathanael Herreshoff's boatyard in Bristol, Rhode Island, which deeply impressed him. Back home, Rasmussen took those practices he admired and innovated still further. "The Abeking & Rasmussen full-framing method was entirely new to me," Waldo wrote, "but very appropriate—that is to say, extremely efficient as well as accurate—for the prefabricated construction of identical sisterships. Each pair of frames (originally steam-bent, but in later years laminated) was bent over an individual form of the correct shape on the framing table. After beveling, these frame pairs were assembled in a finished frame unit that included an attached floor timber, shaped and pre-drilled for its bolts, and a finished deckbeam (or a pair of deckbeams), likewise permanently fastened in place."

The result of these and other time-saving practices, together with a good supply of materials, was an ever-greater rate of production for a series of wooden auxiliary sailboats—at the very moment when fiberglass-reinforced plastic was poised to revolutionize boatbuilding. The Concordia Company commissioned two yawls in 1950, including *Suva,* the first from Germany. From 1951 through 1953, Abeking & Rasmussen built four boats per year, then five in 1954. Following *Malay's* Bermuda victory, the yard shipped 12 boats in 1955, and similar numbers annually, for the next decade. When production stopped in 1966, the Concordia Company had 103 sisters and half-sisters to its credit, with changes large and small along the way. With the sad exception of *Halcyon,* hull #3—lost in May 2011 off the coast of Cuba with her owner, Robert Perry—Concordia owners could say with justifiable pride that all 103 were still alive and well, and in good sailing trim.

Through it all, the Concordia Company Boatyard on Padanaram Harbor's South Wharf, close to New Bedford, Massachusetts, served as both a service and a social hub. Several books and anniversary collections gather pieces of that Concordia lore; the loveliest of these is *Concordia Yawls: The First Fifty Years,* published by Elizabeth Meyer's Dreadnought Company in 1988. Waldo Howland

CCA member Queene Hooper Foster has owned three different Concordia yawls over 50 years of sailing, learning new skills from each one. The newest craze for these classic wooden boats is to race them as a One-Design class, getting as many as 15 Concordias on the starting line together.

wrote a memoir in two volumes, published by Mystic Seaport. One volume is titled "The Concordia Years." At press time, the twice a year newsletter, *Concordian,* was on its 70th edition and still going strong.

The Howlands sold the Concordia Company to Bill Pinney in 1969. "I have no idea why Waldo and Llewellyn [Jr., Waldo's brother] sold their company to me personally," Bill wrote in a 40th anniversary dedication. "But I can thoroughly understand why they sold. Any boatyard owner on Thursday before Memorial Day weekend can explain that. Beyond Waldo's Memorial Day frustrations was an even deeper reason for selling out. He felt that the new trend in boat design and in boat building was too great a break with tradition for him to cope with. The problems were: the mass production of fiberglass boats, constantly changing in style to meet the varying tastes of a new generation of boat owners; the pressure to design to beat a racing rule; the short-changing of quality. He could not see himself handling these types of boats or trying to compete with that way of life."

But Waldo Howland had created something from an earlier way of life that still resonates with many sailors today.

Queene Hooper Foster [CCA Boston Station] has owned three Concordias on and off over 40-some years. The first was hull #78, *Matinicus,* circa 1976, "in a partnership with Elizabeth Meyer that didn't work out." The two women were just out of college at the time. "We had different ideas about how the varnish work should be done and where we wanted to go. For both of us it was our first boat, and we were figuring a lot of stuff out. She's still a friend of mine, and we realized that we could still be friends, but *only* if we didn't own this boat. She went on to own the Concordia for years and really came to love the boat—maybe as much as she loved her J-Class, *Endeavour.*"

Queene's next boat was *Moonfleet,* Concordia #49, a boat she sailed happily for 10 years, including a race to Bermuda, before selling it to Greg Carroll [also

Boston Station] so that she could devote her attention to a bigger Aage Nielsen-designed ketch *Saphaedra*. Sailing aboard that big wooden ketch, built by Paul E. Luke, she became the first woman to skipper her own boat in the Bermuda Race in 1992. Although Queene had raced her Concordia *Moonfleet* to Bermuda in 1982, she wasn't approved by the CCA to serve as skipper in that race, so for that race, aboard her own boat, her Concordia competed under a friend's name. "No further comment from me," she said. (The CCA first invited women, including Queene, into the club in 1994.) Queene was listed as the skipper for her bigger boat, *Saphaedra*, in 1992.

She sailed *Saphaedra* transatlantic to compete in the 2001 America's Cup Jubilee in Cowes, England. "And then when I felt my retirement years coming on, I wanted a smaller boat for Maine, with which I would be instantly familiar." Her choice? *Misty*, Concordia hull #66. "I wanted to stay low on the learning curve; my hand would know right where the light switches were, and when to reef, so I could get the best out of her. She has been well owned through her 60 years, and with her refinements, such as the 26 perfectly fitted sails, small diesel, and low-stretch lines, she's been a real pleasure to sail. She is in as good condition as the summer she came over from Germany."

Elizabeth Meyer also reflected on that early partnership and its enduring effect on her life. "In 1975 I was a senior at Bennington College struggling to finish my thesis, trying to figure out where to go and what to do after school. I was befuddled and frantic at the same time—not a good condition," she wrote. "In the middle of this, Queene Hooper, my friend of 20 years, convinced me (somewhat forcefully) to buy a Concordia yawl in partnership. The partnership turned out to be a bad idea for Queene and me, but my eventual sole ownership of *Matinicus* became the greatest positive influence my life has ever had."

At first Elizabeth thought she'd have to sell the boat. "I wasn't ready to own a boat, let alone a 40-footer." But she couldn't bring herself to do it. So with a boyfriend and a cat she set off from Annapolis for Maine. "As we passed under the Bay Bridge, I realized I didn't know how to sail or navigate. Panic!" By her telling, they bungled their way to Roque Island, Maine, hoping that nobody noticed the lousy anchorages they chose, or how badly they trimmed the sails. "Gradually, even with our beginner's lack of sensitivity, we began to figure out how to get her into that gorgeous, rolling, no-nonsense stride all Concordias have."

That was it. She was hooked. "The summer of '76 was the greatest experience I'd ever had, and since I was young and had the fearful aimlessness often experienced by rich kids just out of school, I focused my life around the boat. Since then, everything I have done, every friend I have made and every opinion I have has sprung in some way from my Concordia. Perhaps that sounds like jumped-up

*"Gradually, even with our beginner's lack of sensitivity,
we began to figure out how to get her into that gorgeous,
rolling, no-nonsense stride all Concordias have."*

idolatry or neurotic fixation; but it is neither. It is simply the truth. *Matinicus* picked up my life and turned it around."

In one account after another Concordia owners tell some version of a change the boat has brought to their lives. Like Elizabeth Meyer, Greg Carroll wrote of his initial feelings of inadequacy and how *Moonfleet* transformed them. "The weather was bad and it wasn't going to improve. Had it been June or July we'd have gone home to try again another weekend, what with 25 knots from the northeast (on the nose), a strange boat, somewhat strange waters. But it was late September, and I was determined to bring her home by water, not land. An hour later we started sheets in Buzzards Bay and my apprehension was gone. I had discovered what a Concordia did in 25 knots and how she handles chop! We headed up the Bay for the Canal and I realized what a Concordia was! I realized that yesterday I had bought a boat with classic lines, a long narrow counter, varnished spars and a teak cockpit; but today I owned a world-class yacht capable of taking me to more places on the globe than I had ever dreamed my boat could."

Dan Strohmeier had several occasions to reconsider the choice of the boat he purchased in 1949. Following *Malay's* 1954 Bermuda Race victory, he had almost no time to bask in his well-deserved glory. On August 31, Hurricane Carol tore through New England with 110-mph winds, driving *Malay* from her mooring over the Padanaram Bridge. Her insurer declared her a total loss. But Strohmeier did not. Instead, he commissioned the Concordia Company to rebuild her over the winter and launch her in time for the 1955 Marblehead–Halifax Race—*which* Malay *won*.

For another 17 seasons he cruised and raced her. "We shook up that first *Malay* in the 1972 Bermuda Race, then we acquired the second of our *Malays.*"

Having owned a Concordia yawl for more than two decades, what boat did Strohmeier choose for his second boat? Another Concordia, hull #77.

"We sailed the second boat in six Bermudas, 1974–1984. The race in 1978 was the best of these later campaigns, because we almost pulled off a victory again, 24 years later. Had we done it, there would have been something in 24-year intervals, with my father-in-law's 45-foot schooner *Malay* winning the Bermuda Race in 1930 and my first Concordia doing it in 1954. As it happened, we lost to another Concordia, Arnie Gay's *Babe*. If we had to lose, there was some solace in losing to a well-sailed sistership. It was a one-two finish for the Concordia yawl, and it left us proud of Arnie Gay and *Babe*, proud for ourselves, our crew and our

Commodore Robert Drew, who owned Concordia #70, named *Kristal*, now *Irian*, said wisely, "You never really own a Concordia, you just hold onto her and care for her until, for whatever reason, you must pass her along to the next owner." Here is *Misty*, #66, sailing down Eggemoggin Reach in 2014.

boat, proud for the Concordias."

One after another, across the decades Concordia owners sing the boat's praises. But it may be the original Concordia owner who sings it best. "Though I thought I required no further opinion that *Java* was a good all-around cruising boat as she lay at her mooring in Padanaram Harbor on the evening of June 24, 1954," wrote Llewellyn Howland Sr., "still, I have to admit how greatly enhanced this opinion of her was when I was roused out of bed early next morning to read a message from Bermuda to the effect that a friend and his boat, *Malay*—*Java's* twin sister—had won that blue ribbon of ocean racing, 'The Bermuda Trophy.' This news called for a celebration with my dear old boat, and so once more we sailed out into the Bay."

*Finisterre*: the boat that launched a thousand ships, and then some. In handicap racing, size does not determine the winner, a fact proven time and time again by this 38-foot centerboard yawl— including three Bermuda Races in a row—in a range of conditions.

# 7

# Reconcilable Differences: Carleton Mitchell and *Finisterre*

Being only a little more than twice as long on the water as she was wide,
my dream ship looked remarkably like a watermelon.
—Carleton Mitchell
Owner, *Finisterre*

She does seem to sail faster than a boat of her size should.
—Seth Persson
Boatbuilder, *Finisterre*

If the early years of the Cruising Club of America were most shaped by the yacht designs of John Alden, Philip Rhodes, and Olin Stephens, Carleton Mitchell's career in sailboat ownership reprised that same evolution. His first cruising boat was John Alden's *Malabar XII*, which Mitchell renamed *Carib* and aboard which he made the cruises evoked in his influential 1948 book *Islands to Windward: Cruising the Caribbees.* Next came the Rhodes-designed *Caribbee*, a 57-foot yawl Mitchell sailed through the Caribbean and Europe, garnering along the way class honors in the 1952 Transatlantic Race, a voyage he captured in the evocative narrative *Passage East* (1953). His progression culminated in the counterintuitive Sparkman & Stephens-designed centerboarder *Finisterre.*

Truly, *Finisterre* was a culmination. Straightaway she made history, winning three consecutive Bermuda Races in 1956, 1958, and 1960—a record that 60 years later still stands. Fifteen years after that final win, *Yachting* editor Bill Robinson deemed her "probably the most successful ocean racer of all time." To this day, in every Bermuda Race the Carleton Mitchell Finisterre Trophy goes to the corrected time winner in the Finisterre division, for amateur entries using cruising sails. Just as ocean racing was only one part of

Carleton Mitchell plied his trade in the snug cabin of *Finisterre*. Mitchell pursued writing and photography to sustain his sailing habit and promote wonderful places best seen by boat, such as the Caribbean and Bahamas. Most of the photographs in this chapter are from his camera.

the Cruising Club's DNA, so too was it only a part of *Finisterre's,* and arguably the smaller part.

Carleton Mitchell—"Mitch" if you were trading tricks with him at the helm—knew early on what he had in this creation. "Clear of the land, *Finisterre* heeled to the wind," he wrote during her shakedown season. "A centerboard yawl, 38 feet 7 inches overall, she was the physical embodiment of dreams spun during lonely night watches through the years, all the doodles on paper transmuted to wood and metal reality. *Finisterre* was the symphony I could not otherwise compose, the vision I could not capture on canvas, the Great American Novel forever unwritten. Before she had even taken form I had confessed I was trying to build a boat that had everything. And now I was not being disappointed."

No one did more to encourage Caribbean and Bahamas cruising in the mid-century than Carleton Mitchell, long before Donald Street Jr. arrived on the scene. Mitch may be credited with spurring the sudden growth in Caribbean chartering that took off in the late 1960s. It was no mere coincidence that Caribbean Sailing Yachts, Caribbean Yacht Charters, and The Moorings were all founded in the Virgin Islands in 1967 and 1968—within a year of the publication of Mitch's influential series of *National Geographic* articles based on extended

Caribbean cruises aboard *Finisterre*. And the dominance of short-handed shoal-draft racer/cruisers that overwhelmingly defined the first generation of composite sailboat building in the 1960s and 1970s was in no small way shaped by the legend of *Finisterre*.

## A Sailor Is Born

Mitch was born in New Orleans in 1910 to a nuclear family of nonsailors. Thank Neptune for uncles—for it was his uncle who first took him sailing.

"Somewhere around the age of twelve," Mitch wrote, "when contemporaries were choosing careers ranging from western sheriffs to railway engineers, I declared my intention of becoming a ship captain and a writer. I had already begun sailing on Lake Pontchartrain—my first nickname was "Skeet," after an uncle was reminded of a mosquito as I hauled on a jib sheet—and had already begun receiving rejection slips as manuscripts made the rounds. Neither goal was achieved as I then envisioned the future, but after all these years I do still find myself basically living my boyhood dream."

Mitch tried college, enrolling at Miami University in Ohio, but dropped out after one year at the beginning of the Great Depression. Riding a motorcycle from one gig job to the next, including a stint of lumbering in Minnesota, Mitch moved to Manhattan, taking a sales job in Macy's underwear department. All the while, he kept sending off manuscripts and collecting rejections.

Two events rescued him from his wandering. First was a $500 gift from his mother, which Mitch used to travel to Miami, where he found stevedore work. The second was an invitation from a friend to sail "the venerable ketch *Temptress*" from Norfolk, Virginia, to the Bahamas. By his account, much of the passage was dreadful, and the boat nearly sank out from under them. But on Christmas Day 1932, they made what was Mitch's first island landfall at Bimini; it inaugurated his lifelong affair with the Bahamas and cemented his love for ocean sailing.

After a rejection slip for one of his travel pieces came back with the suggestion that he submit photographs with his text, Mitch invested in a camera and taught himself to use it, developing his own film. Before long he landed a job writing and photographing for a Bahamian newspaper. When World War II broke out, he joined the Navy, where he taught photography. Toward the end of the war, he moved to Annapolis with his wife Elizabeth ("Zib"). In 1944 they bought John Alden's first ketch, *Malabar XII*, and renamed her *Carib*. John Alden himself made the delivery with them from Marblehead, Massachusetts, to Annapolis.

In the fall of 1946 Mitch shipped *Carib* from Baltimore to Trinidad. The cruise up through the Windwards and the Leewards and the Bahamas that Mitch and Zib and a paid hand undertook that following season became the basis for his first major *National Geographic* article ("*Carib* Cruises the West Indies," January 1948), and his acclaimed book *Islands to Windward: Cruising the Caribbees*, which became a standard text for every East Coast sailor keen to see the tropics. Mitch's publishing career was launched.

Shipmates and colleagues who worked with him agreed on one thing: Carleton Mitchell was a meticulous man. Fellow competitors would describe the chaos around the docks before a major ocean race, while all aboard Mitch's boat was calm. He and his crew had already made their preparations beforehand.

This reflection from *Passage East*, describing the season leading up Bermuda Race, Transatlantic Race, and subsequent European cruise aboard the Philip Rhodes-designed yawl *Caribbee*, gives a taste of how Mitch approached his passage plans.

> The advance planning had worked out. I believe we have aboard every carpenter's, plumber's, mechanic's, and rigger's tool that could possibly be needed for any repair below or aloft, and Cap'n Nick [the bosun] has done an equally good job of providing spares. Last winter I went through my library and copied down lists of gear carried by other people who have made similar passages, which were amended by the Cap in light of *Caribbee's* requirements.
>
> More or less the same system was used in the galley and navigating departments. In the former Henry [the cook] prepared sample menus and a list of stores; the Bermuda Government by special arrangement lifted customs charges, permitting us to store in a bonded warehouse the crates of food shipped ahead from New York, and then load directly aboard in Hamilton Harbor. These crates were numbered against a master list. Therefore before opening we knew the exact contents, and as each item was stowed away its location was noted on the same master list. Henry checks off stores as we consume them. Thus we know exactly where to go for a can of cherries or tuna fish or any other item of food, and exactly how many of each are left aboard.
>
> Frank [the navigator] did the same with the charts and other navigational equipment required, sending to Bermuda what was needed for the race to England. And in both departments additional crates have been shipped ahead to Cowes by steamer to be held for our arrival.
>
> As I write this I see with the clarity of perspective the details that were worked out before we ever sailed from New York for Newport, and now realize why I was so glad to hear the starting gun in Bermuda. Those on the committee boat that day would probably have conceded *Caribbee*

looked ready for the passage ahead, but neither they nor any other casual observer would have realized the planning that brought us to the line, or what we had stowed away on board: food, equipment, sails, spares—an endless list.

What this list omits is that Carleton Mitchell had his perfectly healthy appendix removed before the transatlantic passage—leaving nothing to chance.

It also opens a window into the mind that had been turning over and over and refining the details that would lead to the custom sailboat of his dreams.

## Job No. 1054

Cedar. Mahogany. Bronze. Oak. Spruce. There was nothing magic in the basic ingredients that composed *Finisterre*. These were the standard boatbuilding materials in those last days before stranded glass and thermoset polyester rendered them quaint. Still, there was *something*.

To bring the dream for his one and only custom sailboat to reality, Mitch hired the New York yacht design firm Sparkman & Stephens. Quite apart from the firm's solid two-decade reputation, Mitch had sailed extensively with Rod Stephens Jr., had shared many of his ideas for the perfect boat as he was developing them, and felt comfortable with Rod as an agent between himself and the builder. Before *Finisterre* was *Finisterre*, she was S&S Job No. 1054.

Olin and Rod Stephens Jr., born in 1908 and 1909 respectively, were contemporaries of Mitch. Like him, they were born into a family of nonsailors. Olin's interest in college matched Mitch's; he spent just a single term at Massachusetts Institute of Technology before taking a job as a draftsman at a yacht-design firm while still a teenager. An earlier chapter tells of Olin's creation of *Dorade* and Rod's sailing successes aboard her. From that boat forward, the Stephens' name and fame only grew.

The boat of Mitch's night-watch dreams was no *Dorade*. For two decades Olin Stephens had made his reputation on sailboats that were long and lean, low on wetted surface and displacement, and big on sail area. By contrast, *Finisterre* was a wide, shallow-draft centerboarder with plenty of wetted surface and displacement to accommodate the storage and tankage and other luxuries of a true cruising sailboat.

Mitch had loved his previous boats. But neither was perfect. Toward the northbound leg of a Caribbean cruise, he described one of *Carib's* shortcomings: "At first we were steering north, which would take us to Key West. That wasn't our destination. Our idea was to get east along the Cuban coast to the resort town of Varadero. ... *Carib* was a ketch, 46 feet 8 inches overall, heavy and short

A legend was born with elegance and purpose of fine materials,
and under the watchful eye of Rod Stephens. The name *Finisterre* means the end of the earth,
the place where sailing adventures begin.

rigged. She had begun life as John Alden's *Malabar XII*, and embodied the requisite nautical virtues save one: she was reluctant to go to windward. We came about and did no better than east-southeast."

As for the 58-foot Rhodes-designed *Caribbee*, she required a sizable crew to go sailing, whether cruising or racing.

For his next boat, Mitch wanted something small enough to take cruising shorthanded, in deep and shallow waters, yet commodious enough to carry eight racing crew. And fast enough to compete. In short, he wanted *everything*. A spring 1953 letter to Rod Stephens Jr. fleshes out his aspirations:

> As a primary thesis, I might say that while price is important, we don't want to skimp on the quality of materials, or cut corners in workmanship. Last summer when *Caribbee* lay at Cowes British yachtsmen came aboard to admire 'the latest thing in American boats,' and found it almost impossible to believe she had been built in 1937; even with a Trans-Atlantic passage just behind there was not the sign of a seam in her topsides, and on deck and below not a flaw. To me this is not only a proof of good construction, but of materials, and I would want it understood especial care should be taken in selecting the wood going into the boat.
>
> Another thing is that she must be strong: as an ocean-going

*For his next boat, Mitch wanted something small enough
to take cruising shorthanded, in deep and shallow waters,
yet commodious enough to carry eight racing crew.
And fast enough to compete. In short, he wanted* everything.

gunkholer. It is perfectly possible we might sail her across the Atlantic, as we have always wished to cruise the Mediterranean, but in any case quite definitely would take her in the Caribbean. For this reason rudder and wheel fittings must have maximum strength, as also the standing rigging, mast step, and the rest—these are hidden features but extremely vital, in part depending on the builder.

And finally, she must look well, and last a long time. To me the two go together; if she is built well of good wood and other materials, and beautifully finished—ship carpentry, joiner work, interior and exterior paint and varnish work—she probably will last, too, as it is my experience crude finish is an indication of a second-class job all the way through.

All this amounts to the fact that we want a really top quality boat, and would rather not build than be disappointed. Yet, unfortunately, price must remain a factor. While we know good materials and good workmanship will be expensive, we must have some assurance that if we build on a cost plus basis the job won't run away from either the builder or me.

The job did run away from the builder and the owner. But a close look at the competing bids puts any overage in context. The go-to builder of the day was Henry Nevins yard on City Island, New York. Many winning ocean racers, including a good number of renowned S&S designs were built there. Here's how the Nevins quote for Job No. 1054 came back in 1953 (figures in parentheses correct for inflation in 2020 dollars):

Labor (16,500 hours at $2.00 per hour): $33,000.00 ($320,039)

Material: $21,000 ($203,661)

Payroll taxes: $5,340 ($51,788)

Overhead and profit (25% of labor and material): $13,500 ($130,925)

Total: $72,840 ($706,414)

Figure quoted: $72,000 ($698,267)

Seth Persson, based in Old Saybrook alongside the Connecticut River, was not as well-known but had a strong reputation for craftsmanship. By contrast with the Nevins bid, Persson's initial bid for $30,000 ($290,944), divided into

Mitchell took his own concepts to the Sparkman & Stephens design office, where they developed into Job No. 1054. The inspired, chubby yawl would take shape from cedar, mahogany, bronze, oak, and spruce, built on a cost-plus basis by Seth Persson of Old Saybrook, Connecticut. The physical properties do not explain her fame.

four installments based on stages of completion, looks naïve—as it did turn out to be. By project's end, the job had run $10,080 ($96,981) over budget, for a total construction cost of $40,080.75 ($388,702). Yet in light of the quality—and the $30,000 ($290,944) delta with Nevin's initial bid—she was a bargain. Not included in Persson's initial bid or final bill was any markup for profit or even on materials; Persson passed his discounts on material to Mitch. A letter dated November 17, 1954, lays out Mitch's reaction to the cost overage.

> Dear Seth,
>
> As I told you over the phone this morning, I have decided to pay you the full amount of the bill you submitted to me in Saybrook last week. While a careful accounting of the "extras" requested by me during the progress of the work more or might not represent $10,080.75 more than the contract price, plus the amounts I have paid independently for electric, plumbing and motor work, I have complete faith in your integrity and know if you submit this bill, it represents the actual cost of the boat. I do not want you to lose on the job, especially when you have turned out such a magnificent piece of craftsmanship. Over and beyond anything I can pay, I know it is a labor of love, and that through the years I will benefit from the care with which each piece was put together.

I must admit it was a shock to find out how much we had gone beyond our original estimates of the cost. Both of us were negligent in not trying to assess where we stood as we went along. For your future good, I advise trying to set up some sort of cost control system, and letting the owner know just where he stands. In another case, you might get into serious difficulties.

It was a pleasure to work with you and your helpers. I know *Finisterre* will be a fine little ship for years to come, and will live up to all our hopes.

Mrs. Mitchell joins in regards to you, Mrs. Persson, and the children.

Sincerely,

Carleton Mitchell

In a 1958 *New York Times* profile, Mitch told journalist Gay Talese that *Finisterre* had cost him $65,000 to build (about $630,000). This would have included fees to Sparkman & Stephens, as well as all the racing sails and other extras Mitch himself added.

Mitch's interactions with Olin Stephens weren't without conflict. In early May 1953, Mitch suspected that Olin had been showing the plans for *Finisterre* to other potential clients. "Frankly," Mitch wrote, "I have become increasingly disturbed at the thought that after conceiving a boat of this type, coming to you with the result of years of thought, and then going through the various steps of designing, that other people should have the opportunity of seeing the results practically before I do."

Mitch had learned that the sailmaker Colin Ratsey was considering building a near sister ship at a yard that might even launch before *Finisterre*. "That the basic idea for a boat of this size and type is mine, I don't think can be questioned, inasmuch as no similar boat is in existence. I strongly feel that no duplicate boat should be built within at least a year from the time of the completion of my own boat and I don't think I would proceed with my construction project unless I have the assurance that plans will not be released."

Two days later, Olin sent a mollifying note, which must have done the trick. On May 27, 1953, Mitch wrote to Seth Persson in advance of a formal contract to say that he'd accepted his bid. Clearly, the client was champing at the bit.

"I am sending you this letter in advance of the contract not only to let you know my decision, and how I feel about the boat," Mitch wrote to Persson, "but to suggest that you begin scouting around for that perfect hunk of white oak we discussed. As we all agreed, it is one of the most important items of material that will go into the boat, and I hope you can find a really fine piece of well seasoned timber."

In Rod Stephens, Mitch had found an agent equal to his own obsessions. In letters to Seth Persson, Rod laid out detail after detail about just the right materials for the project. "Want only <u>very best</u> grades of lumber; in comparison to total cost, the differences are negligible." "For all finish below decks, want only Honduras mahogany, top grade." "Oak is important; although hidden, poor oak has caused more maintenance trouble than most other things together." "Plywood worries me most of all; shouldn't it be specified to be entirely of <u>mahogany</u>? (I had some "Marine plywood" in a power boat built just after the war that was mahogany outside, but the inner layers were fir, and it began to rot out in two years.)" And so on—with even more particular admonitions about metals.

As for *Finisterre's* unorthodox design, it presented both challenges and surprising boons. Uncommonly wide for her waterline length and split down her middle by a hollow centerboard trunk, *Finisterre* was full of quirks. But more often than not, her quirks became her strengths. For one thing, she required massive bronze transverse floors to stiffen the hull structure against dynamic rig loads and to keep forestay tension. The CCA rule of the time included a ballast-per-displacement penalty. But *Finisterre's* heavy bronze floors, fitted so neatly below the waterline, went uncounted as ballast. Later, the Rule Committee would tighten this loophole and introduce an incline test. But for the years of her racing life, *Finisterre* profited from the oversight. Together with the initial stability conferred by her uncommon width, that bonus ballast meant that *Finisterre* could carry more sail longer as the wind increased past the point where competitors were wisely reefing down.

It should be noted that initial stability in a wide, shallow boat is not universally a good thing. Harvey Conover's *Revonoc III*, designed to similar lines, was lost without a trace in a 1958 January storm off the Florida Keys one year after her launch. *Doubloon*, another similar centerboard yawl, was rolled twice in the Gulf Stream; the Monday morning quarterbacks suggested that she might not have rolled if her centerboard had been raised.

All of which is to point out that *Finisterre's* sparkling record certainly owed something to her skipper. As Bill Robinson noted in *The Great American Yacht Designers*, "Stephens is the first to admit that a designer is fortunate when his brainchild is in the hands of an owner who knows what it takes to win big ones—infinite attention to detail, a crack crew, and the desire to keep driving hard at all times."

### A Hybrid for the Ages

Quite apart from the shorthand accolades described in collected silverware, *Finisterre's* greatest contribution to the sport was more broad: it was in practically demonstrating an integration of two natures—racing and cruising—that had at

Mitchell joined the Cruising Club of America in 1947.
A year later he became rear commodore of the Chesapeake Station,
and in his later years he was a fixture at Florida Station gatherings.

times seemed wholly incompatible in oceangoing sailboats. From its earliest days, the members of the Cruising Club struggled with the question of whether or not to have anything to do with racing. The debate was already hot just one year into the Club's life. Two founding members, Henry Wise Wood and Frank Draper, articulated the split.

Should the Cruising Club support racing in any way?

On the *pro* side of the argument, Wise Wood wrote in his formal 1923 *Report—Committee on Plan and Scope*, "I am among those who believe that in a sailing craft speed is decidedly a useful factor, as it was in the clipper days, and that it must be cultivated if we are to increase to the uttermost our radius of action. The greater the speed of a sailing craft, the less its operating cost per mile covered, and the less the bulk, the weight and the cost of its supplies for a given voyage. Here lies one of its indestructible advantages over the power craft. I am convinced, therefore, that it is our duty to stimulate the production of fast, as well as comfortable, boats for long-distance, offshore work."

Wise Wood went on to advocate for putting Cruising Club resources behind racing, "provided, however, the racing countenanced is of the nature of cruising; that is to say, provided it be offshore, and over long distances."

Draper gave the *contra* argument. "I am of the opinion that the whole spirit of racing is radically opposed to the spirit of cruising. They are as oil and water," he wrote. "The cruiser approaches the subject of the ideal craft with a wholly different point of view from that of the man with a thirst for racing. The cruiser chooses his rig, the type of hull and fixes upon the details with an eye single to the comforts, conveniences and safety of cruising. After all these ends have been accomplished he will add all the features contributing to speed that are not inconsistent with the demands of his ideal cruiser. The real fact must always remain that the cruising boat cannot be a racer. It is a contradiction in terms. From its nature, purpose and spirit the Cruising Club cannot be a racing club."

Even as the Club went on to revive the Bermuda Race and to initiate the CCA Rule for race handicapping, the controversy grew. In 1939, it came to a full-blown schism. "I am certain that the Club is divided into two groups, whose conflicting philosophies cannot be reconciled under one burgee," wrote William Coolidge in a report dissenting from the majority opinion in favor of racing.

Carleton Mitchell demonstrated better than anyone how the two natures of sailing could be reconciled, not merely in a club, but in a man—and even in a boat. Throughout much of his published work, Mitch reflected on the Jekyll and the Hyde in himself.

"I don't know when in my sailing career it happened to me, this craving for speed," Mitch wrote in *Passage East*. "From a lazy character who would just as soon loll in the cockpit watching Portuguese men-of-war sail through his lee I became the wild-eyed type who laughs demoniacally as the lee rail disappears and looks around for something else to set. So long as the boat is moving I'm happy; when she slows, I die. A terrible thing to confess. Yet now I pity the cruising man I used to be: you get more real sailing—more of the real feel of the wind, the sea, and a boat—in a week of racing than in a year of cruising."

Yet clearly Mitch's soul never finally settled there. In a piece published not much later, the racing man was singing a different tune.

Perhaps the greatest distinction between the cruising and racing yachtsman lies in a sense of pace. Your true cruiser sails by the calendar, not the clock. The moment is what counts: the fact he is afloat, a good little ship carrying him to another place; there is no need to be impatient, nor to fret—only to enjoy. But your racing sailor never escapes the ticking of the second hand. It is probably his most necessary competitive attribute. In any given set of conditions, he feels how his boat should be going. When she is not doing her best, he suffers. He is goaded into action by an overwhelming compulsion: he fiddles with the trim or changes the headsails. If nothing helps he glares at sea and sky, feeling some malign force is at work. He must be efficient to be happy.

Dr. Jeckyll and Mr. Hyde: In Carleton Mitchell the irreconcilable natures
of the cruising man and the racing man found a home. *Finisterre* cleverly
combined attributes that would rate well under the CCA rule and handle easily
for short-handed cruising, solving for a time the CCA "oil and water"
quandary over racing vs. cruising.

As these thoughts came to me I looked at the Kenyon speed indicator
in the cockpit. It stood a hair over 3 knots. Generous. In the St. Petersburg–Havana Race it had read 10 percent high. Change from cruising jib

The view from *Finisterre*'s helm, one that Mitch saw for thousands of miles.
The boat sailed "on her feet" rather than heel excessively, like the earlier, fashionably narrow hulls.
In many views of the boat underway, the sails seem to lift the hull over the waves.

to light genoa, and we might go up to 5 knots. Shift to ballooner, maybe 5 ½. Break out the Hood red-head spinnaker, probably touch 6 knots. Maybe with the 'chute trimmed just right, plus the mizzen staysail, maybe reach 7. Maybe. Close, anyway. Suddenly I found myself grinning. I realized I didn't give one fractional infinitesimal damn. It would be enough to start caring in June when Brenton Reef Lightship came abeam, with the finish line in Bermuda over the bow. Now we were cruising.

In article after article and chapter after chapter, Mitch evokes the special joys of simply experiencing the world from a sailboat's cockpit, sailing under an afternoon of silver haze that intensifies every other color, "the massed trees, turning russet and copper, the brown of cornstalks drying in the fields, the contrast of white barns and silos against evergreens, the steel gray of the water over which we crept"; ghosting past "gently rolling countryside in which sleek cattle browse behind rail fences"; following a river to a creek to a pond where the anchor splashes down and the sail slides rattle home only to be replaced by "the sound of birds, wing beats and voices by the thousand, like the hum of a bumble bee's nest."

Perhaps Mitch was at his most succinct when he wrote, "A race without a

"I became the wild-eyed type who laughs demoniacally as the lee rail disappears and looks around for something else to set." With the wind to pull *Finisterre* along, Mitch and his crew knew how to make her go.

windward leg is no race at all, but cruising to windward is a pain in the neck."

It was in the smithy of these seemingly irreconcilable differences that *Finisterre* was forged.

## The Legacy of *Finisterre*

Carleton Mitchell chose the names of his boats carefully. It was the first thing he changed on the first cruising boat he owned. "A boat is a personal thing, and the name *Malabar* seemed to me personal to John Alden, who had sailed the name to fame. It had all the meaning in the world for him, none for me. We went through the usual pangs and uncertainties, trying for a name that we liked and that would have some meaning. Our dream of sailing through the islands suggested 'Carib,' the native who had been in possession of the Windwards when the Spaniards first came, and whose fierce courage had so left its stamp that even after they had been exterminated the area was referred to as 'The Sea of the Caribbees.' "

For his second boat, his imagination still tended south, and so was *Caribbee* christened.

But by the time he'd conceived his ultimate custom boat, Mitch's wandering imagination had strayed yet further. *Finisterre*—"finis terre"—westernmost point of the European continent, it was to the Ancient Roman mind quite literally "the

"The moment is what counts: the fact he is afloat, a good little ship carrying him to another place; there is no need to be impatient, nor to fret—only to enjoy."

end of the world." For a thousand years, the pilgrims on the Camino de Santiago de Compostela walked another four days west beyond the remains of St. James to end at the mythical shore where the apostle's martyred body was spirited into Iberia.

Mitch ended his sailboat-racing career with his 1960 Bermuda win. By that time, he'd entered 50 major ocean races and brought home 40 pieces of silver. Throughout the 1960s he cruised *Finisterre* both south to the Caribbean he loved and east to Mediterranean he'd dreamed of.

When Mitch died in 2007 at age 96, *Practical Sailor* Editor-at-Large Nick Nicholson recalled finding for the first time at age 10 one of Mitch's *Finisterre* articles in *National Geographic*—which spurred his own love of sailing and made Mitch a personal hero. He wasn't alone. In the articles he published all through the 1950s and 1960s—"To Europe, With a Racing Start," "*Finisterre* Sails the Windward Islands," "A Fresh Breeze Stirs the Leewards," "More of Sea Than of Land"—Mitch and *Finisterre* exposed a whole generation of landlubbers to the deepest pleasures of traveling by sailboat. And many a reader was converted.

For most, it wasn't the racing that stirred their sailor's souls. It was the lyrical, in-the-moment experience of being aboard a wonderful waterborne home in the company of one who could sing the true experience of it into life.

"Feeling the breeze, *Finisterre* began to walk and talk. There was a gentle plash from the bow wave, and tiny little slaps along the hull, and a low murmur under the stern. Quietly but sibilantly insistent sounds came from the mainsheet and blocks. Above the flags moved languidly, ends not whipping, but lifting and snapping in idle flips. Astern, the roiled water of our wake was cut by our tender's sharp bow, while behind her the combined wakes lay as a trail of tiny bubbles.

*Finisterre* flies everything she's got. Spinnakers and mizzen staysails
allow a "cruising" boat like *Finisterre* to eat up miles in light air,
without the drone of an engine to spoil the glory of an expanse of ocean.

Mitchell and his crew prepared *Finisterre* for sea meticulously.
It allowed them to drive the boat hard trusting that everything
would work, and that they had the tools and spares if it didn't.

"As I mused the breeze freshened. *Finisterre* leaned to it and spurted ahead. Gone was the introspective indolence, to be replaced by the exhilaration of motion. Cruising is like that: a matter of mood stemming from weather and circumstance. Now we wanted to feel the boat go. The main was slacked a hair, the jib trimmed a few clicks, and *Finisterre* boiled along with the wind on the quarter, all hands fully awake to the perfection of the moment."

After one lifetime of world-girdling adventure, wartime heroics, and spy craft,
Hod Fuller spent the rest of his life as a charter boat owner and captain in the Mediterranean,
entertaining his ever-widening circle of friends.

# 8

# A Most Extraordinary Chap:
# Hod Fuller's Mid-Century Life Abroad

Grecian waters are the choicest cruising area anywhere: great beauty of sea
and sky, water just the right temperature for swimming, innumerable cozy
anchorages, untold remains of the civilization on which our own is so largely based,
vivid reminders of the time of Christ. Hod Fuller's concern for his companions
transforms these attributes into poignant experiences.

—Peabo Gardner

*Hard Alee*


I looked up, and here was one of the handsomest guys you ever saw.
We went down to Miami, and he was a great shipmate offshore,
as he turned out to be many other times when we cruised together.
And he was a great social success. We formed the kind of friendship
that you can only find on a boat. He was one of the
most extraordinary chaps I ever met.

—Carleton Mitchell

Mystic Seaport Museum, Oral History with John Rousmaniere


Hod Fuller was the best assassin in the OSS.

—Overheard, after drinks, aboard *Velila* on the Dalmatian coast


"No sooner had the 1969 cruise on Hod Fuller's *Velila* ended (it being my
ninth in Grecian and adjacent waters) than I began laying plans for 1970."

So begins the final chapter in *Hard Alee*, George Peabody "Peabo" Gardner's posthumous 1977 memoir that tells of a series of seasonal European sojourns spent mostly aboard boats owned and chartered by Horace W. "Hod" Fuller, a U.S. Marine brigadier general who had served at Guadalcanal and with the French Resistance during World War II.

"My sixtieth reunion and Hod's fortieth at Harvard were to be celebrated in June, so the cruise was postponed by a week to enable us, if desired, to attend Commencement. As I am Chairman of the famous Class of 1910, it meant that there was much for me to do in the way of planning and preparation, and I was therefore particularly desirous of attending the festivities."

After preliminaries about back spasms and travel delays, Peabo's final chapter, "This Is Number Ten: Let's Do It All Again," eases into an idyllic succession of swims, siestas, ouzos, luncheons, cocktails, and dinners, with Hellenic place names scrolling languidly across the screen, and all the meals exquisitely prepared by *Velila's* full-time chef. "The day of our arrival was hot and the water inviting, so while the others swam I went down the companionway and splashed myself with healing salt water. Ouzos, etc., under the awning on deck, anchor up and a choice luncheon while under way. Afterwards I climbed into my bunk and the next thing I knew, nearly four hours later, we were dropping anchor at our old familiar island of Euboea not far from Port Buphalo. It was a bit too late for a swim but not for cocktails, chicken dinner, Rhodes wine and champagne."

On the second evening, "Henry Laughlin seemed much aggrieved—what in a child one would call petulant—because no champagne made its appearance due to the hard-hearted Commodore's reluctance to have it become too commonplace."

Though short on real drama, *Hard Alee* is awash in tone, taking us into a lost time and place and milieu—running concurrent with but entirely separate from the hippie invasion of Joni Mitchell's "Matala moon" and Mykonos, and other Greek island communities as the 1960s gave way to the 1970s. Men like Peabo Gardner and Hod Fuller were the very culture to which young people in those days were running counter.

"George Peabody Gardner embodied the virtues and complexities of the New England character," recalled his frequent shipmate Mason Hammond, a Harvard Classics professor. "Though fully appreciative of feminine company, he blossomed in that of men. On his cruises he preferred an all-male ship's company. Those who were privileged to cruise with Peabo appreciated not merely his friendship but also his tact and firmness as 'commodore.' He found in Hod a remarkably congenial captain whose seamanship is combined with great good fellowship as a member of the afterguard. He knows Greek waters thoroughly, particularly the small, isolated coves which Peabo preferred not only for their quiet beauty but also because of the opportunities they offered to swim in the nude without shocking the still old-fashioned sensibilities of the Greek farmers and fishermen. Hod regularly indulged Peabo's great pleasure in taking the helm on entering or leaving port."

The list of CCA members who sailed with Hod in Greece is long,
and one after another they sing the praises of "the temper of the skipper
who is a joy to sail with." The islands were his familiar playground,
first with the schooner Aegean and then with the big ketch, *Velila*.

The *Cruising Club News* through the 1960s is peppered with accounts of members' Mediterranean charters with Hod. Frederick Ayer, Lawrence Lombard, Howard Wright, Andy Hepburn, Mason Smith, Jack Parkinson, Carleton Mitchell, John Rousmaniere—the list of CCA members who sailed with Hod ran long. One after another, they sing praises for, as Mason Smith wrote, "the temper of the skipper who is a joy to sail with."

Peabo and company signed on for the first of 10 three-week Greek summer charters with him in 1957. "Hod's yacht, appropriately named *Aegean,* was a stout schooner with wide beam and had been built in Florida some years before. She was capable of good speed when off the wind, and with her brown sails made a pleasant picture."

While Peabo and Hod were born a generation apart, Carleton Mitchell and Hod were close contemporaries and fast friends. These two met shortly after World War II and spent the 1946–47 winter season together sailing Mitch's John Alden-designed ketch *Carib* (ex-*Malabar XII*) down the West Indies and back.

Hod introduced Carleton Mitchell to the Dalmatian Coast of Communist-run Yugoslavia in 1970, where rare visitors were welcomed with open arms.

"Let me show you something different in the way of islands," wrote Hod to Mitch more than a decade later, an invitation that spawned many shared explorations of Aegean and Adriatic waters. As Mitch tells us, "Hod had married a Greek girl, spoke Greek, felt Greek, was knowledgable and enthusiastic about everything Greek, past and present, so wanted to show me some of his favorite Greek isles on a postman's holiday."

With his intimate ties to the local culture, Hod opened a curtain to his American guests.

"What sets the Greek isles off by themselves is perhaps a quality which exists as much in the mind as in reality," wrote Mitch for a 1961 *Sports Illustrated* article called "Cruising the Wine-Dark Sea."

"Transcending all, there is a sense of the flowering of the human spirit. The humble lives of the people away from the centers of wealth have a dignity worthy of their distinguished past. They are proud of the imposing marble reminders that here western civilization first flowered, and they remain proud of their islands. Perhaps the key to their attitude lies in the simple word *xenos*. It not only means stranger, but guest. Implicit is the thought that a visitor must be made welcome."

Hod bought the Rhodes 77 that had been built post-war as *Windjammer II*, pictured here.
He renamed her *Velila*, and in 1964 sailed her from San Diego to Greece,
with a young John Rousmaniere soaking up every bit of seamanship and wisdom he could absorb.

*. . . They were all in uniform and never came aft of the foremast*
*except when working and really knew their jobs.*
*Peabo and his shipmates saw the best years*
*for cruising in this part of the world.*

Mitch's acquaintance with Hod's first charter yacht, *Aegean,* ran deeper even than Hod's. "Almost a quarter century before, in the Bahamas, I had a part in her inception; she was the dream ship of my first deepwater skipper, Cy Strong, and many nights we sat around the cabin lamp discussing details on paper. She had later taken form as *Centurion,* solidly put together with natural crook frames of horse-flesh [mahogany] and madeira from Abaco, and planking of Florida long leaf pine."

For some two decades, Hod ran first *Aegean* then *Velila* as fully crewed charter yachts. When in 1976 he traded his 77-foot Rhodes-designed *Velila* for the 38-foot center-cockpit ketch *Velila II,* Hod offered bareboat charters exclusively to his fellow CCA members. But by then times had changed.

"All the foreign charter yachts which are now forced to operate on the Turkish coast are crewed by British or French skippers with their girlfriends along, plus crews of wild-looking long-haired and bushy-bearded youths," wrote Hod for the *Cruising Club News* in January 1978. "During the years I ran the big *Velila* one could still find capable Greek sailors and crew members, and I operated her with two sailors, a first-class chef, plus a steward who waited on table and made up the cabins and gave a hand on deck. They were all in uniform and never came aft of the foremast except when working and really knew their jobs. Peabo and his shipmates saw the best years for cruising in this part of the world."

Peabo Gardner closed his preface of *Hard Alee* with a long personal dedica-tion to Hod.

A word or two about Hod may not be out of place here. Full of charm, he is above all a sailorman, having gained early experience with sail and engine in a cruise around the world as an engineer and hand on a friend's yacht. On board his own yachts he takes skillful care of his ship, fixing the engine or even the head when necessary. He is always willing to try out new anchorages, but with careful approach; eager to rely on sail whenever possible, but again a believer in not taking unnecessary risks—which, after all, is the mark of a good seaman.

Hod has a distinguished military record, which he can seldom if ever be persuaded to talk about except in flashes. Suffice it to say that he was dropped into France well before D-Day and subsequently took part in numerous amphibious landings in the Pacific. [*Author's note:* A more accurate chronology follows.] As a result of his outstanding service, he was eventually retired as a Brigadier General in the Marine Corps, a most unusual accolade for a Reserve officer.

By his friends—and there are many of them in all parts of the world—he is looked upon with admiration and affection. To them he is both loyal and tender, and I am proud to feel that I am one of them. My association with Hod has been one of the high points of my life.

CCA member, marine historian, and National Sailing Hall of Fame inductee John Rousmaniere observed the same reluctance in Hod to speak of his military past. John was 19 years old in 1964 when he first met Hod, just as Hod was first taking ownership of the 77-foot Rhodes-designed *Velila* in San Diego. A self-described college dropout—today we'd say he took a *gap year*—John signed on for the delivery with a crew of men all 30 years his senior, including Donald Starr (about whom, more later), and sailed from California through the Panama Canal, and across the Atlantic Ocean to the Mediterranean Sea.

"While in the Med, coming up toward Greece," John recalled, "Hod would point off toward the beach and say, 'That's where I was, doing something. I'm not going to tell you what it was.'"

Say, how did Hod end up over there in Greece, anyway?

"He had gone into the charter business, so the story goes," said John. "There are two stories about why he was in Greece. Do you know the second story?"

## Riding Out the Great Depression

Hod Fuller graduated in 1930 from Harvard College straight into the Great Depression. While in college, he pursued automobile racing and aeronautics; today, he is regarded as one of the fathers of the Harvard Flying Club. After college, he worked briefly as a transport pilot, but the company that employed him soon went bankrupt, and other jobs proved hard to find. Meanwhile, Hod's close association with internal-combustion engines brought him to the attention of the Massachusetts assistant attorney general, Donald Starr, whose newly built 85-foot Alden-designed schooner had been fitted out with an 85-horsepower Winton diesel auxiliary engine, plus a generator for onboard electricity. Donald was assembling a crew for a world circumnavigation beginning in the summer of 1932. Hod signed on as chief engineer—a role that earned him the lifelong nickname Chief—and spent the next two years doing what few people at that time had ever done: sail all the way around the world for the pure fun of the thing.

Not to say that every moment of *Pilgrim's* circumnavigation was fun. In the posthumously published *Schooner Pilgrim's Progress* (1996), Donald Starr described the genesis of his first transoceanic yacht.

Due to my lack of experience in deep water then, I was looking for a somewhat larger vessel than I would want now for the same purpose. In 1931, the gaff-schooner rig had still not been displaced by the new type of offshore sailing vessel typified by the Sparkman & Stephens yawl *Dorade* as a dependable and easily handled rig for deep-sea cruising in foreign waters. The idea then was not, as now, to go off in a small boat that is part of a flotilla connected by radio, but to have a vessel that could go safely off on its own over the seas of the globe.

Warwick Tompkins and *Wander Bird*, his famous 85-foot North Sea pilot schooner, were working out of Boston at about that time. They confirmed my ideas regarding the size, rig, and accommodations of a vessel, and suggested many of the elements that went into *Pilgrim*. Tompkins himself attended the launching of my schooner in Boothbay and became a life-long friend. Another schoonerman in Boothbay Harbor then was Sterling Hayden. A boy of about 15 then, he lived there and took a great interest in *Pilgrim's* construction. He wanted to go along with me, but I felt at the time that it was too much of a responsibility to take along a lad so young. I subsequently felt sure that he would have been a great addition to the crew.

I had the schooner designed by John Alden primarily because he had revolutionized yachting by adapting the fishing schooner of New England waters to the abilities and requirements of yachtsmen. He also admired Tompkins' schooner, having written: "I consider *Wander Bird* the best-designed and best-built vessel of her size in America." Alden's own highly regarded *Malabars* gave yachtsmen the ability to go offshore with the assurance that their boats were designed for that purpose while also affording the speed every yachtsman appreciates, provided it is not purchased at the price of his idea of minimum comfort and ability. Alden's *Malabars* were proving very successful in ocean racing then, but he could not have been more pleased than by my order for a strictly cruising design. No one could have done a better job of it.

If only the same could be said of her build quality and fit-out. She'd been built to Donald Starr's order by Reed-Cook Construction of Boothbay Harbor, Maine—and not well, as subsequent events revealed. *Pilgrim* and company set off from the Boston waterfront at the start of the morning ebb of the summer solstice

Freshly graduated from Harvard, Hod Fuller rode out the Great Depression
as chief engineer on a pleasure cruise around the world from 1932 to 1934,
aboard the 85-foot Alden schooner, *Pilgrim*.

of 1932. "As the hurricane season grew closer," wrote Donald, "those things which ought to have been done, and those things which had been done as they ought not to have been done, reared their mocking heads. Due to several serious defects in the installation of the engine, the after part of the vessel had been a workshop for a corps of mechanics who left their occupational spoor on the crisp white pine decks and fresh paint work."

*Pilgrim* had been at sea for barely a week when a second major defect in the engine installation showed itself. "Had a hell of time with the engine all day today," wrote Hod, age 24, in his journal. "It is either building up too much hydraulic pressure or not enough. I was in the engine room all day long goosing it along. I finally had to give up about 8 o'clock, it was running so rotten."

Subsequent examinations revealed that the builder had installed the exhaust piping directly from the engine to the transom, with no loop above heeled waterline and no siphon break. During commissioning, the addition of 10 tons of movable lead ballast had lowered *Pilgrim's* waterline substantially. The result was that, underway, unimpeded seawater was now invited into the engine's cylinders. Despite Hod's best efforts, *Pilgrim* had become an engineless sailboat and would remain so till she reached Panama, where the exhaust system could be redesigned and rebuilt.

Another problem with consequences still more grave revealed itself in that first week offshore.

*Pilgrim* leaked.

"Harold Peters ambled over to the leeward deck pump and gave its handle a few tentative heaves. The result? Fresh sea water spilled onto the deck and down the scuppers. Twelve gallons taken in a few hours, while no great amount, was more than normal *weeping,*" Donald wrote.

When *Pilgrim* did finally arrive in Panama, two separate surveyors inspected her hull, and both declared her unfit for ocean voyaging. As the efforts played out to stop the leaks, the weeks in dry dock turned into months. Even to examine the hull, workmen had to bust out massive sections of cement ballast.

"God, what a way to build a boat," wrote Hod. "The whole job looks pretty useless & as though the trip might be called off right here."

A parade of diagnoses followed—all accurate but none sufficient to stop the leak.

Caulked seams? "There appeared to be little oakum in them: I judge two thin threads. It was considered necessary to recaulk the entire hull up to the water line."

Materials selection? "I found several places in the forefoot keel and stern where stopwaters were needed. There were two old wormholes in the false keel. I also found one 14-foot-long plank under the port fore rigging about halfway from the keel to the water line which was badly split through to the inside. This was removed and replaced with a new plank."

Fastenings? "I could pass a hacksaw blade between the planks and the frames, striking the main fastenings. At these points the planks were not tight against the frames."

One by one, these and other exhibits of poor build quality were discovered and corrected. Still, *Pilgrim* leaked.

The final diagnosis was the most accurate but also the costliest, as it called into question nearly 5,000 plank-to-frame fastenings. "The diameter of the holes bored in the planking to receive the square-shanked spikes was slightly larger than the square thickness of those shanks."

Meanwhile, Hod was hearing news from his family back in Boston that put *Pilgrim's* troubles in perspective. "I got a letter from home & things sound terrible up there. I'm lucky to be out of it all. Simpson & Co. say they will fix us up in several days. They plan to cover the hull with tar or asbestos under the copper sheathing. This will stop the leaks while we lie at anchor but will be the same old story when we get to sea again & the vessel starts working. Hell, I'd take a chance in an unseaworthy vessel. What's the use in worrying whether you get home with

*"What's the use in worrying whether you get home with your neck or not? There's nothing when you get there but worry & trouble and hard times & you might as well see what you can."*

your neck or not? There's nothing when you get there but worry & trouble and hard times & you might as well see what you can."

In the end a Balboa shipwright proposed a strategy—forcing a mixture of lead and lead-oxide paste into 1,750 of the 4,900 total bungs under great pressure with a specially designed tool—that, while not perfect, did send *Pilgrim* out the Pacific side of the Panama Canal with the Port Captain's shaky blessing. By then she'd become an embarrassment to all involved, including the builder, a Mr. Wells, who traveled to Panama, assessed the situation, and after hazarding an ineffectual solution, returned to Maine with two maddening words: "I'm sorry."

"After five months of frigging around we are off at last with the schooner still leaking after all this time & money that has been spent on her," wrote Hod. "She makes from 8–10 gals an hr, but we are going on just the same and hope for the best."

All the waiting and the pluck to leave paid off for *Pilgrim's* crew. For the next 18 months, to the Galapagos Islands and across the Pacific, through the Dutch East Indies and Southeast Asia and the Red Sea and the Med, the ship's company enjoyed visiting those places that before World War II and subsequent globalization were so emphatically exotic. On her homebound leg, *Pilgrim* stopped at Bermuda just as the boats of the 1934 race were arriving.

"On 27 June, the ketch *Vamarie* crossed the finish line of the Newport to Bermuda Race, followed by the schooners *High Tide, Water Gypsy, Grenadier,* and several dozen more yachts. Afterwards, their combined crews gathered in the bar of the Royal Bermuda Yacht Club, a room designed to accommodate a much smaller number of guests, and talked it over. The *Edlu,* a [Sparkman & Stephens-designed] sloop, won the race on corrected time. We of the *Pilgrim* listened and enjoyed the company but had little to contribute."

Hod was happy to see familiar faces. "It was great to see the boys from home after being away for two years," he wrote. "We had a good many coming aboard & being very interested in the vessel & hearing about the trip. They all made very good time on the way down, the weather being fine & plenty of wind rather than lack of it. The corrected time of *Edlu* was 69 and a half hours, which is some going."

During the entire circumnavigation Hod spent $400 in expenses. He reckons he would have spent far more looking for a job in Boston.

## Codename Fansul

After *Pilgrim's* 1934 return, Hod Fuller settled back in Boston, where he did take a salaried job at Bethlehem Steel Fore River Shipyard, heading up the department that tested diesel and gasoline engine designs. Within his first year back home he acquired the 36-foot William Atkin-designed schooner *Spalpeen*, built in 1924, which he and his brother and friends sailed between Buzzards Bay and Boothbay Harbor in every weather, chasing rendezvous, regattas, and ducks. In a 1936 November nor'easter he grounded her on a shoal off the Annisquam River entrance from Ipswich Bay. After a clumsy towing attempt by the U.S. Coast Guard, she sank in six fathoms, and Hod might have lost her but for a lucky encounter with a Gloucester fisherman, master of the *Anna F. Clark*.

"The condition of this boat left much to be wished for," wrote Hod, "but when her owner quoted a charter price of fifteen dollars for the whole job whether she sank or not, we decided to take her."

Their salvage gambit paid off. Using two boats and four 12-inch by 12-inch timbers, Hod's crew was able to drag hawsers around *Spalpeen's* hull; over the next five days, they let the tides do the heavy lifting. "Once we had succeeded in beaching her, it was a simple matter to caulk the seams of the sprung leak, bail the water out, refloat her, and tow her to Boston where she was hauled out for the winter."

On September 1, 1939, Germany invaded Poland. Great Britain and France immediately declared war on Germany, but U.S. popular opinion overwhelmingly opposed getting into the fray. Hod Fuller did not.

"As soon as the Nazis attacked, I joined a group of Americans and went to France to volunteer my services," Hod wrote to a U.S. Marine lieutenant colonel in May 1941. He had joined the American Field Service, and drove an ambulance. "I was attached to the 19th Transport Regiment, 10th Division, 10th French Army Corps and served at the Front all through the battles for Flanders and on the Somme. When the Armistice came [the June 1940 French surrender to Germany], I was demobilized, a heartbreaking experience since I had just received an appointment for the next officer's course and a posting to the Foreign Legion."

A year after the French Armistice but still more than six months before the United States entered the war, Hod received the commission in the U.S. Marine Corps that he'd been seeking. For the next year he trained and instructed Marines. When the 1st Marine Division landed on Guadalcanal on August 7, 1942, he commanded one of the companies. Only after one of his legs was crushed under a collapsing bunker did he return to the United States. After several months of rehabilitation, he taught tactics in Quantico, Virginia. But he always wanted to be back in the action.

So far, Hod's military career could be described as traditional soldiering. That changed in September 1943, when General William "Will Bill" Donovan, commander of the newly established Office of Strategic Services, precursor of the Central Intelligence Agency, personally recruited Hod to join his mission.

Before the OSS, the United States had no central clearinghouse for intelligence-gathering, let alone clandestine operations. In 1929 Secretary of State Henry Stimson shut down a code-breaking operation in his department, famously saying, "Gentlemen don't read each other's mail." But as the war progressed, President Roosevelt grew increasingly convinced that U.S. war planners needed better intelligence. He established the OSS in June 1942.

By the spring of 1944, as the Allied forces planned to invade Europe *en masse*, the OSS had come to add clandestine activities to its portfolio. One of the earliest and most wide-reaching of these was a scheme called Operation Jedburgh. Named for a town on the Scottish border, Jedburgh consisted of about a hundred teams of three people each. Each team consisted of one British or American officer, one native-speaking officer, and one radio operator. These teams were to be armed and in uniform—in theory. The goal was to drop them behind enemy lines where they could assist local resistance forces to carry out military operations. Strategically, the whole ploy was initially meant to distract German generals from what the Allied commanders were calling Operation Overlord: the D-Day invasion of Normandy.

"Each man was to be hand-picked for his high intelligence, his skills as a partisan, his personal courage, his ability to command respect, and his fairness," wrote one chronicler of the Jedburgh Operation, "for a Jed was expected to be captain, judge, confessor, and quartermaster—to say nothing of demolitions expert, gunsmith, linguist, marksman, poacher, and doctor."

Forty American officers joined Operation Jedburgh; among them was Marine Lt. Col. Horace W. Fuller, code-named "Fansul," leading a three-person team known as the Bugatti Mission. At dusk on June 28, 1944—three weeks after the Normandy invasion—the Bugatti Mission parachuted into Nazi-occupied France, in the mountainous Hautes-Pyrénées region near the border with Spain. Their mission was to rally and support the *maquis*, the French resistance fighters on the ground. Indeed, they were immediately greeted by *maquisards* and led to a farmhouse for hiding. Next morning, Hod departed alone to rally other resistance leaders in the region. His hosts let him know that the Gestapo were searching nearby houses for agents like him, so Hod changed into civilian clothing—a decision that he knew would result in his trial as a spy, and his certain execution, if he were caught. For two frustrating months his team struggled to operate with inadequate supplies, squabbling factions among the *maquis*, and civilians who informed the Germans of their positions. "At this time we had more to worry about from the French than we did from the *boche*," Hod wrote, using a slang word for German soldiers. When an Italian informant was discovered in the village, it was Hod who ordered his execution.

But by early August Allied troops had taken much of northern France, and a second invasion was underway from the Mediterranean coast. Hod tells what happened next:

On the night of the 14th of August we received the BBC radio broadcast message for all *maquis* to enter full-scale open guerilla warfare. We moved our headquarters the following day down into the village of Saint Bertrand-de-Comminges on the plain below. Patrols were sent out to cover the main bridges and narrow mountain passes where they succeeded in bagging a few stray enemy vehicles and motorcycles during the following days without suffering a single casualty. We received word that the *boche* garrison of 400 at Luchon were preparing to make a break to the north to join their troops who were packing up and hot-footing it back to the *Vaterland* by any means possible. At a later date, I watched long columns of krauts all heading eastward on foot, in peasants' oxcarts, on bicycles, pushing baby carriages filled with gear, and even riding on donkeys. It was quite a contrast to the once proud German Army I had seen enter France in May and June of 1940.

It was decided to attack the garrison at Luchon at once, and I sent one group of 100 *maquis* under the command of Lt. Marchal south through the adjoining valley to begin the attack, while I moved south down the parallel valley of Luchon with 60 men to occupy and hold the narrow gorge at Port Chaud through which the enemy had to pass to reach the main highways to the north. Large trees were felled across the narrow road, which was bounded on one side by the Garonne River and on the other by steep rocky cliffs.

The *maquis* were well installed and hidden among the rocks and cliffs which bristled with Sten guns [British submachine guns], six Bren guns [British light machine guns on a tripod], potato masher grenades, and shotguns loaded with buck shot. I installed my command post together with our first-aid station behind the stone embankment of a bridge about 200 yards north of the roadblock. It was well protected by our heavy artillery, which consisted of an enormous single-shot antitank rifle for which we had only nine cartridges. The following morning we received word that Lt. Marchal's group had made contact with the *boche* and had them running toward our reception committee. News of the fighting traveled like wildfire through the valley. We were soon joined by old men and young boys armed with everything from old hammer-type shotguns to homemade grenades—all spoiling to kill a *boche*.

About 1 o'clock we heard the sound of approaching motor vehicles, which presently appeared around a bend in the road about 500 yards away and continued in our direction. I had given orders to hold all fire until they rounded the next curve and were stopped by the road-block, then the anti-tank rifle would be fired as a signal to let them have everything we had. However, the temptation was too much, and all hell broke loose from the cliffs while the enemy was still 200 yards away. Two trucks started burning, the convoy stopped, and men tumbled out of the vehicles like rats leaving a sinking ship. They withdrew their remaining vehicles, and the fire fight was on. Bullets whined overhead and ricocheted off the rocky cliffs as the *boche* got into position and returned fire. Our men were so well hidden among the rocks and in the cliffs that I felt quite confident that we had little to worry about unless the *boche* started to work us over with mortars.

Intermittent small-arms and machine-gun fire continued during the afternoon, and a few minor wounded were brought to our dressing station to be patched up once we had located our Corsican medic, who had disappeared with his small *boche* grenade launcher and rifle to join in the fight. About 4 o'clock we discovered a group of the enemy were climbing up around our positions in the cliffs in an attempt to outflank us. Four Bren guns and the doctor with his grenade launcher went into action from the crest of a ridge, which seemed to discourage any further efforts on their part to continue this plan of attack.

The fighting continued intermittently through the night. Meanwhile, a messenger brought word that Lt. Marchal's group had liberated Luchon, where the Germans had been garrisoned. Next morning, a delegation from the town came to Hod's position in the hills to present him with a captured German flag. In a later ceremony in town, Hod and his men were celebrated as heroes. One *paysan* presented Hod with 48 bottles of vintage Champagne.

From there, Hod's Bugatti Mission liberated Tarbes, another town where the German army was garrisoned, then provided tactical support for the Allied invasion of the south of France and the Seventh Army penetration into central France. For his service, Hod was awarded the Silver Star, the French *Croix de Guerre*, and other honors.

## Greece Needed Looking After

Hod Fuller was demobilized in December 1945 with the rank of lieutenant colonel in the U.S. Marine Corps. In 1957 he retired from the U.S. Marine Corps Reserves with the rank of brigadier general. As Peabo Gardner said, this was "a most unusual accolade for a Reserve officer."

Declassified documents—personal letters, operational synopses, many held in Federal Records Center files—tell us more now than Hod was willing to tell his friends after the war. On August 14, 2008, the National Archives released the names and files for some 13,000 OSS personnel. The same is not true for all undercover work performed later, after the OSS transitioned into the CIA.

In brief biographical sketches, a common refrain is that Hod went to Greece under the auspices of the Marshall Plan. John Rousmaniere reckons that was a euphemism.

"Hod had been in the OSS during the war, so he was used to undercover work," he said. "He had a sibling who was in Greece in some sort of government position, and Greece needed looking after. If Greece had turned to Communism, there would have been a lot of trouble."

Hod's nephew, CCA member Henry Fuller, runs Cape Breton Boatyard in Baddeck, Nova Scotia. "Hod's younger sister, Anne, followed him to Greece. She was in WACS during the war, and I believe she had some OSS connection when she first went to Greece."

Henry remembers sailing with his uncle and Peabo and the gang aboard *Velila* before his 17th birthday. "A few years ago I came across a quote from a former CIA agent who stated to his son that Hod Fuller was the best assassin in the OSS. This was after the father had had a few drinks on board *Velila* on a father-son cruise along the Dalmatian coast."

Surely there are people who still recall more about what kept Hod busy through his retirement from government service in 1957, and perhaps documents yet to be declassified will add to the details of Hod's service.

In the meantime Hod took his friends sailing. "Let me show you something in the way of islands," Hod Fuller would say to the guests who would visit him aboard *Velila* in the Aegean or the Adriatic Seas.

"The ancient battlements of Dubrovnik lifted with the sun," wrote Carleton Mitchell for *Yachting* in a 1970 article called "A Rift in the Iron Curtain."

"Earlier, golden rays had outlined the crests of the mountain range beyond, like surf strongly backlighted, while the shore remained in shadow. It was a landfall holding special promise. After the Iron Curtain clanged down at the end of World War II, the Dalmatian Coast assumed some of the mythical quality of a modern Atlantis. Earlier yachtsmen, who had known it during the final days of

*"Let me show you something in the way of islands,"*
*Hod Fuller would say to the guests who would visit him*
*aboard* Velila *in the Aegean or the Adriatic Seas.*

the Austro-Hungarian Empire, sang praises sounding suspiciously like nostalgic dreams of a never-never land, combining the islands of Greece, the dramatic slopes of Italy, and the charm of an unspoiled French Riviera. Yet it remained out of reach until the Communist government decided to open Yugoslavia to tourism. Roads were built, hostels and hotels blossomed, and restrictions eased for that arch symbol of capitalism, the cruising yacht."

As Hod had introduced Mitch and friends—and a large American readership—to Greece, now he was doing the same for Marshal Tito's Yugoslavia.

"When I came in during 1957 the officials couldn't understand what you could want, going around in a boat," Hod told Mitch. "I was only allowed to anchor where police were stationed. As we sailed along the coast, look-outs signaled each other with mirrors. Boarding parties armed with tommy-guns came aboard, usually around midnight, to demand our *papiera*. When I came back in '62, they were friendly, but not well organized. Since they have improved. Now we'll see."

Hod Fuller, a good man to have on a boat—here repairing sails on Carleton Mitchell's *Carib*.
The list of CCA members who sailed with Hod runs long.

For over four decades, *Carina* has collected trophy silver in major races, crossed oceans,
and circled the globe under the ownerships of three distinguished CCA members.

# 9

# Raising Sons, Raising Fathers:
# The *Carina* Story

Sailing and *Carina* provided the foundation for my father and me
to share something of enormous value to us both.
—Richard B. Nye
*Carina's* co-owner

My brother and I felt doing the Bermuda Race was really good quality time
with our dad. As much as my dad worked, and our lives were crazy with sports
and everything else, it was a tradition that he wanted to create for us.
You don't realize how special something like that is until you're a bit older.
—Allen Potts

As long as they want to do it and as long as I'm physically able, we'll keep doing it.
This is one of the joys of owning a boat and one of the joys of being a father.
—Rives Potts
Owner, *Carina,* the three-time St. David's Lighthouse Trophy winner
(1970, 2010, 2012)
Circumnavigator, 2011–12

At the awards ceremony for the 2010 Newport-Bermuda Race, Rives Potts, skipper of the fleet-winning boat, invited to the stage anyone who'd ever sailed aboard *Carina*—whereupon the stage soon groaned under a Who's Who of offshore sailboat racing, two and three generations deep.

*Carina,* launched in 1969, had been conceived in the cyclone of bitter debate between the keepers of the CCA and RORC measurement rules and at the dawn of the International Offshore Rule. As it happened, she won the overall fleet prize in the 1970 Bermuda Race, the first ever raced under the

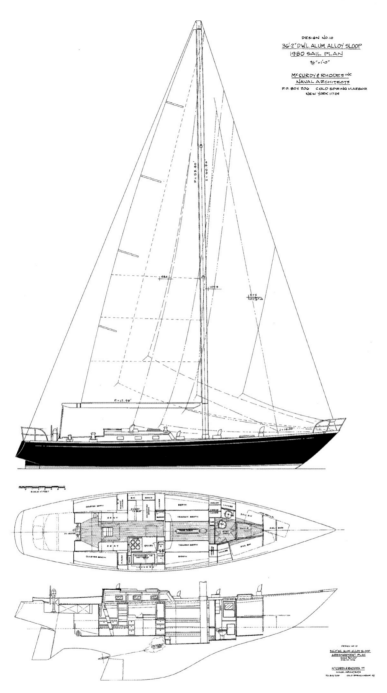

*Carina*, born in the transition from the CCA to the IOR handicapping rules,
won the first Bermuda Race she sailed in 1970.
This drawing shows a rig modified in 1980.
Her aluminum underbody was also modified for more speed.
She won her second and third Bermuda Races in 2010 and 2012.
Design No. 10 came from the drafting tables of McCurdy & Rhodes
for Richard and Dick Nye, in 1969. She is a sea boat in every way,
from her snug accommodations to her rugged hull and rig.

The changing of the guard from Richard B. Nye, on the right, to Rives Potts, on the left. After 27 years of father-son ownership, *Carina* found a new home with an accomplished sailor who knew her well, after caring for her in his boat yard for several years.

IOR. At 41 years of age, she had just collected the St. David's Lighthouse Trophy for the second time. Add to that her record-number 18 Bermuda Races sailed, her wins in the 1969 and 1972 Transatlantic Races, her successful finish in the calamitous 1979 Fastnet Race, almost too many Block Island, Seawanhaka, Monhegan, Long Island Sound, and New York Yacht Club wins to keep straight, and you might say that *Carina* could now go gentle into the quiet life of an esteemed Hall of Famer.

But that's not what she did.

## Head and Shoulders Above the Rest

When Rives Potts bought *Carina* from her owner, Richard B. Nye, in 1996, he took on a legacy almost too great to carry. Richard B. Nye ("Sonny," "B is for boy") was the younger of a father-son duo whose legend in offshore-sailing circles dated back to their first Bermuda Race win in 1952. Richard S. Nye ("Dick," "Pop," "S is for Senior") had gotten the family into sailing a decade earlier than that, and entirely by accident.

"I didn't know my father had any particular interest in boating or sailing," the junior Richard Nye recalled. "Lloyd Georgeson was my father's senior partner in their brokerage business—the stock market. Lloyd died in the spring of 1944, and my father bought out his interest in the firm. He came home one night and said, 'By the way, I've bought a boat.' I believe it was part of the business deal to

*Knowing nothing, the Nyes, father and teenaged son,*
*set off on Long Island Sound with outdated charts, dodging rocks*
*and sometimes spending whole tide cycles firmly aground.*

purchase the company. We were all dumbfounded."

The boat was *Vanward*, a 40-foot wooden cutter designed by Philip L. Rhodes. Knowing nothing, the Nyes, father and teenaged son, set off on Long Island Sound with outdated charts, dodging rocks and sometimes spending whole tide cycles firmly aground. Together, the two learned to sail, while the Nye sisters pursued different interests, equestrian and otherwise.

"As the only boy in our family," Richard recalled, "I can describe the relationship I had with my father in one word—tough."

Yet aboard the boat, a different kind of dynamic evolved between them, a democracy of sorts, and from the beginning the son shared real authority with his father. The Nyes joined the Indian Harbor Yacht Club in Greenwich, Connecticut, and tried racing. In 1947, Dick Nye bought a Rhodes-designed yawl with a proven record. Dick's enthusiasm was piqued by the knowledge that this boat had won the Port Huron-Mackinac distance race, but he got fleeced in the sale. After he handed over his check for the boat, the previous owner told him, "Of course, you realize the racing sails are extra." In the end, Dick Nye spent $30,000 on a boat that had been built for $10,000 just a couple of years earlier. Her first owner had christened her *Carina*, and Dick kept the name. From then on and appended to two more boats, that name would be forever linked to the Nye family. Beginning there, the Nyes created something that would grow through all the remaining decades of both men's lives. A letter from the headmaster of the Brunswick School congratulates the 15-year-old student and his father on *Carina's* victory in the 1947 race to Nantucket, giving a shy boy an indescribable sense of accomplishment upon which he could build the rest of his life.

Off the boat, the Nye's relationship grew no less difficult as it grew ever more entwined. Richard attended Dartmouth University, as his father had done, then after business school joined Dick's brokerage firm. "One of the chief problems we had was that he didn't know what to do with me. My father was a formidable presence in that office, and everyone was cowed by him. But he wasn't a very good teacher." Knowing nothing of the Wall Street proxy-solicitation business, the boss's son was relegated to mailroom status. Yet on their railway commute into the city, which they also shared, Dick granted his son leeway if the topic was boats. "Whether it be adapting a simple piece of equipment or proposing a major

Richard B. Nye sits with his father Richard S. "Dick" Nye, who enjoys his signature cigar. The two took up sailing at the same time when Dick bought out his late partner's interest in their financial firm. A boat, the first *Carina*, came with the sale.

overhaul, we'd review plans together," said Richard. "I might have to argue with him a couple of times to convince him to do what I thought needed to be done, but I usually prevailed."

Aboard three *Carinas* across four decades, the Nyes fostered a spirit that attracted talented sailors, young and old, and left indelible memories of goodwill that would be told and retold long after the event. "There was something unique in my father's style that was in some ways transferred to me," wrote Richard, "something that was, in effect, greater than the sum of its parts."

"To sum it up," said Larry Huntington, who first crewed aboard *Carina* in the 1963 Transatlantic Race and many others afterward, "you sailed *seriously* with friends. Once I started sailing with the Nyes, I realized that there was a very happy home on board there with a wonderful group of sailors and fantastic management. Both father and son made the ship totally hospitable and fun."

The Nyes were among the first to sail distance races with women as crew. Hope McCurdy, daughter of yacht designer Jim McCurdy, lobbied Dick Nye to take her on as crew for the 1966 Transatlantic Race to Denmark. Her sister, Sheila, recalls the deliberation. "My sister had this incredible ambition to sail transatlantic. At the tender age of 19, she made her case to Dick Nye, and he told her he'd have to think about it. The forecast for the race was rough—it was going to begin in a gale—so Dick Nye probably thought that by adding another crew member it would free everyone up a bit and give them a little more rest.

*"No matter what, you just kept on sailing as though you were the first boat. That meant that if you were in the lead, you were going to cover that guy and luff them to Spain if you had to, but if you weren't doing well you would split tacks with the leaders."*

Dick consulted Irving Pratt, who was an elder statesman of yachting at the time, and who was also doing the race. Dick asked him, 'So, Irving, what do you think about this idea of taking a girl along on the race?' Irving replied, 'A boat is no place for a girl!' On the basis of his response, Dick Nye decided to invite the girl!"

Through the 1970s and 1980s, as other race crews became more professional, the Nyes mentored young amateur sailors who only later would go on to make names for themselves. "A few years ago a friend of mine who happened to work at North Sails said one of his regrets was never to have sailed on *Carina,*" said Stephen Lirakis, a frequent crewmember in the 1970s and the founder of an offshore safety equipment company. "I responded by saying that he would likely never have been invited to sail on the boat as the Nyes never found the need to have 'rock stars' as part of the crew."

Rock stars or not, beginning with the 1952 Bermuda Race victory, *Carina's* offshore racing record grew more impressive by the season. "From the very beginning," wrote Richard Nye, "I had a philosophy that you go for the home run every time. The upshot is that we never gave up on a race." His wife, Patricia, elaborated on the theme. "No matter what, you just kept on sailing as though you were the first boat. That meant that if you were in the lead, you were going to cover that guy and luff them to Spain if you had to, but if you weren't doing well you would split tacks with the leaders."

The tales of Dick Nye's unconventional ocean-racing strategy are legion. During the 1982 Bermuda Race he popped his head out the companionway, rubbed the sleep out of his eyes, and called, "Tack!" The crew on watch couldn't believe what they were hearing; *Carina* was just 10 degrees off her layline to the finish. "Tack," he ordered. "There's lightning to windward. The Gulf Stream's up there." They did tack, and for the next two hours sailed *away from Bermuda—* but into warmer water and a three-knot boost. *Carina* won her division by 34 minutes.

In *Nowhere Is Too Far*, the 1960 history of the Cruising Club of America, Jack Parkinson reflects on the 1952 Newport-Bermuda Race win and those that followed. "It was only the first in a series that established Dick Nye as one of the great ocean racing skippers of all time. If we count only Bermuda, Fastnet, Trans-Atlantic, and Honolulu Races as classic events, certainly Dick Nye, John Alden and Rod Stephens stand head and shoulder above the rest."

For some 20 years the Nyes campaigned two Rhodes yawls built of wood, then in 1968 commissioned their final sailboat—"the Black *Carina,* "the third *Carina,*" "the new *Carina*"—the subject of a story now 50 years old and counting.

## The Black *Carina*

The coffee-table book *Philip L. Rhodes and His Yacht Designs* by Richard Henderson features the first *Carina* on its cover. That 46-footer was said to be Rhodes' favorite of all his designs; it was also the lifetime favorite of Uffa Fox, the British yacht designer and Bill Nutting's transatlantic shipmate. This was the boat in which the Nyes first made their name. But after a lackluster showing in the 1954 Bermuda Race, Dick commissioned from Phil Rhodes a new 53-foot centerboard yawl. The so-called "second *Carina*" served the family well through 1968, earning Transatlantic and Fastnet fleet wins and a host of class wins in major ocean races. During the particularly rough 1957 Fastnet Race, the second *Carina* took a pounding that broke three of her ribs and threatened to separate her deck from her hull. Hour after hour as the boat sailed on, the crew pumped vigorously, several men at a time. When they finally crossed the finish line and affirmed they'd taken first in the fleet, Dick Nye said, "OK, boys. You can let her sink."

Instead, *Carina* was repaired and lived on to gather silver for another decade.

By the late 1960s, though, things were rapidly changing in the world of offshore racing and, correspondingly, in the boats. Broadly speaking, the first two *Carinas* would have been at home among a fleet from the 1930s. Through nearly four decades, the rules for handicapping ocean-racing sailboats, and hence the trends in yacht design, had remained largely stable—proof, in its way, that the charter members of the Cruising Club of America had met the stretch goals they'd set for themselves from the very beginning.

"We encourage the development of that type of craft which is most useful to our work," Henry Wise Wood wrote in a 1923 CCA report on the Club's plan and scope. "I am among those who believe that in a sailing craft speed is decidedly a useful factor, as it was in the clipper ship days, and that it must be cultivated, if we are to increase to the uttermost our radius of action. The greater the speed of a sailing craft, the less its operating cost per mile covered, and the less the bulk, the weight, and the cost of its supplies for a given voyage. Here lies one of the indestructible advantages over the power craft. I am convinced, therefore, that it is our duty to stimulate the production of fast, as well as comfortable, boats for long-distance, offshore work."

The Club's revival of the Bermuda Race in 1923 was an explicit expression of its goal to develop sound offshore boats for both racing and cruising, as well as to develop talent among sailors. In the earliest races the boats were handicapped solely on their overall length. Then in 1934 the Club adopted the Cruising Club Measurement Rule based on work by Wells Lippincott of Chicago—a rule that would dominate American yacht design until the International Offshore Rule replaced it in 1970. Robert N. Bavier Jr., the winning America's Cup helmsman and veteran marine journalist, reflected on the CCA Rule in a 1960 essay.

> Perhaps the greatest contribution which The Cruising Club has made to American yachting is the development of the Cruising Club Measurement Rule. And it is safe to say that without this rule and without the Bermuda Race which our club sponsors, the Cruising Club could hardly be so widely respected.
>
> The Cruising Club Rule is, however, as frequently condemned as it is appreciated. Its critics complain of its length and complexity, and avow that it takes a math major to understand it. They point out, also, that close and fair racing is often had under much simpler rules which everyone can understand, and which local measurers can figure ratings from with ease. What the critics lose sight of is that *any* simple rule could easily be "beaten" by designers if boats were built to it. The simple rules work out well only because the truly major distance racing events are conducted under the Cruising Club Rule, and hence designers create boats to fit that rule rather than a simple one which could be circumvented by some extreme design. Because the Cruising Club Rule would penalize such an extreme design properly, designers are kept from building freaks which would have no chance in the biggest events of all. Just so long as the big events are sailed under "our" rules, the simple rules will continue to work well for more local racing.
>
> To rate boats of diverse size and type fairly, and to plug loopholes which clever designers and owners are always (and rightly) trying to find, it is inevitable that the rule be long and apparently involved.

By today's standards, the CCA Rule isn't very difficult to understand. It starts from the premise that (except in planing hulls) potential speed increases in proportion to the square root of the boat's waterline length. It further recognizes a sailboat's other features that either produce or constrain speed: beam, draft, displacement, sail area, freeboard, ballast, propeller. The Cruising Club rating formula balances these factors, then returns a rating. From this rating, boat

*The Club's revival of the Bermuda Race in 1923 was an explicit expression of its goal to develop sound offshore boats for both racing and cruising, as well as to develop talent among sailors.*

owners and race organizers enter a table showing the number of seconds per mile of course length allowed by a boat of a given rating.

As Bob Bavier noted, this scheme functioned beautifully through the 1930s, 1940s, and 1950s, with adjustments large and small along the way to plug loopholes and discourage unseemly bumps, hollows, or outright freak designs. The broad result was a venerable fleet of yachts, including the first two *Carinas*, that could successfully race *and cruise* in the ocean.

By the 1960s major ocean races were drawing more and more entries from foreign countries. British boats, designed to race under the Royal Ocean Racing Club Rule (hence, typically narrow and deep-ballasted), fared poorly in the Bermuda or Honolulu races under the American rule. And American boats, with their relatively wide beams and low ballast-to-displacement ratios, faced a disadvantage under RORC rules in the Fastnet Race, for example.

In 1966 an international group was created to harmonize the measurement rules used in different countries. Yacht designer Olin Stephens represented the CCA. Looking back many years later, the agreement reached by the Offshore Rules Coordinating Committee left Olin with grave misgivings, particularly after the fleet-wide disasters of the 1979 Fastnet Race in which five boats were lost, 24 boats abandoned, and 15 sailors drowned. The iconic 1970s and 1980s scenes of crews lined up and hanging their bodies over the windward side—*rail meat*—to keep every boat on her feet even on days of fine sailing dismayed Olin.

"In the end," Olin wrote, "the new International Offshore Rule (IOR) combined most provisions of the RORC hull measurements with sail area measurements right out of the CCA Rule. Scantlings and stability were then, and remain still, very difficult to handle. We provided a center-of-gravity factor (GCF) to discourage excessively deep, heavy ballast. I am disappointed to realize that the GCF has worked opposite to what we intended. It now seems to encourage ballast so high that many boats have inadequate stability. This problem is now recognized and should be corrected."

When Dick and Richard Nye decided in 1968 to commission a new boat, all this change was in the wind and entirely unsettled. Having owned two good boats designed by Philip L. Rhodes, the Nyes now chose a younger firm to create their new boat: McCurdy & Rhodes Inc., Naval Architects, established in 1965. In fact, the Nyes were keeping it in the family. Jim McCurdy had been the chief yacht designer in Philip L. Rhodes's firm, and Philip H. "Bodie" Rhodes was his son. The McCurdy & Rhodes firm would come to be lauded for its fleet of Navy 44 sail-training craft and a host of Hinckley Sou'westers, among others; still, Black *Carina* (Design No. 10) remains one of its earliest and most enduring achievements.

Unlike the first and second *Carinas*, the sloop-rigged aluminum Black *Carina* could not have gone undistinguished from a 1930s fleet. Though radical in some aspects, she remained modest in other ways that the coming generation of IOR boats were not. Her standout feature for that era was arguably her underbody.

"The separation of the rudder from the keel was one of the most radical changes to be found in the development of yacht design during the late 1960s and early 1970s, at the beginning of the IOR," wrote Olin Stephens in a 1987 book on trends in yacht design. "It was widely used around the turn of the century, and for many years was familiar to us through its use on the Star Class one-design. For whatever reason (evidently not a good one), it was out of favor on larger boats from about 1905 to the late 1960s, although it was used on many New Zealand boats. Bill Lapworth, a yacht designer from California, pioneered the feature's return to favor in America with his highly successful Cal 40 racer-cruiser sloop. Dick Carter put a separate rudder on his *Rabbit*, which won the 1965 Fastnet Race, and our office took it up, with a trim tab as well, in the 12-Meter *Intrepid* in 1967. Before long, it was seen on many racing boats. In the context of speed, it has two real advantages over a long keel and attached rudder. First, it has less wetted surface, which means a faster boat, especially at lower speeds—for example, when sailing to windward in light weather. Second, a short fin keel with a high aspect ratio has less 'induced drag,' which is the drag resulting from the side force resisted by the keel."

A letter dated May 21, 1968, from Jim McCurdy to Dick Nye, offers a status report on the new *Carina*, as bids had started coming in from various builders capable of fabricating the boat's aluminum hull. The letter opens a window into that circumscribed time in yacht design when models were physical objects you shaped with your hands and tested in water tanks—before they referred to the virtual product of a velocity-prediction program generated by computers.

The Stevens tank expects the modified model tomorrow and plans to run it right away. The tests should therefore be completed this week and the results in our hands before the end of next week.

As Bodie has told you, the final lines are being drawn so that we will be ready for action. I have come to the conclusion that the 3" of additional beam we have had under consideration from the beginning will make the boat a more suitable instrument for your particular use. It produces an eight percent increase in ability to carry sail—something you enjoy doing, I understand. Thus it could be expected to produce a noticeable improvement in speed to windward in heavy weather, with little harmful effect in light air.

Bear in mind that the tank tests to date show a marked superiority to windward in winds of up to say 16 knots. We might almost give a little away here, if we had to, in order to crank up performance in the 16 knot plus wind speed range. The alteration to the underbody aft that is about to be tested is supposed to be effective in this respect from a resistance point of view. The extra 3" of beam will provide more power, which combined with the lesser resistance should have a doubly beneficial effect.

To build the boat, the Nyes hired Harold Paasch of Erie, Pennsylvania, a builder regarded more highly for its metalworking in aluminum than its yacht finish. In 1969, her first season out, the new *Carina* won the Transatlantic Race to Ireland, then as team captain won that year's Admiral's Cup. Season after season she notched one win after another: Onion Patch, Vineyard Race, Northern Ocean Racing Trophy, Long Island Sound Season Championship, New York Yacht Club Regatta, Block Island, Stratford Shoal Race, Larchmont Annual Distance Race, Monhegan Island Race. Under the Nyes, Black *Carina* kept winning ocean races well into the mid-1980s.

Toward the end of his life, Richard reflected back on some of the standout moments from all those days on the water—with one memory standing out in particular.

The Fastnet Race in the summer of '79 was supposed to be like any other we'd competed in over the span of our sailing experiences up until that time. Tracing, as it does, the southern coast of England for half its 605-mile distance, with its turning point at Fastnet Rock, off Ireland's south shore, there are some tricky currents and other factors that make it especially popular among serious yachtsmen.

In the *Carina* sailing tradition, our crew was mainly made up of family and friends. In addition to my father, who was then 76 years old, my son Jonathan was aboard, as was Larry Huntington and his son, Chris.

Three-hundred-and-three boats started out from the Cowes Royal Yacht Squadron that Saturday afternoon, August 11. No one anticipated the kind of weather we would encounter the next day and throughout the remainder of the race. In fact, the BBC had issued reports of relatively calm seas with gradually increasing winds.

The gales that soon descended upon that largely helpless fleet of boats during the race reached what is known as "Force 10," which means that the wind speed roared upwards of 50 knots or about 58 miles per hour. What wind of that nature does to the surface of the water and the general sailing conditions can only be described as pure chaos: whitecapped seas swelling and churning, and wind and water pounding the boat and crew in mercilessly driving sheets.

The crew was doing its job as always; they didn't appear panicky at all, although I'm sure the thought crossed their minds, as it did mine, that we were in for the ride of a lifetime. I myself wasn't worried until one point when I sent some members of the crew forward to get a jib down, which, even under the best conditions, is one of the most difficult jobs on board. I was holding my breath because I thought that at any moment someone could have been washed overboard. Keep in mind that we were in a 50-knot breeze. It was particularly nerve-racking because my son, Jonathan, was one of the crew I'd sent forward.

Ultimately, of course, we made it back—finished the race. I have to attribute our success in completing it to both our crew and the *Carina*. The boat was beautifully designed, well built, and well sailed; three reasons I believe we finished relatively unscathed.

Patricia Nye tells of her anxious night ashore in Plymouth while the storm decimated the fleet. Her son and her husband and her father-in-law were all still out there. She'd already been to the RORC office and seen the disaster reports coming in. Sleepless, she walked down to the hotel lobby at 2:30 a.m. just as winning skipper Ted Turner walked in with an entourage from the *Tenacious* crew and a band of marine journalists. She congratulated him, then added something else.

"I can't believe I'm about to ask you this question, but I'll go ahead and ask it anyway. You didn't see anything of *Carina* out there, did you?"

Looking her straight in the eye with what she felt was a kind expression, Ted Turner said, "You're the last one who needs to worry, Nye. Go to bed."

### He Wanted It to Be Kind of an Adventure

This was the boat and these were the stories that Rives Potts inherited when he took on *Carina* in 1996.

Richard B. Nye, having decided that it was time to retire from sailing, sought

*The gales that soon descended upon that largely helpless fleet of boats during the race reached what is known as "Force 10," which means that the wind speed roared upwards of 50 knots or about 58 miles per hour.*

not merely a buyer for his boat but a curator: someone who could keep *Carina* in fine trim and perhaps even continue racing her into her fourth decade. Rives Potts, for his part, had cared for *Carina* in the off-season going back many years, first as project manager at Derecktor Shipyards in Mamaroneck, New York, then as general manager at Pilots Point Marina in Westbrook, Connecticut—experience that was informed by his roles crewing and project-managing grand-prix racing campaigns, including Dennis Conner's America's Cup syndicate beginning in 1979 in Newport, Rhode Island, and continuing through five campaigns in Australia and San Diego. For the 1979 Fastnet Race he was one of those crewmembers aboard Ted Turner's *Tenacious.*

When Rives took ownership of *Carina*, he wanted to sail her as the Nyes had done: competitively, yes, but in a Corinthian spirit, crewed with family and friends. His two sons sailed their first Newport-Bermuda Race in 1998. Allen Potts was in eighth grade; Walker, in seventh. For both boys, it was the first of many Bermuda Races to come. Rives described to *Soundings* journalist Jim Flannery a dynamic he witnessed in those early years.

"The boys start the race reserved and wary of each other, not sure what to expect. As the wind picks up and darkness sets in, they stand their first night watch—nervous and often seasick. 'It's like the first day of boot camp,' Potts says. But then they change a few sails and stand more watches and start gaining confidence and competence. 'By the third or fourth day, they are good friends. By the time they get to Bermuda they are lifelong friends.'"

The boot-camp reference was apt. In 2003, fresh out of high school, Walker Potts joined the U.S. Marine Corps. Allen, with one year of college under his belt, straightaway followed his brother into service. "Walker was two and a half months ahead of me in boot camp, then we went into infantry units," said Allen. "After that, we both ended up in the same Reconnaissance unit, sort of a special-operations group in the Marines, but in different platoons and with different deployment schedules." Over the next four years, Walker deployed once to Haiti and twice to Iraq. Allen deployed to Iraq, then to a U.S. Navy ship based in the Med as part of a quick-reaction force. They each served four years, then spent another four in inactive reserve as they made their way through college.

With only a couple of exceptions during their stints in the Marines, both Potts boys continued to sail in every Bermuda Race with their dad and his friends. The crews included some of Rives' old mates from America's Cup and maxi-racing days, as well as his brother-in-law Bud Sutherland—and their sons.

"One of those guys' son, Will Gahagan, is now the godfather of my newest boy," said Allen in 2019.

It was sometime around the 2010 Bermuda Race that Allen and Walker noticed something new. "My dad started getting more serious about the success of *Carina*," Allen said. "By then we were all older and stronger, and it was more possible to actually have a crew that could do everything on the boat. All of a sudden, it was like, 'All right, we've got something to prove. Let's make the Nyes proud.' "

Winning the St. David's Lighthouse Trophy in 2010 surely did that. But Rives wasn't finished there. Next, he set his sights on the 2011 Transatlantic Race to England and the Fastnet. Could the boys take the time to do those races with him, then deliver the boat back to the U.S. East Coast? Allen had just earned a business degree and started his first real job in commercial real estate; he didn't feel he could take the time. But Walker said yes. So did their cousin, Rives Sutherland ("RS," "Little Rives")—born the same month as Walker. They would both turn 26 that year. To prepare for the voyage, RS moved from South Carolina to Connecticut over the winter to work at Pilots Point Marina by day and refit *Carina* in his off hours. Walker joined his cousin that spring, and for two months they both put in 20-hour days, stripping the boat down to bare aluminum and building her back up for a transoceanic summer. The refit included a thorough rebuild of *Carina's* engine and plumbing; all new running rigging and navigation electronics; a relocation of the binnacle and helm; a new watermaker; and the conversion of one water tank into a fuel tank. "The watermaker allows us to shed a significant amount of weight for racing," said Walker. "And it means we don't need to ration our fresh water quite so carefully, especially nice given our diet is primarily freeze-dried food, which is mixed with water before eating." They added a second 200-amp alternator with its own bracket, as all electrical gear on the boat—autopilot, refrigeration, nav electronics and weather forecasting—was powered from the engine.

Sometime during that spring Rives Potts ("RP," "Big Rives") started thinking still bigger. *Carina* and crew were prepared to sail to England, and then in the Fastnet Race, come August. But what if that same December she also competed in Australia's Sydney-Hobart Race? And *what if the boys delivered* Carina *to Australia on her own bottom, then home again in time for the next Newport-Bermuda Race in June 2012?*

*Carina*'s crew in the 2010 Newport Bermuda Race received the trophy
from the Governor of Bermuda, with the Commodore of the CCA,
Sheila McCurdy, center, and Commodore Peter Shrubb of the Royal Bermuda Yacht Club.
Patti Young, second from right, was the winning navigator.
Owner Rives Potts, soon to become Commodore of the New York Yacht Club,
is shown kneeling by the port winch.

"The whole plan," said Rives Sutherland, "was initially to do the Transatlantic Race and the Fastnet, and Walker and I were going to bring it back with somebody to Newport. But at some point RP got a little idea in his head and said, 'Hey, what about doing this?' And I said, 'Well that sounds pretty cool.' We talked about shipping it, but RP wanted it to be kind of an adventure."

Big Rives gave no more detailed instructions than this: arrive in Sydney (December 2011) and Newport (June 2012) at least 10 days before the start of the next race. He would ship a container full of the boat's racing sails and other gear to each destination. The only thing the boys had to do was arrive in time to prep for racing. How they did it was up to them.

### Once Around the Planet

As the poet said, life is what happens while you're busy making plans. The plans that Walker Potts and Rives Sutherland made for a speedy circumnavigation were dashed just before the Fastnet Race in August when Walker fell and injured his knee, tearing his anterior cruciate ligament: his ACL. Instead of sailing back west across the Atlantic Ocean after the race, he would board a commercial flight at

Heathrow Airport and fly home for surgery—but not before sailing the Fastnet, a race in which *Carina* took first in class and fifth in a fleet of 350 boats. A month earlier she'd led the Transatlantic pack nearly all the way to England, but then sailed into a hole 17 days out, and got rolled by the trailing boats just shy of the finish. Still, *Carina*, age 42, finished second in her class.

The recovery period for an ACL surgery is two to six months. Walker scheduled the procedure, blocked out an eight-week window from that date, and made plans to join *Carina* and his cousin somewhere on the far side of Panama. Meanwhile, Little Rives and a revolving cast of twentysomethings left England in early September, sailed south to the Azores, then across the Atlantic to the Virgin Islands; across the Caribbean Sea to Panama; and across the Pacific to the Galápagos and the Marquesas and Tahiti.

As every armchair sailor knows, September is not the favored month to set off from Europe across an Atlantic Ocean actively spinning up tropical cyclones. "We really didn't have much choice," said RS. "We just had to go and make do with the weather we had."

Smart or lucky, they crossed in mostly blissful fashion. Rives Sutherland's post-passage log gives the flavor of life aboard *Carina* in cruising mode, beginning in the Azores, where they touched ashore for six hours before continuing west.

The next 2500 nautical miles would be the long leg of this trip, but we had some good luck right off the bat as we left Flores. Within the first few days we caught 3 Tuna (2 yellowfin, and 1 blue fin) and even hooked into a huge Marlin just after sunrise. I regret to inform the fisherman reading this, however, that we didn't land the marlin. Unfortunately, it hit our lure that was connected to a reel mounted on the stern pulpit, and without a rod to fight the beast, we were no match for this massive fish. But for the record, the fish would probably have weighed in at 500 . . . no, 800 lbs.

The days passed quickly, and we enjoyed some nice sailing days during that two-week period. It didn't take long for us to realize that as we headed south it was going to get hot. REALLY hot. This necessitated daily searches for nearby swimming holes. As it turns out there are plenty of swimming holes in the middle of the Atlantic, and even though the commute to reach them is a bit of a hike, we hit them hard and often. The rest of our days were filled with sweating, reading, eating, sweating, playing chess, sweating, and sleeping, until you inevitably woke up because you were sweating again.

Long-distance voyaging means a long string of maintenance in interesting places.
Jeremiah Ellis Garland and Rives Sutherland make a headsail repair at sea.

Jeremiah "Ellis" Garland was one crewmember who came aboard in England and stayed for the full circumnavigation. He'd attended the Landing School in Arundel, Maine, and like RS had worked on the classic Fife-designed *Sumurun*. "Luckily, he's pretty clever," said RS. "He was really good with all the engine stuff and electronic stuff, maybe where I lack a little bit in that. But I could do all the sailing."

Meanwhile, as the miles of ocean passed beneath her keel, *Carina* evolved from a race boat into a true cruising boat. "They built a platform that made the cockpit just one big seat," said Allen Potts, who joined the boat briefly in Australia, then for her homeward leg from St. Thomas. "They had quick-drying beanbag chairs, and a big awning, and stuff like that that made cruising on *Carina* actually quite comfortable. Anybody who's sailed on *Carina* for any period of time knows that it's not a very comfortable boat above deck. We would always joke that you can never find an area where it's big enough for your butt to sit down without having, like, a track under it." Aft of the helm they built bench seats that doubled as a fish-cleaning station.

Belowdecks, *Carina* underwent a transformation from race mode to cruising mode, as well. "Everyone likes to make Asian food," said Allen, "so in one of the compartments that usually stores foul-weather gear, they had all their curry-making ingredients. There was an Italian corner where they had all their pasta sauces. And there was a ton of fishing. They were catching mahi-mahi and tuna, and either eating sushi or making great fish dishes. They ate like kings. That's not something that you usually do when you're racing."

And so the days rolled through early November in French Polynesia. Somewhere east of Samoa a gear failure occurred that threatened the entire project.

"We were trying to go Tahiti to Fiji to pick up Walker," said RS. "But we had a little issue a couple of days out of Tahiti and burned up the starter motor. The engine on that boat runs everything. And for about 24 hours we were just bobbing around with no wind."

By the end of the first day items in the freezer were melting. The forecast was windless. Mid-November was coming on; *Carina's* crew still had half the Pacific Ocean to cross before their deadline in Sydney, and less than a month to do it in.

Ellis recalled something he'd heard in the Marine Systems program at the Landing School about a couple who'd started their boat's diesel engine like a lawn mower by wrapping line around the flywheel, attaching the other end to the boom, and crash-jibing the boat to pull the cord. The jibing trick wouldn't work without any wind, but Ellis and RS tried something similar. A large opening hatch in the main saloon provided a clear shot from the flywheel to the boom. First, they removed any unnecessary belts from the engine. Then they removed the core from a length of double-braid line; this way, the line's cover fit tightly in the groove of the flywheel. "What we did," said RS, "was we centered the boom and hung a block off the boom. We wrapped the line around the flywheel, passed it up through the block, then made a handle with a solid bilge-pump handle that was about two and a half feet long. We wrapped the line around that and rolled it up to the cabin top, as high as we could get it. And then Ellis and I just got on it and basically did a pull-up—or a pull-down. And it started."

*It started?* After how many attempts?

"One," said RS.

"If the engine had been any bigger, it probably wouldn't have worked," he reckoned. "But it did on this one. It ran like that for two days while we motored to Bora Bora. Walker met us there with two new starters."

Walker Potts was finally back with his mates, and together they sailed nonstop to Sydney Harbor, arriving on December 3—plenty of time to prepare for a race that wouldn't start till Boxing Day.

Allen Potts was able to take time over the holidays to join his dad and brother and the rest of the *Carina* crew for the Sydney-Hobart Race. "It was a great experience," he said, "an unbelievably beautiful race. The start of that race was just really something, to have a country where the general public cares way more about sailing than we do over here. It was cool to have this spectator experience while you're in the washing machine of the Sydney-Hobart start."

*Carina*'s crew, enjoying the night watch.

There was something else Allen noticed, now being back aboard *Carina* after a hiatus of more than a year. "The amount of experience that Rives and Walker gained over those few months was very apparent. My brother and I had always sailed together, growing up. I realized I wasn't on the same playing field as them anymore. They had far surpassed me in every way when it comes to knowledge and experience. They took it to a different level."

As for the racing, an early glitch in the communications protocol slowed them down and they never recovered. *Carina* came in seventh in class. "I remember us getting the award for the boat that traveled the farthest by sea to participate," said Allen. "We got that. So it wasn't all for naught."

Nor was the experience of sailing and traveling with his family. "Down in Hobart we went on a hike one day. It was just a great experience—another great experience with our dad."

After the race crew, including Allen, all flew home, *Carina*'s round-the-world delivery crew tightened up. "We'd had a mishmash of crew," RS said of the Atlantic and Pacific crossings. "Other than myself and Ellis, we had a bunch of friends come when they could. Not everybody could stay for the whole time. But going down there is kind of a real nice trip. You're in the Pacific. It's sunny and

*After a compressed pitstop to change back from cruising
to racing mode,* Carina *did the unthinkable:
for the second consecutive race and for the third time in 43 years,
she again won the St. David's Lighthouse Trophy.*

warm and everything."

Knowing that the route home from Australia would entail longer legs in often cold conditions, RS thought, "You know what, we're going to slim this down a bit. So going home it was just four of us: Kit Will, Ellis Garland, Walker, and myself." With that crew, they rounded the bottom of Australia and crossed the Indian Ocean to South Africa, around the Cape of Good Hope, then across the South Atlantic to the Caribbean.

At St. Thomas, Kit and Ellis got off. "Ellis and I were with each other every day for a year. Every single day we slept six feet apart. He's one of my best friends, and I couldn't have done it without him."

Meanwhile, Allen Potts quit his first real job and on the very next day high-tailed it to St. Thomas, where he joined his brother and cousin for *Carina's* last leg home. "That was just really cool to see *Carina* in full cruising trim—the best way a boat like *Carina* could cruise. It was like an identity shift. We anchored across the channel from St. Thomas, and we stayed there for a few days, before we got going on the way back. And that was beautiful. From there we stopped once in Charleston, which is where my cousin Rives lives. He got kind of a hero's welcome from his friends."

His hero's welcome continued several days later when *Carina* landed back at Pilots Point Marina in Connecticut and a contingent of the Cruising Club of America was on hand to present Rives Sutherland with the circumnavigator's flag.

How did it feel to be a circumnavigator?

"Frankly, I would love to do this trip and take like three years," said RS. "Ideally I would have really loved to have gone around Australia the other way and checked out the Great Barrier Reef and that kind of thing. But I was on a mission, you know? All our stops were really three to five days: unload the trash, clean the boat, go provision, load the boat, and leave. But, oh, man—I love that boat. I wouldn't do it on any other boat."

## Bermuda, and Beyond

In the 2012 Newport-Bermuda Race, after a compressed pitstop to change back from cruising to racing mode, *Carina* did the unthinkable: for the second consecutive race and for the third time in 43 years, she again won the St. David's Lighthouse Trophy. Only *Finisterre* had ever won three times. But *Finisterre* didn't circumnavigate the globe between consecutive wins.

"I think it was really cool to see as I got older and started to understand what an important thing it was for my dad to continue such a legacy that the Nyes had established. And I don't even mean racing success," said Allen. "I've got two young kids of my own. I live in landlocked Montana, and I don't sail nearly as much as him. But I'm hoping that I can continue to sail often enough, and maybe through my brother and cousin we can create those kinds of experiences for our kids. That's really kind of at the forefront of what I'd like for them."

With enough wind and a will to win, even a Cal 40 can try to break the bonds of gravity,
here at the finish of the Transpac Race in 2003. *Illusion* found new life in 1988
when Stan and Sally Honey customized the derelict hull to race and cruise,
mostly doublehanded, in the Pacific and Atlantic.

# 10

# *Illusion* and the Honeys:
# Oh, What One Couple Can Do
# with a Stock Fiberglass Boat

She gets prettier every time she wins.
—C. William Lapworth, Cal 40 designer

To say that *Illusion* was a stock production 40-footer when Sally Lindsay and Stan Honey found her in 1988 would be overselling it.

"We found a derelict Cal 40 in Santa Cruz, California," said Stan. "She was in a yard next to the freeway and had sat out of the water for seven years. It had bullet holes, and the bilge was full of oil and water."

Rudder tube? Broken.

Engine? Nope.

Boom? Go find another.

"She had homeless people living inside her and fleas all over it and exploded cans of undisclosed stuff in the bilge," said Sally.

Yet despite *Illusion's* execrable condition, she did have good bones—and, it turned out, a pedigree. She was hull number 57 of a line of production fiberglass sailboats first launched in fall 1963 by Jensen Marine of Costa Mesa, California. Straightaway, these Cal 40s brought home the top prizes from the world's most prodigious ocean races, including overall wins in the 1964 Southern Ocean Racing Circuit (SORC); three successive wins in the Transpac Races from California to Hawaii in 1965, 1967, and 1969; and an overall win in the 1966 Bermuda Race. In fact, in that 1966 Bermuda fleet of 167 boats, *five of the top 15 overall finishers* were Cal 40s.

But by the late 1980s, when Sally and Stan found *Illusion*, the Cal 40 wave had long since crested. Swans, Tartans, C&Cs, then later J/Boats and

*Illusion*, a stock production cruiser of the Cal 40 line,
racing in the doublehanded Farallones Race, some 50 years after she was launched.

other fiberglass production models had come along to beat the Cal at its own light-displacement ocean-racing game.

How, then, was this couple able to refit a 25-year-old wreck and go on to set the singlehanded TransPac record in 1994? How did they win overall honors sailing doublehanded against a fleet of fully crewed boats in the 1996 Pacific Cup? And, perhaps most intriguingly, how did they set up this boat to live aboard and commuter-cruise for more than two happy decades and counting, from San Francisco to Hawaii to Alaska, then Mexico and around through Panama, the Caribbean basin, and on up U.S. East Coast to Maine?

The Honey's *Illusion* stands as an example for us all.

## Ordinary Boat. No Ordinary Couple

Let's just get one thing out of the way. Sally Lindsay Honey is a two-time Rolex Yachtswoman of the Year, honors she garnered in 1972 and 1974 as a champion skipper of one-design 505 planing dinghies. Stan Honey is the man Gary Jobson has called "the most successful offshore navigator of the modern era." Stan was navigating when the catamaran *PlayStation* set the record day's run of 687 miles

No ordinary couple: Stan and Sally Honey have been winning together
since the 1970s. Each has also served on national and international committees
to make the sport safer and more competitive.

in 2001; also when the trimaran *Groupama 3* broke the world speed circumnavigation record in 2010, circling the globe in 48 days and change; also when
*Comanche* set the monohull record day's run of 618 miles in 2016—on its way
to setting the fastest monohull transatlantic passage of 5 days, 14 hours, and 21
minutes. In 2010, Stan was named Rolex Yachtsman of the Year for his role in
*Groupama 3's* record circumnavigation. Of that honor Stan said, "It was nice to
get 50 percent caught up to Sally."

So Sally and Stan Honey are no ordinary sailing couple. But what they did
with a down-and-out production fiberglass boat already more than a decade past
its sell-by date is no different from what any would-be sailor could do with one
of the legions of classic plastic sailboats that populate the brokerage listings today.
Between 1963 and 1971 Jensen Marine built 170 Cal 40s, and these boats still
come on the market in the $50,000 range. At press time, the 1966 Bermuda Race
overall winner was listed at $20,000—with a note that says "needs work."

The Cal 40 was created just after the dawn of fiberglass boatbuilding. Truly
speaking, "fiberglass" is a shorthand for fiberglass-reinforced plastic (FRP). Thermosetting polyester was invented in 1936; glass strands suitable for weaving into
laminates, in 1941. In *Heart of Glass*, a history of composite boatbuilding, author
Dan Spurr reckons that Ray Greene of Toledo, Ohio, was the first person who
put the two materials together to make a boat. That was in 1942. "The boat, in all
likelihood, was a dinghy, perhaps the 8-foot Tubby dink or 12-foot Nipper, which

*The 42-foot Sydney Herreshoff-designed* Arion *was built as a one-off by The Anchorage in Rhode Island—the same yard that build Dyer dinghies—and launched in May 1951; she's considered the first FRP auxiliary sailboat.*

Ray had been building for some years in plywood."

The marriage of those materials worked. While the polyester alone could be molded into complex shapes, it was too brittle to withstand significant loads; the glass strands provided working strength. Over the next few decades, the component materials would improve by degrees—vinylester or epoxy improving on polyester resins; aramid and carbon improving on glass fibers; cores of wood or foam sandwiched between FRP skins to reduce weight while adding strength—but by the end of World War II, the basic ingredients were in place. Modern "composite boatbuilding" boomed. Between 1950 and 1960 boat ownership in the United States doubled from 3.5 million to more than 7 million boats. Much of that growth was in the new FRP boats, through still mostly small outboard-powered runabouts and sailing dinghies of less than 20 feet.

By the late 1950s, ocean-capable auxiliary sailboats were built in ones and twos, but not yet in the kind of series production that generated large fleets. The 42-foot Sydney Herreshoff-designed *Arion* was built as a one-off by The Anchorage in Rhode Island—the same yard that build Dyer dinghies—and launched in May 1951; she's considered the first FRP auxiliary sailboat. The 40-foot Phil Rhodes-designed *Bounty II*, adapted to FRP construction from a pre-war design for a line of series-built wooden boats, debuted at the 1957 New York Boat Show. She was the first stock FRP cruising auxiliary produced by the dozen. The FRP Bill Tripp-designed Vitesse 40 was launched later the same year; that centerboard yawl became the Block Island 40, of which American Boatbuilding of East Greenwich, Rhode Island, built nine more over the next few years, followed by a line of smaller Sea Sprites. Also that same year in California, Bill Schock built the FRP Schock 22, which won the next season's Ensenada Race and starred in a *Yachting* magazine Sea of Cortez cruising feature article. In 1958 George O'Day started building Rhodes 19s in Massachusetts, on his way to bigger auxiliaries. The big breakthrough for series-built FRP cruising auxiliaries—*production boats*—was the Pearson Triton. Designed by Carl Alberg and built in Rhode Island by cousins Clint and Everett Pearson, the 28-foot Triton debuted at the 1959 New York Boat Show. The Pearsons took orders for 17 Tritons, at $10,000 each (about twice the cost of a Ford Thunderbird at the time). Pearson Yachts and other licensed yards built 700 of them over the next nine years.

From 1960 on, modern industrial production boatbuilding was truly underway. In the transition from wood to FRP, it wasn't that wooden boats couldn't be series-built. The builders of the New England fishing fleet had long ago devised jigs and templates that allowed them to quickly repeat steps and build multiple boats of similar design. The German builders at Abeking & Rasmussen had refined their tools and techniques to build 99 nearly identical Concordia yawls in wood between 1950 and 1966. But even with these tricks of the trade, the job of building wooden boats still required a team of skilled shipwrights.

The transition to FRP represented a step-change in the process of building boats, as well as the market for them. The principle investment for a builder of FRP boats was to create "tooling"—the usually female-shaped molds in which FRP parts would be laid up. Those parts might be big, such as the hull or deck; or they might be small, such as locker hatches or molded interior bulkheads or modules. Once good tooling had been created by skilled (expensive) workers, yard owners could employ relatively unskilled (inexpensive) labor to lay up the fiberglass parts and wet them out with thermosetting resin—and they could do this by the dozens or even hundreds from one mold. The per-unit cost of FRP boats diminished dramatically as the unit number increased. The effect? It encouraged the middle class in America and Europe to take up sailing. In 1967, some 28,000 sailboats were sold in the United States; in 1973, the historical peak, 120,000.

## Birth of a Classic

Before Olin Stephens' *Dorade* became a classic, she was a wild child, breaking all the rules. So too was George Griffith's Cal 40 three decades later. And just as Olin was abetted by a father and brother who helped him mix old ideas in new ways, George was abetted by a willing designer and builder. Both boats set a new trajectory that would shape all future yacht design, either *with* or *against*.

A member of the Cruising Club of America, the Los Angeles Yacht Club, and the Transpacific Yacht Club, George Griffith messed about in boats his whole life. He built his first dinghy at age 10. In 1941 at age 20 he sailed his first TransPac Race from California to Honolulu and came in second on corrected time. In 2012 aboard his motorboat *Sarissa*, underway between Catalina Island and Long Beach, he died at age 91. In the meantime he left a mark on sailing and boatbuilding that can't be erased.

George graduated from the California Institute of Technology and had a good grasp of materials and structures. A Standard Oil engineer, he'd spent the war years in Houston designing Navy craft. After the war he enjoyed a long friendship with fellow CCA member Charles William "Bill" Lapworth.

*Illusion* finishes the 2003 edition of the Transpac Race to Hawaii, celebrating 40 years of Cal 40 sailing. The reduced wetted surface of the fin keel and separate rudder allowed Cal 40s to shine in the largely downwind race. They also have done well close reaching from Newport to Bermuda.

Bill Lapworth, for his part, had come to Southern California with the U.S. Navy, having earned a degree in marine engineering and naval architecture from the University of Michigan. The two often sailed together, including in the 1950 Bermuda Race aboard the relatively diminutive Lapworth-designed *Flying Scotchman*. Because she was shorter than the 35 feet required by the race committee, Lapworth added a temporary extension—a so-called "zipper bow"— to qualify. This was just one early example of fresh thinking to come.

When George began working out his ideas for new 40-footer in those early days of FRP boats, he'd already owned and enjoyed a wooden Lapworth 36 for years; with more than 70 L-36s built, this was the largest one-design class of the time. The new boat, George reckoned, shouldn't do any worse. "I knew damn well what I wanted, and I would not accept anything else," he told a *Cruising World* editor in 2004. A man who expressed himself clearly, he was unmoved by the conventional wisdom of his contemporaries. "With Bounty, they copied a

*Because she was shorter than the 35 feet required by the race committee, Lapworth added a temporary extension—a so-called "zipper bow"—to qualify. This was just one early example of fresh thinking to come.*

turkey," he said of the traditional CCA 40-footer, one of the most popular FRP racer-cruisers of its time.

George didn't want a fiberglass copy of a boat that had already been designed for wood. Eschewing round bilges, he sketched out a hull with flat sections. "Walking on the bottom of the boat wasn't exactly normal," he quipped, comparing his idea to other boats of the time. Still, the Cal 40's canoe-shaped flat bottom wasn't her greatest affront to the tastemakers. That distinction was reserved for her split underbody: a fin keel and a separate spade rudder.

"Dinghies had free-standing rudders and were easy to control," said George, "and Chinese sailors have used this concept for 2,000 years." Only after the Cal 40's proven results started coming in did other forward-thinking yacht-designers begin to entertain the idea. Dick Carter used it in his revolutionary 1964 *Rabbit*. Olin Stephens tried it for the first time in the 12-Metre *Intrepid*, the America's Cup winner in 1967 and 1970 and arguably his finest yacht; all subsequent 12-Metres adopted it.

In designer Bill Lapworth, George found a willing accomplice. He took George's sketches and added his own spin. Compare, for example, the Cal 40's modest overhangs fore and aft with other designs from the early 1960s. While designers for decades had exploited the CCA rating rule by keeping the at-rest waterline short compared to overall length, resulting in long overhangs at the bow and stern, Lapworth simply drew the boat that he believed would get up and go. If she suffered a little in the handicap, she more than made up for it in her performance—particularly off the wind and in the waves.

A less-willing accomplice, at least initially, was the builder Jack Jensen. When George took Lapworth's design for the new 40-footer to his old CalTech pal, Jensen told him, "You're out of your bleeping mind. The biggest boat I have going is 30 feet, and I lose my shirt on each one of them." He held out until George famously guaranteed that he would sell 10 boats. Over the next eight years beginning with the first launch in fall 1963 Jensen Marine exceeded that stretch goal by a factor of 17.

A decade after the first Cal 40 won a race, yachting journalist Bill Robinson reflected on that creation and its effects. "Perhaps the biggest eye-opener of all

*"At that time, breaking the 20-knot barrier was unheard of. When a Cal 40 catches a ride, her bow wave reaches as high as the spinnaker pole, yet even moderately experienced drivers retain control."*

was how the Cal 40 exceeded all previous expectations of what speeds a boat that size could attain and maintain at sea. A 40-foot boat surfing along for hours on end at 14 to 16 knots, with wings of water arcing out from her hull like a water-skier's wake, was mind-boggling to traditionalists, and virtually a new breed of sailors was created by this type of sailing. Young athletic crews who could stand the constant tension and exhilaration of rides like this drove the Cal 40s as ocean racers had never been driven before, and the TransPac was their place to shine, with its days of downwind surfing."

The Cal 40 entry in the American Sailboat Hall of Fame puts it even more plainly: "With its clean, canoe-shaped hull and fin underwater appendages, the Cal 40 defied the constraints of hull speed." It goes on to record sustained boat speeds of 15 knots and a top speed of 25 knots.

"In one fell swoop, Messrs. Griffith, Lapworth, and Jensen turned ocean racing into an exciting sport by introducing a fast, seakindly, and affordable boat," wrote yachting journalist Dieter Loibner for the boat's 40th anniversary. "At that time, breaking the 20-knot barrier was unheard of. When a Cal 40 catches a ride, her bow wave reaches as high as the spinnaker pole, yet even moderately experienced drivers retain control."

Or as Stan Honey puts it, "The Cal 40 has no bad habits."

### From Good Bones to a Fleshed-Out Winner

Stan grew up as the 1960s gave way to the '70s around the Los Angeles Yacht Club where Griffith and Lapworth were members. He knew those early TransPac winners firsthand—*Psyche, Holiday Too, Argonaut, Montgomery Street*—and between college semesters he earned money delivering Cal 40s back from Hawaii.

"The Cal 40 was kind of a legendary local boat," said Stan. "There were dozens of them at L.A. Yacht Club. I grew up sailing on them and really liked the boat. It was just a nice all-around good sea boat with great manners."

When he and Sally first went looking for a boat to take ocean sailing in the late 1980s, a Cal 40 is what they went looking for. "At that time we weren't super long on funds," Stan said, "and we weren't smart enough to know that you never saved money buying a cheap boat."

Stan and Sally found just such a cheap boat in 1988 at Ron's Reef in Santa

Cruz, California, home of the West Coast ultralight-displacement movement. It had been sitting there for at least seven years. The yard's proximity to the highway, they reckoned, accounted for the several bullet holes they found in the hull. It was unclear who actually owned the boat, and after some digging, a yacht broker stepped forward and accepted their $20K lowball offer on behalf of an anonymous owner.

Stan and Sally then set off on what they thought would be a six-month refit. "We were down there in Santa Cruz over Christmas, going through our notes on what we had to do that weekend. There was a huge amount of rain and we were sitting down below and seeing all these waterfalls coming down the inside of the cabin. We thought, 'Uh-oh.'"

They weren't the first owners of an old leaky fiberglass boat. "Back when we were first racing on Cal 40s, all we knew prior to that were wooden boats," said Stan. "Of course, you always had leaks here and there, and ocean racing was kind of an experience of knowing which bunks were dry and how to stay away from the water. People hadn't yet figured out that it was possible to have a boat that was dry below."

Jensen Marine had emphasized light weight when it built the Cal 40. Over time the hull and deck and bulkheads came to move rather independently of one another. Where the deck sat bolted on the hull's inward-turning flange, water would find its way past the fiberglass mat and bedding compound and into the boat. And Jensen Marine's original hatches were never entirely waterproof.

So Stan and Sally went to work. "We stripped the deck—took off all the handrails, stanchions, the pulpit, all the fittings. There's not a single bit of metal on deck that was there when we bought the boat. We reglassed the hull-to-deck joint. We tapered the deck and ran biaxial mat and epoxy all the way around, which made the boat a lot stiffer. And then we replaced the old Jensen hatches with Lewmar hatches. We replaced all the portlights, too, and the portholes. It's really nice now to have a boat that's as watertight as we've grown to expect with modern boats."

During the refit, they added such details as a transverse bulkhead under the companionway bridgedeck to support the loads from the mainsheet traveler, and they moved the engine and tanks forward to redistribute the weight. Sally made all the new sails. At a gathering for the Cal 40's fortieth anniversary, Lapworth said he wished he'd considered some of Stan and Sally's modifications when he first conceived the boat.

After the low original purchase price, how much did *Illusion* actually cost? "We have no idea," Sally told Peter Isler during a 2020 American Sailing Association webinar. "We don't think about how much it cost."

With their two-year refit complete, Stan and Sally did not take *Illusion* cruising straightaway—to the South Pacific, say, where they'd dreamed of going from the beginning of their relationship in the mid-1970s.

"Old habits die hard," said Stan. The couple had been racing 505s together at the championship level for all that time, while also starting new businesses—Sally as a sailmaker at first, then taking on ever greater technical challenges for clients as diverse as the Grateful Dead and NASA (she built Kevlar straps for the space shuttle after the Challenger disaster); and Stan developing the first vehicle navigation system, a precursor of Google Maps. (Let that sink in.) In 1990 they weren't yet ready to chuck it all and go cruising. But they could go racing.

To Hawaii.

"We ended up sailing the boat about three times before the 1990 Pacific Cup," said Stan. "It was pretty last-minute. I don't think we'd recommend that approach."

"I finished the third of our three spinnakers the night before the start," said Sally. "And we had a brand-new autopilot that Stan had just put together, and although I grew up sailing, including a Bermuda Race and a transatlantic delivery, I hadn't raced double-handed with an autopilot. So it was definitely a learning experience."

What about that autopilot that Stan "had just put together"?

"It's a Spectra from Alpha Marine," said Stan.

Just any Alpha Marine autopilot?

Not quite. In fact, Stan applied some of knowledge he'd picked up on his way to a master's degree in electrical engineering from Stanford, and some of the technical chops that would eventually earn him three Emmy awards for inventing the lines we see in televised sports coverage: the yellow first-down line in football, the strike zone in baseball, the laylines in America's Cup racing. Stan Honey is one of the few sailors you'll meet who is in both the National Inventors Hall of Fame and the Sports Broadcasting Hall of Fame.

"I wrote a program that runs on a PC which controls the autopilot so that it'll steer to our optimums from the Cal 40's polars," said Stan. "It'll bear off in the puffs and come up in the lulls and, you know, follow wind shifts. In all the Hawaii races we've done it's never rounded up and never rounded down. It's never jibed. In the daytime it doesn't steer quite as well as Sally steers because she can see the waves. But at night it steers absolutely as well as a human. And it never gets groggy, and it never makes a blunder."

Stan calls it their secret weapon.

This was the autopilot that was steering *Illusion* in 1994 when Stan set the Singlehanded Transpac record of 11 days, 10 hours, and 52 minutes—beating the

*"In the daytime it doesn't steer quite as well as Sally steers because she can see the waves. But at night it steers absolutely as well as a human. And it never gets groggy, and it never makes a blunder."*

passage times of the more than 100 Cal 40s that have sailed that same route, fully crewed or otherwise. At press time, his singlehanded record is still the one to beat.

Two years later, the autopilot steered when Stan and Sally, sailing double-handed, came in first overall in the Pacific Cup, this time beating all the fully crewed boats in that fleet. "The interesting thing is that doublehanded, the boat's about 10 percent lighter, which makes it faster for a downwind race. With the autopilot steering really well, Sally and I could concentrate on trimming and aggressively sailing the boat. I think we jibed 50 times in that race, and on one of those really shifty nights a third of the way through, we jibed 15 times. At the next roll call, we learned we'd gained 25 miles that night."

Perhaps the Cal 40 hadn't exceeded her sell-by date after all. "We found that the Cal 40 is still very competitive under rating rules that are fair to a diverse set of boats, like the Offshore Racing Rule," said Stan.

## Commuter Cruising—Or, Tacking on the Shifts

After the 1996 Pacific Cup, for the first time ever, Stan and Sally tried cruising.

"The funny thing about bringing a boat back from Hawaii is that it doesn't really matter where you go," said Stan. "By the time you get north of the Pacific High, you've done the hard part. From there it's just as easy to go to Los Angeles or San Francisco or Seattle. So after the '96 race, we just figured we'd put the boat up on the wind and see where we ended up."

Where they ended up was the north end of Vancouver Island in British Columbia. They planned to cruise down Queen Charlotte Strait and the Strait of Georgia, then out Juan de Fuca Strait and down to San Francisco. "But then we had so much fun cruising down the inside of Vancouver Island that we left the boat for the winter. The next year we sailed the TransPac on other boats, then went back to *Illusion* and cruised it all the way up to Glacier Bay, Alaska."

That same year, after two decades together, Sally and Stan married on the beach at Half Moon Bay. "That was a good party," Sally told Carol Cronin for *Seahorse* magazine. "We decided we were going to spend three years sailing around the world. We thought it might be better in foreign countries, or if one of us got sick, to have the same name. And the nice thing about waiting 20 years is that you

*Illusion*'s outbound leg: leaving San Francisco Bay in 2014 on a planned delivery
that's turned into seven years—and counting—of wide-ranging commuter cruising.
Demands ashore kept Stan and Sally returning the Bay area
even as *Illusion* remained in new cruising grounds, first south to Panama,
then through the Caribbean and up the East Coast.

have a similar group of friends."

As for the honeymoon cruise, Stan said, "It may have been the most fun we'd
ever had."

Following their extensive refit, *Illusion* was clearly set up to race in the ocean
and win. But to cruise? Not so much. "We didn't have a dodger at all, so we spent
that first summer standing in the rain. We had no heater and no windlass," said
Stan. What they did have was a German shepherd who loved to swim. "Every day,
she'd jump in the water."

*Illusion* sails away from Cuba, 2019. Just because they are cruising,
and there are only two aboard does not mean the spinnaker should stay in the bag.

This cruise would have been the beginning of a several-year hiatus, except for one thing. "On the way back down the coast," said Sally, "as we got close to San Francisco we got into cell-phone range, and Stan got talked into starting another company."

One opportunity followed another, and 18 years passed before the next time the Honeys set off cruising. But set off they did.

"We took a delivery trip to Newport, Rhode Island, and made that into a five-year cruise," said Stan. "We had the plan to do a Bermuda Race, but we hadn't really figured out which year it was going to be."

"It took longer than we thought to go around because we got stuck in the Sea of Cortez," said Sally. "We just loved it. One of our favorite places is Isla Isabel, just northwest of Banderas Bay. They call it the Galápagos of Mexico, and we actually went there twice because it has zillions of boobies and frigate birds and so many iguanas that it's hard to walk around there without stepping on them."

With ongoing commitments back in the Bay Area, they found they could cruise for a month or two, then leave *Illusion* in La Paz or Tapachula, Mexico, or later in Panama on the Caribbean side, all rather inexpensively. "The funny thing we discovered about commuter cruising is that there's a lot of marinas that are

Thinking like a racer when cruising keeps the boat moving efficiently, while the slower pace is easy on gear and the crew.

perfectly safe places to leave your boat, and cheaper than a slip back home."

"There were a couple of times when we left the boat in La Paz for hurricane season, we had some people watching the boat for us," said Sally. "If there was a hurricane coming through, they would double up docklines and make sure the canvas was off and be in touch with us the whole time."

Stan describes sailing *Illusion* in cruising mode as a "cakewalk" after doing five Hawaii races and some 20 Farallon Races and other regattas in and around gusty San Francisco Bay.

"We knew we wanted to set up *Illusion* to sail shorthanded," said Sally, "and since we'd been sailing dinghies for so long, we kind of set this boat up like a dinghy. So steering at the helm, I have the traveler and the mainsheet and the afterguy and the foreguy all within reach while I'm holding on to the tiller. I can handle the back of the boat. And then we've got all the halyards up at the mast, so Stan can handle the front of the boat."

If you compare *Illusion* to a typical cruising boat, you'll miss many of the usual suspects: the biminis, dinghy davits, wind generators, radar arches, barbecues, fenders, and jerry jugs. "It's an interesting cultural discrepancy," Stan said. "Because we enjoy sailing, we take the approach of carrying everything below deck. The Avon Redcrest dinghy deflates and goes below in the lazarette, and the 2-horsepower motor stores below. That way, it's easy to sail because we don't have

*Illusion* in full-on cruising mode at Block Island, 2019.
Note the usual cruising-boat items that do not clutter her cockpit and deck:
no permanent Bimini, no wind generator, no dinghy on davits.

all the clutter on deck. And we don't have all that windage."

This was a lesson they learned in Alaska. "We had the dinghy upside-down on the foredeck, and we got into a lot of breeze when we were beating," said Stan. "With a dinghy on the foredeck, we can't set our staysail stay. So then in order to go to a number four, we've got to take the number-three headsail off the headstay, then hank the four on the headstay. It's a lot more work to sail. So we timed it and discovered that we can tear down the dinghy in five minutes. For us the right answer is, whenever we're going for a sail, we just get rid of the damn thing. The Cal 40 is a small boat for a 40-footer, but for two people there's plenty of room to stow it all away."

Sally's sailmaking experience and their many years of racing instilled in the Honeys a refined appreciation for sail shape—and the second major decision that differs from that of most of the cruising population. "For almost the entire time we've owned *Illusion*, we've used hank-on headsails," said Stan. "When you're shorthanded, you can change sails and it's a really seaworthy change. Because, you know, you drop the jib, you tie it down, you unhank it, then you hoist up the new headsail that was hanked on underneath. And then your sails, including the smaller ones, are all the right shape. Whereas with roller-furling, you either try to change sails—in which case you're dealing with a sail on the foredeck that's not attached at the luff—or you try to sail with the thing partially reefed, which doesn't do well in many cases."

Another of *Illusion's* secret weapons is a reefable hank-on headsail—with a second clew and tack installed four feet above the normal tack. "The reef zips in so that it's 125 percent when it's unreefed and 100 percent when it's reefed," said Sally. "It saves room below for one sail. That sail has done really good duty for us." The zipper works better than reef lines, they've found, as it keeps seawater out of the rolled sail.

For all of their sailhandling maneuvers Sally and Stan carry a set of cheat sheets. "That kind of descends from sailing 505s, because it's got to be choreo-graphed and each person has to know even when the other person is going to move. So in the Cal 40 we took the same approach."

Sally has investigated sailing casualties and edited US Sailing's *Safety at Sea Handbook*, experience that has informed the doublehanded practices she and Stan employ aboard *Illusion*. "Our crew-overboard practice has evolved over the years," said Stan. Today, it starts with good jacklines and good habits of wearing a harness and clipping in on deck. Each of them wears a personal AIS transponder. "The person who remains on the boat takes all the sails down and takes their time, because if they panic and get a line in the propeller or get the spinnaker tangled in the rig, then the person in the water is in real trouble. Then, assuming you've got the AIS, you can find the person."

Stan learned another trick sailing maxis. "You motor back to the person, deploy the Lifesling, and drag the Lifesling past them until the person has it. And then you just let the boat drift with the helm hard over, slowly towing the person in the water. Then you clip a halyard around the line going to the Lifesling so that the halyard shackle can slide down on the Lifesling line. And then you hoist up on the halyard so that you're pulling the person up and into the boat on a 1-to-2 disadvantage. The nice thing about that approach is that by the time the person gets close to the boat, they're being pulled up enough to where the boat can't drift over them."

From Panama, the Honeys sailed to Newport to strip off the boat all the cruising kit they'd accumulated and get back into race mode for the 2020 Bermuda

Race. And they did, too—only to learn that the event would be cancelled in that first wave of the Covid pandemic.

But if there's one thing the Honeys know, it's how to tack on a shift. And that's what they did, trading a summer in Bermuda for a summer in Downeast Maine. The future holds as many vagaries. Maybe they'll go back down to the Caribbean. Maybe Nova Scotia. Or maybe up through the Saint Lawrence Seaway to the Great Lakes.

*Belvedere* took John Bockstoce everywhere he needed to go for his research
of the Arctic and its indigenous communities, including through the
Northwest Passage west-to-east. She is a 60-foot, 39-ton,
steel motorsailer that her owner has pushed and pampered for over 40 years.

# 11

# Cruising the Northwest Passage Deeply: Travels with John Bockstoce and *Belvedere*

> Beginnings are important, and the first thing I did was to rename and register
> her as *Belvedere* of New Bedford, Massachusetts. Her namesake was one
> of the greatest New Bedford whaleships, a steam auxiliary bark that spent her
> working life in the Arctic fishery, a long-lived, sturdy, and lucky ship that was
> one of the first commercial vessels to enter the eastern Beaufort Sea.
> I hoped some of her good fortune would encompass my boat,
> and as far as I can tell, it has.
> —John Bockstoce
> First yachtsman to transit the Northwest Passage from west to east (1988)

To understand *Belvedere*, you must first understand the umiak.

When *Belvedere* became the first yacht to transit the Northwest Passage from west to east in 1988, New Englander John Bockstoce had already spent more than two decades in the North. He spent his first several seasons conducting archaeological digs, employing trowel and measuring tape and camera to decode the contents of 4,000-year-old middens in such places as the Diomede Islands and Cape Nome where once a land bridge connected Siberia with Alaska. He spent a decade crewing with a group of indigenous whalers. He spent a season piloting a 20-foot freighter canoe down the Yukon River from Fairbanks to Nome. And he spent nearly another decade exploring the Chukchi and Beaufort Sea shorelines aboard an open 32-foot walrus-skin umiak.

> I have spent twenty seasons in those waters, studying the history
> of the fur trade and the whaling industry in the western Arctic. In
> 1969, when I began my research, I understood that merely burrowing
> away in libraries and archives would yield only a pallid record of

Whither the umiak? Through the Northwest Passage—or maybe not quite. Here the crew
traverses the Russell Inlet, Beaufort Sea, in 1978. The 32-foot, 600-pound open boat
was light and flexible, made of a wooden frame covered with five walrus skins.
It could carry a ton of crew and gear and had the added benefit of doubling as shelter ashore.

what I considered to be a vibrant, energetic, and self-reliant age, populated with heroes. I knew that I would have to work in those waters, see
the land and feel the wind in my face to achieve an understanding of
what it was like to have been there in those days: I would have to go back
and forth in those sinuous waterways and poke into every corner where
people had been, searching for historical sites, graves, shipwrecks, and
the living participants of those long-gone industries.

## Why the Umiak

During those years before *Belvedere*, the young doctoral candidate in ethnology
embedded himself deeply among the "northerners"—the name John Bockstoce
prefers for all the people of any ethnicity or nationality who live and work and
adapt to the environment of the far north. As for the indigenous people of that
region, some of whose languages he learned to speak, John later wrote: "My use
of the ethnonym *Eskimo* is carefully chosen. In Canada *Inuit* has largely replaced
*Eskimo*. If applied to all Eskimo peoples across the Arctic, as it often is, the term
*Inuit* is inexact. For example, in Greenland the natives refer to themselves as
*Greenlanders* or *Kalaallit*; in western arctic Canada they refer to themselves as

John Bockstoce patrols the whale camp in Point Hope, Alaska, alongside the Chukchi Sea, in 1972. He was not there as a yachtsman: he lived among the northern people, gained their trust, and studied the history and culture of the hunting communities.

*Inuvialuit*. In Alaska, however, *Eskimo* is commonly used as a broad reference to include the Iñupiat (adjective: Iñupiaq) of northern and western Alaska, as well as the Siberian Yupik of St. Lawrence Island and a few settlements on the coast of the Chukchi Peninsula, the Yup'ik [*sic*] of southwestern Alaska, and the Alutiiq (Sugpiaq) of the Pacific coast. In Alaska the Eskimos prefer to be called Eskimo."

In April 1971 John joined an Eskimo whaling crew led by Laurie Kingik of Point Hope, Alaska. Kingik became John's *qumnaaluk*, his teacher.

It didn't take me long to realize that at Point Hope I was among some of the most consummately skillful hunters on earth. Their entire lives were centered on whaling—and when they were not actively engaged in the hunt, they spent much of their time reflecting on it, preparing for it, or teaching their children about it. They understood full well the enormous achievement of capturing a fifty-ton animal and of providing the settlement with so much food. They knew that their lives depended on this exhausting and glorious adventure, for it provided them with food and fuel, a sense of community, and personal pride. And, having carried it out so successfully for more than a thousand years, they considered themselves to be superior people—and they wasted no time telling me so."

The work was hard, and the lessons often painful. With pickaxes, in the dark of the Arctic early spring, they cleared their way through the ice to the shoreline, then by hand hauled to the camp all their whaling gear, their tents, and their umiak—the open seal-skin boat aboard which they would paddle, quick and quiet, away from the ice and toward the gargantuan bowhead whale. John's seasons of rowing on the heavyweight varsity team at Yale University, then later at Oxford, had at least partially prepared his body for the stamina this work demanded. When they caught a bowhead, the job of butchering all those tons of whale meat and blubber lasted through the night and all through the next day. Then they'd haul their load down into ice cellars laboriously dug beneath the permafrost.

Working with the Eskimos was hard not only physically but emotionally too. John's crewmates teased him. Relentlessly. After one particularly long and dreadful night in his first weeks among them, the Kingik family bestowed upon him the nickname *Siqpan*, forever memorializing a humiliating moment when his biscuit fell into a disgusting blubber pot—and he ate it anyway. Time after time, while his fellow whalers-in-training sat silent, John, ever curious, would pepper the more experienced hands with questions. "Occasionally my questions were answered with silence or, less frequently, by being told to shut up." In moments of duress he would recall the advice of his mentor Froelich Rainey back in Philadelphia, an archaeologist who'd known the Kingik family 30 years earlier: "Remember, keep your mouth shut."

As John came to realize, this constant teasing—hazing, even—was a crucial test.

"I remembered Rainey's advice and never let my anger show," John wrote, "and I am glad I didn't because, of course, that is what they wanted to know: Was I steady under fire? Was I there for the long haul? Could they count on me when they found themselves in danger? Would I be a member of the team? They must have decided in the affirmative, because after three or four seasons of this everything changed and life on the whaling crew became really enjoyable."

John Bockstoce was utterly fascinated by the Point Hope whalers, whose methods blended tools from thousands of years earlier with industrial-age bomb-lance shoulder guns manufactured in New England. That fascination led him to spend the next dozen years researching and writing *Whales, Ice and Men*, a history of whaling in the western Arctic, published in 1986.

Through all this work, he steeped himself in the oral history of the polar region that since childhood had held sway over his imagination.

And, meanwhile, something else was tugging at his attention.

*As John came to realize, this constant teasing—hazing, even—was a crucial test.*

Above all in my first whaling season, I was riveted by the umiaks. They were covered with five or six *oogruk* (bearded seal) skins, making them lighter and more maneuverable than the Bering Sea boats [the walrus-skin versions aboard which he'd traveled between the Diomede Islands and Nome two years earlier]. But like the Bering Sea boats, they were tough and flexible. During the lulls in the chase, as I sat beside the boat, waiting for the whales to pass, I thought about how, a thousand years ago, the Eskimos had spread from Alaska to Greenland with boats like these, and it gradually dawned on me that I wanted to travel in an umiak along the same route. I felt a powerful urge as I gazed across the ice at Cape Lisburne, low on the horizon, fifty miles to the northeast, and I found myself desperately wanting to visit it. But I also began to realize that each time I might reach one of these capes that had barely been discernable in the distance, there would be another far away beyond it, and another beyond that, and another. As my thoughts flew forward it suddenly dawned on me that I wanted to confront the greatest Arctic boating challenge of them all—the Northwest Passage. I knew that only a handful of vessels had ever made the transit of the northern waterway between the Atlantic and Pacific Oceans, and I wanted mine to be one of them.

## Whither the Umiak

The Northwest Passage.

Coined by the English in the earliest days of the Age of Discovery, the Northwest Passage had for centuries remained merely mythical. John Cabot went looking for it in 1497—just five years after Columbus first found a new world on the far side of the Atlantic. With a commission from King Henry VII, Cabot sought a sea route to China at those higher latitudes where the physical distances between longitude lines shorten. Sir Francis Drake and John Davis both tried and failed in Queen Elizabeth's name. In 1609 Henry Hudson thought he'd found it when he worked his way past Weehawken and saw the river that now bears his name widen at Tappan Zee, but he turned back when the water petered out at Albany. Two years later, in Arctic James Bay, Henry Hudson's crew mutinied and set him and six loyalists adrift in an open boat on icy waters, never to be seen again by European eyes. The names Bylot Island and Baffin Bay attest to how close Hudson's crew came to finding the passage's front door—if only it had been open. In 1745 the English Parliament proclaimed its strategic aspirations when it enacted a twenty thousand–pound prize for the first person to find the Northwest Passage. James Cook, William Bligh, and George Vancouver all grabbed for that brass ring. Alaska's Cook Inlet memorializes a moment in 1778 when *Endeavour's* captain thought he had it. Another burst of imperial enthusiasm followed some 70 years later with the doomed John Franklin expedition of 1845, whose remains were later found on King William Island. When Robert McClure set off from England to find Franklin, McClure's own crew nearly starved in the ice at Banks Island before still another band of searchers pulled them out by sledge. Yet McClure, who in several years of searching for Franklin had entered the waterway from both the Pacific and Atlantic sides, was able to look out from his icy imprisonment at Banks Island and recognize Melville Island, which he'd visited from the west. His ship couldn't reach it across all that frozen sea; still, that moment in 1854 marks the European discovery of the Northwest Passage.

Modern history begins in 1906 with Roald Amundsen. In the 45-ton auxiliary sloop *Gjøa*, Amundsen of Norway completed the transit from east to west, wintering over three seasons in the ice. It took till 1941 for the second vessel to make the transit. By the early 1970s fewer than a dozen well-financed surface vessels and nuclear submarines had ever done it, many of them with massive icebreaker support. In 1969, the oil tanker *SS Manhattan* became the first vessel to test the viability of a commercial route. After the discovery of oil at Alaska's Prudhoe Bay the previous year, the Humble Oil Company (later renamed Exxon) bankrolled the *Manhattan* experiment, but it proved so costly and so risky that Humble and its partners decided instead to build the Trans-Alaska Pipeline System to the ice-free port of Valdez. At that time, there had never been a season on record when the entire Northwest Passage was free of ice.

This was the state of play as John Bockstoce began to contemplate transiting the passage in that late spring of 1971. But first he needed an umiak. His initial thought was to build one himself. Knowing he'd want to travel with crew and carry all the provisions and equipment he'd need to continue his research and document the trip, he was drawn to the larger umiaks he'd seen on the Bering Sea. To learn more about the boats and their materials, he signed on with a crew of walrus hunters out of Nome.

> When we spotted a group of walrus we would cut the outboard
> motor and paddle quietly toward them from downwind. Soon we would

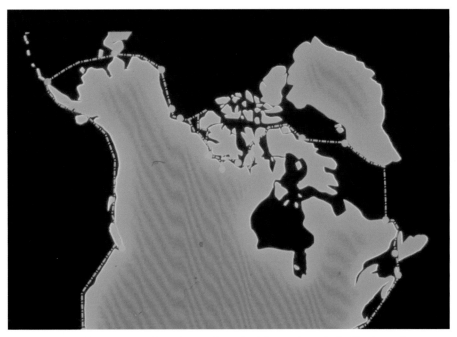

There's more than one route from the Pacific to the Atlantic through the Northwest Passage; this shows the route *Belvedere* took over several seasons. Bockstoce's earlier attempt in his umiak fell short, due to impenetrable ice.

smell their particular odor ("Like a dead horse," said one of the hunters) and see their white tusks, their broad muzzles sprouting thick bristles, their small, bulbous, bloodshot eyes, and their huge, thick necks covered with warty, scarred skin. There were the magnificent old bulls carrying tusks nearly a yard long and weighing more than three thousand pounds, the cows with their thinner, more delicately curved tusks and the pudgy calves lying next to or on top of their mothers or woofing and scrambling along after them.

When the animals had been shot, the back-breaking work of butchering them began. The skins had to be carefully stripped off in one piece so that they could be used for boat skins.

Once we were back on shore, the raw hides, weighing two hundred pounds or more, were stored in cool places until the end of the hunting season in June. The Eskimos would then scrape the remaining flesh and blubber from them and roll them up, leaving them in a warm place for a week or more. The hide would thus begin to rot a little and the hair could then be removed easily with a scraper.

While John was going out on the walrus hunts and conducting his field research in that early summer of 1971, he puzzled over how to build an umiak that would take him and a crew 4,500 miles through the Northwest Passage. Conversations about his project led him to a man who had a beat-up 1930s-era umiak from Little Diomede Island perched behind his house, a veteran of Bering Sea hunting expeditions and trading trips across the strait to Siberia. But this boat's recent years in Nome hadn't been kind. The town's plows had alternately battered its gunwales—parting the lashings, breaking some ribs—and heaped it full of snow. The boat's blackened, rotting walrus hide hadn't been viable in years. But here was a start. For a hundred dollars John bought the remains.

The umiak was 32 feet long with ribs spaced every 12 inches. "She was an evolved form of umiak," John wrote, "built with bent hardwood frames." He asked a local friend about this. "He said that this type was stronger and faster with an outboard motor than the traditional, hard-chine, flat-bottom type of boat."

When John expressed surprise about the Eskimos' use of outboard motors, his friend replied, "Do you think we were crazy? Would *you* want to paddle twenty miles across Bering Strait to the island?"

And, so, John and his friend set about rebuilding. They sawed a piece of oak into the dimensions of ribs. They built a steam box out of stove pipe and an old fuel drum; they sealed the ends with rags when the water commenced to boiling. Twenty minutes in the steam box proved sufficient to soften the oak for bending. With rope his friend made from seal skin, they lashed the joints. The umiak's frame was now ready for skins.

The process of shaping the skins of an umiak requires extraordinary skill. The Eskimos almost invariably selected female hides for the boat skins because, although these were slightly smaller than the male hides, they were not warty or scarred from fighting. Walrus hide, which can be up to an inch-and-a-half thick, must be split in half to achieve a workable thickness for boat skins. The task is done by the Eskimo women who work with an *ulu* (a crescent-shaped blade) carefully opening the skin along its edge. Once the skins were split in half, they were laced at the edges on a ten-by-ten-foot wooden frame and stretched as tight as possible for drying.

Harold Ahmahsuk had sold me two good walrus skins along with the umiak frame, but with a boat of that size I needed three more to complete the cover. I managed to buy them from the King Island Eskimos in Nome. All five skins were stiff as boards, so before they could be cut and sewn together they had to be softened. We drove out past Cape

Nome to Safety Inlet and weighted the skins down with rocks in the shallow lagoon. They became soft and rubbery after being submerged for five days. In this waterlogged state, each weighed more than a hundred pounds. With some difficulty we hauled the squishy, slippery skins back into the van (which did not improve its odor) and returned to the boat frame. We then draped the skins side by side on the overturned frame in the order in which they were to be sewn together, putting the toughest hides at the bow and stern.

To cut and shape and sew the skins, John worked with Stanislas Muktoyuk, an elder of the King Island Eskimos.

He was now bent with great age, but as he whetted his knife it was clear that he was still skillful. He trimmed off the irregular and crenelated edges of the hides till the margin of each skin was exactly parallel with the next. Stan actually trimmed away so much from the edges that he left a gap the width of his hand between the hides as they lay on the overturned frame. It looked as if the covering would be far too small to fit the boat frame when the skins were sewn together. But this was intentional: By making the covering a bit small Stan insured that the skins would fit tightly when we stretched them on the frame. We then carried the trimmed skins indoors, where seven or eight Diomede and King Island women were sitting on the floor, ready to begin sewing.

It took them all day to finish the job because each seam was eight feet long and had to be sewn twice—in a double or "blind" seam, with locking stitches. They used large thimbles and triangular-pointed glover's needles. It was hard work pulling the long strands of braided linen thread through the tough hide, as they had to take great care that no stitch went entirely through the skin. By not piercing the skin—that is, by leading the thread through only about half the thickness of the hide—they created a waterproof seam.

When the sewing was done, and the women got stiffly to their feet, we carried the cover outside and stretched it over the frame. We laced it drumtight, running heavy walrus-hide rope between the holes in the edge of the skins and the stringers on the inside of the frame. It was now evening and the cover dried slowly and evenly during the night. In the morning the cover was so tight that when I snapped my finger on the hide it gave a deep reverberating boom.

By the time John finished rebuilding his umiak, the 1971 season had come and gone. He stored his 600-pound craft in a friend's barn for the winter, then returned to England to work on his doctoral dissertation. In spare moments over

*His research on past transits—harrowing gales, fatal groundings, expedition after expedition stopped by ice—at once chastened and reassured him.*

that winter he visited London chandleries and libraries and learned what was known about the Northwest Passage—about the Beaufort Sea, the Canadian Arctic Archipelago, Baffin Island, Davis Strait, Greenland. He learned that while four possible routes had been identified, only the southernmost was viable to a small boat operating without icebreaker support: south around Victoria Island, south around King William Island, past Somerset Island by whichever route was open, then into the eastern Arctic.

His research on past transits—harrowing gales, fatal groundings, expedition after expedition stopped by ice—at once chastened and reassured him.

> I had developed a very healthy respect for those waters. But while my level of caution had risen considerably, I also began to realize that the umiak would be a very safe boat for the voyage, not only because of its flexible construction, but also because, when fully loaded with a ton or more of people and gear, it would draw only a little more than two feet. That way we would be able to stay close to shore in shallow water and would often be able to work inside the grounded pack ice where it had come pressing down on the coast. Also, if a gale were to blow up, we would be able to land quickly and haul the boat up the beach, rolling it on sausage-shaped boat fenders as the Eskimos did, before the seas became too rough to get ashore.

For shelter, he did what the Eskimos do: camped under the up-turned umiak and slept on reindeer skins for a mattress. Also following Eskimo tradition, he brought a gasoline pressure stove for cooking and gasoline pressure lanterns for light.

For the 1972 season, John pulled together a crew of five: a friend from Connecticut, two friends from England, and two Eskimo friends. And as plans came together, they were joined by a two-man television crew in a 16-foot Boston Whaler. "Off duty, when they were not asleep, each crew member had his own pastime," John wrote. "Bib frequently played his harmonica, Mickey took photographs, Jim and I endlessly discussed navigation and Arctic history, Tony kept us all laughing with one ribald story after another, and Robin rarely lifted his head

*"We had no idea how far we would go that summer,
nor did I have any idea that the adventure would consume
the next seventeen years of my life."*

from a Latin or Greek text—and I think it was this diversity of interests that made for an easygoing and cooperative crew."

In fact, the crews Bockstoce assembled for his voyages over the next several seasons became legendary. "I would have loved to have been with Bockstoce," said David Thoreson, who successfully transited the Northwest Passage east-to-west in 2007 and west-to-east in 2009. "He had musicians and writers and all kinds of folks with him. Craig George, who is now the world's foremost authority on the bowhead whale was with him for a few seasons; at the time, Craig was a young up-and-coming scientist who didn't know what he was doing. John Bockstoce had a big impact on a lot of people, and I think he was a real pioneer for the new era of exploration that we're in now—exploration with a higher mission, instead of just being on a quest to be first."

How many seasons John would devote to his quest even he couldn't know, as his merry band set off from the beach at Nome on July 1, 1972.

"We were ready and only waiting for good weather to get started. We had no idea how far we would go that summer, nor did I have any idea that the adventure would consume the next seventeen years of my life."

Over the next nine summers the umiak carried John Bockstoce and a revolving cast of crewmates over 6,000 miles. For the first three seasons, they worked back and forth along the Chukchi and Beaufort sea shorelines, as far as Cape Bathurst in the Canadian Northwest Territories. In three short years, they witnessed the utter transformation of Prudhoe Bay, where oil had been discovered in 1968. From his research, John had learned about massive boom-and-bust cycles in the Arctic, following the fur trade, the whaling industry, and mineral extraction, especially gold and lead-zinc. Now, he watched a region booming in real time.

"Shortly after midnight we were off Prudhoe Bay," John wrote. "In 1972 there had been little to see, but now, with the advent of oil drilling, the scene was dramatically changed. In the twilight of midnight, cranes stood out from the horizon and everywhere were the orange beacons of the oil wells' gas flares. It was depressing to think that now that a road had been built from Fairbanks to Prudhoe, it would be possible to drive right to the shore of the Arctic Ocean. If a person hopped into a taxi in New York City with enough money he could now be carried to this wonderful wilderness without any of the problems or logistical difficulties that all previous travelers, including myself, had had to endure."

The umiak was serving John as well as he'd initially hoped. After the 1974 season, it was damaged in winter storage; the following year, he painstakingly rescued the boat and again rebuilt it. He continued his research for several projects, including his new position as curator for the Arctic collections at the New Bedford Whaling Museum in Massachusetts. All the while, John and his crew continued pushing eastward. Most seasons—which end near Labor Day—they simply ran out of time. In others they met an impassable wall of pack ice. As late as August 1980, John still believed that his umiak and crew would complete their transit of the Northwest Passage.

> When the wind finally died we pushed on for the final ninety-mile leg to Barrow Strait. Unfortunately, however, the calm and cold had allowed the formation of great mile-long patches of skim ice. This was only an eighth of an inch thick, and was very hard, being formed from a thin layer of fresh water, from rain or melt, floating on top of the salt.
>
> Many years before, on Diomede Island, Dwight Milligrock had told me how this condition could be the most dangerous of all for an umiak: As the boat moves through the glassy skim ice, its edge acts like a razor blade on the walrus hide, slicing through it at the waterline in no time.
>
> At sunrise on August 20 we finally reached Barrow Strait, which separates Somerset Island from Cornwallis Island. The town of Resolute, population one hundred seventy, lay only thirty miles across the water. We were all restless and eager with anticipation. "Big city, here we come," said Pat with a grin—and then we saw the ice, a long, dense river of it flowing out of the Viscount Melville Sound, through Barrow Strait, and into Lancaster Sound. It was so closely packed that we had no choice but to turn back to the Somerset Island shore and to make camp, hoping for a change. But this time we had to break young ice to reach the shore, and we knew that the summer was just about over.

A helicopter pilot dropped in on their camp, giving John a chance to go up several thousand feet to have a look at what lay ahead. What he saw wasn't promising. Three days later, John and his mates climbed to the top of Limestone Island to survey the scene from 800 feet above.

> A vast band of drift ice stretched from horizon to horizon in the strait. As I stood at the top of the island with my three friends I began thinking about the future of our trip. We all wanted to complete the

*"To make a recorded transit," Capt. Pullen told John,*
*"you have got to start at one end and come out at the other.*
*You've got to go all the way in one voyage,*
*whether you have to winter over or not."*

Northwest Passage, but it had grown increasingly clear that this would not be possible. The umiak's walrus skins now had three years' worth of wear on them, and I remembered how Dwight Milligrock had told me, point blank, not to use them for four because they would lose some of their strength and resiliency. I knew that I could not take this chance, because the rest of the trip to Davis Strait would be in very deep water, past long reaches of bold cliffs and glaciers; if the skins started to give out and leak, there might be absolutely no place to land, and we certainly wouldn't last more than a few minutes in that cold water.

As we walked back down the steep slope of the island, the four of us, who had come so far together, sensed that our voyage was over, and each grew quiet, thinking sadly, I suspect, that we would probably never have a chance again to experience our unique teamwork and camaraderie.

## Enter *Belvedere*

The 1981 season had its depressing moments as John crated his umiak for shipping across the continent to Connecticut where it would join the Mystic Seaport collection. He watched the town of Resolute on Barrow Strait, staging hub for oil exploration and lead-zinc mining in the Canadian Arctic islands, grapple with its own new boom cycle.

"I could not have known it then, of course, but the changes I was witnessing as I completed those last chores of my umiak expedition would precisely foreshadow my Arctic voyages of the eighties—that wrenching change, both historically and in the recent present, would be the central theme in my research work as well as in my quest to complete the traverse of the Northwest Passage; in fact my travels from now on would seem simultaneously to be through time and across large distances."

All the while, John continued his conversations with the most knowledgeable Arctic explorers of the day. One of these was with Thomas Pullen, retired captain in the Royal Canadian Navy, veteran of several transits beginning in 1954, and renowned as the leading pathfinder and arbiter of Northwest Passage record-keeping.

*"Soon it dawned on me that what I needed was a sailboat."*

"To make a recorded transit," Capt. Pullen told John, "you have got to start at one end and come out at the other. You've got to go all the way in one voyage, whether you have to winter over or not. It can take any number of years, but it's got to be one discrete voyage, beginning at Bering Strait and ending at Davis Strait, or vice versa."

In 1977 Belgian sailor Willy de Roos in his 43-foot steel ketch *Williwaw* became the first yachtsman to transit the Northwest Passage, largely following Amundsen's route. He continued on to circumnavigate North and South America, earning the CCA's Blue Water Medal in 1980.

John now saw the weaknesses of the umiak for his goal of completing the transit. "Although the umiak voyages had allowed me to travel safely along huge stretches of Arctic coastline," he wrote, "I had been unable to cross big bodies of water. But to complete my field research on the history of the Arctic whaling industry and fur trade, I still needed to reach the islands far offshore. Soon it dawned on me that what I needed was a sailboat."

And so began John Bockstoce's lifelong relationship with *Belvedere*, now 40 years on and still counting at press time. He abandoned his 600-pound walrus-skin open boat for a seagoing vessel of 39 tons.

"The solution came in April 1982 when a marine broker sent me a prospectus for a sixty-foot cutter-rigged motorsailer that was berthed in San Diego," John wrote. "I learned that she had been both designed and built by George Sutton, who was well known as a skilled naval architect specializing in seakindly and very livable long-range cruising boats. Better yet, she was heavily built of steel with big water and fuel tanks, and she carried a [Gray Marine] 6-71 marine diesel engine—the DC-3 of marine propulsion, steady and very reliable."

"George Sutton specialized in manufacturing steel structures out there in Newport Beach, California," John said. "He built landing craft and tanks and barges. But he was a man of many parts, and he had a good eye for a seaworthy boat. He built four yachts of which *Belvedere* I think was the last one. He was very skillful in forming steel. So *Belvedere* looks like a fiberglass boat, because it's such good rounded lines."

Speaking in May 2020 from his home in Padanaram, Massachusetts, he said, "And God willing she'll be down here in about two or three weeks, and I'll go sailing again."

In that inaugural summer of 1982, John and his mates sailed her to Puget Sound for a refit worthy of the Arctic: extra ballast, heavier anchors, radar, satnav,

John Bockstoce and his crew had to make up his own travel guides through the wilderness of the high Arctic, often relying on oral histories. They were well aware of the perils of an offshore lead to a dead end, with no way through the ice pack.

single-sideband radio, and an enclosed pilothouse. "I often thought fondly of how simple the umiak had been—all she needed was a compass—but of course in the umiak we were always near shore and could haul the boat out at a moment's notice. Now I would be in a heavy boat, sometimes far from shore, and I had to plan for occasionally violent weather."

These musings gave John a still greater respect for the 19th-century whalers who needed to prepare for all the same conditions, but without the radar, the satnav, or the radios. Reckoning with the mindshare it would require to maintain this boat's many systems—electrical, mechanical, hydraulic—John brought on a captain so that he could devote himself to the archaeological and historic research that had brought him to the Arctic in the first place.

"*Belvedere* performed wonderfully," John wrote. "With her mainsail and jib drawing she had the feel of an ocean rover, moving effortlessly over the big, long swells of the North Pacific, and during calms or periods of headwinds the diesel engine drove her easily ahead at a steady seven knots."

In the summer of 1983 *Belvedere* passed through Bering Strait and worked into the icy waters near Barrow, rejoining the umiak's former track. In the absence of published cruising guides for this wilderness, John and his crew relied heavily on the oral history he'd been gathering now for almost 15 years. His heavy, deep-draft boat couldn't be hauled up on the beach, and he was now discovering a whole new set of problems.

We set off and almost at once found loose, drifting pack ice as we worked our way eastward. I pulled on my parka and climbed to the spreaders with a hand radio to talk to Sven, who was on the helm as we picked our way through it. One thing I definitely did not want to do was to take an ill-advised turn and run off down a lead—only to find that it was a cul-de-sac. The old whalemen knew that the waters off the north coast of Alaska can be dangerous; for offshore leads usually close up, and when they do, any ship caught in the ice is carried away in the great clockwise gyre that slowly grinds round the Beaufort Sea.

Standing at the spreaders I remembered how, ten years before, I had met one of the last of the old Arctic whalemen who, as a sixteen-year-old, had been the engineer of the schooner *Polar Bear*, going after bowheads in these waters. Ben Kilian was eighty years old then, but his mind was sharp and his eyes flashed as he told me how his captain, Louis Lane, had avoided being caught in the pack in 1913. Others were not so skilled. That same summer, 1913, the old whaleship *Karluk* was carrying the main party of the Canadian Arctic Expedition eastward in the Beaufort, when her captain, unused to the ways of the western Arctic, took the chance of making progress by running down one of these offshore leads. The *Karluk* was caught in the pack and swept away to the western Chukchi Sea, where the ship was crushed, far from shore, and many of the crew and passengers perished on the ice floes.

Louis Lane had been tempted to follow the *Karluk* offshore, and for a while he did head down one of these leads, but when he found it a dead end—and planned to wait there in the assumption that it would open further—an ancient retired whaleman, Captain William Mogg, who happened to be taking passage aboard the *Polar Bear*, stepped forward and advised returning to shore and staying as close to it as possible. Ben Killian recalled his words: "Captain, don't tie up here. I always like to sleep with the mud on one side of me." Lane turned the *Polar Bear* back to shore and safety.

In 1983 *Belvedere* sailed 4,000 miles from Puget Sound to boom-time Tuktoyaktuk near the Mackenzie River in the Northwest Territories, where John and a crew from the Northern Transportation Company Limited built a skid and hauled all 39 tons of her out with bulldozers.

For the next three seasons, *Belvedere* and crew traveled eastward, but never farther than Amundsen Gulf. John began the 1984 season without expecting to complete the transit: the winter had been exceptionally cold, and the breakup of ice through the Northwest Passage was forecast to come late that year.

As it turned out, the forecast proved accurate. The ice had not melted much, and we were forced to work along inside the ice edge in very shallow water, within only a mile or two of the delta islands. Normally, this wouldn't have been a problem, because the silty bottom is very flat and uniform there. But as the search for oil intensified, the oil companies moved from onshore exploration in the delta to offshore drilling—and the simplest way to do this was to build an artificial island. They built these islands by using dredges to suck up sediments from the sea floor and to deposit them, either by dumping them through floating pipes or by using a hopper dredge. The island-building is economical in water up to ninety feet, though at the outer range the sediments are pumped into a retaining metal caisson rather than being merely heaped into a pile and protected from wave erosion by plastic 'berm bags' full of sediment. The theory goes that, once the drilling is completed, the caisson or berm can be removed and then the island will simply wash away. But if in fact this is true in the long run, it was clear to all aboard *Belvedere* that it certainly was not so in the short—for we saw these islands awash and unmarked."

These man-made hazards weren't the only navigational quirks *Belvedere's* crew experienced in the western Arctic, particularly in the Mackenzie delta. *Pingos* are earthen mounds, as high as 200 feet, that form naturally when, for example, erosion drains a lake that had previously insulated the surface. With this insulation gone, the wet sediments underneath then freeze and push upward. Some grow as fast as 18 inches per year. In 1969, the Canadian escort for the *USS Manhattan* was shocked to discover uncharted underwater pingos jutting dangerously upward from an otherwise uniform depth in the Beaufort Sea. A sharp eye on the depth sounder and a safe speed are the only remedies.

John used the slow going of that 1984 season to begin work on a sequel to his history of the western Arctic whaling industry; the new book would explore the Arctic fur trade that grew as whaling died out. To meet the traders who were still alive (or their children) meant visiting many remote villages along the Beaufort Sea shore and in the Canadian Arctic Islands. "*Belvedere* was perfectly suited to take me to all those remote settlements," John wrote.

At a forum of yacht designers hosted by *Cruising World* magazine in 1999, W. I. B. "Bill" Crealock said, "The challenge of cruising boats is they're a fixed platform operating in a variable environment. You really need one boat for passagemaking and another one for port."

Two decades earlier, John had cracked that nut by conducting his voyages in two entirely different boats. "The combination of the umiak first, for inshore work, followed by *Belvedere* for offshore work was a good one," he said.

Breakup for the 1985 season came on schedule, but that year a long spate

*Belvedere* anchors in Rae Strait, King William Island, in 1987.
The skipper's grandson and namesake, John G. Bockstoce, age 11,
explores the surroundings on an ice floe.

of northwesterlies pushed the pack ice close to shore. For *Belvedere's* Northwest Passage aspirations, the season was largely a bust.

The 1986 season was more successful. *Belvedere* carried its crew for the first time to Banks Island, where Robert McClure's crew had wintered over (then inadvertently summered over, still frozen in the ice) and nearly perished before another expedition arrived by sledge to lead them back to safety. *Belvedere* tried to pass northbound through the Prince of Wales Strait on the eastern side of Banks Island but was stopped cold by solid ice that hadn't broken up since winter. Further attempts to reach Holman on Victoria Island proved impossible, and for the third consecutive year *Belvedere* returned to Tuktoyaktuk.

Would the 1987 season offer any better openings? When John returned to Tuk in July, the town was strangely quiet. The price of oil had dropped below the $24-per-barrel threshold that made Arctic drilling profitable, and the oil companies had precipitously moved out. With his long historical view, John recognized what he saw. "We were witnessing the same boom-and-bust cycle in the oil industry that had happened in the fur trade, and before that, in the whaling industry." He hoped that this would be *Belvedere's* time to move on, too. Even though the winter had been cold, auguring a late breakup, and though polar ice still choked crucial straits, he thought it was worth the try. And if he didn't complete the Northwest Passage transit this year, he figured he could still gather research for his book on the fur trade. This time, they were able to reach the northern end of Banks Island. "We passed the latitude of 74º20', and we were in the waters now where as far as I know only four other surface vessels had ever been—an ice-strengthened whale-ship, an ice breaker, a canoe, and Robert McClure's HMS *Investigator*, which, as I mentioned earlier, never returned."

Crossing from Banks Island back to the continental shoreline was slow going.

The ice cover was denser than the ice chart we received on the weath-erfax had indicated, and we quickly became enmeshed. I was at the helm, backing and filling and trying to work through it, and when that proved futile, simply trying to get out of it. It was dead slow, neutral, reverse—over and over—as we maneuvered our way in and out of the tightly packed floes. After an hour of this we began to notice a slight swell in the water, indicating that we were getting close to the windward edge of the ice field. Farther on, the swell grew to about two feet, heaving the floes around a bit, a situation that could easily become dangerous if a piece got under the stern and tore off our rudder or bent a propeller blade. We all knew, and I most of all, that *Belvedere* was not built to be an icebreaker and that the steel of most of her hull was only about a quarter of an inch thick.

Near midnight a day later the skies cleared and we saw the sun set, only to rise 14 minutes later, giving us a beautiful morning. But as the sun continued its progression across the eastern horizon, it was soon right in our eyes, making the waters dance and sparkle and visibility extremely difficult. In order to see and avoid the scattered ice we began to "tack" across the path of the sunlight. Even so, I hit a low, waterlogged piece of ice that gave a hiss and rumble as it passed under the hull breaking in two without any damage to the boat.

Painstakingly, *Belvedere's* crew worked their way through Queen Maud Gulf, a "navigational nightmare" of marginally charted rocks and shoals—"all drum-lins and glacial erratics." They spent "a tormented week" trying to find a passage through to King William Island where Amundsen had wintered over, but found their way blocked by an impassable mass of multiyear ice and "never-ending streams of ice feeding down from the north." Exasperated, they retreated to Hat Island. A pilot friend landed at an abandoned base of the Distant Early Warning line, a vestige of the Cold War nuclear brinksmanship between the United States

After 2,700 miles traveled in 1987 through largely uncharted waters,
*Belvedere* was stopped before James Ross Strait when the ice and weather
conspired against them in late August.
The crew had to backtrack a 1,000 miles for winter lay up.

and the Soviet Union. Flying a thousand-mile loop around the Boothia Peninsula, John believed he saw a navigable waterway through the ice. Back aboard
*Belvedere* they tried it, and indeed made it as far as Gjøahavn for a visit with old
friends. But on August 30 at James Ross Strait, the obstacle they met was total.

"Although we had covered 2,700 miles from Tuk, it was clear we weren't
going any farther that summer," John wrote. "The weather forecast was gloomy
for the near future—strong northwesterlies that would really pack the ice in hard
in Larsen Sound and James Ross Strait. The autumn in the Arctic is no place to
be wasting time, for the gales increase in frequency and ferocity, and up there
autumn begins in mid-August. On September 1 *Belvedere* turned west to begin
the 1000-mile return to her winter quarters in Tuk."

## The Northwest Passage

Warm winds blew through the Northwest Passage in the spring of 1988, hastening
the melt and promising an early breakup. *Belvedere* and crew sailed from Tuk to
Cambridge Bay, and from there John again flew with his pilot friend, as he'd
done the year before, to scope out the waterways as far ahead as Somerset Island.
"To my joy I saw only fifty miles of ice blocking the route north of James Ross

*"To my joy I saw only fifty miles of ice blocking the route north of James Ross Strait—and it was in a fairly advanced state of melt.*

Strait—and it was in a fairly advanced state of melt." *Belvedere's* passage across Queen Maud Gulf, with neither ice nor fog nor wind, was immeasurably easier than it had been a year earlier.

On August 21 *Belvedere's* crew encountered their first pack ice of the season at the entrance to James Ross Strait. But this time it wasn't nearly as dense as they'd found it the previous season, and weather conditions were now more auspicious. To bide time, they fell back and anchored in an unnamed bay on the west coast of the Boothia Peninsula. While anchored, they dinghied ashore and built a cairn in the style of one that *St. Roch's* crew had erected on Victoria Island in 1941 as they made their way toward the second-ever successful transit of the Northwest Passage. John's crew dubbed the place Belvedere Harbor; any traveler coming along who toppled the monument would find a Tupperware treasure box containing *Belvedere* business cards.

> The time passed with agonizing slowness, but the next day the ice had started to move a bit, and we pushed on in a narrow shore lead past Cape Victoria into Kent Bay. Suddenly Craig [George] and Richard Olsenius let out a whoop from the spreaders. "I can see another sailboat coming toward us!" Richard shouted. It was the small yawl *North Hangar* of England, and I believe it was the first time eastbound and westbound vessels have met in the Passage. An hour later we met another, the motor lifeboat *Mabel E. Holland*, also of England, with my friend David Cowper aboard. He had wintered the boat for two years at Fort Ross at the east end of Bellot Strait, waiting, like us, for an opening. He was underway to circumnavigate the world, alone, under power. It was a series of ecstatic greetings, frantic toasts, and hurried goodbyes—for none of us wanted to waste time with that menacing pack ice lurking out there to the west of us in Larsen Sound. (Both *North Hangar* and *Mabel E. Holland* were stopped by heavy ice just west of Herschel Island and wintered at Inuvik, completing their traverses to Bering Strait in 1989.) [David Cowper would go on to earn the CCA Blue Water Medal in 2012, honoring his six circumnavigations and five solo transits of the Northwest Passage.]
>
> Less than twenty-four hours later we reached Bellot Strait, which is the

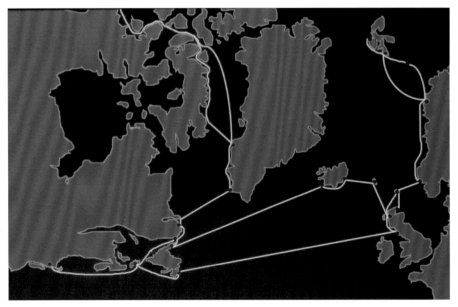

The world according to *Belvedere*. The unique motorsailer
could handle open ocean and narrow ice leads under the expert navigation of her owner.

fulcrum point of the Northwest Passage. This is where the waters of the
western Arctic meet those of the east, and it is the first meeting of the tides
of the Atlantic and Pacific north of Tierra del Fuego. The strait is narrow
and deep: twenty miles long and less than half a mile wide at its narrowest,
where it separates Somerset Island from the Boothia Peninsula, which is
the northernmost point of the continent of North America. Tidal currents
race through its fjordlike, rocky walls at more than nine miles per hour,
which is about as fast as *Belvedere* can go under full power.

On that day, August 25, 1988, they serendipitously entered Bellot Strait at
slack tide—just as if they'd planned it. And, with that, John achieved a goal he'd
set for himself 17 years earlier. Of course, *Belvedere* hadn't yet officially completed
its transit. There were still miles and days and icebergs and polar bears and whales
and ocean swells to reckon with before that happened. But the impenetrable pack
ice was behind them now.

"On September 2 we crossed onto Store Hellefiske Banke and saw one or two
Greenlandic trawlers at work," wrote John. "I couldn't sleep at all that night I was
so excited. I can say without fear of contradiction that we were a happy crowd
when the massive granite headlands of Holsteinsborg Harbor showed above the
fog. We had reached Davis Strait, the eastern entrance to the Northwest Passage,
and *Belvedere* had become the first yacht to traverse the Passage from west to east."

These days *Belvedere* dresses up the entrance to Padanaram Harbor in Massachusetts. John takes her out sailing most every week in the summer.

A lot has changed since that September day in 1988. The oral histories that guided northerners so successfully for so long are now ever more stressed by accelerating changes in the climate and the environment. A historic tipping point came in 2007—the first season the ice opened through the entire Northwest Passage, followed by another in 2012. Yachts in unprecedented numbers have now made the transit, some of them wondering, "What's the big deal?"

Still, the mark Bockstoce left on the region remains indelible. As George Porter Jr. of Gjøahavn told him in 1988, "John, we really enjoy your visits. You are helping to preserve our history, and no one else cares about it."

As the intervening years have shown, people do care. "If you look at the recent history of the Arctic from when Amundsen went through the Northwest Passage to now," said David Thoreson, who transited by yacht in 2007 and 2009, "you'll see that people like Bockstoce were pioneers in creating an understanding of place by most white people. The transmission of local knowledge and science and understanding has come from people like him exploring in small boats and spending time with local people and communities and having an experience like no one will ever have again."

A boat can be an adventurous world to a child,
and the child can become a responsible part of the operation of that world.
A boat can also introduce a child to the vastness of the world and the universe beyond.

# 12

# Around Again, This Time with Children: The Kuhner Family's *Tamure* Voyage

I always wanted to show the kids there's more to life than Fairfield County.
—Scott Kuhner

It is the thing I'm most grateful for in life, other than the basics.
—Alex Kuhner

Alex Kuhner, age 44, lives with his wife and daughter in Westport, Connecticut, the town right next to the one where he was raised. If that were all there was to it, this would be a different story, or maybe no story at all. But a wrinkle runs through the fabric of the Kuhner family life.

This is the story of that wrinkle.

*Tamure* is a Valiant 40 built in 1976, the go-to production performance cruiser of her day, even though this boat had first proven herself as Francis Stokes's *Mooneshine* in the 1976 and 1980 OSTAR races.

## Dancing the *Tamure*

"The *Tamure* is a fast, sexy dance," said Scott Kuhner, father of Alex and his younger brother, Spencer. "And our boat is a fast, sexy boat."

Scott and Kitty Kuhner first encountered the *Tamure* back in prehistoric 1972, long before the boys were born. As newlyweds they'd sailed *Bebinka*, their 30-foot Allied Seawind ketch, from Connecticut to Panama, then across the eastern half of the Pacific Ocean to the islands of French Polynesia: Hiva Oa, Nuku Hiva, Takaroa, Tahiti, Bora Bora. "We had a marvelous time because we can't help but like the Polynesians," Scott recalled of those long-ago days. "What a musical lot they are. Every night the locals would come out with their guitars and banjos, and we either just listened to the beautiful Tahitian songs or tried to dance the *Tamure* on the wharf." Over four years, Scott and Kitty completed a world circumnavigation, then returned to their lives in Connecticut and Scott's career in Wall Street finance—but not without becoming changed forever by what they'd seen and experienced along the way.

Alex was born in 1976; Spencer, in 1978. Almost from the beginning, Scott and Kitty knew they wanted to sail around the world again, this time with their boys. "Frankly," said Kitty, "it was such a wonderful experience for us the first time that we just wanted to share that with them: the chance to see these wonderful cultures around the world."

It was a dream shaped by mentors. On their *Bebinka* voyage Scott and Kitty cruised in company with the Bercaw family aboard the 38-foot Sea Wolf ketch *Natasha*, raising three teenage kids as they circumnavigated in the early 1970s. "Jay had been first mate on Irving Johnson's Brigantine *Yankee*, and Gretchen was one of the passenger-students," said Kitty. "They fell in love and got married, and then sailed around the world with their kids. They were a big influence on us after we started a family. We thought, 'Gee, we should do this with our kids, too.'"

With that goal in mind, they felt they needed a boat more family-friendly than the 30-foot Allied Seawind they'd come to know so well. The boat they found was *Mooneshine*, already famous among passagemakers and the sailors who followed them. Built in 1975 in Washington state, she was the 22nd hull of the Valiant 40 line. *Mooneshine's* owner, Francis Stokes, had sailed her to class honors in the 1976 OSTAR singlehanded transatlantic race, then again in 1980. Scott and Francis had become acquainted as they competed on separate boats in the 1979 and 1981 Bermuda One-Two Yacht Races. By 1982, Francis was setting his sights on a new boat to sail in the inaugural BOC Challenge singlehanded round-the-world race—an event in which he would go on to join the pantheon of world-class sailors for his rescue of fellow competitor Tony Lush from a sinking boat in the Southern Ocean.

*With that goal in mind, they felt they needed a boat
more family-friendly than the 30-foot Allied Seawind
they'd come to know so well.*

"Francis sold his boat to us for a real deal," said Scott. "I'd always had this desire to go off cruising again with the kids. When we bought the boat in 1982 the boys were still really little. But he gave it to us for such a good price that we couldn't turn it down."

The boat the Kuhners bought was a model that had sparked a small revolution in the market for oceangoing sailboats. Beginning in 1973 the Valiant Yacht Corporation was formed as a partnership between Nathan Rothman, Sylvia and Stanley Dabney, and the yacht designer Bob Perry, still in the infancy of his career. When the early fruit of that partnership appeared at the 1975 Seattle Boat Show, visitors were treated to that rarest of all things: something new under the sun. Then and now, the Valiant 40 was widely touted as the first production-built offshore performance cruiser.

That said, her creator was never one to fall for his own press. "Some sailors think the Valiant 40 was an innovative design, but I'm not among them," wrote Perry in a 2008 memoir. To hear him tell it, the Valiant 40 was composed like a folk song, mixing bits and pieces of existing boats, and arranging the parts in a new way. That canoe stern? It came from a boat Perry first saw on a *Soundings* magazine cover, *Holger Danske*—a Scandinavian-style double-ender designed by Aage Nielsen (aboard which CCA member Rich Wilson, age 28, would become the youngest Bermuda Race overall winner in 1980). That midsection? It came from the IOR Two-Tonners that Perry was contemporaneously drafting for Carter's yacht design firm. The bow? It was from William Garden's *Bolero*, with its *soupçon* of concavity and arguably too much flare—a bow that kept the decks dry on a power-reach but probably retarded the boat's all-up speed potential.

"I could trace each design element back to a boat from my past," Perry wrote.

Above all, the Valiant 40 was created in reaction to that darling of CCA founder Bill Nutting, the Westsail 32 (which was based on quick-and-dirty sketches of a 47-foot Colin Archer Norwegian rescue cutter that Nutting scaled down to 32 feet in 1923 and passed along to his yacht-designer friend Billy Atkin; Nutting's sketches became Atkin's *Eric* design, which Robin Knox-Johnston sailed to fame in the 1968–69 Golden Globe solo nonstop round-the-world race, which with tweaks from designer W. I. B. "Bill" Crealock became the series-built fiberglass Westsail). In 1973, as Perry was working out his ideas for a fast, comfortable, safe 40-foot cruising boat, *Time* magazine had just featured the Westsail 32 as the quintessential platform for a countercultural chuck-it-all cruising way of life. Perry and his friends, in their youthful derision, referred to the plodding Westsail as a "wet snail." And these youngsters weren't alone in their critique. "Westsail lines were taken from the Colin Archer designs for Norwegian lifeboats and were undeniably salty," wrote Stokes. "The problem was that these boats, with long keel and heavy displacement, were designed to heave-to with contentment, not to cross oceans upwind."

More broadly, Perry created the Valiant 40 in reaction to the entire fleet of production cruising boats at the time. "The bottom line was that I knew racing boats far better than I knew cruising boats," he wrote. "I also knew racing boats were nice to cruise. They were fast, and in the early 1970s their interiors were designed to work well for a crew. The typical cruising boat of that time was a pig."

Inspired by an article from veteran yacht designer Ted Brewer, Perry learned to focus obsessively on two non-dimensional ratios in his designs: displacement-to-length (D/L), which is how heavy a boat is relative to its waterline length; and sail-area-to-displacement (SA/D), which calculates how much sail a boat carries relative to its weight. Working backwards from the ratios he desired, Perry resolved that the key to a lighter, more powerful boat was in the underbody. He had to "get rid of the full keel and replace it with a fin keel and skeg-hung rudder." This last decision was the ultimate heresy for a boat marketed to sail over the horizon. Sure, ten years earlier yacht designer Bill Lapworth had separated the rudder from the keel of his Cal 40, and Perry had enough experience with Carter's IOR racing boats to know that a well-done split underbody could deliver exemplary directional stability and helm response. "With a D/L of around 260," wrote Perry, "the Valiant would be a radically light cruising boat compared with the D/L of 400 for the Westsail types." The wags were slow to accept such flights of recklessness. When the Valiant 40 had been in production for five years, a *Yachting* magazine piece described it as "too light to be considered a serious offshore boat." Never mind that Bill and Mary Black of Seattle had happily sailed their Valiant 40, *Foreign Affair*, around the world, to say nothing of Francis Stokes' several successful transatlantic passages.

Given that the Valiant was built not of today's engineered composites but of the "bulk fiberglass" standards of the mid-1970s—resin-rich inch-thick hand-laid fiberglass mat and woven roving at the keel, tapering to 3/8 inches at the caprail, no core in the hull, and scant attention to the direction of the fibers—21st-century observers can chuckle at the too-light criticism. For comparison, consider that among the 22 cruising sailboats nominated for *Cruising World's* 2020 Boat of the Year awards the average D/L was 169. The only new sailboat in the 2020 fleet

*No one was more critical of the boat's square coachhouse lines than her creator: "like a shoe box on a banana," Perry wrote of his early effort.*

with a D/L greater than the "radically light" Valiant 40 was an Island Packet 349, with its D/L of 278: hardly a light boat by today's standards.

Within the year that Stokes sold *Mooneshine* to Kuhner, Dan Byrne successfully finished the inaugural BOC Challenge singlehanded round-the-world race aboard the first Valiant 40 ever built. And National Sailing Hall of Famer Mark Schrader with his Valiant 40 became the first American solo sailor to circumnavigate by way of the five Southern Capes, picking up several world speed sailing records along the way.

Of course, not everything about the Valiant 40 was perfect. No one was more critical of the boat's square coachhouse lines than her creator: "like a shoe box on a banana," Perry wrote of his early effort. In later versions of the 40, he moved the mast two feet forward, rendering her more sloop than cutter, and reducing some of the Valiant's weather helm. In other derivative models, both larger and smaller, Perry fixed the excessive flare in that bow.

The ultimate problem in some of the Valiant 40s came not from the designer but from the builder. Between 1976 and 1981, Uniflite of Bellingham, Washington, used a proprietary polyester resin called Hetron that had been tested by the U.S. military in Vietnam and proved to be flame-retardant. Though Uniflite had warranted the boats free from failure "for the lifetime of the boat's original owner," some Valiants built in those years blistered catastrophically over time, both above and below the waterline, a fact that drove Uniflite into bankruptcy in 1984 and still mars the resale value of Valiants built during that period. Under new ownership, Valiant Yachts continued building boats in Texas through 2011. In all, 200 Valiant 40s were built, plus another 70 slightly modified Valiant 42s. In 1997 the Valiant 40 was inducted into the Sail America Sailboat Hall of Fame.

When Stokes made the 1982 offer that Scott Kuhner couldn't refuse—on a Valiant that had been built just before Uniflite adopted Hetron resin and which therefore suffered none of the massive blister problems—a new member entered the Kuhner family picture. At press time in 2021, four decades later, Scott and Kitty still own hull number 122 of the Valiant 40 line. (Hull numbers on the Valiants started at 101.) Francis had named his boat *Mooneshine*, with its archaic spelling, in honor of a ship sailed by the Elizabethan explorer, John Davis, whom he'd read about in a book by CCA member and Harvard historian, Samuel Eliot

*The Kuhners took the boat into their hearts*
*and straightaway renamed her* Tamure, *forever memorializing*
*their encounters with the good people of Polynesia.*

Morison. The Kuhners took the boat into their hearts and straightaway renamed her *Tamure*, forever memorializing their encounters with the good people of Polynesia.

"She's such a wonderful solid boat, really comfortable at sea," said Kitty.

"She's a perfect cruising boat," said Scott.

## The Gales of November

Alex Kuhner remembers keeping a secret. He was in 6th grade in the fall of 1987, enrolled in the Norwalk public middle school. But not for long, not that year. "I remember having a conversation with an adult and telling them, 'Yeah, when we leave—' and then being like, 'Oh, I'm not supposed to tell you.'"

The leaving he was not supposed to talk about was a world circumnavigation aboard *Tamure*, set to begin early in October. It was a trip that over the next three and a half years would carry the Kuhner family to the Virgin Islands, Panama, Galápagos, Marquesas, Tahiti, Suwarrow, Tonga, Fiji, New Zealand, New Caledonia, Australia, Indonesia, Thailand, Sri Lanka, Oman, South Yemen, Egypt, Israel, Cyprus, Gibraltar, the Canary Islands, and back to North America by way of the Eastern Caribbean.

"I certainly didn't have a grasp of what we were getting into when we cast off," said Spencer, 8 years old at the time. Now in his early 40s, he recalls bedtime stories his parents would tell about the places they'd visited and the people they'd met on their earlier *Bebinka* voyage, but no clear announcement about just what lay in store for him and Alex that fall.

Still, for more than a year, Scott and Kitty had been preparing themselves and their boat for a second circumnavigation. Scott had rebuilt *Tamure's* engine and reinstalled it himself. He replaced plastic portholes with more robust aluminum ones. He replaced the boat's standing rigging and terminals, adding a bowsprit and moving the headstay forward two feet to reduce weather helm. He replaced a kerosene stove with a new propane stove, including a new vented LP locker for two 20-pound tanks and all the lines to deliver propane safely. He added refrigeration and radar.

Stokes had optimized his boat to race east-to-west across the Atlantic Ocean, upwind against the prevailing westerlies. The Kuhners, by contrast, looking forward to a trade-wind circumnavigation, adapted their boat for extended down-wind passages. They added a second headstay and a second pole; this allowed them to fly twin headsails, wing and wing, a trick they'd picked up on *Bebinka* and still loved. They also removed the Monitor windvane self-steering device Francis had installed and replaced it with *Bebinka's* original Hasler windvane. Apart from a few replacement parts, that same marvel of 1960s servo-pendulum engineering still steers *Tamure* today. "We didn't like the Monitor as much because you couldn't get the oar out of the water as easily," said Kitty, "for example, if you got a line around the oar."

Other preparations were more social than mechanical. The summer before they set off on the big trip, the Kuhners sailed to Midcoast Maine to meet another cruising family with kids. CCA members Cabot and Heidi Lyman, founders of Lyman-Morse Boatbuilding in Thomaston, were preparing their Seguin 49, *Chewink,* to sail around the world with their three boys, Alex, Zach, and Drew, similar in age to the Kuhner boys. (Cabot and Heidi Lyman earned the CCA's 2016 Far Horizons Award, recognizing their 150,000 sea miles together, 95,000 of those aboard *Chewink.*)

"The fact that we knew the Lymans made a difference," said Alex Kuhner. "It was like: OK, we're not alone. There are other kids out here. Our family isn't crazy."

Still, that departure from Connecticut wasn't easy—not for anyone. "Even though we were finally ready to leave, I didn't feel relaxed," Scott wrote. "The incredible stress and frantic pace of the last few weeks before quitting my job at Donaldson, Lufkin and Jenrette and leaving the dock in Rowayton was almost impossible to cope with. As we motored the half mile down Five Mile River to Long Island Sound, three of our kids' friends were running along the beach waving goodbye. They followed us all the way to the mouth of the river, where they stood on the rocks at the point and waved until we were out of sight. A few tears welled up in my eyes as I went below to get out the chart book, and there was Alex lying on his bunk, crying too. I sat down next to him and we talked for a while about how sad it was to leave all our friends, but now we could look forward to the adventure and new friendships that lay ahead."

Scott and Kitty's earlier circumnavigation had taught them that the transition zones between the higher latitudes of variable weather and the tropical trade-wind belt often produced the roughest passages, especially near the spring and fall equinoxes. So the Kuhner family traveled south by way of the protected Intracoastal Waterway as far as Charleston, South Carolina. From there, Kitty and the boys left the boat to enjoy a couple of weeks in Florida with Scott's parents, including a trip to Disney World, while Scott and a friend sailed *Tamure* to the Virgin Islands.

They didn't want the boys' first major offshore passage to be excessively rough.

Their instincts were spot on. When *Tamure* had been at sea for nine days, Scott made this entry in the log:

> It's blowing a near gale out, as it has been for the last three days. This is our second bout with the North Atlantic during the winter. The seas are only about 10 to 13 feet but are steep and coming from abeam. Now they are slamming against our side and rolling us over as much as 45 degrees. We have only a small storm jib set and nothing else, still making six to seven knots. Every so often a wave breaks over the whole boat and cascades down the deck, completely covering the ports, giving the illusion we are actually on a submarine, not a pleasure yacht. Consequently, all hatches are battened down hard, making it a little like a steam bath below. Sleep is impossible between the heat, the violent rolling, the crashing of the waves and the constant screeching of the wind in the rigging.

If Scott's departure timing hadn't been perfect in that season of turbulent weather, it surely was in light of turbulent economic winds, and not for the first time. Barely a week after *Tamure* left Rowayton, the news came of a 508-point drop in the stock market—more than 22 percent, the highest one-day drop in Dow Jones history. Scott had made his career in Wall Street finance. Before the *Bebinka* voyage, he and two analysts had started E. F. Hutton's Institutional Department, which quickly took off. It was his 1969 Christmas bonus that bought the Allied Seawind ketch. When at age 30 he told his boss he was quitting his job to sail around the world, his boss replied, "Are you out of your mind? If you want to go sailing, work for another four or five years. Then if you want to quit, you can quit for good." Nevertheless, Scott and Kitty carried on with their plans; they were more than a year into their voyage when the stock market crashed in January 1973, the worst loss since the Great Depression. Meanwhile, *Bebinka* was crossing the Tasman Sea from New Zealand to Australia.

And now in October 1987 here was Black Monday, the new worst crash since the Great Depression. "I was missing history being made, and for a brief moment I wanted to be back at my desk to watch the happenings. But I was even more relieved to be exactly where I was." Before setting off, Scott Kuhner had sold all his stocks.

The family reunion in the Virgin Islands was sparked up by the nearly simultaneous arrival of *Chewink*, just in time for the Lyman and Kuhner families to celebrate Thanksgiving together and for the kids to spend a day playing on the beach. But the subsequent month, as Scott recalls, was "a nightmare." It began

*Enjoy life now. That philosophy was one reason behind our decision to make this trip. We wanted to spend time with our kids before they grew up and went off on their own.*

with a week of torrential rains. On the rough passage south, Scott had noticed kidney problems. Overland treks in a sputtering rental car through washed-out roads from Puerto Rico's southeast coast to an unclean hospital in San Juan produced more medical questions than answers. Finally, Scott and Kitty resolved to fly to St. Louis with the boys, spend the holidays with Kitty's family, and consult a family doctor they knew and trusted.

"Even though it all turned out well," wrote Scott, "I was once again reminded to enjoy life now, be thankful for each day and not waste it. That philosophy was one reason behind our decision to make this trip. We wanted to spend time with our kids before they grew up and went off on their own. On December 23rd we found out all was okay with me, and Christmas 1987 at Kitty's parents' home in St. Louis was an especially happy, warm family gathering."

## Westbound, Together

On January 4, after their unplanned reset, the Kuhner family set off on what would be their first real offshore passage: 960 miles westbound across the Caribbean Sea to the San Blas Islands, just off the coast of Panama.

"Our deal when we went off cruising was, well, if one of us doesn't like it, then we go home," said Kitty. "We didn't set out to sail around the world no matter what. We only set out to sail and to have fun and to head west. And that was the deal with the kids. If one of us wasn't happy, then forget it; the whole boat's not going to be happy."

On that first real night at sea together, the jury was still out.

We left the harbor at noon, and by 4 p.m. Puerto Rico was beginning to fade from sight. Alex sat in the cockpit looking back at the vanishing shape of terra firma. I could tell he was somewhat anxious, so we talked about what we should expect for the next six or seven days, about how safe the boat was, and about how our friends the Lymans with their three kids were already in the San Blas Islands waiting for us.

That night Alex got seasick, and then at least once a day thereafter. It lasted only a few minutes and didn't affect his spirits or his appetite. Still, as I watched him blow lunch, I wondered whether we had done the right thing taking them out of school and starting out on this adventure. Was it really fair for me to be putting him through all this?

Alex remembers that first offshore passage—sort of. For all the years since the Kuhner family's "great escape," Scott has presented slide shows relating stories from the trip. "We've probably messed up my memory a little bit with the slide show, because we put a joke sequence in there about me getting seasick," says Alex. "Maybe I did. But we intentionally made pictures to make it look like I was getting seasick. And Spencer was laughing at me. Now, was Spencer laughing at me because I was seasick? Or because I was play-acting seasick? I don't know."

Whatever the answer, that passage was the beginning of some new direction in the Kuhner family. "There were times like the two or three dark, cloudless evenings when the stars glittered in vast profusion," wrote Scott. "On those nights we got out books about the stars and spent hours picking out such constellations as the Gemini Twins and Orion holding his shield. Alex and Spence loved learning about the constellations and would come out every night before bed to pick out some more."

Compared to many later passages, this one was rough, with easterly winds over 30 knots and peaky 10- to 15-foot seas. But Scott and Kitty were feeling pleased with their choice of boat. In one 24-hour period, *Tamure* broke the mythical 200-mile-per-day mark. Later, in more benign conditions, they found the boat comfortably averaged between 150 and 170 miles per day.

On their third night out, *Tamure* raised *Chewink* on the single-sideband radio, a ritual they repeated nightly, and those conversations with the Lymans cheered the boys. It became the highlight of each day.

And then—landfall!

"At 9:30 a.m. on January 10th we dropped anchor next to *Chewink* between two idyllic islands of the San Blas in stunningly clear, calm waters. In a flash the kids joined the three Lyman boys in the water, seasickness and angry seas instantly forgotten."

"I do remember arriving at the San Blas, how cool it was for it to come over the horizon," said Alex.

"San Blas was our first real exotic, tropical paradise," said Spencer. "It just wowed me—these white sandy beaches and tall palm trees and thatched huts all along the shore, and, you know, their traditional sailing canoes all around. It was really wild."

Here, finally, in the San Blas Islands, the Kuhner family's great escape had truly begun.

School day, *Tamure*-style. The routine included the arts and sciences, as well as learning from the ever-changing world around them and ever-present boat chores.

## A Whole New Lesson Plan

*Tamu*re's crew now settled into two sets of daily routines: one in port, another on passage. It was in the San Blas Islands that the Kuhners developed the first of these routines.

Kitty recalls the details as they were emerging:

> In the mornings we had school, and in the afternoon the kids sailed their Dyer dink ashore by themselves and played with one of the boys, Elezier, who was 12 and spoke a little Spanish (no English). He was very bright and friendly. The kids didn't talk together as much as they imitated each other. Ours taught Elezier to make potholders and braided bracelets, play with Legos, and throw a Frisbee. He taught them how to use a machete to make a sailboat from a palm frond stem or from half a coconut. They spent hours together sitting in the shade of palm trees, carving and then improving on what they had whittled or carved before. After a few hours, the surfboards came out, and all three messed around in the water.

The boys remember Elezier, too. "We got to know one local kid from an island with a family on it—like, it wasn't a town. So there wasn't *every* kid," said Alex. "There was just one kid on the island. We showed him Legos. And clearly he had heard radios before, but he hadn't heard one built into things. So when we turned on the stereo in the boat—the speakers were on a bulkhead, and the head unit was at the nav station—he was like, 'Where is the radio?'"

In the San Blas village islands, Alex and Spencer would go ashore in the afternoon. "Every time we came ashore with the boys," Scott wrote, "there would be a group of Kuna children waiting for them on the dock. Then they would all go and play together."

On one afternoon soon after *Tamure's* landfall, Scott took the boys snorkeling. "Swimming along with a kid on each side, watching them discover the wonders of skin-diving was truly a great experience," Scott wrote. "The whole afternoon was punctuated with cries of, 'Look! Look! Lobster!' Both of them became quite proficient at diving and were able to get down to look into a hole in the coral for fish. By the end of the afternoon we were able to actually get two lobsters and had a great lobster dinner that night."

Scott recalled another moment, just as they were preparing to leave San Blas. "Alex talked about how little these people have, how simple their life was, and how rich we must have seemed to them. And yet, they were so happy. Alex said that happiness came from within, not from how much money you have. This was certainly a better education than reading a Social Studies book!"

The second set of routines aboard *Tamure* was established on passage—first on the six-day run from Panama to the Galápagos, then on the 20-day run across the eastern Pacific to Hiva Oa in the Marquesas Islands.

> At about 10 a.m. every morning school started. Kitty taught English, spelling and reading while I tackled math, geography and science. At noon we normally broke for recess and lunch. After lunch, school started again with Alex and Spencer switching places so that Alex, who had been learning math on deck with me went below to study English with Kitty. Spencer, who had been below, now came up to study math with me.
>
> Normally after "school" they would close their textbooks and grab one of their story fiction books and read for pleasure while I tried to accomplish some boat maintenance chore. Alex had been reading at least 100 pages a day and went through almost all his books. One of his favorite books was *Tales of the South Pacific* by James Michener.

"I read a lot of Michener," said Alex, 11 years old at the time. "Even though some of the themes were more adult, I wanted to read all about the South Pacific. Now I think reading it would be a bit cringy—as a white guy reading another white guy writing about the Pacific islands back then. But then it was fascinating."

The school work that Alex and Spencer completed most mornings was a curriculum from the Calvert School, based in Baltimore, Maryland. Founded in

Crossing the equator, King Neptune promotes a couple of pollywogs
into shellbacks. Even the unbroken ocean has milestones.
Entering a new hemisphere deserves a celebration.

1897, Calvert offered a homeschool component as early as 1905. In the 1940s
and 1950s Exy Johnson taught her sons, Arthur and Robert, from the Calvert
School curriculum when their family was underway aboard Brigantine *Yankee*.
"It's tough!" said Robert Johnson. "It was always much easier when I was ashore
at a public school." In the 1970s and '80s, Calvert's K–8 curriculum became the
go-to homeschool program for the growing cohort of cruising families, as it was
for American diplomats and ex-pats living abroad, as well as many rural families.
As rigorous as the curriculum is, parents appreciate the clear step-by-step daily
guidance it offers. As of 2013, Calvert's homeschool component was sold to a
private owner and is known as Calvert Education Services. It is no longer affiliated
with the day school in Baltimore.

"We left when the boys were in fourth and sixth grade and came back when
they were in eighth and tenth," said Kitty. "Calvert was a fantastic program. We
would usually do schoolwork in the morning from, say, 9 to 12. But my feeling
was that we did school on the boat if there was nothing more interesting to do on
shore. So what if we don't get all four years done? That's not the end of the world.
So they keep them back a year when we get back. We just didn't worry about it."

For Alex their school schedule stands as a running gag. "We were just
constantly behind," he said. "When I was midyear through sixth grade, everyone
else was looking forward to getting out for the summer. Eventually we realized

*"And if it doesn't matter that it's Tuesday to go to the waterfall,
then it doesn't matter that it's Saturday and you have school.
Because really who cares what day it is, anyway?"*

that we should keep it moving when we can, because there are also times when school would not be the right choice. 'Let's hike to the waterfall today. It doesn't matter that it's Tuesday. The weather is good for it.' And if it doesn't matter that it's Tuesday to go to the waterfall, then it doesn't matter that it's Saturday and you have school. Because really who cares what day it is, anyway?"

When the boys weren't doing schoolwork, they found ways to entertain themselves. "We read a ton of books," said Spencer. "And I got into ropework. We had a knot book on board, and I started learning how to make Turk's heads and all kinds of decorative knots."

"Spencer and I started to do things—like, when we did have a rationed soda, we would take the can and cut it apart to have a sheet of aluminum," said Alex. "We'd fold it into a little boat and tow it behind *Tamure*. And those went from just a little boat with a rudder so it would go straight to a little boat with a folded-up square rudder to make it do a rooster tail. Eventually they had hydrofoils. In the Red Sea it would blow so hard that we then started putting sails on these. It had to be very flat but also very windy for a soda can to hydrofoil and not just flip over."

## Cruising in Company

All around the world Spencer and Alex Kuhner never lacked the company of other children.

"Upon our arrival in Wreck Bay on San Cristobal Island, Galápagos," wrote Scott, "there were five other yachts in the harbor, including *Chewink*, who had left Panama two days before us, and a steel sloop from Canada named *Windwoman*, that had two children, a boy aged 7 and a girl aged 10. That made six kids between 7 and 11 years old. Alex and Spencer were ecstatic!"

At Fakarava in the Tuamotu archipelago, Scott and Kitty went ashore to watch a spear-throwing competition. Meanwhile, Alex and Spencer joined a group of kids playing tag and swimming off the pier. "They may not have been able to talk to each other," Scott wrote, "but the language of play and laughter seems universal, and the kids were having a great time."

At Suwarrow Atoll, a lonely coral outpost between Polynesia and Samoa, *Tamure* spent five days in an anchorage populated by boats with six cruising kids. While the adults fished the reef, the kids spent their days ashore building an elaborate palm-frond fort, complete with opening doors and woven mats to sit on.

After a long Pacific crossing, Kitty Kuhner finds a terrestrial friend in the Marquesas islands. After the blues and grays of the ocean, land can feel Eden-like.

Kitty remembers the crowds of kids that gathered around *Tamure* in Niua-toputapu. "Most afternoons after school, a group of Tongan kids swam out to the boat to take turns jumping off the bowsprit or paddling around with Alex and Spencer on their Styrofoam surfboards. The younger boys would often strip naked and carefully hang their shorts on the lifeline, while the girls swam fully clothed in long dresses and then sat there dripping wet in the cockpit as we chatted, played cards or ate popcorn which I had made and passed out. If they weren't swimming off the boat, all of them, including Alex and Spencer, would be ashore jumping the 10 or 12 feet off the dock into the water and climbing out again via the big truck tires hanging as fenders alongside."

*Tamure's* New Zealand sojourn was emblematic of the ways cruising families adapt to changing circumstances. Their *plan* had been to get out of the tropics for typhoon season in the western Pacific, spend a couple of months in New Zealand's Hauraki Gulf near Auckland, make some boatyard repairs, and tour the South Island by car. But those plans changed even before *Tamure* made landfall in Opua. By radio Kitty learned that her mother had died back in St. Louis. A Kiwi friend whom the Kuhners had known from their *Bebinka* voyage quickly arranged to meet *Tamure* at the dock as soon as they cleared in and drive Kitty to the airport in Auckland. That plan was then interrupted when Scott slipped on a greasy ladder and broke two ribs. Kitty's airport run now included a detour to the local hospital until she knew Scott would be OK. For the week she was away and Scott was initially recuperating, Spencer stayed with the Lymans aboard *Chewink*,

Kitty said "We didn't set out to sail around the world no matter what.
We only set out to sail and to have fun and to head west. And that was the deal with the kids.
If one of us wasn't happy, then forget it; the whole boat's not going to be happy."
Half way around the world they were still happy.

and Alex stayed with another cruising family.

The more consequential change in plans came a couple of week later when the Kuhners were heading out on a car-camping excursion to the South Island. On a day-hike in a cow pasture, Kitty stepped into a hole and tripped, breaking her leg. X-rays revealed a spiral fracture of her tibia and a clean break of her fibula near the ankle. With the range of treatments including the possibility of a bone graft, the Kuhners now realized they needed to recalibrate entirely. They enrolled the boys in a local school, and Scott took a job with the Auckland merchant-banking firm Fay, Richwhite Equities—whose founding partner was Michael Fay, the man who in 1987 challenged Dennis Conner's San Diego Yacht Club for the America's Cup, inaugurating a Kiwi dynasty in America's Cup racing that continues today. Scott soon found himself doing a job he really liked.

Both boys remember that period fondly. "It was a great time," said Alex. "We and the Lymans all ended up in the same marina outside of Auckland, and we all went to school together. It was a tiny school, three grades in one classroom."

"I remember there was a shortcut on the way to school," said Alex Kuhner. "It was to walk over a four-foot-wide pipe over a valley where we were then above these small trees. It was probably 30 feet up. And the Lyman kids were a little bit dangerous. My first way across the pipe was to put my legs on the side and shimmy across. But the Lyman kids would walk across bouncing a basketball. So eventually I was walking across, too."

After seven months Kitty was healed enough to be able to continue on, but it was now too late in the season to sail around the bottom of South Africa, as *Bebinka* had done. They recalibrated again, retraining their sights on Indonesia, Singapore, Thailand, Sri Lanka, and the Red Sea. From there, they would return home through the Mediterranean Sea, Gibraltar, and the North Atlantic Ocean.

In the end, the Kuhners' modified plans amounted to one of the happiest periods of their lives. "Years later, I often wonder why we left New Zealand," Scott said. "The kids loved their school, we had made a number of very good friends, and I had a job with the most innovative and probably the best brokerage in the country. Everything was perfect. I guess it was the desire to finish what we had started that made us willing to move on."

After yet another rough passage from the zones of variable winds to the tropics, once again the *Tamure* crew found plenty of kids when they arrived in New Caledonia. "On the Fourth of July, 13 yachts, nine Americans, three Kiwis, and an Aussie went to a deserted bay to celebrate with a good old barbecue," Scott remembered. "For two days we relaxed, swam, snorkeled and played on the beach. Half the boats had kids. One morning all 11 kids went ashore and cooked their own breakfast over an open fire. That night Alex and the girl on the boat next to us stayed up for hours, each sitting on the bow of their own boat, talking away as 13-year-old kids anywhere do."

Yes, the boys were maturing—partly as the inevitable consequence of growing older, but also in ways that were uniquely shaped by their uncommon environment. "If there were no kids, we'd just hang out with the adults," said Alex. "I learned to talk to adults much earlier than other kids did."

Alex most vividly remembers piloting up the Red Sea. "There was one time when I was annoyed with Mom for not trusting me. She came up and said, 'There are ships everywhere!' And I'm like, 'I know. I have my eye on all of them. I know where they all are and where they're headed.' Obviously we didn't have AIS then. But we took sights on the ships. And listened to music in between."

Still, meeting other cruising kids was always a highlight. And Cyprus proved the best place for doing just that. "I don't feel like there was ever a point where we were starved for other kids to hang out with," said Spencer. *Tamure* spent two months in a Cyprus boatyard while Scott sorted through engine problems and other items on the maintenance checklist. "For whatever reason, there were a bunch of kids on boats. There must have been 20 of us, just roaming around the marina causing a ruckus and having a grand old time."

Alex and Spencer still keep in touch with those kids with whom they spent eight weeks in Cyprus 30 years ago.

## Bringing It All Back Home

When *Tamure* returned to Connecticut in April 1991, Alex was near the end of 9th grade; Spencer near the end of 7th. With just six weeks left in the term, Kitty put them back in school to determine which grade level was the best fit.

"It wasn't a particularly hard transition," said Spencer. "I got to be friends with a lot of my old friends. Not to say that Alex had a hard time, but I think the socialization was a little bit more of a shock to his system than it was for me. The cliques are really formed in high school, not quite as much in middle school."

"When I first got back, no one knew how to categorize me," said Alex. "'Is he a popular kid? What are those weird clothes?' For a little bit the popular kids and the alternative kids were open to having me around. And then I decided that the alternative kids were more fun."

Kitty had to jump through several hoops to make sure Alex got credit for the work he'd done. "I found out that Alex needed certain things to call 9th grade behind him. The English teacher said, 'Well, he hasn't read *Romeo and Juliet.*' I said, "No, but he's read every single thing that James Michener has ever written.' The kids read *all the time* on the boat."

Alex and Spencer both ultimately graduated in the top five percent of their class. That said, the true measure of their education—and the experience underpinning it—showed up more in the broad range of their studies than in numbers measured by grade point average or test scores. Alex enrolled in an innovative Japanese Studies program for his final two years of high school, traveling twice to Japan before going to college.

"I got Spencer into that program, too, because who wasn't bored of high school?" said Alex. "So then Spencer and I traveled to Japan—our first time traveling without our parents."

It's so often fascinating to see how siblings from the same household go on to lead lives that differ fundamentally from each other. And so it is with Alex and Spencer.

"I just decided I like a paycheck," said Alex. "I like that stability." His family's favorite mode of travel is to explore "cities with nice museums from a base in a hotel." While living in Japan he even convinced his parents to come try traveling his way for a change.

Spencer, by contrast, has traced a more peripatetic life path. "For all my 20s I don't think I spent more than a year in any one place." At age 18 he backpacked solo in Europe for several weeks. Since then, he's worked in the music industry, as a sailmaker, as professional yacht crew, as a licensed captain, and as a consumer-advocate lawyer. "A highlight of my professional sailing career was a six-month cruise in 2005 aboard an Outremer 55, sailing from Los Angeles down to the

South Pacific and ending in New Zealand," Spencer said. "I got to revisit many of the islands that we had been to on *Tamure*, and was even able to track down a number of locals we had been friends with, including some my parents had met during their trip in the 1970s."

A common thread Alex and Spencer still share with each other and with their parents is *Tamure*. Scott and Kitty took her back out for an Atlantic Circle from 2003 to 2005 after the boys finished school, which together with their two circumnavigations earned them the CCA's 2017 Far Horizons award. For many seasons after 2005, they sailed north and south, from Maine to the Bahamas. But since 2018 they've stepped back from sailing. "I've had bad neuropathy in my feet after knee surgery, which means my sense of balance is off," Scott said. "I don't feel comfortable on the boat anymore."

Yet the boys still do. Alex and Spencer spent the summer of 2020 in a refit project they deemed "a transfer of captainship." In November, Spencer set off southbound with a friend—through one of those raucous blows where the variables meet the trades—once again taking *Tamure* back to the latitudes the whole Kuhner family came to love so well.

*Cloud Nine*, a Bowman 57, took Roger Swanson and company around the world
for the trip of a lifetime—then again, in ever-widening circles.
Curiosity, persistence, and good fellowship marked over 200,000 miles at sea.

# 13

# Thirty Christmas Letters:
# Recalling 200,000 Miles
# with Roger Swanson and *Cloud Nine*

A typical circumnavigation is about 27,000 miles. Roger's circumnavigations
would be 80,000 or 100,000 miles, because he doesn't take the traditional route.
That's what makes his cruising so interesting. He'll go by way of Antarctica
and Alaska and South Africa, and he just trots all over the world.

—David Thoreson

*Cloud Nine* crewmember on nine voyages over 16 years


He wasn't necessarily an explorer, although he would have been a good one.
He wasn't necessarily an ecologist, but he still had an interest in the world
he was sailing in. He was an adventurer. He just liked to have adventures,
and he liked to share those adventures with people, and he had a lot of fun doing it.
People enjoyed his company and he enjoyed theirs, and if they had a good sense
of humor, he enjoyed that a lot.

—Steven Swanson

Roger's son


Gaynelle Templin asked her husband how he'd like to spend his 80th birthday.

"What I'd really like to do," Roger Swanson replied, "is gather as many as
possible of the 310 former crewmembers who have sailed aboard *Cloud Nine*
for a party to celebrate our shared sailing experiences."

The word went out for the summer of 2011, and to Dunnell, Minnesota—homeport of Swanson's world-girdling Bowman 57 ketch, *Cloud
Nine*—proceeded 169 vagabonds and wanderers and grizzled seafarers from
all over the United States, Canada, and the British Isles. The number of party

"How would you like to celebrate your 80th birthday?" Gaynelle Templin asked her husband. By gathering as many past *Cloud Nine* crewmates as possible to Dunnell, MN, he replied. One hundred and sixty-nine showed up.

guests exceeded Dunnell's population, according to the 2010 census, by two souls.

"We couldn't find all of our shipmates," said Roger, "and we learned that 22 of them had made their final passage. But the others came to attend our weekend pig roast among the Minnesota cornfields. The gathering was informal, and guests spent idle time browsing through my collection of artifacts from distant cruising destinations, including an eight-foot-long 'spirit house' carving from Vanuatu's Ambrym Island, a set of masks from New Guinea's Sepik River, and a lion spear from Kenya. The walls of our bathrooms are also papered with previously used charts, and over 400 framed photos are hung on the corresponding places on the charts where the pictures were taken."

Many of the guests had never been to sea before coming aboard *Cloud Nine*, and many were the lives that were deeply altered for that experience. "Because crew changes often took place in remote spots to accommodate work and vacation schedules, I hadn't seen many of these faces for many years," wrote Roger, "not since leaving them on a distant dock in Mozambique or Papua New Guinea or maybe even Dutch Harbor, Alaska."

Cynthia Bowell was one of Roger's shipmates who came to Dunnell. "The beauty of this event," she said, "was that no matter who you were sitting next to, you had so much in common, and the stories were so easy to share. Everyone had unique experiences in places that most people can only dream about."

### The Trip of a Lifetime (So Far)
Let's flip the calendar back to 1982, the year Roger first tried voyaging. "It has not been my custom to send a Christmas letter, but this year it will be the most

*This was the first of 30 Christmas letters Roger sent
to an ever-growing list of friends and family
in ever-widening circles of geography.*

practical means to communicate," he wrote. "It is a bit lengthy, but touches on the high spots that may be of interest to you. So bear with me for getting a little carried away with detail on a project that has occupied my attention the past several months."

This was the first of 30 Christmas letters Roger sent to an ever-growing list of friends and family in ever-widening circles of geography. Three years after Roger made his own final passage at age 81—he died on Christmas day, 2012—Gaynelle gathered and edited these letters, and the photos that accompanied them, and published them in a lovely book called *Cloud Nine: A Christmas Update*.

Born and raised in St. Paul, Roger had joined the U.S. Navy after graduating from the University of Minnesota with a degree in electrical engineering. While stationed aboard the destroyer *USS Henley*, he befriended a fellow officer who loved to sail. As the ship landed at ports all around the world, Roger's friend somehow found boats for the two to take sailing, and these outings kindled something in the once dirt-bound Midwesterner. Home again after his service, Roger started a family on the Minnesota farm he took over from aunts and uncles he'd often visited as a child—a property that under his stewardship grew to 1,400 acres and 1,800 pigs. He married and had three children. He started some businesses, including such light-manufacturing companies as Glasstite, which made fiberglass truck toppers; others made snow blowers and tractor cabs and snowmobiles and farm equipment. He became the president of a local bank his relatives had started. In 1976 Roger's wife, June, died. Their children—Steven, Lynne, and Philip—were 18, 12, and 7 at the time.

It was on Roger's 50th birthday in 1981 that his high-school-aged daughter posed the question that, as he says, "hit me between the eyes."

"When are you going to sail around the world?" Lynne prodded. "That night I started planning," said Roger.

Planning, it turns out, is something that Roger Swanson was very, very good at. He set up managers to run his farm and his businesses. He bought a 1975 British-built Bowman 57 ketch. He organized sailing crew to round out his family foursome. And then he set off.

"Last spring Lynne graduated from Sherburn High School, and Steven received his bachelor of architecture from the University of Minnesota," wrote

A sailor can never catch up to a rainbow or an horizon: reason enough to keep sailing.

Roger in that first Christmas letter. "This seemed like quite a milestone, so we decided to celebrate by sailing around the world."

On July 18, 1982, *Cloud Nine,* with a crew of ten including Steven, Lynne, Philip, and me, set sail from Miami hoping to sail west until we arrive back in Miami again, possibly two years or so later. We headed into the Bahamas, stopping at Nassau and San Salvador (paying respects to C. Columbus), on through the Windward Passage between Cuba and Hispaniola.

We spent a pleasant week in Jamaica where Lynne and two other crew members left us as planned. Lynne had to get back to her horse shows and make final preparations to enter the University of Minnesota in the fall. After she left we set sail for Cartagena, Colombia, a passage that included some fairly heavy weather with seas running up to twenty feet. Five weary days later we passed under the guns of several old Spanish forts that once guarded Cartagena. This was a major port of call for the Spanish treasure fleets that returned untold riches to Spain from the New World so many years ago. In fact, they brought back so much treasure that Spain had no need to tax its people for over 300 years.

*Already in his first Christmas letter Roger was setting out themes that would guide the next three decades of his life—a wide-ranging cultural and historical curiosity, a willingness to trade rough passages at sea for rich experiences in new places, and an enduring connection to his home and family back in Minnesota.*

Already in his first Christmas letter Roger was setting out themes that would guide the next three decades of his life—a wide-ranging cultural and historical curiosity, a willingness to trade rough passages at sea for rich experiences in new places, and an enduring connection to his home and family back in Minnesota.

*Cloud Nine* transited the Panama Canal, then called at the Galápagos Islands en route to the Marquesas and the Tuamotus and the rest of French Polynesia. "Bora Bora is considered by James Michener to be the most beautiful island in the world. It is also the mystical Bali Hai of *South Pacific* fame. In any case, we like it very much and will find it hard to leave.

"We want to wish you a Merry Christmas and a Happy New Year from the South Pacific. You are very much in our thoughts. In a remote part of the world such as this, one often reflects on his relatives and friends, probably more so than one would normally do in the hustle and bustle of everyday life at home. We do miss you and would enjoy hearing from you."

In that first year, Roger and *Cloud Nine* were following the typical trade-wind route traced by so many cruising circumnavigators of that time. But by his second Christmas letter, Roger began to tell of passages that distinguished his voyaging from others.

I will bring you up to date on our sailing saga aboard *Cloud Nine*. My letter last year was written from Bora Bora in French Polynesia. From there we visited Rarotonga in the Cook Islands where we saw the bones of the brigantine *Yankee* of *National Geographic* fame high on the reef. [Under her third set of owners after Irving and Exy Johnson, *Yankee* broke free from her anchor during a July 1964 gale and shipwrecked.] Next came American Samoa, the only U.S. territory south of the equator.

At this point there were four of us who had sailed all the way from Miami: Steven, Philip, Tami (Steven's fiancée), and I. The other crew members rotate about every three months on a prearranged schedule.

My daughter, Lynne, joined us in Guam to spend six weeks with us. We also met a Japanese woman, Tamie Hishinuma Jacobs, who sailed with us to Japan. Her knowledge of the language and Japanese history was invaluable. During the following days we visited many WWII sites including the marine landing areas on Guam, the bomb pits on Tinian where the two atom bombs were loaded aboard B-29s headed for Japan, the battlefields and suicide cliffs of Saipan, the prison where a persistent rumor claims that Amelia Earhart may have been held prisoner, and many other familiar names and places. It was a thought-provoking experience to visit these wartime sites with a descendent of a Japanese Samurai family who was old enough to remember as a child of ten the skies glowing red from the firebombing of Tokyo and Yokohama.

We arrived in Japan running ahead of typhoon Abbey and found refuge in Yokosuka Harbor, which was familiar to me having anchored there in 1953 during my navy days. After several days in the Tokyo–Yokohama–Kamakura area, we sailed through the Inland Sea of Japan and down the west side of Kyushu to Okinawa. En route we visited Kobe, Osaka, Kyoto, Nara, Matsuyama, the Island of Shikoku, Hiroshima, Sasebo, and Nagasaki. We learned much about Japanese Imperial history, particularly in the Kyoto–Nara area with Tamie Jacobs explaining many interesting personal highlights.

The hospitality of the Japanese people was unbelievable and we were treated like royalty wherever we stopped. One of the high spots was a tour of a Toyota factory after they had machined a replacement stainless steel fitting for *Cloud Nine* without charge. All around us we saw overwhelming evidence of Japan's industrial progress. It is also interesting to note that we see many Japanese tourists wherever we stop. Lynne left us at Osaka, informing us she would be back as soon as school was out in the spring.

The coming and going of different crew members would emerge as one of the keys to the whole *Cloud Nine* project. "A lot of the crew were not sailors at all," said CCA member David Thoreson, who sailed 40,000 miles aboard *Cloud Nine* over 16 years. "Many of them were friends of Roger's from around Dunnell. They might have been farmers or physicians or somebody who really wanted the experience. They might be a great cook. Roger was really kind of a genius at putting people together."

The way Tamie Hishinuma Jacobs opened the perspective of everyone aboard in light of the places they visited in Japan—that became a hallmark of *Cloud Nine's* voyages.

Two years and three months after setting off, *Cloud Nine* closed the circle of

*But something his sailing friend Rona House wrote to him
from chilly England stuck with him: "It is possible
to have remission from sea fever, but it is incurable."*

her first circumnavigation. Swanson had satisfied his long-held dream.

"Several months previously we set Friday, November 2, as arrival day in Miami," Roger wrote in his third Christmas letter, sent in 1984. "My friend Paul Buhler (who introduced me to sailing twenty-eight years ago) set up a party for 5 p.m. at the same berth we left in July 1982. Paul and his brother, Peter, met *Cloud Nine* at the sea buoy outside Miami harbor in two power boats with Mother, Dad, Lynne, and several good friends aboard. It was an emotion-filled moment as we cheered and waved across the water to our family and friends after being away for so long. With all sails including spinnaker flying, we entered the channel and at 5:05 docked at slip 240, Miamarina, where the rest of our friends and a gala party awaited.

"Our trip was over! 838 days, 36,612 nautical miles, and many, many experiences were behind us. Steve and Phil made the entire trip with me, while other crew members rotated with time on board varying from six weeks to fifteen months. At any one time we had as few as four and as many as ten aboard. In all, thirty-two crew members participated, and it was a learning and sharing experience for everyone. We were glad to be back and thankful for the blessings and protection we had received along the way."

## Nowhere Is Too Far

Roger may have been glad to be back home after all those miles at sea. But something his sailing friend Rona House wrote to him from chilly England stuck with him: "It is possible to have remission from sea fever, but it is incurable."

And so it was for him. His (short) fourth Christmas letter of 1985 told mostly of Minnesota. "It is now thirteen months since we returned to Miami aboard *Cloud Nine* completing our circumnavigation. Since then we have been absorbed by the day-to-day world around us that seems to demand all our energies.

"Steven has started a small business in Santa Fe and is making his debut in the architectural world. Lynne is still at the University of Minnesota, feverishly trying to cram four years into five. Philip is back with his old classmates as a junior at Sherburn High School, trying to concentrate on matters other than football and social activities. I stay busy with the routine responsibilities of work and trying to keep up with the kids.

Roger Swanson divided his life into alternating segments: three months on the farm, three months underway on *Cloud Nine*.

"As we look out the window at the unseasonably early white world of Minnesota, memories flood back. Bora Bora, Chi Chi Jima, Hong Kong, Sri Lanka, Santorini, Madeira, and many more."

The 1986 Christmas letter reveals the stirrings that would become the stuff of Roger's and *Cloud Nine's* worldwide reputation. "The big news for me," he wrote, "is selling my business, Glasstite Inc., to Raven Industries of Sioux Falls last April. The company has grown nicely the past few years, and it seemed to be a good opportunity for me to walk away.

"With the kids settled, I gathered a crew of friends last January and island-hopped aboard *Cloud Nine* from Grenada to St. Thomas. It was a nice trip made particularly interesting by running into friends we had met earlier in various parts of the world: New Zealand, Australia, Thailand, Sudan, Turkey, Madeira. Rona, the English girl who found sea fever incurable, lives on *Cloud Nine* and takes good care of her."

Roger and his crew sailed *Cloud Nine* transatlantic by way of Bermuda and the Azores to Southampton, England, for a refit after 10 years of ocean voyaging—a work list that grew still longer after one particular rogue wave during heavy North Atlantic weather.

The 1987 Christmas letter recounts 13,000 miles of sailing that brought Roger and *Cloud Nine* from England, across the Atlantic to the Caribbean, then down the coast of South America to Ushuaia, Argentina. Whether Roger knew it or not at the time, this landfall marked the beginning of his second circumnavigation. His Christmas letter from four years later (1991) tells the last chapter of that saga.

"On December 8 we passed through the Straits of LeMaire between Staten Island and the southeastern tip of Tierra Del Fuego. The last one thousand miles has been pretty heavy going at times with continuous reefing and sail changes in strong and erratic wind patterns. We were glad to enter the relatively calm waters of the Beagle Canal, and the anchor splashed down at Ushuaia at 1225 on December 9 after thirty-seven-and-a-half days at sea.

"This also marked another milestone for me as it was the completion of my second circumnavigation: Ushuaia westward around the world to Ushuaia again in a little under four years. I can't help but wonder how many have used Ushuaia as the beginning and end of a circumnavigation. Probably not very many."

It was during this second circumnavigation that Roger perfected *Cloud Nine*'s voyaging routine. He now divided his life into three-month segments that alternated between time in Minnesota and time at sea. When he was away from *Cloud Nine*, one or more of the seasoned crew would remain aboard to take care of the boat, keeping her ready for the next voyage. For the sailing Roger arranged crews of six that constituted three experienced hands, including himself, plus three others who may or may not have had prior sailing experience. David Thoreson laughs when he reads about how many people *Cloud Nine* carried on her first voyage. "Man, I can't even imagine 10 people aboard," he said. "Somewhere through that voyage, Roger kind of settled in on six people being the perfect crew size."

In that arrangement, the three most experienced sailors became watch captains in a four-on, eight-off system; the three others would also take four-hour watches but with the cycles offset by two hours. In this way, each time a new person came on deck, someone was already on who had become acclimated to the situation and conditions; information flowed seamlessly through the watches. All crew except Roger shared cooking duties in a cycle that rotated every five days: dinner and the next day's lunch, with that day's cook responsible for cleanup. Every day, even in dirty weather, everyone except the on-deck watch gathered for meals at 1200 and 1800—the only times of the day that all crew members would see each other. "When you sailed with Roger, you basically threw in for expenses, but it wouldn't break the bank," said David. "Roger wanted to keep the cost of sailing on *Cloud Nine* accessible to anyone who was willing to create the time in their lives to be aboard. He wanted others to share in the experience."

In this way *Cloud Nine* sailed to Antarctica, Pitcairn Island, Polynesia, New Zealand, Australia, Papua New Guinea, Indonesia, Thailand, Sri Lanka, Kenya,

When a German freighter dismasted *Cloud Nine* at a dock in Polynesia,
the insurance company declared her a total loss. But not Roger Swanson;
he created a jury rig and crossed half the Pacific to New Zealand to install a new rig.

*"He worked through problems like a scientist, you know,*
*just dissecting what the problem was and what we needed to do,*
*and then to engage the crew."*

Zanzibar, Madagascar, and South Africa before crossing the South Atlantic back to Argentina.

The flexibility of this rig faced its ultimate test in October 1988 when the German container ship *Urte* collided with *Cloud Nine* as she was docked in Rarotonga, bringing down the main mast. After complicated international negotiations, the ship's insurance company offered Roger $300,000 to declare *Cloud Nine* a total loss. But Roger wasn't done with her yet.

"We jerry-rigged the boat using a spinnaker boom to extend our mast stump from 22 to 36 feet," wrote Roger. "By so doing we could carry our two staysails as jibs, our storm jib as a staysail, and our storm trysail as a main. On November 3 we headed for New Zealand via Tonga. We fine-tuned our jerry-rigged boat and found it quite satisfactory, giving us five or six knots in moderate trade winds."

This event was just one step in the ladder of ever-greater challenges Roger encountered and sometimes even sought. "Roger had a calm, methodic demeanor," said David. "He worked through problems like a scientist, you know, just dissecting what the problem was and what we needed to do, and then to engage the crew. And we worked through whatever it was we needed to do, trying to get something fixed, or working hard to get from A to B with a process that he put in place."

David first joined *Cloud Nine* in Cape Town, November 1991, toward the end of her second circumnavigation. He'd never sailed on the ocean before that. Raised near Lake Okoboji, Iowa, just 35 miles away from Roger's farm, David had known the Swansons by reputation; they'd raced small boats on each other's lakes. "Before *Cloud Nine,* Roger and Steven sailed C-Scows and wanted to get better," said David. "That was during an era when we had seven or eight national champions right here from Okoboji. Our C-Scow fleet was one of the best in the country, and Roger had a lot of respect for the sailors here."

By 1990 David had become interested in Antarctica, and he called the Swanson farm in Dunnell. Before that, he'd traveled cross-country and internationally by bicycle and other means, and he'd built a successful photography business. He'd also done some journalism.

The Bowman 57, featured as one of the stand-out examples in Arthur Beiser's 1978 edition of *The Proper Yacht*, proved ideal for Roger's style of voyaging.

Bowman Yachts of Hampshire, England, commissioned the 57 design in the early 1970s from the British firm of Kim Holman and Donald Pye, a partnership best known for Oyster Yachts' early models. *Cloud Nine* was either hull number three or four of a total 14 Bowman 57s built; there was always ambiguity about which slots were held by *Cloud Nine* and her 1975 sister ship *English Rose* in that progression. The Bowman's interior layout provided double bunk-bed sleeping cabins for for four, plus an owner's suite aft, while preserving the forepeak for storage and the main saloon as a public social space for the whole crew. Two cockpits and separate helm stations provided hydraulic steering near midships for optimal docking visibility, and cable steering farther aft for better feel under sail. The staysail ketch rig divided the boat's 1,300 square feet of sail area into manageable sails that even new sailors in their middle age could handle at sea.

"So I interviewed Roger for a story, and then he interviewed me about sailing with him," said David. "Because it's so windy here on Okoboji, Roger knew that if I was racing Scows, I had a really good background for sail trim and the way boats work efficiently."

David wanted to sign on for Roger's next trip to Antarctica. "He told me, 'You can't go to Antarctica until you make a long bluewater passage with me so I can see how you operate.'"

Before David ever stepped aboard *Cloud Nine,* he faced Roger's first test.

"Be in Cape Town, South Africa, and meet us in the marina," Roger said.

"How will I find you?"

"You'll find us," was Roger's only reply.

"So I fly into Johannesburg to clear customs," said David. "This is during Apartheid, and I have 10,000 frames of film and 20 hours of video tape and mountains of gear with me. And, you know, this is at a time when they're killing journalists. So they pull me into a side room where these guys in military dress with guns start opening my bags and staring at me and asking, 'What are you doing here?' And I say, 'I just want to let you know that I'm here to meet a sailboat. I have a letter right here.' And I pull out the letter on *Cloud Nine* letterhead and say, 'This explains what I'm doing.' I hand it to the official, and he goes, 'Oh, I know about this boat. She just rounded the Cape of Good Hope recently, and she's sitting down in the harbor right now in Cape Town. If you are on that vessel, good luck to you, and have a nice voyage across the Atlantic.' And they never even check my bags. The power of a letter from Roger and *Cloud Nine* opened that door for me."

For the next 38 days, David sailed 6,000 miles, and he never wanted it to end. "That trip across the South Atlantic opened up a world that I had only dreamed of as a boy, and I loved it. I learned that I don't get seasick. I was young

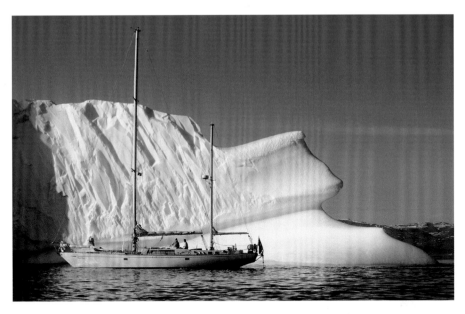

*Cloud Nine* spent some of her last voyages with Roger in the ice: first Antarctica,
then the Northwest Passage, which she successfully transited in a single season in 2007.

and dancing around the foredeck and having fun. If ever Roger needed somebody
anywhere, including up the rig, I'd say, 'Send me up there.' I was happy doing it."

When Roger left *Cloud Nine* to spend Christmas 1991 with his family, David
stayed with the boat in the Beagle Channel. And then came Antarctica.

### Learning to Love the Ice

"How different from a year ago!" wrote Roger in his 1992 Christmas letter. "Last
year I started my letter aboard *Cloud Nine*, beating our way south into the 'roaring
forties' in the South Atlantic Ocean en route to Cape Horn. My study here in
Dunnell is much more peaceful and the lack of excitement is somewhat welcome
for a change.

"The good news in our family is the marriage of Philip to Laura Lausen of
Estherville, Iowa, last May. The rest of the family is continuing much as before
with Mother active and well. Steven and Ana are following their art careers. Ana is
selling art in Santa Fe and Steven is showing in Minneapolis, Chicago, New York,
and Santa Fe. Lynne continues to work in Stillwater managing a fleet car division.

"For those interested in following the *Cloud Nine* saga, I will go on," Roger
wrote. "This was probably the most exciting year ever for us."

I returned to Ushuaia from Minnesota on January 5, carrying a
new cylinder head for the engine in my hand luggage. We had the head

installed and the engine running that night. Unfortunately, the engine was still below par as it was using far too much oil, but we felt we could make it. Another problem was that the new diesel heater we had installed in South Africa to prepare for this trip was not working. This meant no heat in Antarctica. We weighed our situation carefully. There was no way to get spare parts or repairs down here in time to make the January time window for Antarctica. We either had to go now or give up the trip. We decided to go for it.

Quite by accident we met John Ridgeway in Puerto Williams. He is a very well-known Scot who has made two circumnavigations in *English Rose*, a sister ship to *Cloud Nine*. The first was an early Whitbread around the world race. In 1984, his second circumnavigation set a world record for the fastest double-handed non-stop around the world passage in history [203 days], beating the previous record by eighty days.

We headed south, reaching Cape Horn in the usual miserable, rainy, windy weather so typical of this infamous cape. We passed within two miles, so we got a good look at old "Cape Stiff" before setting a south-easterly course to cross the Drake Passage from Cape Horn to Antarctica.

The Drake is six hundred miles of the most challenging waters in the world. The winds were from the south making for heavy going under double-reefed mainsail and working staysail.

We were battered pretty hard the first 48 hours by 35- to 40-knot headwinds with rain or sleet much of the time. Waves would frequently break over the boat and flood the cockpit, which might compare with having bathtubs full of cold saltwater dumped over our heads every few minutes.

One of our goals was to try to cross the Antarctic Circle, an achievement that had escaped us in 1988. To the best of my knowledge, only one other American yacht has crossed the Circle, and that happened about three years ago. We knew the only way we could accomplish this was to stand well out to sea because the sheltered channels between the islands along the west side of the Antarctic Peninsula and the mainland were filled with ice. We decided to go for the Circle first and try to work our way into the islands and channels as we headed back north.

Because of our concerns about our engine, we decided to use sail power only, except for emergencies and to charge our batteries. We continued south and were starting to see a lot of ice, huge sculptured masses of white that came looming out of the fog. Cherie exclaimed, "That berg is bigger than Dunnell, Minnesota!" She was right. Many bergs towered above us, some 200 to 300 feet high.

Downwind from the large bergs were many small fragments or "bergy bits" that break off and form a trail of debris. These small pieces were the most dangerous to us. In rough weather it is difficult to distinguish them from whitecaps, and many of them were large enough to easily punch a hole in our fiberglass hull, which would sink us.

Only 30 miles from the Circle we were confronted by a line of large icebergs that looked bad. We finally found a pass between them, hoping it would be better on the other side. We did get through the big bergs, but on the other side we found ourselves in a sea of brash ice. As we went south it got worse. Finally, only 25 miles from our goal, we reluctantly had to turn back. It was too dangerous. We had to get out of here while it was still possible. If a wind came up causing rough seas, it would take only one of these Volkswagen-sized bergy bits to do us in.

After several anxious hours on a northwesterly course, we were able to work our way free of the ice and we could breathe more easily.

We were headed west in open water about five miles and decided to try one more time. The weather was reasonably good and with the wind behind us we headed south again. Finally, at 0519 on the morning of January 9, WE MADE IT. The Antarctic Circle, 66 degrees, 33 minutes south!

We had a temporary clearing in the weather and we could see the Antarctic mainland in the distance on our port bow, but we knew the coastline was choked with ice and we would have to return 100 miles or more north before we could approach it. After a brief celebration, we turned north into the wind. The deck was covered with snow and ice and all lines were wet, making for soaked mittens and cold hands.

As we clawed our way north, close-hauled into a biting wind, a northeast gale descended on us. The next four days were the toughest I have ever spent at sea.

Roger's 1992 Christmas letter tells in harrowing detail what came next: the lack of cabin heat, the dripping condensation, the soaked clothing, the cold, the fatigue. Meanwhile, *Cloud Nine* crashed through 20-foot seas studded with solid ice. Sleet stung the faces of those on watch. The wind's roar drowned out the screaming of the person standing by the shrouds watching for ice. Meanwhile, small fragments scraped ominously, continually, along the fiberglass hull.

"By the time we were allowed into Palmer Station, the U.S. scientific base, we were barely operational as a vessel," said David. "We just got absolutely hammered by storms down there: big, big winds and seas and icebergs and ice all the time. We had no heat on board. The warmest the cabin got was 37 degrees. We had open saltwater sores on our faces from exposure. Cherie had a black eye and a head contusion. It was old-school the way we entered the harbor there: telltales and compass. We called it the Shackleton tour."

With all that behind them, the *Cloud Nine* crew spent the next days ashore on the Antarctic Peninsula, days that Roger described as "wonderful." They supped with the Palmer Station staff and enjoyed hot showers and changed out of their clothes for the first time in two weeks.

"One of our friends at Palmer took us up on the glacier above the station (something one does not do alone) where we could look out over the Bismarck Strait and east across the Gerlache Strait to the Antarctic mainland," wrote Roger. "It was indescribably beautiful."

Thoreson published a sumptuously illustrated book called *Over the Horizon: Exploring the Edges of a Changing Planet* (2016). His description of leaving Dorian Bay to cross the Drake Passage back to the South American continent captures the way moments like these can work on a certain kind of soul. "It is snowing as hard as I have ever seen it snow, and we are sailing through slush. I cannot ever recall a more uncomfortable stretch of bad weather, combined with stress, in my life. I learned that I can take a hell of a lot of punishment and still keep an optimistic attitude. This has made me a stronger person, and I can face life with a renewed sense of confidence. Lastly, I know I want to do more sailing, which I find a wonderful way of existence."

The Antarctic had changed everyone aboard.

David recalls rejoining previous crew in Argentina. Jamie had been first mate on earlier *Cloud Nine* passages, including David's first transatlantic crossing. But having broken her arm, she was unable to make the Antarctica trip. "By the time we got back to Cape Horn," said David, "we'd endured 80 or 90 knots of wind and 40- to 50-foot seas and icebergs and ice. We were so well-versed in heavy wind that when we started sailing back up the coast shorthanded with only four of us aboard and the wind kicked up to 55 knots, Roger and I started experimenting with different sail sets for heaving to. Jamie and Carl hadn't had all that heavy-air experience, so when we started turning back into that wind on purpose—to find the best way to heave to efficiently and comfortably—they thought we were absolutely bonkers."

Something else happened under all that stress: Roger and David and others began planning for their next adventure—a transit of the Northwest Passage.

That's where Gaynelle Templin comes in. "How I met Roger is I crewed for him," she said. "I had a boat up on Lake Superior, a 27-foot Erickson, and I

*"I cannot ever recall a more uncomfortable stretch of bad weather, combined with stress, in my life. I learned that I can take a hell of a lot of punishment and still keep an optimistic attitude."*

wanted saltwater experience. I was going to sail around the world down the line after I retired. Well, I crewed for Roger one year on *Cloud Nine,* and then I crewed for him again the next year. The third year we got married."

A registered nurse, Gaynelle was working as a computer-systems analyst when she first joined *Cloud Nine*. Because she hadn't yet retired, she could sail for only monthlong stints in those first two seasons. Looking back after almost 30 years—having subsequently taken on the role of first mate for the longest of *Cloud Nine's* three circumnavigations, Gibraltar to Gibraltar, against the trade winds, and with seven years' worth of detours that more than trebled the distance of the earth's circumference—Gaynelle still fondly recalls her first passage aboard *Cloud Nine* in 1994. "That was a good one for me. It was from St. Thomas up to Nova Scotia. It was in preparation for Roger's first Northwest Passage."

Roger's summary of that trip, as told in his 1994 Christmas letter, is brief. "In early May we headed north to visit the Arctic and to attempt to transit the Northwest Passage from the Atlantic to the Pacific. We made it as far as 70° 40' north, 95° 25' west before we were turned back by the ice. That is ten miles west of Dunnell, Minnesota—but nearly 500 miles north of the Arctic Circle. Our tale is covered in the enclosed booklet, which speaks for itself. We left *Cloud Nine* in England with tentative plans to cruise the Baltic next spring. Happy holidays and remember, reef early."

The booklet he mentions, *An Arctic Experience Aboard Cloud Nine,* is included as an appendix in the book *Cloud Nine: A Christmas Update* that Gaynelle published in 2015. It is an indispensable record of a world that no longer exists. Though Gaynelle wasn't aboard for that first attempt, she and Roger tried the Northwest Passage again in 2005, and again *Cloud Nine* failed to penetrate that quasi-mythical waterway.

In 2007—with Gaynelle and David aboard—*Cloud Nine* was back in the Northwest Passage again, this time to bear witness to the moment that everything changed. "We are the first Americans to complete Roald Amundsen's route in a single year," David wrote. "The golden age of exploration, Amundsen's, has come to a close, and a changing climate will be the focus of a new era of exploration. We on *Cloud Nine* have bridged the two eras. We were solidly stuck in the Arctic's vast pack ice in 1994. And now we have sailed through the same route."

*"More than 200 people without any sailing experience
came through* Cloud Nine*," said Gaynelle.
"That's what he felt was an accomplishment."*

The DVD *Cloud Nine Returns to the Northwest Passage Once Again*, produced by Roger and Gaynelle, shows comparative video footage from 1994, 2005, and 2007. Bays and straits that are impenetrable in the earlier years are open water in the final version. It is another indispensable record of a world that no longer exists.

"More than half of all successful voyages through the Northwest Passage have taken place since 2007," David wrote in *Over the Horizon*. "In 1994, when we first attempted it, ours was one of two sailboats to try and fail, although four ice-breaking vessels succeeded. In 2007, there were five successful attempts, including two ice-breaking vessels. In the three years since, hundreds of new adventurers have flocked to the Northwest Passage."

Since that 2007 passage David has devoted his life to witnessing the changes in the far North. In 2009 he joined the crew of *Ocean Watch*, skippered by CCA member Mark Schrader, for a 13-month expedition called Around the Americas—a circumnavigation of North and South America. In so doing, David became the first American yachtsman to transit the Northwest Passage in both directions.

David was aboard *Cloud Nine* in Alaska's Inside Passage in 2000 when he got word from back in Iowa that his dad had died. It took two days to arrange a seaplane to get him off the boat and back home. "Take good care of yourself," David said to Roger before leaving the boat. "You're the only father I have left in the world."

## No Place Like Home

Roger did take good care of himself, for 12 more years. "Roger Swanson was one of the greatest long-distance voyagers of this era or any other era," wrote Herb McCormick in *Cruising World* magazine after he made his final passage at age 81. "Few sailors have gone from the Arctic to the Antarctic and everywhere in between. He was one of a kind."

Roger's accomplishments weren't merely what the hikers call peak-bagging. "More than 200 people without any sailing experience came through *Cloud Nine*," said Gaynelle. "That's what he felt was an accomplishment. Let me tell you: having all these people come out to a farm in southern Minnesota for his 80th birthday party—we had to roast two pigs."

Now living back on Lake Mille Lacs, Minnesota, just seven miles from where

Roger Swanson, three-time circumnavigator and farmer/manufacturer
from Minnesota, looks astern from *Cloud Nine*.

she started first grade, Gaynelle fondly recalls her years aboard *Cloud Nine* with Roger. "All of the voyages had their merits," she said. "I enjoyed the long hauls, crossing oceans. It was interesting being up in the Arctic; that's such a different terrain, and you're really alone up there. One year we left the boat in Alaska, and the next year we had grandchildren aboard for the first time. We went up and did Glacier Bay and the whole thing, and they were just in a fun age to do that."

Among the children and grandchildren, is there a sailor in the bunch today?

"Not a one," Gaynelle laughs.

But that doesn't mean they weren't touched, as so many others were, by the experiences aboard *Cloud Nine*. Roger may have summed it up best in his 1984 Christmas letter, the one he sent shortly after completing his first circumnavigation.

"People sometimes ask if it was worth it, or if I would ever do it again. One recent evening, Philip and I were standing in the yard watching a magnificent pink and red sunset through the trees west of our farm. Phil said, 'Dad, of all the places we've seen, I think this is the most beautiful of all.' I think perhaps that acquiring this knowledge and attitude is well worth the effort of sailing around the world."

*Night Runner*, in her silver-collecting mode. The Bob Perry-design
is faster than her varnished topsides would suggest.

# Doug Fryer and *Night Runner*: Mixing a Dram of Safety into the Spirit of Adventure

Doug raced *Night Runner* in the Single-Handed TransPac race. Doug cruised *Night Runner* around Cape Horn. Doug has taken *Night Runner* to just about every anchorage in the Pacific Northwest all the way to Alaska. I think it's accurate to say that of all the boats I've drawn, *Night Runner* has the most miles under its keel.
—Bob Perry, yacht designer

Sailing on *Night Runner* with Doug was like being a movie star. It was great fun! We seldom went anywhere without friends and strangers coming by the boat to chat or admire the boat. *Night Runner* and Doug Fryer were almost synonymous.
—Karen Fryer, Doug's wife

For 15 years I was the organizer of what The Sailing Foundation did. But you've got to hand the whole thing to Doug Fryer, because he's the guy who got it started.
—Tad Lhamon, past CCA commodore and chairman of The Sailing Foundation

A fall 2020 Yachtworld listing marked the end of an era.

*Night Runner.* Perry Custom 42. 1980

Asking price: $99,000

"Possibly no other yacht has achieved greater success in the realms of both cruising and racing as *Night Runner*," read the description provided by the Seattle brokerage Swiftsure Yachts. "Designed by Robert H. Perry for Seattle sailor Doug Fryer, she is a well-known 'wolf in sheep's clothing' in Pacific Northwest waters with a classic appearance above the waterline and modern lines below. Under Fryer, she won just about every notable race in the Pacific Northwest. She is a veteran of 38 Swiftsure International Yacht Races (three times first overall), a singlehanded Transpac, four Victoria to Maui races (including a first in class) and four Van Isle 360 races. At the same time, she served her owner as a comfortable and capable cruising platform, extensively exploring Pacific Northwest waters north to Alaska and a dozen circumnavigations of Vancouver Island. As if that is not enough, *Night Runner* completed a 21,000-mile voyage around South America by way of Cape Horn and the Panama Canal for which Fryer received the Blue Water Medal from the Cruising Club of America in 1998. To say that *Night Runner* knows her way is an understatement."

People frequently ask yacht designer Bob Perry which boat of all his creations is his favorite. "I try my best not to answer," he said, "but when pressed, I usually say *Night Runner.*"

What exactly was this boat? And what legacy did her owner leave the rest of us? Truly, the community of ocean sailors who've plied the seas since the last decades of the 20th century are lucky to sail in Doug Fryer's wake.

## The Seafarer's Apprentice

In the course of these tales we've heard from several boat-mad kids—John Alden, Olin and Rod Stephens, Irving Johnson, Ross Sherbrooke—young ocean-sailing prodigies who knew from their earliest independent steps just where they were meant to go.

Doug Fryer was one of that crew.

"Early on at age 15, I began to sail in small boats," Doug wrote in *Justice for Wards Cove,* his memoir of a 27-year legal case that ultimately went to the United States Supreme Court and involved all three branches of government, a case

that Doug himself led. There can be precious few maritime lawyers so steeped in the lives of working seafarers.

Doug Fryer was not afraid of hard work. As a teenager, he cooked on a schooner and served as a seaman on cargo vessels, before turning to fishing vessels and tugs. Those experiences informed his approach to his career in maritime law.

"My early sailing led me in 1950 to obtain a workaway position dishwashing on a 97-foot schooner, *Gracie S*, which operated as a boy's camp, and I took my first trip to Southeast Alaska that year, traveling to Ketchikan, Juneau, Petersburg, Wrangell, and Sitka. It rained most of that trip; we ate salt beef and stood watches four hours on and four hours off on an open deck, and I was glad to get home."

Yet home wasn't a place the adolescent would remain for very long.

The next year, I graduated from high school and embarked on a more enjoyable trip on the schooner, this time to San Francisco, Los Angeles, and the Hawaiian Islands and return.

I wanted to see more of the world rather than entering college after graduation from high school. I found a couple of wintertime delivery trips on the Pacific coast, one southbound on an 87-foot yacht to San Diego and then northbound on the 101-foot pilot schooner *Adventuress*. Like Joseph Conrad's "Youth," I wanted to see the East and, in 1952, found a job as acting able-bodied seaman on the liberty ship *David B. Johnson*, carrying grain to India by way of Honolulu and Singapore. I was not prepared for the rampant disease, or the starvation in India. My first view of India was at Cuddalore, where we anchored the ship in a roadstead about four miles offshore and at daybreak saw a fleet of perhaps 30 lateen-rigged sailing lighters headed toward our ship, carrying some 300 thin longshoremen, who were to sack 2,000 tons of grain by hand and discharge it into the lighters in three days' time. After that, we sailed up the Hooghly River to discharge the balance of the cargo at Calcutta.

The next year, I went to Anchorage, Alaska, as a second mate on a converted 110-foot subchaser, carrying groceries, and then a three-month trip as ordinary seaman on the Bureau of Indian Affairs knot ship *North Star,* carrying supplies to the Eskimos in 46 towns and villages in the remote areas of the Bering Sea and the Arctic as far north as Point Barrow.

This work was interrupted by some college courses at the University of Washington, but I found work at George Broom's Sail and Rigging Loft at Maritime Shipyard for the summer of 1954 and on the purse-seine fishing boat *Molle* for the summer of 1955. The *Molle* (Croatian for "let go") was an Alaskan limit salmon seine boat 51 feet on the keel with an eight-man crew owned by Nakat Packing Company. We fished Excursion Inlet, Icy Strait, and the west side of Noyes Island in Southeast Alaska. Our home port in Alaska was the Waterfall Cannery on Prince of Wales Island touted to be the largest salmon cannery ever built.

The next spring I worked out of the Alaska Fisherman's Union as a longshoreman and, in the summer of 1956, returned to the *Gracie S* and worked as a rigger for her new owner, actor Sterling Hayden, who renamed her the schooner *Wanderer.*

My last seagoing job was the summer of 1957, when I worked on the 112-foot ocean tug *Justine Foss,* towing barges to Southeast Alaska, Kodiak, Anchorage, and Bristol Bay.

Karen Fryer was married to Doug from 2001 till the end of his life in April 2020. She believes some of those experiences in the Far East set him on his professional path. "Doug had barely started college when he decided to pause his education and devote his life to sailing," she said. "He got a position on a boat that went to India and was given the job of chipping the paint on the steel hull. He told me, 'Right then is when I decided I'd better go back to college.' So he went back to his studies in Business Administration. One of the required courses was Business Law. He so enjoyed the course that he changed his major, and this was the start of his career in law."

That career was forever infused with the experience of working on or near the sea. "In the process of these jobs," Doug wrote, "I worked out of two closed-shop hiring halls, the Sailors Union of the Pacific and the International Longshore and Warehouse Unions (ILWU). The closed-shop union has the right to do the exclusive hiring for employers. As a result, I witnessed firsthand overt discrimination in the Sailors Union and long-standing nepotism in the ILWU."

Doug thrived in law school. He loved the history of the law, and he loved the lawyer's case-by-case process of arriving at a decision. "The Socratic method of teaching got my full attention as nothing else had ever done." Graduating with honors, he was recruited into the Admiralty and Shipping Section of the United States Justice Department. His next recruitment came 15 months later to the post of Assistant U.S. Attorney in Seattle—a transfer that was signed by Attorney General Robert Kennedy and Deputy AG Byron White, who would soon become a U.S. Supreme Court justice.

By 1965 Fryer left government work to join the firm of Broz, Long, and Mikkelborg, where for the next 47 years he practiced law, Admiralty and otherwise. Along the way, Doug's own name was appended to that of the firm.

"Doug was very, very revered in the fishing community," said Linn Larsen, a longtime friend and shipmate. "I have roots there, being from a Seattle halibut-fishing family. You mentioned Doug's name, the floor shook."

*Night Runner* looked like a traditional Atkin design above the waterline—
but below the waterline she shows the separated rudder and shallow hull.

## The Three Things

Practicing law, compelling as it was, wasn't everything.

"Doug's life was really divided into three areas. He was very passionate about all three and excelled in all of them," said Karen. "One was his career as a maritime attorney. One was his family. And then there was sailing."

On that last topic, let's start with Bob Perry, whose memoir, *Yacht Design According to Perry,* devotes a full chapter to Doug and his boats.

> *African Star* [a 34-foot William Atkin-designed Tally Ho Major] was bought by Seattle Admiralty law attorney Doug Fryer, who began racing the boat. Doug had a huge, ugly, yellow spinnaker with a green star on it, and the rule of thumb was that at the end of the race, if you could see that spinnaker, *African Star* had beaten you on corrected time.
>
> Many years later, in 1977, I was comfortably ensconced in my Shilshole Bay office and business was good. Doug came in one afternoon and said he wanted to build a new boat, a version of Bruce King's *Unicorn* ketch. But he was concerned about the boat's handling characteristics off the wind. The last thing I wanted to do was to be given the job of "fixing" a Bruce King design. But I told Doug to come back in three days. I was confident I could draw something that he would like. At that precise

instant, I had no idea what that would be.

As I stood before the drawing board staring down at the big sheet of blank paper, an idea came to me. Make Doug's new boat as modern as possible under the water without resorting to IOR shapes, but topsides, give him something with which he was familiar—something I knew he liked. I drew a 41-foot, 24,000-pound displacement, fin-keeled, skeg-hung-rudder version of *African Star*.

This was the "wolf in sheep's clothing" described in the Swiftsure Yachts fall 2020 brokerage copy, by which time Doug and she had collected silver—including the CCA's 1998 Blue Water Medal—for four good decades.

Below the waterline, the boat looked like a modern two-tonner without the IOR influence. The hull shape was based upon a big International 14. The boat would have some tumblehome because it looked good. I would try to do a pretty transom without introducing so much hollow in the garboards that it would slow the boat down. I wanted the run to be straight and on the full side. I gave the hull an arc-like midsection that went tangent at the centerline so that there was no deadrise through the middle of the boat. I did this expressly because I wanted to use multiple veneer layers in the cold-molding process, and I wanted to wrap those veneers across the middle of the boat so that there would be no "seam" where the veneers butted on the centerline.

Shape-wise, the hull was beautiful and very dinghy-like. I gave *Night Runner* a deep, Petersonesque keel fin and a rudder hung on a deep skeg.

*Night Runner* wasn't built exactly as she was designed, and Perry's telling doesn't go easy on her builder, Cecil Lange of Port Townsend, Washington, who made changes in the build to save money. Yet something in the combination worked.

"Once the *Night Runner* build began, Doug spent every spare moment he had over the next 18 months assisting at Cecil Lange's yard in Port Townsend," wrote Andy Schwenk for a profile in *48° North*. "There is a rumor that once a tool was turned on in the morning, it was not shut off until work was completed for the day in order to complete the build as expeditiously as possible. Doug was the king of the unskilled labor department. He pushed brooms and held the dumb end of measuring tapes, in order that the skilled folks could concentrate on the tricky stuff. To his credit, he did all the plumbing, varnishing, and mounting of the deck hardware. Doug describes this time as a carpenter's assistant as 'one of his best summers.'"

*Night Runner*'s cold-molded construction of wood and epoxy
was carried out by Cecil Lange of Port Townsend, Washington.

The boat was completed in time for the 1980 sailing season, and she straight-away joined that year's Swiftsure fleet. Sailboat racing in the Pacific Northwest dates back to the 1850s, some three decades before Washington became a U.S. state. At that time members of the British Royal Navy raced colonists out of Victoria, British Columbia. In 1930, six boats raced from Cadboro Bay, home of the Royal Victoria Yacht Club, around Swiftsure Bank at the Pacific Ocean entrance to the Juan de Fuca Strait, and back up the strait. Versions of that roughly 140-mile course grew into the annual Swiftsure International Yacht Race, the premier Pacific Northwest sailboat-racing event. By its heyday in the early 1980s, Swiftsure was attracting some 400 boats.

Doug sailed the Swiftsure an astonishing 50 times, 38 of them aboard *Night Runner*. Three times the pair took fleet honors.

Certainly, the boat's many race wins had something to do with the way she was sailed. "I sailed with Doug aboard *Night Runner* waist-deep in white water through Race Rocks as the 1.5-ounce spinnaker blew up," recalled Schwenk. "Doug was one of a kind. He sent me forward with the 2.2-ounce with wire luffs. Soon, we were back underway and headed for victory."

*Night Runner*'s inaugural season wasn't constrained by the inside passages of Puget Sound. "On June 6, 1980, less than one month after her first race," Andy wrote, "Doug set sail from San Francisco in pea-soup fog. He was bound for Hanalei Bay, Hawaii, in the Singlehanded Transpacific race. He covered over 600 miles in the first three days, beam-reaching in over 30 knots and heavy seas. By the end of the third day, the autopilot had enough and packed it in. Doug brought his toothbrush on deck and put his sextant where he could reach it soon as the sun broke through the cloud deck. Sixteen hours was about the limit he could handle at the helm. He continued this way until he had one of those Eureka! moments, and packed the autopilot fuse with aluminum foil. He sailed into Hanalei Bay with it still functioning 15 days later."

## The Blue Water Medal Voyage

In August 1995 Doug and *Night Runner*, with a revolving crew, set off from Port Townsend on a voyage he'd long been dreaming of.

"Inspired by Joshua Slocum," Doug wrote, "I had always wished to sail the passages of Southern Chile. This led to a planned voyage on *Night Runner* around South America to be accomplished in ten months to a year's time."

He set a goal of rounding Cape Horn in the middle of the southern summer, but that meant sailing through Mexico in hurricane season. "We thought that with modern tracking and forecasting, any tropical disturbances could be avoided."

They thought wrong.

The first thousand-mile leg from Cape Flattery to San Diego was uneventful. From there, the next planned stop was the Galápagos Islands. "As we departed from San Diego, a new tropical storm named Henriette was developing in the Gulf of Baja California. We sought avoidance by sailing well offshore and to the west of the projected position of the navigable semicircle. Henriette developed into a hurricane and changed course gradually west as if it had us in its sights. On September 5, we passed within five miles of the center. By then Henriette had been downgraded to a tropical storm with maximum winds of 60 knots."

After an unplanned stop in Cabo San Lucas to fix a watermaker, *Night Runner's* crew promptly sailed into its next tropical disturbance, Ishmael. "We suffered winds of 65 to 80 knots, took a knockdown, and the spinnaker pole was ripped out of its mounts, tearing a winch loose; a small section of the deck house was taken with it. After 24 hours on the Gale Rider, the wind moderated and we proceeded to Puerto Vallarta for repair, arriving on September 16."

Longtime crew Doug Hannam recalled details of that incident, as told to him by Bruce Katter during a late-night watch aboard *Night Runner*. "When the overtaking wave hit *NR* while running downwind during the hurricane, Doug was pressed against the binnacle, lucky to not be seriously injured. The wave forced the 22-foot-long spinnaker pole out of the chocks. On its way up, it tangled in the preventer lines on the port side, twisting the lines into greater tension as the rotating pole hit the shrouds. The tension on the preventer pulled the dedicated winch off the top of the cabinhouse, along with about a square foot of the cabinhouse itself, leaving a direct hole into the boat. Bruce Katter came on deck to retrieve the spinnaker pole, and then, in breaking waves, nailed down some spare canvas over the hole as a temporary fix while Doug kept the boat in control. That fix lasted until they were able to do a proper repair."

From the Galápagos to Chile, Doug and Bruce Katter double-handed. Seasoned sailors voyaging from Mexico to the Pacific Northwest often quip that the simplest route is by way of Hawaii: it avoids beating that interminable distance against a foul current. A southbound trip down the coast of South America poses the same problem.

"We left Santa Maria on October 26 and headed west-southwest to sail around the South Pacific High. The alternate route along the west coast of South America would have been dead to windward and in the teeth of the Humboldt Current. By sailing west we were gradually lifted, and on day six were headed south in position 12S, 95W."

When they were a week out, the bolt holding the lower shrouds failed, nearly bringing down *Night Runner's* rig. "We immediately headed dead downwind, dropped the sail, and then spent a difficult day setting up a jury rig," wrote Doug. "This rig consisted of a pair of spinnaker guys as lower shrouds on each side, attached to a chain bridle around the forward side of the mast, and wrapped around the port and starboard spreaders. The fresh trades rolled both rails under while I hung in the bosun's chair for about three hours installing the bridle and seizing the shackles with wire mousings."

The stretch in the polyester line, even with block-and-tackle advantage and cranked down hard on the primary winches, meant that on every wave the mast deflected six inches at the spreaders. The only answer was to set minimal sail, storm trysail and reefed staysail, and continue on a beam reach till they gained the confidence to try bigger sails. If their jury rig failed, the next help—Hawaii or Tahiti—was still mighty far to travel downwind with only a spinnaker pole for a mast.

As it was, their path took them to within 350 miles of Easter Island before the westerlies properly kicked in. "We broke out of the High at 38S 85W on November 18, with cold freshening westerlies and the appearance of Southern Ocean birds, the wandering albatross, cape pigeon, storm petrels, and giant fulmars."

*Night Runner's* passage to Valdivia took 29 days. After pulling the mast and replacing all of the standing rigging, fixing the sails, and taking on new crew, they spent the next month and a half voyaging south through the channels of southern Chile that had so captured Doug's imagination. "It was spring in Chile, and the countryside was reminiscent of western Oregon with evergreens and green rolling hills," he wrote. "The terrain changes remarkably as one moves south from Valdivia. First, the farms disappear and the forest thickens, then the mountains are bolder and closer to the channels. Squalls and rain increase. The snow line lowers, waterfalls become more prevalent, ice and glaciers appear and anchoring becomes more difficult as kelp—unseen from the surface—thickens and grows to a depth of 30 fathoms. The compass balanced for the northern hemisphere sticks when rolling in the swell."

The great-circle distance from Valdivia to Cape Horn measures 900 miles; *Night Runner* logged 2,100 miles along that same stretch of coast. For 40 days, they anchored or moored with shorelines every night but two. Happy hours were sparked up with readings from Bill Tilman's *Mischief in Patagonia.*

And then—Cape Horn.

"We left Magellan Strait in sight of Cabo Froward, the southern tip of the continent, and headed south into Canal Cockburn and the ocean again at 54S, then into a hurricane hole at Caleta Brecknock with the boat lashed fore and aft to the rocks, surrounded by massive granite mountains, waterfalls, and freshwater lakes.

"On January 16 we rounded Cape Horn about two miles off to windward in a freshening northerly gale. We found secure anchorage that night in Caleta Martial in the Wollaston Islands. Hal Roth had been shipwrecked just north of here on his Cape Horn trip, but this anchorage was clean sand with excellent holding."

From Cape Horn *Night Runner* proceeded into the Atlantic Ocean for the first time in her life. And Doug sailed on the rest of the way around the South American continent, through the Panama Canal, and on home to Seattle. The homebound passage, like the outbound one, did not lack for incident.

Of those, Perry tells the best story: "Cruising back from Cape Horn in 1996, *Night Runner* lost its skeg off the coast of Mexico. The rudder stayed on but the skeg was gone. Doug called to get me to mail him a copy of the skeg drawing. I asked how the boat handled without a skeg.

"'Better,' he said."

Sailing up the coast of North America now posed the same problem *Night Runner* found sailing down the coast of South America. "But for the necessity of a crew change at San Diego," wrote Doug, "the most effective route north from Mexico is probably a long arc offshore as recommended by *Ocean Passages for the World*, into the Pacific High and a heading breeze, and then tack at about 38N, 135W."

This time they accepted the hard slog up the coast—including 21 days to cover the final 1,000 miles. Rounding Cape Flattery, Doug said, "was a propitious day marking the end of the ocean voyage, my 63rd birthday." And it came with a bonus: "As a homecoming we caught three salmon off the buoy."

Propitious, indeed.

"With *Night Runner*," wrote Schwenk, "Doug's sailing exploits became a blur of enviable activity. He raced and cruised as prolifically as any boat or skipper in the area. These stories could fill a hundred articles, but he says the sailing accomplishment he's most proud of is being awarded the Blue Water Medal by the Cruising Club of America. This was in 1998 for seamanship on his trip around South America."

"They also gave it to the British yachting fleet for the Dunkirk rescue," said Doug, "so I was in good company."

## The Lifesling: Rethinking Safety at Sea

In Bill Nutting's 1921 book, *Track of the Typhoon*, the CCA founder famously posed this question: "Is 'Safety First' going to be our national motto?"

Nutting, just home from the subchasers of World War I, was all for good sport and disdainful of the "safe-and-sane and highly specialized and steam-heated" softness of his generation. "I feel that what American yachting needs is less common sense, less restrictions, less slide rules, and more sailing," Nutting famously wrote. Three years later he and his mates were lost at sea between Greenland and Labrador.

Of course, not all of the early CCA cohort shared Nutting's peculiar brand of bravado. In the club's first report on plan and scope—written in 1923, a year before Nutting's disappearance—author Henry Wise Wood listed a dozen topics around which the club should create a clearinghouse of information, the final item of which was safety. "I mention safety last," he wrote, "because thoughts of it seem to be the scantiest duffel that most of you stow in your heads. This is an admonition."

That said, for the club's first six decades—and, more broadly, in the whole community of offshore sailors at large—seagoing safety generally remained the province of individual skippers and crews. Then in the early 1980s, something in the sailing Zeitgeist changed.

"There was a huge shift of opinion after the Fastnet Race of 1979," said Sheila McCurdy, past CCA Commodore (2010–2012) and one of a small cohort of qualified Safety at Sea Seminar moderators. "After that, it became more of an institutional effort."

Yachting journalist and historian, John Rousmaniere, sailed in that '79 Fastnet. Immediately after the event, he set about interviewing fellow sailors who'd lived through it. The back flap of his best-selling 1980 book *Fastnet, Force 10* sums up what happened out there:

On August 11, 1979, 303 yachts began the 600-mile Fastnet Race from the Isle of Wight off the southwest coast of England to Fastnet Rock off the Irish Coast and back. It began in fine weather, then suddenly became a terrifying ordeal. A Force 10, sixty-knot storm swept across the North Atlantic with a speed that confounded forecasters, slamming into the fleet with epic fury. For twenty hours, 2,500 men and women were smashed by forty-foot breaking waves, while rescue helicopters and lifeboats struggled to save them. By the time the race was over, fifteen people had died, twenty-four crews had abandoned ship, five yachts had sunk, 136 sailors had been rescued, and only 85 boats had finished the race.

The '79 Fastnet jolted the sailing community, including many CCA members, who began to question the boats, the safety equipment, and the onboard skills of the crews who were going to sea. Rousmaniere's book was at once an indispensable record of a defining moment in sailing history and the primary document that spurred an entirely new stance on safety going forward.

Around that same time, Pacific Northwest sailors were shaken by the drowning death of their friend Arnie Bennett. "The project started when a couple of fellow Seattle Yacht Club members went sailing, and the man fell overboard off the foredeck," recalled Linn Larsen. "The woman couldn't get him back aboard and literally drove into the harbor with him strapped to the boat, dead."

Doug Fryer, together with sailors Dick Marshall and Fred Hayes, felt particularly compelled to respond in some meaningful way. The threesome eventually grew into the Safety at Sea Committee of the Seattle-based Sailing Foundation.

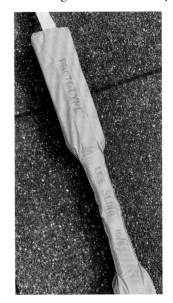

The group's earliest claim to fame was the invention of the Lifesling, both the product and the practice, now so ubiquitous on both sail and powerboats. They conducted many of their early experiments from the deck of *Night Runner*.

Hayes wrote a brief history of the Lifesling's beginnings:

In early 1980 three sailing friends began research into rescue methods for a person who has fallen overboard from a pleasure boat. Doug Fryer, Dick Marshall

In the early 1980s, Doug Fryer and friends conducted MOB-recovery tests, many of them aboard *Night Runner*. An early prototype of the resulting Lifesling is shown here. It solved two problems simultaneously—to secure the MOB to the boat by a line and ability to hoist the MOB back on deck.

*The group's earliest claim to fame was the invention of the Lifesling, both the product and the practice, now so ubiquitous on both sail and powerboats. They conducted many of their early experiments from the deck of* Night Runner.

and Fred Hayes had sailed all of their lives. They realized that, in spite of considerable sailing experience, they knew very little about rescuing a person from the water. Moreover, they knew of no one who did.

They researched all available written and anecdotal information about man-overboard incidents and rescue methods. Almost without exception, they were stories of futile efforts ending tragically.

Tad Lhamon, whom Doug recruited to chair The Sailing Foundation in the early 2000s, recalled some of the rich experience Doug brought to the group's initial search for a better man overboard (MOB) recovery practice. "Part of Doug's law practice dealt with the fishing fleet that went up to Alaska every year, so he had good knowledge of how they operated and the things that could happen to the fishermen," said Tad. "That also links to his interest in safety at sea."

Hayes continues:

> Research into rescue procedures involved on-the-water testing from a sailboat, first with a dummy and then with live volunteers. They found that none of the commonly espoused methods of return to and retrieval of a victim was adequate when put to actual test. Many were dangerous. So the three men set out to develop their own boat-handling and man-overboard retrieval systems.
>
> A retrieval system was essential. A great many boats, perhaps a majority, sail with only two people onboard. If one person goes over the side, the other must make a singlehanded rescue. A person without flotation who is in the water for more than five or ten minutes invariably is exhausted and unable to climb aboard. A lifting method, operable by one person, was needed. After four years of experiment, the original three, by now a Committee of eight, were successful.

Larsen took part in some of those early trials and remembers some of the experiments that failed. "The water on Puget Sound is glacier-fed, and our water temperature here is between 46 and 59 degrees," he said. "So you've got to get a person out of the water, absolute max, in 45 minutes. And the real max is about 25 minutes. We tried an early methodology that had you grabbing and holding the Lifesling, as opposed to putting it over your head and getting it under your armpits in order to be towed to the boat and lifted out. We found that people couldn't hold on in cold water for very long."

Doug patented the product their team developed, and in 1985 he arranged with West Marine to manufacture and distribute the Lifesling. "Royalties, to this day, are paid to The Sailing Foundation," wrote Schwenk in a February 2019 profile of Doug for *48° North*.

As a May 2020 *Scuttlebutt Sailing News* obituary put it, "This was Doug's gift to sailing."

From the beginning, Doug and his mates understood that the solution to their problem involved not just a great new product but something much harder to sell to the sailing population: *the practice to use that product effectively.* Through the 1980s, the new stance toward safety within the sailing community at large came to comprise three legs of a stool: the boats, the equipment, and the skills of the crew. Members of the CCA Technical Committee addressed what they saw as unwholesome new directions in yacht design and construction in the 1987 book *Desirable and Undesirable Characteristics of Offshore Yachts*, edited by John Rousmaniere and featuring chapters by Olin Stephens, Dan Strohmeier, Jim McCurdy, and others. The *World Sailing Offshore Special Regulations* addressed the safety equipment offshore racing boats carried aboard. But that still left a gaping hole for the behavior of individual crew members. An expensive life raft is only as valuable as the crew's ability to use it.

That's where the Safety at Sea seminars came in. They were part of the same broad change in mindset in the 1980s, and their origins have near simultaneous roots in efforts by the U.S. Naval Academy sailing program, The Seattle Sailing Foundation, the CCA, the U.S. Yacht Racing Union (now US Sailing), the International Sailing Association, and others.

Before 1980 the U.S. Naval Academy had regularly hosted a winter lecture series on safety at sea for its midshipmen and coaches. After the Fastnet '79 disaster, the Academy opened its next safety lecture series to the public, expanding it into a daylong event with multiple speakers addressing a range of topics.

"Lieutenant General Robert Taber and Captain Ned Shuman organized a Safety-at-Sea Colloquium on 1 March 1980 as a community service," wrote Robert McNitt in his 1996 book *Sailing at the U.S. Naval Academy*.

Speakers included Capt. J. William Kime, USCG (later the commandant of the U. S. Coast Guard); Dr. Stephen Hiltabidle on

*From the beginning, Doug and his mates understood that the
solution to their problem involved not just a great new product
but something much harder to sell to the sailing population:*
the practice to use that product effectively.

hypothermia; Capt. Robert McWethy on man-overboard recovery; and a
two-hour review of heavy weather safety and the Fastnet Race experience
featuring Captain Ned Shuman, General Taber, and Rod Stephens; John
Rousmaniere, who was writing his book *Fastnet, Force 10,* and Commo.
Richard C. McCurdy of the Cruising Club of America and chairman of
the CCA/USYRU Safety-at-Sea Committee. The latest safety equipment
was displayed, and rescue procedures were demonstrated on the water.
The response to this authoritative program was so enthusiastic that it
became a popular annual event, known thereafter as the Safety-at-Sea
Seminar.

In 1985 Captain John Bonds decided to expand the highly successful
Safety-at-Sea Seminar by offering a second day for the public. The
response was overwhelming, with a standing-room-only audience on the
first offering, leading to a continuation of this plan for the next two years.
As executive director of USYRU after retiring from active duty, Bonds
expanded the concept nationally.

"The Seattle Sailing Foundation offered a safety seminar in 1987 and
Newport in 1988," Bonds recalled. "USYRU combined with *Cruising
World* magazine in that year to co-sponsor the program all across the
country, and since then some 75 events have taken place in sailing centers
everywhere."

Today US Sailing marshals a broad certification program, with a textbook,
online courses, and in-person seminars, often including open-water MOB
retrieval practice. The CCA is one of a handful of organizations that host the
events in venues around the country.

From the start, CCA members were at the center of the new safety initiatives.
"They didn't necessarily have their CCA hats on back then," said Sheila McCurdy.
Still, over time the club came to take on safety as part of its institutional mission.
"What is now the CCA Safety and Seamanship Committee was started around
the hosting of the Safety at Sea events in the late 1990s."

Without setting aside that seminal call for the "adventurous use of the sea,"

"Doug Fryer was at the helm in a courtroom, in a yacht club or social gathering, and certainly aboard his beloved *Night Runner,*" recalled his friend and crewmate Andy Schwenk.

today's CCA members—Doug Fryer, *et al*—have largely answered Bill Nutting's provocative question in the affirmative.

## How Lucky: a 151-Proof Ritual

Larsen sailed many a mile aboard *Night Runner,* including trans-Pacific passages. "She was not an easy boat to sail. Everything manual," he recalled. "She was a man's boat, and Fryer was just that. When he had her built, he was running six miles a day and could do 80 push-ups and the same number of sit-ups, and did every day. He had tremendous strength and capability, as well as sailing wisdom."

But even for a sailor like Doug, *Night Runner* eventually became too much to manage.

"Doug and I decided that if we were going to stay on the water in the way we wanted to, *Night Runner* was getting too much for us to handle by ourselves," said Karen. "The sails are big, and handling them was a lot of work for the two of us as we aged. I'm in my 70s, and Doug was in his early 80s. So I said, 'Let's build a smaller version of *Night Runner.*' Doug agreed, and we contacted Bob Perry who began working on designs. Shortly after that, Doug was diagnosed with cancer, and this changed our focus to his care."

"About six months ago," recalled Bob Perry just after Doug's death in April 2020, "Doug called me on a Saturday and said he wanted to do a new boat. Music to my ears. Sunday evening he called and said he had bad medical news

*Night Runner*'s new owners, together with Karen Fryer (second from left)
at the beginning of a new chapter for *Night Runner*.

and would have to put off the new boat. I kept working on the design anyway.

"The last race I did with Doug was last summer. He was a bit weak, but he drove the entire race, and we took 2nd. In classic Doug style, after the boat was put to bed, the rum bottle came out with the hot-buttered-rum mix, and the crew sat around the cockpit drinking 'Ritual Rums.' Doug liked 151-proof rum because it weighed less for the punch. We drank, and Doug recited nautical poetry, some a bit bawdy. Doug had a resonant, baritone voice, and he delivered the poems with attorney-like panache. Looking back, I think all of the crew knew we were experiencing something that would never happen again."

Andy Schwenk also remembered Doug's 151-proof rituals.

"Doug had a clan that followed him," he recalled. "A crew jacket was his armor, always black, always salt-stained with equal parts sweat and seawater. Captain Fryer was at the helm in a courtroom, in a yacht club or social gathering, and certainly aboard his beloved *Night Runner*. Pour yourself a spot of Lemon Hart 151 rum, a touch of honey, and a splash of hot water from a battered teapot. Take your time. Tell your crew how special they are to you and how lucky each one of us is. Put your hand on the galley rail and thank the designer and builder for bringing the clan in safe. That was Doug's way."

"Doug stood with me and my best man on the foredeck of *Night Runner* for my wedding ceremony about a month before leaving for the South America trip," recalled Doug Hannam. "Doug did this for me, part of his crew, while preparing for his long trip. Doug treated all of those who crewed with him as family."

*Great American III* carried Rich Wilson around the world twice in the
Vendée Globe Single-handed Race in 2008 and 2017, becoming the oldest competitor
in the 28,000 mile race. Why? He did it to excite school children about rainforests,
U.S. history, wetlands, fisheries, islands—and, yes, sailing.

# 15

# Rich Wilson and the *Great Americans*:
# Sailing for Other People, Shorthanded and Alone

The notion was that we can bring adventures to the general public if we keep our
communications on the human level. And if we can engage kids, then we can wrap
a curriculum around that adventure. Why is he in a storm? Because this is how a
storm works. It's geography and mathematics and physics; it's nationalities and flags
and passports spilling over from different countries. Everything is embedded in it.

—Rich Wilson

sitesALIVE!

Sailing in America is dying. Where's the gap? Kids sail 420s until they're 22 years
old, and then what? Unless they are progeny of a yacht-club family, they have no
access to any bigger boats. Having spent so much time in France, I knew that the
fundamental building block for the great French offshore sailors were the Figaro 2s.

—Rich Wilson

Collegiate Offshore Sailing Circuit

*Brutal* is the one true word to describe the 2008 Vendée Globe start.

In any year the simple demands of that 28,000-mile round-the-world
sailboat race—singlehanded, nonstop, unassisted—amount to an endurance
test that fewer than 50 people had ever met. That's 10 times fewer than the
number who'd been to outer space, and 60 times fewer than the number
who'd summited Mt. Everest.

The Vendée Globe begins at the focal point of western Europe's Bay of
Biscay, and when the equinoctial storms come blowing from the west across
the high 40s of North Atlantic latitude, the bathymetry of that coast creates
notoriously vicious seas. The 30 singlehanders in that race's 2008 sixth edition
set off into just such a storm. Among them were 17 French sailors, seven

Aboard the Bernard Nivelt-designed *Great American III*, Rich Wilson, together with the whole 2008 Vendée Globe fleet, sailed into the teeth of a notorious Bay of Biscay storm.

Brits, a Canadian, and a smattering of other Europeans. The lone American, only the third American ever to start the Vendée Globe, also happened to be the oldest.

That sailor was Rich Wilson, age 58—also the *youngest* overall winner of the Bermuda Race in 1980.

## A Fleet Decimated

"Emerging into the Atlantic Ocean, emotionally drained by the French send-off, we found an unsettled sea, larger than expected for the 20-knot southwest wind, rolling in from the west toward the coast," wrote Rich of those first moments of his first circumnavigation attempt.

The second part of that *we*—for by then Rich Wilson truly was alone—was his boat. "I did have one shipmate still with me, our trusty *Great American III*, the Bernard Nivelt-designed, Thierry Dubois-built Open 60 that I'd acquired for the voyage. Her clean white topsides were elegant next to the sponsor-emblazoned topsides of the other boats. Under Thierry and another French skipper, she had raced solo around the world three times already. Hopefully, she had one more good one in her. She couldn't do it without me, and I couldn't do it without her."

Four long months at sea were to begin with a hard windward beat. The first natural rounding mark was Spain's Cape Finisterre, Europe's westernmost point,

Rich Wilson was the oldest skipper in the 2008 Vendée Globe fleet. Eight years later, at age 66, he became the oldest-ever VG competitor—and the fastest American solo circumnavigator.

the place the ancient Romans called "the end of the earth." On that November day the Cape lay dead to windward, and as a starboard tack would put you on the beach somewhere near Bordeaux, the only real choice was to head west on port tack directly toward the center of the coming storm, then tack at the weather front and hope you cleared the continental rocks for your southing.

"It's easy to be brave in a warm, dry living room, imagining some future voyage," wrote Rich. "But will you be brave when the voyage arrives, when you're scared and cold and tired in a storm, seas are coming aboard, and both you and the boat are taking a beating?"

Rich Wilson had run out of time to ponder these questions. Now seasick and anxious and ineluctably heading into the first storm of the voyage, he felt the fear coming on.

Like his fellow competitors, Rich was sailing an Open 60. Administered by the International Monohull Open Class Association (IMOCA), founded in 1991, the "open" class set such basic design restrictions as length (between 59 and 60 feet) and draft (no more than 15 feet), but left other dimensions like beam, mast height, and sail area to the designer. Following a spate of capsizes and sinkings in the class's early years, new restrictions came to include flotation and self-righting capabilities—observed and documented, not merely modeled on a computer. As the Open 60s developed, they came to look like aircraft carriers, or like floating pie wedges with their extraordinary beam carried all the way aft and their flat hull sections to promote surfing down mountainous Southern Ocean waves. To add righting moment, a boat's tendency to resist heeling or capsize, designers added innovations like water ballast and canting keels. (Hydrofoils would come later to the IMOCA class.) In all of this, an arms race develops: every increase in righting moment invites a corresponding increase in sail area. The resulting horsepower in

"I'm 6 feet tall, 160 pounds, and my asthmatic lungs work at 70 percent of normal,"
Rich Wilson told his trainer months before the race start. "I'll never be the strongest
or have the most aerobic capacity, but I want you to be able to say
when we're finished that nobody worked harder."

an Open 60 grows ever more formidable, and so does the human effort required to master it.

Rich describes a typical maneuver: "I rolled out the staysail, grabbed the pedestal handles (think bicycle pedals driven by your hands), hunched over, and muscled in fifty revolutions to turn the leeward winch to trim the staysail, then disengaged the leeward winch clutch, engaged the windward winch clutch, and muscled in seventy grinds on that winch to trim the monster mainsail. Scanning the full 360 degrees of the horizon to be sure we were clear, I dashed below to cant the keel to port to its full 40 degrees from the vertical. Swinging that ton of steel keel fin supporting three tons of streamlined lead bulb at the bottom of the windward side added counterbalance to the wind pressure on the sails. I rushed back to the cockpit, and adjusted the autopilot for our new course."

In these conditions, so early in the race, eating food was the last thing Rich wanted to do. It was also the last thing he wanted *to not do*. "Our nutrition goal was 6,000 calories per day, three times the normal intake: four full meals spaced every six hours, snack in between, hydrate constantly with Gatorade, Ensure, and

*Rich compares Open 60s to the 12-Metre yachts that were raced with 11 crew in America's Cup events from the 1950s into the 1980s. "Open 60s are slightly larger and more powerful in every dimension, yet there are 10 fewer crew aboard, and you don't come home for lunch."*

Nestlé's Nido Whole Milk. If I couldn't or didn't want to eat, that would lead to more fatigue and weakness and would invite the seasickness to linger. Plus, a momentarily weaker state might mean a mistake in a sail maneuver, a missed handhold, a trip and a fall, and rapidly the consequences could multiply."

Meanwhile, the winds built as *Great American III* raced into the storm. Her 450-pound mainsail measured 1,500 square feet up a 90-foot mast; it would soon need to be reefed. Rich compares Open 60s to the 12-Metre yachts that were raced with 11 crew in America's Cup events from the 1950s into the 1980s. "Open 60s are slightly larger and more powerful in every dimension, yet there are 10 fewer crew aboard, and you don't come home for lunch."

The motion of an Open 60 at sea is unthinkably jarring, especially to windward. "These Open 60s have shallow, nearly flat bottoms," Rich wrote. "*GA3's* hull is only 18 inches deep, despite being 18 feet wide. Like a surfer paddling seaward from the beach, they will rocket off a wave, go airborne, and come crashing down—*BAM!* Nine tons of boat landing flat on the water is like dropping your house, with you in it, on concrete."

Every maneuver demands extraordinary physical exertion; more importantly, it demands a practiced protocol that can be repeated under the worst conditions by a lone sleep-deprived sailor. Here's how you reef an Open 60:

> The mainsail has control lines at each of the three corners, plus three additional pairs of control lines spaced along the vertical and diagonal edges which allow the sail to be lowered 20 feet to the first reef (1,200 square feet), or an additional 20 feet to the second reef (900 square feet), or an additional 20 feet to the third reef (600 square feet).
>
> Wrap the main halyard around the central winch of our cockpit's five winches, ease the mainsail out until the boom swings out over the water and the sail is blowing back from the mast like a flag and is therefore under no load. The boat is now sailing under staysail alone.
>
> Ease the 2:1 halyard out ten feet, so the sail comes down five feet.

Then snug the new reef lines at the forward and aft edges of the sail down to the boom. Repeat three times until the sail is down to its new reef.

You could try to lower the entire 20-foot increment between the reefs all at once. But then the lines for the third reef would go slack, with 40 feet of loose line (since it was also 2:1) blowing wildly in the dark, and likely to wrap itself around the end of the boom. Then you'd have to stop the whole procedure, crawl forward to the mast, climb on top of the sail on the boom, crawl on the slippery, wet, and loose folds of sailcloth 30 feet to the end of the boom, which is now swinging over the seas in the dark night like George Clooney on the outrigger in *The Perfect Storm*, and by your LED headlight, untangle the mess that you'd created by trying to do everything too fast. Don't fall off, or you'll be overboard and will die. Don't get your fingers caught in the on-again/off-again loading of the main-sheet block. Don't get knocked unconscious by the flailing reef line.

No, much better to proceed incrementally and keep everything under control. Now snug each of the three control lines and grind another hundred revolutions on the pedestal to pull the mainsail back in till it fills with wind.

A day and a night and halfway into the next day the wind surpassed 40 knots piling up vicious 20-foot seas. The rain, when it came, came in torrents. And then conditions deteriorated. An alarm signaled another vessel dangerously close by, yet radar returned only the rain. "On deck I could see nothing. The rain blowing at 50 knots was like trying to look into a hose being sprayed at your face. You just can't do it. Out there, somewhere, was a vessel of unknown size, direction, speed, or distance from us. My eyeballs were lashed painfully. I tried to protect them with the visor, then with my hand, then gave up and looked only away to leeward to see if there was a ship down there. I could see a few hundred yards, to the tops of the next waves. A fishing vessel or a container ship could be converging from a half mile away, and I'd see nothing because of the big waves between us. I saw nothing to leeward, and couldn't physically look to windward."

It was in these conditions that Rich suffered the blow that nearly ended his race before it properly began. He remembered that he'd stowed construction goggles aboard for a moment like this. Sure enough, with his contact lenses and those goggles, finally he was able to scan the wavetops for 360 degrees around the boat to look for traffic. Thinking a self-portrait in this getup would amuse the folks back home, he reached for his camera.

I took the digital camera out of its cubbyhole, removed my on-deck gloves to better manipulate the tiny switches, aimed the camera backward at my face, still holding firmly onto the post with my left hand, and took a picture. OK, did I aim it correctly? Let go with the left hand, turn the camera around, holding it with both hands to check that last image.

BAM! The boat was hit by a vicious uppercut wave. I felt myself airborne, flying and twisting across the cabin, back first. In mid-air, I knew what was about to happen but couldn't do anything to prevent it. BAM! My back hit a horizontal stainless-steel grab bar above the bulkhead opening to the starboard bunk. In a one-point, full-bodyweight impact after six feet in the air, it jack-knifed me, chest to knees, through that opening, rear end first, to slam against the inside surface of the hull. I crumpled in a heap underneath the bunk, with a sharp pain at the point of impact on the left side of my spine and near the bottom of my ribcage. My whole back cramped to protect the area. I'd hit so hard I feared for paralysis. The boat was laying over 50 degrees on its side. My legs were trailing upward through the bulkhead opening into the cabin from my heap underneath the bunk. I tried to move extremities, fearful of the results. But my fingers worked. Then wrists and elbows. I could scrunch my toes, rotate my ankles, and bend my knees.

Wracked with pain, Rich could neither lie in his bunk nor move to sit at the nav station. He couldn't go on deck. The barometer was still falling and the conditions still worsening, but luckily the sailplan was down to three reefs and the storm jib. *GA3* could manage herself. For 10 hours Rich was unable to reach the satellite phone. When he finally could, he placed a call to an emergency-medicine expert back in Massachusetts.

His call went to voicemail.

Meanwhile, to distract from the pain, Rich checked for messages from race direction back in Les Sables d'Olonne. What he learned stunned him. In fact, he was one of the lucky ones. Bernard Stamm had collided with a fishing boat; Jean-Baptiste Dejeanty discovered a crack amidships. Derek Hatfield, Dominique Wavre, and Michel Desjoyeaux all suffered electrical problems. In Michel's case, the water-ballast tank had separated from the hull and sprayed seawater into his engine's starter motor, preventing him from making power. Worse news followed. Kito de Pavant, Marc Thiercelin, and Yannick Bestaven had all dismasted. Alex Thomson discovered two skins of carbon fiber delaminating from a foam core in the pounding conditions; he literally watched as his boat peeled apart. After two days of sailing, four of the 30 sailors retired entirely, and five others returned to port with hopes of restarting well behind the fleet.

"*Great American III*, nicknamed GA3, was a complex system
of advanced technologies that needed to function flawlessly for the next four months
in a relentlessly hostile environment," said Rich.

The start of this sixth edition of the Vendée Globe was without equal the most disastrous—and the Southern Ocean still hadn't yet had its say. Before the finish, 19 of the original 30 sailors would retire in conditions more or less dire.

Meanwhile, Rich was still sailing. But only barely.

## A Special Kind of Motivation

Rich not only finished that race (in just over 121 days), but he returned eight years later and sailed it again (finishing in 107—two days faster than Bruce Schwab did it in 2005). Rich's 2017 result made him both the fastest American solo circumnavigator and, at age 66, the oldest competitor in any Vendée Globe ever sailed.

Why on earth would a person do such a thing? *Twice?*

"You've got to have the right reason to go and do that race, because it is godawful hard," said Rich. "It's physically demanding. Emotionally. Mentally. The boats are huge. You're alone. It's incredibly hard. But we had a reason."

That reason had been 30 years in the making, or even longer, depending on where you start the clock. For this telling, let's start it in 1974, at a time when Rich had finished college but hadn't yet entered graduate school.

"I taught math one year in Boston, at Hyde Park High School," said Rich.

By the finish of the 2016–17 Vendée Globe race, Rich Wilson had circumnavigated solo and unassisted twice—and excited 500,000 students in 45 countries. He had also become beloved by the tight-knit, single-handed competitors for his grit and graciousness.

That year happened to coincide with a U.S. District Court decision that ordered administrators of the Boston Public Schools to achieve racial parity by busing students to neighborhoods distant from where they lived.

"I was in the second-worse school for racial violence," said Rich. "I got the job because 25 percent of the faculty quit. They refused to teach Black kids who would be bused in from Mattapan. For me, growing up in Marblehead with normal white privilege, which people are slowly becoming aware of now, it was outside my comfort zone."

After a rough start, Rich found that he deeply enjoyed working with the students. "It was appalling in one sense, but it was great in many other senses," he said. "The kids were great. If you could have taken all the parents and shipped them to Nevada, the kids would have figured it out."

Though in the course of that year Rich concluded that classroom teaching wasn't his calling, he carried within himself a deep commitment to education as he pursued graduate degrees in ocean-resources management and business, then ran a scientific-research startup through much of the 1980s.

All the while, Rich sailed. He'd grown up cruising with his family, and in college he raced dinghies round the buoys. His family's boat was *Holger Danske*, the now-legendary 42-foot double-ended Scandinavian ketch, commissioned by Rich's father, John Wilson; designed by Aage Nielsen; and built in 1964 at

Walsted's Baadewerft in Denmark. This was the boat that Rich, age 28, sailed in the 1980 Bermuda Race, winning the St. David's Lighthouse Trophy—the overall win—from a fleet of 162 boats. Aage Nielsen toward the end of his life deemed *Holger Danske* the favorite of all his creations, and yacht designer Bob Perry freely cribbed the lines of her stern sections for his Valiant 40 in 1973.

Following Rich's Bermuda win, administrators of the Sea Education Association in Woods Hole, Massachusetts, invited him to join that organization's overseers, then the board of trustees. Through those relationships, Rich also came to know and join the board of the School for Field Studies, which ran six permanent field-research stations around the world.

"SEA and SFS students returned utterly transformed by these academically rigorous, hands-on, team-oriented semesters, far from society's normal land-based support systems," Rich observed. "Bored of your four-walled classroom? Go to sea on a ship, or trek into the rainforest to learn your science. You will work within teams, overcome physical hardship, adapt to foreign cultures, and do serious real-world academics."

In 1986 Rich visited Newport, Rhode Island, to watch the start of that year's BOC singlehanded round-the-world race. His friend, singlehanded racing sailor Phil Steggall, invited Rich to help one of the competitors make final preparations. While they were stowing an anchor, Phil said to Rich, "You know, we ought to be doing this ourselves."

Solo voyaging had never been something that Rich believed he could do. For one thing, he'd suffered debilitating asthma since infancy. Simply doing normal activities demanded extraordinary training. As a teenager, Rich had read books by the great singlehanded voyagers Joshua Slocum, Francis Chichester, Robin Knox-Johnston, and Bernard Moitessier. "I wondered if I could ever be brave enough, strong enough, or smart enough to sail a significant singlehanded voyage—not like theirs, of course, because theirs was around the world, and that was beyond imagination—but a shorter one, an overnight, or maybe a few days alone over a few hundred miles, if I really got up my nerve."

Yet something in Phil's comment spurred something in Rich. Two days later he went shopping for a boat to compete in the 1988 Carlsberg Singlehanded Transatlantic Race. The namesake of his father's boat had been Denmark's national hero from the days of Charlemagne; Rich named his own boat *Curtana*—the name Holger Danske bestowed on his sword.

As a tech-minded teenager, Rich had learned ham radio. Racing *Curtana* back across the North Atlantic Ocean from England in 1988 he rekindled that skill, checking in with friends from the high seas. One friend put him in touch with Bill Smith, host of a radio call-in show on WZLX in Boston. Rich called in. During their first on-air conversation, the host clearly didn't understand the circumstances on the other end of the call. But the second call, during the daily commute, was different.

"I was in a Gulf Stream gale," said Rich. "I was in my survival suit, fearing capsize. Hearing the fear and fatigue in my voice, Bill *got it*. There is a guy out there alone, a thousand miles from land. He's tired, cold, scared, and in a storm. And no one is sure what's going to happen next."

"We could hear your voice going up and down with the radio waves," Bill later told Rich. "We could hear the wind and the sea in the background. It was the theater of the mind."

For years afterward, Rich encountered people in the Boston area who still remembered his exchange from the North Atlantic as they drove in to work that day in the summer of 1988. Some kind of revelation began to stir in him. "This proved the critical point that even though sailing was relatively unknown to the public, if you kept the communication on a human, nontechnical level, you could excite and engage that public with a dramatic adventure—which happened to be at sea."

Then he carried that notion one step further. He connected the dots. "Real-world problem sets in the Boston Public Schools; the transformational real-world experiences of the SEA and SFS students; the "theater of the mind" of live, interactive broadcasts—could these be combined into new and potent school programs?"

That initial musing set off nearly three decades of interconnected questions, problems, and solutions; a succession of emerging ends and means; and a string of thrilling adventures on ever greater scales. The result was an education-based company that Rich called sitesALIVE!

In the late 1980s, the idea was constrained on all sides, not the least being the problem of delivering timely stories to large populations of students at once in those years before the internet came to households and classrooms. Still, Rich had a breakthrough. It came from a conversation with a fellow CCA member, Stephen Taylor, whose family published *The Boston Globe* and who alerted Rich to a program called Newspapers in Education.

"This was a program set up by the Audit Bureau of Circulation, which keeps track of publications' circulation figure toward setting advertising rates," said Rich. "They said, 'You can sell newspapers into schools and charge half the newsstand rates, but you can't dump them.'" It was a program that was little used when Rich first learned about it. But he knew that Joshua Slocum's regular stories to newspapers had captivated a large and devoted readership as he made his way round the world on that first-ever solo circumnavigation. Rich conceived of something similar, while also adding school curriculum.

As his plan developed, Rich recalled a book called *Greyhounds of the Sea* about the great American clipper ships of the late 19th century. Two things stood out. One, the speed records were typically set between places like Boston or New York and San Francisco—cities with large print-media circulations. And two, the passage times for those record-setting runs tended to be about 10 weeks or 12 weeks—an ideal duration for a semester of learning.

In 1990 Rich mortgaged his condominium and bought the 60-foot trimaran *Great American* aboard which George Kolesnikov and Steve Pettengill had just broken *Flying Cloud's* New York–San Francisco record from the Gold Rush era.

"When we started that first pilot program, we planned three clipper-route voyages. The first one was San Francisco to our home town of Boston set in 1853 by *Northern Light* in 76 days," says Rich—with a pause to say, "That was a hell of a pilot program."

Indeed, it was. "The voyage and program would last 11 weeks, race history on an important American trade route, and risk the peril of Cape Horn," wrote Rich. "It would overflow with science, math, and geography. Audio reports would provide our 'theater of the mind'; daily ship's logs would provide data for math problems; our journals, written at sea, would enliven the classroom activities in the teachers' guide."

As with all of his clipper-route record attempts, Rich sailed double-handed. The 1990 voyage with Steve Pettengill started well enough, with a television story aired nationally on NBC Nightly News. But it ended disastrously—with a somersaulting double capsize 400 miles off Cape Horn on Thanksgiving Day. In 65-foot seas Rich and Steve were rescued by the crew of the *New Zealand Pacific* containership and delivered 18 days later to Holland. Still, as harrowing as it was to live through that event, the sitesALIVE! concept demonstrably worked. Returning home, Rich visited schools that had participated in the program, all the while planning his next voyage.

In 1993 he tried for the same record again with a new boat—the 53-foot Nigel Irens-designed trimaran that Rich named *Great American II* in honor of the boat that had been lost. He remembers one call from Colorado on the same day he signed papers for his new boat. It was from a woman named Jill Scott at *The Denver Post*, saying she wanted in. Rich asked why. "We're a thousand miles from the ocean, and a lot of our kids will never see the ocean," she said. "What better way can there be to learn about the ocean than to follow a live ocean adventure?"

This time Rich and his team succeeded on both fronts—successfully breaking *Northern Lights'* record by more than six days, and growing the scope of the site-sALIVE! program in schools. For 12 weeks they communicated with more than 13 million readers.

Over the next dozen years, the school program grew both in reach and in the

*"With the unique symbolism of this globe-circling event, perhaps we could create a truly global school program and move beyond our US-only constituency."*

subjects featured. Partnering with accredited field schools, sitesALIVE! featured live semester-long programs tied to rainforests, U.S. history, wetlands, fisheries, islands—and, yes, sailing. In 2001 and 2003, Rich and his team took on two more clipper ship records, sailing double-handed: New York–Melbourne (*Mandarin* in 1855 set the record of 69 days during the Australian Gold Rush) and Hong Kong–New York (*Sea Witch* set the 1853 record of 74 days in the China tea trade). Of the more than 70 programs, Rich built six around his own large-scale ocean adventures.

As the internet grew, Rich found himself often frustratingly ahead of the curve of actual computer screens and internet access in students' hands. Still, by the mid-2000s he began setting his sights on something larger. "It occurred to me that the Vendée Globe could provide an opportunity to produce the next generation program for sitesALIVE!" he said. "With the unique symbolism of this globe-circling event, perhaps we could create a truly global school program and move beyond our US-only constituency."

Which is how Rich Wilson found himself just outside the Bay of Biscay in November 2008, alone, with four broken ribs.

## Sailing in America Is Dying. Long Live Sailing

After successfully completing his second Vendée Globe in 2017—the triumphant culmination of the sitesALIVE! program, reaching 500,000 students in 45 countries—Rich felt a 30-year cycle drawing to a close. Meanwhile, all the time he'd spent among that cohort of exceptional French ocean sailors had revealed a problem he could no longer ignore.

"Sailing is kind of dying in the United States," he said. "College dinghy sailing may be strong, and Olympic dinghy efforts may be strong. But not ocean sailing. The Cruising Club has the same problem. They did a survey, and the average age was 71, and aging out."

A hundred years ago when the CCA was founded, its charter members set themselves a goal of developing talent among new ocean sailors. "We popularize the use of the open sea for pleasure," wrote Henry Wise Wood in 1923. "By turning into a gigantic playground three-fourths of the earth's surface and training our youth to use it for sport, we shall recover the seagoing impetus that we lost at the close of the clipper ship era."

"Our country didn't offer the plethora of solo ocean races that fill the French calendar and act as the sport's minor league." Aiming to fix that, Rich started the Collegiate Offshore Sailing Circuit (COSC), based around a one-design fleet Beneteau-built Figaro boats, shown here in the 2021 Monhegan Race.

For several generations, the reintroduction of the Bermuda Race in 1923 and other initiatives, effectively introduced young Americans to the ocean for sport. Yet lately those introductions had tailed off—in the United States.

But not in France.

Reflecting on his own college sailing, Rich began thinking about how much more there was to offshore sailing than there was in sailing dozens of times around the same windward mark. "The things you have to learn to go offshore," he said, "that's what's interesting. You have to learn navigation and learn about the tides and the currents and the lights at night. How do you forecast the weather? How are you going to put the weather in your routing? How are you going to make repairs, and respond to a medical situation? You've got to stand a watch. You got to wake up at midnight and stay up till 4 am. It's just a big adventure."

With other sailors and friends, Rich began to examine the problem with the same analytical attention he'd brought to so many complex problems before. Those conversations started from a single question: "Where's the gap?"

"It seemed like the gap was after college." Kids may sail 420s till they're 22 years old. But then what? "Unless they are progeny of yacht-club families, they have no more access to bigger boats," said Rich.

Rich's experience with the Vendée Globe gave him a chance to watch the latest generation of top offshore sailors up close, sailors like Michel Desjoyeaux and Jean le Cam and Samantha Davies. Among them—but not among young U.S. sailors—was one common denominator: the Solitaire du Figaro single-handed sailing event. Sailed annually from Brittany, the Figaro comprises four legs of at least 500 miles each sailed in strict one-design boats. To get a sense of the scale, some years the notorious 600-mile-plus Fastnet Race is merely leg three of a Figaro event.

"That's why the French are so good at this stuff," said Rich. "They've all scared the daylights out of themselves a gazillion times in Figaros, by pushing them to the limit. Then they get the confidence to do the same thing in the Open 60s, to be able to push that. Jean le Cam was in the 2020 Vendée, and he's up there at the front of the fleet—with no foils! He's a three-time winner of the Solitaire du Figaro."

To respond to this gap, in 2017 Rich and others created the Collegiate Offshore Sailing Circuit (COSC). Their aim is to bring at least 20 Figaro 2s to the United States. "Beneteau built them in lots of 50 in 2004," said Rich. "If you wanted to buy one new, you sent in your deposit, and they randomly drew numbers and you got whichever boat came up. You couldn't order one and have it built to your specifications. They're super-one-design."

In France, a subsequent generation of Figaro 3s feature lateral foils to increase righting moment and therefore power. But for the COSC's purposes, the second-generation boats are ideal. "They're not new," said Rich, "but they're still bulletproof." The boats all have jackline and life rafts and other offshore safety gear. Among other uses, they'll be ideal for teaching hands-on safety-at-sea courses.

Each boat costs $100,000 to purchase, ship, and commission to the COSC one-design standard. Since 2017, individuals or groups, including several CCA members, have made tax-deductible donations sufficient to bring 12 Figaro 2s to the United States. The boats are then leased, preferably two at a time, to college programs with a goal of participating in at least one offshore regatta per semester. At press time, boats had been deployed to Massachusetts Maritime Institute, Maine Maritime Institute, Webb Institute, SUNY Maritime Academy and the U.S. Merchant Marine Academy at Kings Point.

"Our goal is to expand the pool of offshore-capable mariners," said Rich. "That first time you're offshore at night, out of sight of land, when you can't see lights, you don't ever forget that. The word _overnight_ is probably more important than _offshore_ because that's just a whole different ball game. That's the adventure, and the adventure is the hook."

Rich Wilson knows that adventure—and he would like his fellow Americans to experience it for themselves.

Harriet and T. L. Linskey look out from the bow of *Hands Across the Sea*,
their 46-foot cruising catamaran, a substantial upgrade
from their first boat that took them across the Pacific as newlyweds.

# 16

# Saving the World, One Book at a Time:
# *Hands Across the Sea*, with Harriet and T.L. Linskey

*People say that one book can take you to the future,*
*and that is what I would like to thank you for.*
—Obed
Pupil at Giraudel Primary School, Dominica

It was in the South Pacific, probably Tonga circa 1988, that the germ of an idea first sprouted in the minds of Harriet and Tom "T.L." Linskey. They wanted to do *something*. They just didn't know what.

Harriet remembers a shaky arrival into Niuatopatapu aboard *freelance*, their 28-foot Bristol Channel Cutter that T.L. had built from a bare hull. Their existence at the time was minimalist. They'd left California as newly-weds a year earlier with "50 bucks in cash and 250 bucks in the bank," plus the promise of a monthly retainer from *SAIL* magazine, where T.L. was a contributing editor. "We had a boat full of food, and we left," Harriet said.

They made their passage across the Pacific—23 days from Acapulco to the Marquesas Islands—with the analog tools of that time, and their wits. They spent that season learning to live together in a small, simple space. At the same time, they were learning to solve problems together.

"The chart shows three mountains. Do you see three mountains?

"No, I only see a mountain and a plateau."

"So maybe we're not there."

After the mountainous Marquesas, landfall in the low-lying, reef-strewn Tuamotus taught them to pay attention to *everything*. "We had everybody's books," said Harriet. Most of the time, the water's flowing out of the lagoon through the pass, flowing out, flowing out. There's only an hour a day where the water's actually flowing *in* through the pass; and it's going in when the

*"We were watching with the binoculars, and gradually the pass died down. No more dolphins. So we sailed in, with the current pushing us, and the wind. The moon did that. Isn't that wild?"*

moon is either directly overhead or right under your feet. So we calculated when the moon was under our feet."

"Good old *H.O. 249*," said T.L., referring to the book of tables that helps navigators find the positions of celestial bodies at any given time.

Harriet described sailing back and forth outside Rangiroa, with binoculars trained on Tiputa Pass through the breaking reef and into the lagoon. In the middle of the pass they could see dolphins leaping from wavetop to wavetop. The outflowing current against the incoming breeze had set up a massive standing wave. The pass was all but impassable.

"And then the moon went underneath our feet," said Harriet. "We were watching with the binoculars, and gradually the pass died down. No more dolphins. So we sailed in, with the current pushing us, and the wind. *The moon did that.* Isn't that wild?"

Experiences like these honed the Linskeys' appreciation for their analog tools. "Oh, my goodness," said T.L. "That was the most amazing illustration of the tidal system there. When you use the sextant, you realize that things don't happen by accident out there. I think with GPS, you lose touch with all that stuff."

These were the conditions aboard *freelance* as the Linskeys approached Tonga several months later. "We were sailing up to Niuatopatapu," recalled Harriet. "It was a couple of days' sail from Niue, and we were using the SatNav. At one point we got this fix that had us like five miles from Niuatopatapu. It was sunset, and we were like 'Ahhh, this can't be right.' That island is fairly low, with a reef around it, and you have to go around the back side of it. Plus, the chart was one of those Captain Cook things, which can be off, so there was not really a chart. So we hove-to most of the night. And we were lucky because twilight had three planets: like, Mars, Venus, and Jupiter, or something. So I wake up T.L., and I'm like, 'OK, let's do this.' We've got this planet, and this planet, and this planet, and the little asterisk on the chart shows we're like 30 miles away. It was telling us the same thing our Walker log and dead-reckoning were telling us. We had to sail really hard, but we finally got in. That was a typical situation where our sextant worked better than the electronics."

Passage making is about the ocean and landfalls, but it also about the people along the way. In 1988 Harriet and T. L. sailed across the Pacific Ocean aboard *freelance*, their home-built 28-foot Bristol Channel cutter, stopping in Tonga where they first got the idea to "do something."

## We Weren't Equipped to Do Anything

It was one thing to solve the problems of learning to function in the simple, self-imposed confines of a 28-foot sailboat. But the Linskeys' arrival in Tonga opened their eyes to a far more complex set of problems, one that would emerge two decades later and grow into a nonprofit corporation with a half-million-dollar annual budget and nearly two dozen international staff serving 125,000 schoolchildren.

Their revelation began shortly after that 1988 landfall in Niuatopatapu.

"This chief came out to the boat," recalled Harriet, "and he said, 'I want to throw a ladies' tea. Might you have any flour? Because I think I'd like to make some scones.' And I said, 'Sure, we have some flour.' And then he said, 'Well, might you have some butter and jam?' And I said, 'Yes, here's a big tin of Anchor butter from New Zealand, and here's some jam.' And then he said, 'Oh, by the way—would you have the tea?'"

The Linskeys had seen relative prosperity as they crossed the first half of the Pacific. The French government had substantially supported the Marquesas and Tahiti and the rest of Polynesia's Society Islands. And in the Cook Islands and Niue, the New Zealanders had delivered a certain level of material comfort. But by Tonga the Linskeys started to see the real poverty that afflicts so much of the developing world, as well as its effects.

Harriet and T.L. left a wake of thousands of miles crossing the Pacific.
The adventure ended in Japan where they sold the boat to return to the U.S.
and to careers. Twenty years later, they took up the cruising life again.

In Vava'u, they met an eye surgeon, an American sailor on a Valiant 40, who was donating his services in the local hospital. "It was amazing," said T.L. "The Tongan fishermen, especially, had a lot of sun damage: pterygiums—you know, the white growth that creeps over your eyes. So they'd go in to see this doctor, and he'd get them out. And you could tell that the Tongans weren't receiving medical care anywhere else."

Before setting off from the United States, the doctor had coordinated with Rotary Clubs to collect eyeglasses. "He had sailbags full of reading glasses and prescription glasses," said T.L.

"He was doing vision tests," said Harriet, "and people could grab into this bag and find glasses. So you'd see big Tongan men with their black tops and their

*"We gave away pots and pans and shampoo and things like that. But we weren't equipped to do anything. We thought it would be nice to do something while we're out here enjoying all this wonderful world on our yacht. Our 28-foot yacht."*

grass skirts wearing these glasses. This one looks like Clark Kent; this one looks like Linus or Lucy. But they could see!"

That experience and others like it affected the Linskeys deeply, and it got them thinking. "Once you leave the U. S. of A. in your yacht, there's a lot of poverty out there," said T.L. "We'd go to other villages in Tonga and just realize how poor everybody is—which planted the seed in our mind: Someday we want to sail to places like this and actually do something constructive. We gave away pots and pans and shampoo and things like that. But we weren't equipped to do anything. We thought it would be nice to do something while we're out here enjoying all this wonderful world on our yacht. Our 28-foot yacht."

Do something, sure. But exactly what that something was would take another lifetime to work out.

### The Case for a Cruising Catamaran

Fast-forward 20 years. T.L. and Harriet have lived and worked for several seasons in New Zealand: he as a sailmaker, she as a schoolteacher. They've sailed to Australia and then Japan—47 days from Melbourne to Osaka—and sold *freelance* to a Japanese architect keen on classic American cruising boats. They've moved back to the States and embarked on new careers in the Boston area: he as a *SAIL* magazine staff editor, she in a corporate job with a global marketing firm. They've bought and refurbished several homes. They've raced their J/32 around the buoys and cruised Buzzards Bay and the Maine coast.

By 2007 a new idea bubbled up. "We thought, OK, both sets of parents have passed, and we never had any kids," said Harriet. "Maybe it's time to sell the house and go cruising again."

In 2007, they commissioned a new Dolphin 460 catamaran and named her *Hands Across the Sea*. They didn't start out dead-set on a catamaran, just curious. They were looking at such monohulls as a Pacific Seacraft 40, a J/46, a Valiant 40 and 46, and some Hallberg-Rassys. But T.L. had previously raced smaller catamarans—Hobies, Prindles, Tornados—and his stint reviewing boats for *SAIL* magazine gave him a good taste of the cruising cats on the market.

"I've always been fascinated by Chris White's boats, the Atlantic 46 and such,"

*Hands Across the Sea*, a 2008 Dolphin 460 catamaran, was built in Brazil. While not a thoroughbred racer, she's a solid performer whose top speed with the Linskeys stands at 19.8 knots. More typically, they dial back for comfort and reel in steady 200-mile days.

he said. "And we just wanted to keep an open mind."

Of course, not any cat would do. "There's a schism in the cat world," said T.L. "Most cats are designed for chartering: four big double cabins, 500 or 600 gallons of water tanks so everybody can shower every day of their charter. And then the Gunboats are designed for Antigua Race Week. They make a thing of 'Oh, fly a hull.' 'Are you nuts? Get this hull down, right now!' I've flipped cats. Even in a Hobie or a Tornado, it's game-over. It's tough to get back upright."

The Dolphin, in T.L.'s reckoning, is a middle-of-the-road cruising cat: neither a charter boat, nor a thoroughbred racer. "Our boat's dialed down enough where it's really not going to flip," said T.L. "The sail-area-to-displacement ratio is just not up there like on a Gunboat."

Still, the boat had to sail well. "We decided we wanted daggerboards so it would be a boat that was a sailboat. At the time there was really only Outremer or Catana doing that, or a custom boat. Or it was a Dolphin 460, which was near to a custom boat, because they would do anything you wanted."

The Dolphin 460, no longer in production, was the brainchild of a French designer and builder, Philippe Pouvreau, and a Brazilian partner, Junior Pimenta. Based in Aracaju, Brazil, the yard employed state-of-the art composite-building techniques—vacuum-bagging, resin-infusion—but not particularly exotic materials: not carbon and epoxy but tried-and-true fiberglass and vinylester. They employed unidirectional glass and Divinycell core smartly to reduce weight and maximize stiffness. The boat's 20,900-pound displacement on a 45-foot, 9-inch waterline adds up to a displacement-to-length ratio of 97, quite light by the standards of most ocean-cruising boats, and even many cruising cats. The Dolphins were imported into the United States for several years by Phil Berman at The Multihull Company.

The Linskeys' top speed stands at 19.2 knots, surfing under main and jib in 28 knots of wind and with the autopilot steering. But top speed is seldom what cruising couples care about most. "On *Hands* we've averaged 8 knots on passages of 1,000 to 2,000 miles without pushing the boat or taxing our mom-and-pop crew," said T.L. "As a doublehanded team, it's crucial that we stay well rested, so our focus at sea is concentrated not on all-out speed but on off-watch comfort and not breaking gear. Harriet and I have both been seasick on *Hands*, and each time it's because we've been driving too fast down a bumpy road. Taking your foot off the gas—reefing down—always eases the ride."

"Averaging 8 knots on passage, more than 200 miles a day, is really handy-dandy when you're leaving New Bedford and trying to get to Bermuda in late October or early November," said Harriet, to which T.L. added: "It's good to have some speed when you need it."

The Linskeys have sailed *Hands* double-handed on many of their passages between the U.S. East Coast and the Caribbean, although lately they've enjoyed sailing with others. "I think we're getting tired of the watches," said T.L. "It's a little demanding to get up, try to sleep, get up, try to sleep. A third person really makes it much easier."

Over the years, T.L. has come to feel that modest cats are safer than mono-hulls. "Our boat has five collision bulkheads in each hull," he said, "and we have four areas under the cabin sole that are completely sealed. If we smash into some-thing, parts of the boat may flood, but the entire boat's not going to flood. I just think a cat's safer because it has two engines, two rudders, and it can't sink. I would no longer feel good going offshore in a monohull that could sink."

## A Fuzzy Mission Statement

All that time the question nagged: Do what? Harriet and T. L. knew that this next cruising phase wouldn't simply be about the adventure for themselves; this time, it would be driven by a mission.

Over that spring of 2007 they created the structure of a nonprofit, if not an entirely fleshed-out goal for it. "It was really fuzzy," said T.L. "Doing something while we're sailing around."

"T.L. came up with the name *Hands Across the Sea*," said Harriet, a name they applied both to their new boat and their new venture. "We got an accountant to help us with the IRS application to set up a 501(c)(3) corporation. And we created a mission statement that was very broad—something like, 'We're going to help coastal communities where we sail with medical, educational, girls-empowerment, environmental help.'"

"Saving the world, you know," quipped T.L.

Toward the end of 2007 the Linskeys traveled to Brazil to take delivery of *Hands,* and they spent the early months of 2008 sailing north to Trinidad and through the islands of the Eastern Caribbean, slowly getting to know their new boat. Meanwhile, they were also getting to know the islands they visited. Because Harriet had taught school for a couple of stints during their earlier vagabonding years, the Linskeys were drawn to visit some schools in the Grenadines.

"We arrived at this one little school on Union Island," she said. "It was a typical school. You know, beautiful children in bright and shiny uniforms, but very few resources. It had these really dilapidated desks and chairs left over from British Colonial days."

When the Linskeys asked what the school needed, the principal responded, "Could you get us a photocopier and paper? And could you get us some library books?" Harriet and T.L. spent some time that day going through the school's library. As they came to learn, it was the principal herself who had created the library.

"She had this room, and she had some bookshelves made," said Harriet. "She had books on the shelves, but the books were whatever she could find. What was left on the island were spy novels and these romance bodice-rippers and an old encyclopedia set from the '50s or '60s. You'd pull a book off the shelf and open it up, and these insects would come out. I mean, it was disgusting."

The more they explored, the more they learned about how schools in the Organization of Eastern Caribbean States are organized. The OECS comprises such former British colonies as Antigua, Dominica, Grenada, St. Kitts and Nevis, St. Lucia, and St. Vincent and the Grenadines. Teachers in these countries would typically have some community-college training—possibly a teaching certificate but seldom a degree. Following a series of education reforms in the early 2000s, the OECS ministries of education added a new requirement: that principals hold a post-secondary degree. To comply, many principals had completed an online Bachelors of Education Administration program at the University of the West Indies.

"The degree—and this was very clever of the university—required that these principals do a school-improvement project," said Harriet. "I almost think of it as sinister. Right? Because school principals don't have a budget. They have to demonstrate that they can improve their school without any help from the

*They told the principals of these schools that they could get them books for their libraries. At the end of that season they returned home to the States and set about asking people to make donations for the schools they'd visited.*

Ministry of Education. The ministry gives them teachers, and maybe they'll give them an allotment of toilet paper and cleaning supplies and chalk, but that's it. The principals have to get parents to chip in, and they have to get teachers to help. Fund-raising is a skill set for a school principal in the Caribbean."

Now the Linskeys' mission was starting to come into focus. In 2008, they identified three schools—one in St. Vincent and the Grenadines, one in Dominica, and one in Nevis—that needed help. They told the principals of these schools that they could get them books for their libraries. At the end of that season they returned home to the States and set about asking people to make donations for the schools they'd visited.

Before they sailed south again, Harriet realized that all their work had created a new problem. "I had 10 boxes of books, plus some supplies, that we had collected for these three schools," said Harriet. The load they'd gathered was larger than their boat could carry. So Harriet called a buddy at Harte Hanks, the marketing-fulfillment firm where she'd worked near Boston. Among other things, Harte Hanks has a sophisticated logistics department.

"No problem," her friend replied. "I'll send a truck."

In the course of her research, Harriet found an organization called Boaters for Books; that group, in turn, had a relationship with Tropical Shipping, which transports cargo between the United States and the Caribbean islands. If the Linskeys could deliver their load to the Tropical Shipping dock in Medley, Florida, Boaters for Books would consolidate the Linskeys' load with their collection.

In that first year, the Linskeys identified two thirds of what Hands Across the Sea now calls its Logistics Angels. Harte Hanks provides warehousing and receiving in Massachusetts; AIT Worldwide Logistics provides one 18-wheeler from Massachusetts to Florida per year; and Tropical Shipping transports the load from Florida to customs authorities in each of the countries where Hands Across the Sea works. Together, they can ship roughly 25 palettes of books to the Caribbean islands each year.

The Linskeys had established the bare bones of what would become their mission for the next 12 years and counting. But along the way they learned that there were still a few more problems yet to solve.

In 2020, the Hands Across the Sea nonprofit organization sent 20,441 new books
to 508 schools in six Caribbean nations, benefiting 20,000 children.
Harriet and T.L. have stopped by as often as possible during the school year.

## Beyond Donation Dumping

The Linskeys figured all they'd need to do is get the books to the schools where
they'd been promised, and everybody would know what to do with them. "That
turned out to be not the case," said Harriet. "We'd come back a year later, and the
books would still be in boxes in the principal's office."

The unpacked boxes, it turned out, were not a sign that school administrators
didn't care enough about the books; it's that they cared too much. "They don't
get new anything," said Harriet, "and so the Caribbean way is to hoard—to keep
whatever you have in shrink-wrap, to protect it, and to not let anyone touch it—
because you never know when you're going to get something again. This is when
we realized, 'Oh, we have to help them set up a lending library.' "

In their visits to schools in St. Lucia and other islands, the Linskeys would run
into Peace Corps volunteers. "By 2010 we'd met enough of them," said Harriet,
"that we realized they had a lot of collective knowledge. So we actually visited the
Peace Corps headquarters in Washington, DC, and they had all these resources
about how to create a school library."

Together with some of the volunteers they'd met, Harriet and T.L. conducted
interviews and compiled bits and pieces from the experience of many volunteers.

Meanwhile, they learned of a UNICEF program called Child Friendly Schools. "UNICEF came in and said, 'We don't want you to beat the children anymore. We're going to teach your teachers positive behavior-management techniques that avoid corporal punishment.' So we found a UNICEF checklist, and some of the items were things like, 'have a student council; have students run part of your school; have a school library; make the library a nice place; have students run the library.' "

Compiling tested practices from these and other sources, the Linskeys created the *Hands Across the Sea Library Manual for Primary Schools*. The key, they found, *was to appoint students* to become the librarians. "The kids are dying for some responsibility at school," said T.L. "There's no one more excited about books in the library than the children. Running the library is a big thing for them. They get status, and acclaim."

Of course, the idea of letting students run something found plenty of push-back: "You don't know our children." Or, "We can't do that here; they'll tear the books apart." But the Linskeys treated these challenges as an education process, beginning with teaching kids how to turn the pages of a book without bending or tearing them.

Posted on the Hands Across the Sea website (www.handsacrossthesea.net) is a series of videos from kids describing their experience of running a library, and if you're feeling down, do yourself a favor and spend some time with these kids as they describe what it feels like to run the library. It'll light up your day. Or listen to Shundalyn Niles-Scott, principal of the Constantine Methodist Primary School in Grenada: "I am impressed to see students from as young as Grade 1 taking charge of the library," she said. "The teacher doesn't necessarily have to be there because these children know exactly what they have to do. They maintain law and order at the library."

Child-friendly schools? Consider this: "The student-run library creates a very friendly atmosphere," said Principal Niles-Scott. "One child will teach another child to read, or one child will show other children where to find books, from the very easy books to the most difficult books. The children know the library inside-out. One doesn't have to venture far to find illustrations of the benefits to the kids. They got together, and they created the solar system, and they had the planets and so on. And they were inspired by the books that came from Hands Across the Sea about the solar system. And afterwards they had lights, and they had astronauts and so on. Eventually everybody wanted to read those books. It wasn't like a teacher came and said, 'You need to read this for a book report, or you need to do a project.' It's just by that little project that the student librarians did, people just started to read on the solar system. And I think that is quite commendable."

As for the books themselves, the Linskeys learned early on that gathering castaway books from well-meaning people was far less effective than going straight to publishers to ask for new books. "We gave up trying to give old books or donated books," said T.L. "We saw with donation-dump books that they were so inappropriate, so horrible, they were actually turning kids off of reading. We'd throw out about 95 percent of them. So we started a Wishlist system where we ask the schools to give us their lists." Wishlists are drawn from school principals, teachers, librarians, U.S. Peace Corps volunteers, and the students themselves.

"We've really become experts on children's literature," Harriet said. "First of all, you want to get books that kids want to read. Everybody wants to read *Diary of a Wimpy Kid*. Well, this leads you into *Dog Man*. It's an early chapter book that leads you into that. And then there's series books with these Black characters. The goal is to get kids reading fluently."

To date, Hands Across the Sea has shipped over 500,000 new books to schools in six countries, reaching 125,000 children. To do so, they work directly with two dozen publishers of children's literature. Each May, staff gather that season's catalogues from the publishers; then, steered by the Wishlists from their contacts in the islands, they place orders for some 20,000 to 100,000 books. The larger publishers offer discounts of as much as 60 percent, plus free shipping to the Harte Hanks warehouse in Massachusetts; books from smaller niche publishers may be more expensive but also more targeted to young Caribbean readers. The average cost per book is between $3 and $4. From its half-million-dollar total annual budget, Hands Across the Sea spends between $50,000 and $100,000 on books.

In the 12 years from 2007 to 2019, Hands Across the Sea has grown from helping those three original schools to serving 380 lending libraries in six countries. As the nonprofit grew, the Linskeys brought on a board of directors, with Harriet serving as executive director and Tom as marketing director.

"It's very intensive," said Harriet. "I'm focused almost 100 percent on administration and fund-raising. We write grant reports, and I pitch foundations and donors for money. And T.L. does all our marketing materials—all our email and all our design and all our photography and videography." The corporation pays Harriet and T.L. each a salary that would be similar to a teacher's income in the U.S. Southeast but not the Northeast.

As the organization has grown in size and reach, Hands Across the Sea hired staff on each of the islands where they have a presence. They call these staff members Literacy Links. "We used to visit all the schools," said Harriet, "but we can't do that anymore. It's too big. So we have 10 Literacy Links in six countries, and we have a program manager who manages them." The Literacy Links are mainly retired educators who live on-island and work for Hands Across the Sea on a part-time basis.

In all, 800 schools in the eastern Caribbean take part in the Hands Across the Sea program. The students take pride in running the school libraries

Avoiding mission-creep has been a challenge as the nonprofit grows. Particularly after such disasters as hurricanes or earthquakes, strident requests come in for items beyond children's books, as well as offers from well-meaning donors. "Everybody wants to help in a disaster," Harriet said, "but I've become really cynical about it. The government technocrats in the ministries are overwhelmed. They've lost their home, too. They haven't had a shower. And then they're having to deal with all this incoming. And people want to give, give, give. But they don't realize that unless a project is done in a certain amount of time, these organizations are gone. And if the project's not done, who's going to finish it? And then what are these materials that were left behind? Meanwhile, another group is coming in and saying, 'You have to hurricane-proof everything.' But how do we know these leftover materials are hurricane-proof? It's donation-dumping *of construction materials*! It's mind-boggling what these islands are dealing with."

After Hurricane Maria, one donor offered $10,000 to Hands Across the Sea for emergency aid. "I bought diapers," said Harriet, "because I thought, 'We have people working down there for us, and they need help with their families.' And so here are some emergency lights, and here is some peanut butter and food. We did one shipment. But never again."

*"And when you have PTSD and you're in this horrible situation, a book is a wonderful thing to have.*
*You need something for your brain. You need something to take you out of that situation. That was an eye-opener for us, seeing the power of books after the hurricane."*

"We're just not set up for any of that," said T.L.

There's one category of questions that the Linskeys encounter again and again: "Why are you sending books? Why are you doing libraries? Why don't you send iPads? Everything's on the computer."

But the Linskeys have stood firm. "Our mission is not teaching computer skills or connecting kids to YouTube or social media," said T.L. "Our mission is teaching kids how to read. How to think. How to speak. How to write. That all comes from reading."

He describes seeing graveyards of dead computers and tablets that had been donated by one group or another. "Microsoft doesn't support Windows XP anymore, and the Caribbean is littered with Windows XP machines. You need IT people to keep it all together, and ministries just can't afford IT people. Or then it rains, and the Internet goes down."

Books, by contrast, always work. "We toured the southeast of Dominica in January of 2018, and that area didn't get electricity until well over a year after Hurricane Maria," said Harriet. She described passing a house by the side of the road with no roof, no doors, no windows, just an empty shell. "Out in front, there was a lady on a chair reading a book. There was no electricity, no television, no Internet. And when you have PTSD and you're in this horrible situation, a book is a wonderful thing to have. You need something for your brain. You need something to take you out of that situation. That was an eye-opener for us, seeing the power of books after the hurricane."

## Looking Over the Horizon

In 2019 the Linskeys feel that Hands Across the Sea is the right size for its mission. A single 18-wheeler can handle no more than 27 palettes of books. When McGraw-Hill Education sent them 35 palettes of books one year, it was more than their logistics structure could reasonably accommodate. When a corporate sponsor asked them to expand into Jamaica, they realized that country's nearly three million people numbered more than twice that of all the inhabitants in the six countries they were already serving. Today their goal is not so much to grow

Harriet and T.L. Linskey aboard their catamaran named
for the nonprofit that they founded, Hands Across the Sea.

but to sustain what they've already built.

They've summarized their mission with the acronym CLASS, for Caribbean Literacy and School Support program. The three steps of that process are 1. send great new books; 2. create or rejuvenate lending libraries; and 3. sustain the literary gains.

That third item is their main focus now, set down in a five-year strategic plan. "We have to sustain what we've built; that's what I'm telling donors now. So our next budget is less about books—we've reduced our book budget to $50,000, because the books are in place now—and more about the program, the people part. That's all about getting the books to be used."

In recent years, the Linskeys have noticed a lot more attention being paid to Caribbean writers. "There's a new OECS project that's working really hard on getting children to write and publish books, which is really cool," said Harriet. "There are a couple of Caribbean writers' festivals. It's neat that more attention is being paid now to literacy and literary efforts."

These are the initiatives the Linskeys want to continue to foster. From that germ of an idea in Tonga, circa 1988, to a presence that extends through most of the English-speaking Caribbean, T.L. and Harriet have well and truly figured out how to "do something constructive while we're out here enjoying all this wonderful world" on their boat.

"Without sailing," said T.L., "we wouldn't have done any of this."

In 2016, Jeanne set off on her second solo, unassisted circumnavigation.
Both attempts were thwarted.

# 17

# Navigating Life, and the Five Great Capes: with Jeanne Socrates aboard Two *Nereidas*

We think we know maybe where we are. But are we?

—Jeanne Socrates

Four-time circumnavigator

Oldest person to sail solo nonstop unassisted around the world from North America

Jeanne Socrates was not born to sailing. She was 48 years old the first time she tried it. With George, her husband, she bought her first boat at age 55. The boat was struck by lightning. They sailed across the Atlantic. George died. Jeanne learned to sail alone. In mid-Pacific she lost her engine. She learned to change fuel injectors at sea. She sailed solo around the world—almost. She lost her boat on a beach. She bought another boat, then sailed around the world again. And again. And again. At age 70, Jeanne Socrates became the oldest woman to sail solo nonstop unassisted around the world from North America by way of the Southern Ocean. At age 77, she became the oldest *person* to do it.

How did she do it?

"You push yourself, and you gain confidence as you go, and you can do more and more," she said. "Basically, it's lots of little steps, and they become bigger and bigger steps."

Sounds simple enough. But the Southern Ocean? The Cape of Good Hope? *Cape Horn,* for crying out loud? *Three times?*

We probably need to look a little more closely at those steps.

## A Star Is Born
Jeanne Socrates, trained in physics, lectured at London's Brunel University, then taught at the same boys' secondary school that her stepfather and

Over 29 years, Jeanne Socrates went from stepping on a boat for the first time
to circling the world solo—almost four times—finishing when she was 77.
In *Nereida*, her Najad 380, Jeanne Socrates found the boat that fit.

uncles and son had attended. After exams each summer, Jeanne would take a group of her students on a weeklong outdoor excursion. It was a total break from academic work.

"I've always been a very active person," Jeanne said. "I was always in for anything—tennis, hockey, you name it. Music. Languages. Singing. Bird watching. But I never had the chance to sail."

In 1990 a colleague in the mathematics department offered the students a beginners watersports course in the south of France and gave her the chance to join as a leader. It included a bit of canoeing, a bit of dinghy sailing, a bit of windsurfing. George was able to take a weeklong holiday from his lecturing at Brunel University, where he taught spectroscopy and nuclear magnetic resonance. Immediately it was the windsurfing that really excited her. Jeanne was 48. George was 53.

Four years later, Jeanne found herself actually running her school's sailing and windsurfing program. Three of her students wanted to take a course called Competent Crew, offered by the Royal Yachting Association (RYA). As the minimum course size was five students, George was recruited once again. Jeanne was 52. George was 57.

*"It was just so enjoyable—because there's so much more to it than I'd realized. There was the sailing, which obviously I enjoyed. But then there's working the tides, the weather. You've got to live onboard. You have to learn the night lights and the day marks and the collision regulations. And, of course, as a mathematician, the navigation side of things is intriguing. It really got me!"*

The RYA course was Jeanne's first experience with a big boat—a Sigma 33, as it happened. "I wasn't that bothered," she said. "We were going in and out of Cowes, doing our courses, and I'd look at these people coming in to the docks in their yachts, and they're not doing very much, and it's all looking very static. I kind of thought it would be boring."

But they caught a lucky break with the weather that June on the Solent, and the UK Sailing Academy assigned them a very good instructor. "I was totally taken," she said. "It was just so enjoyable—because there's so much more to it than I'd realized. There was the sailing, which obviously I enjoyed. But then there's working the tides, the weather. You've got to live onboard. You have to learn the night lights and the day marks and the collision regulations. And, of course, as a mathematician, the navigation side of things is intriguing. It really got me!"

For the next couple of years, step by step, Jeanne and George progressed through the RYA curriculum. "These are fantastic sailing courses, the best in the world," Jeanne said. "And George was only too happy to come along and join in with me, learning everything as I did. We were very aware that we had not grown up sailing. We were trying to make up for lost time, as it were."

They found inexpensive deals on weekend sailing courses offered in the English wintertime. They joined a weeklong flotilla charter aboard a 25-foot Beneteau they called a *Baby Ben*. On a monthlong windsurfing trip to Greece, they spent their mornings beside their camper van studying theory for the RYA Yachtmaster course.

In 1997 Brunel University offered George an early retirement. Around that time, Jeanne's school made a change to its pension scheme. She totted up some figures and reckoned that working longer would add no financial benefit whatsoever. "Well, damn that," she said. So she retired too.

"Having suddenly, unexpectedly realized that we were about to be facing early retirement together, we went to the London Boat Show," she said. Jeanne was 54. George was 59.

## Of Magic Carpets

In their six years of experience, they'd formed a few opinions about the sailboats they'd observed. "We'd seen Beneteaus and Jeanneaus and Bavarias—they were the popular ones—because we'd gone through all these different courses in different school boats. And they were very easy to maneuver. Whenever I took a practical exam in a boat for the various RYA qualifications, I'd choose to go happily in a Beneteau or a Jeanneau. If you wanted to take the boat backwards, you just turned yourself around, put then engine in reverse and yourself at the wheel, and you pointed it and it went. Whereas with a heavy-displacement long-fin keel, that often doesn't happen."

By now Jeanne and George had decided they'd like to try some ocean sailing. "We wanted a sturdy, comfortable oceangoing boat," Jeanne said. "We just read up, and what we discovered seemed to be the general consensus: for good seakindly ocean-crossing boats, the heavier the better."

Having begun their big-boat experience in a 33-footer, Jeanne and George figured that was probably the right size for their needs. "We looked around at various 33-foot boats. Then you open a locker and suddenly realize there's no beam to the boats and very little depth to the lockers. Storage became a problem. So from 33 we moved up to thinking about a 36-footer. Every time we opened those lockers, there was more space in them."

Step by step, decision by decision, their research led them toward sailboats built in Sweden: Malö, Hallberg-Rassy, and Najad. "The Malös were lovely," Jeanne said. "But they were aft cockpit, not center cockpit. We looked at the center cockpit and realized you could get that lovely aft cabin. The aft cabin really drew us to the Hallberg-Rassy and the Najad."

This was the state of play when Jeanne and George set off for the 1997 London Boat Show, having suddenly, unexpectedly realized that they were both simultaneously about to retire. With a lump sum. Each. At the Najad stand they learned something else: that one boat had been started but that its prospective owners had abandoned the deal. Here was a Najad 361 already partly in build, and would they like to take it on?

"We jumped at the idea," said Jeanne. "That's how we got our first boat." A secondhand 36-foot Najad it would be.

## One Step at a Time

*Nereida's* log entry. Thursday, January 3, 2013. Approaching Cape Horn:

> Slept very little overnight, with worry of broken forward lower starboard shroud connection—felt like a "sword of Damocles" hanging over

me... a time-bomb, waiting to bring the mast down....!! Was interesting to see that the sky never got really dark—maybe partly the moon shining from behind the overcast, but more a matter of being well south in "high summer" now. Sunset is late and sunrise, early! Must have dozed off because woke up at 4am, in broad daylight already, and promptly got up to see to the problem. We were making around 6kt in quite heavy following seas which threw us around constantly—and rain had just started!

It was a bit of a struggle removing the split pins holding the broken "fork" fitting and the normally-connected top screw of the bottle-screw fitting, not helped by finding blood everywhere from a deep cut in my thumb from a sharp metal edge—couldn't feel anything in the cold, but bleeding wouldn't stop!! Placed a shackle on the swaged eye to form a rounded edge and used Spectra braid to lash to the bottle-screw fitting 3-4 times. Final result was certainly strong—but not very well tensioned.

Going back down below in the heavy rain, I had the broken fitting to hand—and discovered an almost identical fitting in my rigging spares, together with its clevis pin...! So a short while later, I was back on deck, undoing my previous efforts and soon had the shroud connected up and back in place properly, nicely tensioned using the bottle-screw in the usual way!!—relief—and jubilation!! By the time I'd finished putting everything away, it was gone 2pm! Time for a welcome, late breakfast in lovely warmth, having switched on the Eberspacher diesel heater to warm both me and my wet clothing—and then had a deep 2-3 hr sleep!!

On that day in early 2013, Jeanne was approaching Cape Horn for the second time, both times sailing solo. She was 70.

Jeanne had trod many steps since July 4, 1997—the very day after she retired from her teaching career—when she and George flew to Sweden to take delivery of their first boat. In the interim she did push herself, and she did gain confidence, and her small steps did indeed become bigger and bigger steps.

Najad is the Swedish spelling for the category of nymphs who inhabit fresh-water fountains, springs, and streams; Jeanne and George named their new Najad 361 *Nereida* for the sea nymphs who accompany Poseidon. They spent a lovely summer cruising Sweden and Norway and Denmark and getting to know their new boat before returning to England by way of Germany's Kiel Canal, the Frisian Islands, and the Netherlands, Belgium, and France. "It was brilliant," Jeanne said. "We had no autopilot at the time. We had no GPS. So it was really basic sailing and navigation."

On July 8, 2013, Jeanne Socrates completed her third circumnavigation, and her first nonstop, unassisted solo sail around the world. Her passage time was 259 days.

Their son and his fiancée joined them for a long weekend in Holland, but neither of them shared his parents' new pursuit. "They've never actually become sailors," said Jeanne. "It's a pity. It put the dampers on the family coming down and getting the grandkids involved. I think kids love being on boats. But they've missed out on a lot of enjoyment."

Still, Jeanne and George forged friendships with other sailors who understood the steps they were taking as they broadened their horizons in ever-widening diameters. After completing the commissioning of their new boat back in England, the two set out in 1998 for the warmer waters of the Mediterranean. It was on their first transit across the Bay of Biscay, approaching La Coruña, that *Nereida* was struck by lightning, destroying all the new electronics they'd just spent the last season installing.

A devastating setback, no?

"Here we were, suddenly caught, as it were, in northwest Spain for three weeks," said Jeanne. "But, you see, we hadn't planned to spend that long. We thought we were going to spend maybe two nights, then amble down through the *ríos* of Spain, and down Portugal, and so on. Well, it gave us a chance to learn a bit of Spanish. There's a beautiful castle there and a medieval fair was held over the king's birthday while we were there. It gave us a chance to go and visit a few

*Throughout all the tribulations known to every sailor
who ever untied a dockline and set off from solid ground,
Jeanne and George were* game.

places, and enjoy the town."

Throughout all the tribulations known to every sailor who ever untied a dockline and set off from solid ground, Jeanne and George were *game*. For every step they took, they took still another—always a little bigger, and always in a spirit of enjoyment. They replaced their electronics and carried on. In 1999 they joined the Atlantic Rally for Cruisers in the Canary Islands and sailed 2,700 miles south and west down the northeast tradewinds to St. Lucia and the Caribbean Sea. They spent the millennial year exploring the Windward and Leeward Islands, then set off for Bermuda and New York and eventually the Canadian Maritimes as far as Baddeck, Nova Scotia, before heading back south in September. They spent 2001 as typical North American snowbirds do, following the U.S. Intracoastal Waterway south to Miami, then island-hopping from the Bahamas to Cuba, Puerto Rico and the Virgin Islands, all the way on down to Grenada. They were loving their retirement.

But their initial instincts had been all too sound, and George's retirement was all too brief. Increasingly, he began to notice a pain in his lower back. In September 2001 he went in for a physical examination and came out with a diagnosis of prostate cancer.

"It was not until May 2002 that he got back on board," wrote Jeanne on her blog, "and we headed for Tobago & Trinidad, finally setting sail for Venezuela in late August, enjoying the uncrowded island anchorages and spending time in Puerto La Cruz and Merida. By late December, we had reached Bonaire, via the beautiful Los Roques and Las Aves. We had hoped to return in the New Year but that was not to be—George's body gave up the fight in March 2003." George was 65.

## Solo
*Nereida's* log entry. Friday, January 4, 2013. Approaching Cape Horn:

Around midday the wind started increasing slowly from the F3-4 of earlier, and pressure started dropping—from a steady 993 in the morning more rapidly in the evening—to 984 by 11pm, when I made my usual contact with Pacific Seafarers Net.

By that time, we were in very strong conditions, with genoa furled away, small stays'l and 3 reefs in mains'l. Seas were pretty big—around

5m or more—and were tossing us around—but they were fairly well spaced and not breaking. With the wind on our beam we were making speeds of around 7kt or more and Fred [*Nereida*'s Hydrovane self-steering gear] was happily keeping us on course (autopilot had gone down, again, earlier that morning!). My worry ahead was a steep seamount peaking at around 300m depth, rising abruptly from 2000-3000m depths! Seas were likely to be nasty in that area in these conditions—so definitely to be avoided.

We were making directly for our waypoint due S of Cape Horn and the day had been grey with frequent rain—but I had seen the occasional birds—a pair of prions and, later, a wedge-tailed shearwater.

I was debating whether I'd have to stop the boat—but was not inclined to do so while we were coping with the conditions. Winds were around 30kt or more (I recognised the sound in the rigging!) and our speed showed the wind strength also—with so little sail up, to be making over 7kt shows a strong wind! Eventually, with no sign of the wind increasing further (I also kept checking the gribs and weather info!), I got to sleep for a few hours—with an alarm set to wake me up well before we could get anywhere near the seamount—and also to check on our course, should the wind have changed direction…

When I awoke, it was daylight, with a patch of blue sky overhead among the grey clouds—and the wind had died totally! Adjusted Fred and unfurled the genoa and stays'l to give us speed—from 4kt, we increased to 6kt! Pressure is still very low at 982 hPa—and wind set to increase possibly a bit later but then die back. We're 13ml SW of the seamount, heading ESE, so that's a safe distance away.

In June 2003, Jeanne Socrates, newly widowed, traveled from London to *Nereida* in the southern Caribbean with her husband's ashes. She was 61.

It was a difficult time. Yet no thought of abandoning the boat or the sailing ever entered Jeanne's mind. "It was just too much enjoyment," she said. "There were boat friends around who were able to support me. There was no hint of giving up the boat. It was a matter of how I could continue on with it."

In one sense, she had a good start. As new boat-owners, Jeanne and George had forged a resilient partnership. "One thing I wanted right from the beginning," she said, "was that it's *our* boat. I didn't want pink jobs and blue jobs. In fact, George was only too happy that I would take on the job of keeping the head working. He hated dirty things. And I have a physics degree, so, you know, the electrical side of things was not a problem. I was quite determined that I would

*"I was quite determined that I would be involved in the boat from the beginning. And that was a good thing, really, because obviously when I lost George, I still stood a chance of being able to maintain the boat."*

be involved in the boat from the beginning. And that was a good thing, really, because obviously when I lost George, I still stood a chance of being able to maintain the boat."

Maintaining the boat alone would be a daunting but familiar prospect. More daunting and less familiar was the prospect of making ocean passages without George. "I was worried about sailing overnight and not keeping watch," Jeanne said.

Around that time she learned of a cruising rally being organized by the Ocean Cruising Club in British Columbia for late summer 2004. Feeling ready for a change, she began plotting how to get *Nereida* there from Bonaire. "What are the options?" she wondered. "Well, you can get it to Texas and truck it all the way. Or, you can sail it somewhere and put it on a ship. Or you can sail it all the way. That was rather out of the question because I was only beginning my singlehanding, and it was a long, long way to get up to British Columbia from the Caribbean and through the Canal."

From her research, she concluded that the Dockwise Yacht Transport float-on, float-off system made the most sense. Dockwise could ship *Nereida* from Ft. Lauderdale to Vancouver in time for the rally. Still, she'd need to get the boat to Florida. Several cruising friends initially offered to make the passage with her. But with a wedding here, an unexpected departure there, all those offers fell through. "I suddenly realized that if I wanted to keep sailing, I was going to have to be prepared to go by myself. I was not prepared to have a stranger come on the boat with me, and I couldn't rely on people turning up."

Seeing that she was resolved to get to Florida, cruising friends counseled her to take the shortest possible route, back through the island chain she and George had already visited before. "Well, hang on. That means I miss Curaçao; I miss Aruba; I miss Colombia; I miss the San Blas Islands; I miss the Canal; I miss Providencia," said Jeanne. "I thought, no way. I'm not going to miss any of these lovely places I've been hearing about."

It had been several seasons since Jeanne had sailed *Nereida* hard. During George's illness she hadn't poled out the genoa, hadn't flown the asymmetrical spinnaker. She lacked confidence. As she prepared to leave Bonaire, she heard about a young Dutch man, a good sailor, who was keen to join her. After a couple of missed connections, he caught up with her in Curaçao.

"Daan was a very good sailor," said Jeanne. "We got on fine. We had completely similar music tastes, and he was happy to cook every other day. I don't want to be on the boat with people who can't cook. I knew I could sail the boat. I just needed the confidence of someone who knew what they were doing, just to be with me and go through things and sort things out."

The arrangement worked fine—for a while. Daan was meant to make the trip to Florida but left the boat at Panama. "He was 21 or 22, and he was finding it difficult as a youngster. At that point, I had gained my confidence, and I was now becoming more of a skipper. He was not able to cope with a female skipper."

So Jeanne prepared to leave Panama alone. Along the way, she'd been checking in by single-sideband radio with Herb Hilgenberg, the well-known weather router. She made her preparations and set off. "When I finally went to go, I thought, 'Oh my gosh, it's a bit rougher than I expected.' The waves were breaking over the Colón breakwater wall, which is quite big. So it was pretty rough," Jeanne recalled. "About two hours after I got out, it was my chance to get hold of Herb to see what the weather was like. And he said, 'Oh, my god! You haven't gone, have you? You should turn back.' I told him, no, I'm not aborting. So he wasn't too happy."

But who *was* happy? Jeanne Socrates. "I finally got to Providencia after an overnighter to get there—my first solo overnight—and it was great. After two big G&Ts, I was just so pleased that I had managed. So that became a major thing, the beginning of my solo sailing."

## Round the World
*Nereida's* log entry. Saturday, January 5, 2013. Approaching Cape Horn:

> Midnight! Southern sky near the horizon almost as light as day—but Jupiter shining brightly in the darker sky in the N, along with a few stars. (My body can't get used to all these quick time-zone changes!)
>
> It's been a good day of mainly pleasant, fast sailing, if we ignore the big seas that have continually tossed us around and the frequent grey skies and sometimes heavy rain! But in between, there have been lovely blue skies and several different birds seen—including two different abatross (grey-faced and black-browed), storm petrel, prions and others.
>
> The light N wind of very early morning gave way by mid-morning to stronger wind, NW-NNW around F5-6 (20-25kt), continuing on into evening, when it finally started dying down again—but not completely.

I really felt at one with the Vendée Globe sailors tonight—I had my first dehydrated (freeze-dried) meal!! Beef and pasta hotpot, the foil wrapper proclaimed—and it wasn't too bad at all!

Ice is beginning to pose a problem after rounding the Horn and beginning to head ENE—two icebergs look as though they're drifting onto my path… Will have to keep a good lookout and maybe be prepared to divert around them. Problem is partly the 'bergy bits' that could be up to 20ml ahead of them in the direction of drift—presently, due E or ENE.

Weather is looking distinctly unhelpful in a few days' time—either almost no wind or, after that, way too much—two Lows forming, with us the 'meat in the sandwich'! … and later getting the full brunt of one of them—deep Low of around 970hPa (pressure right now is down at 977hPa—typical of these latitudes).

Time for some sleep—still light in the S…

24hr distance-made-good at 7pm local time (Chile time!) (2300GMT ): 142 n.ml. (good speed last night and from mid-morning ) Cape Horn 197 n.ml. away and my waypoint, off the continental shelf, well S of C. Horn, was 191 n.ml. away. The nearest big island along the channels of the SW Chile coast is now Isla Londonderry (!!!), 135 n.ml. away to NE.

The yachting journalist and Ocean Cruising Club member Liza Copeland recalls meeting Jeanne in 2004 soon after Dockwise deposited *Nereida* in Vancouver. "Small, slight, and social, Socrates immediately invited Andy, my husband, and I below to share our welcoming bottle of wine. I became aware of her constant attention to detail in boat operation, in updating the logbook, and in the preparation for docking and anchoring that's required when one does it alone."

Jeanne enjoyed sailing in the Pacific Northwest and especially enjoyed the company of accomplished sailors. The rally and the conversations gave her still more confidence to push her own boundaries. In October she left the relatively protected inside waterways behind Vancouver Island, exited the Juan de Fuca Strait, and proceeded down the rough Pacific coast of Washington and Oregon and northern California—a boisterous stretch of ocean in which many cruising dreams have come to a dispiriting end. Jeanne was exhilarated by it. She continued on to Zihuatanejo, Mexico, then shipped *Nereida* back north to Ketchikan, Alaska, for the 2005 summer season. In 2006 she entered the Singlehanded TransPac race from San Francisco to Hawaii. *Latitude 38* magazine reported on her passage: "Jeanne Socrates on *Nereida*, a last-minute entry who hails from the British Isles, spent the time reading, chasing chafe, and dancing to Bob Marley tunes on *Nereida's* tiny

Jeanne's adopted home of Victoria, British Columbia,
would become the place she'd return to, again and again.

dance floor." A photo of her with an ear-to-ear grin carries this caption: "Despite *Nereida's* broken bow pulpit, Jeanne Socrates couldn't wipe the smile off her face."

It was on the return passage through the windless Pacific High that she learned to change the fuel injectors on *Nereida's* diesel engine. "After my race finish in Kauai, I headed up towards Sitka, Alaska, beating into big seas and quite strong winds, until finally reaching the calm of the Pacific High when I went to use my motor—nada!" wrote Jeanne on her blog. "Another major learning curve, as I struggled with the result of seawater in my diesel fuel—not a happy engine! Triumphantly, I got the engine going again, after five days of struggling, changing one injector (who me? That was only supposed to be in my spares for a mechanic to deal with!!) and checking the others."

Jeanne had truly become the master of her vessel—confident, competent, and joyfully in command. "As a result of these ocean passages, and having to overcome the many and varied boat problems that cropped up en route," Jeanne wrote, "I gained in confidence tremendously and set my sights on sailing around the world—to be started from Zihuatanejo (Mexico) after their Annual Guitar Festival in March 2007. So, in San Diego from December 2006 on, I prepared *Nereida* for a planned one-year, "stop-everywhere," "cruising-style" circumnavigation."

*"When I lost that boat and I was busy salvaging stuff off it
as it was sinking into the wet sand—it was horrible, because,
you know, this is my teammate dying—I was saving the stuff
I could get off her really for the next boat.
There was no discontinuity in my mind.
I just wanted to keep doing what I had been doing."*

One year had become 15 months when Jeanne and *Nereida* returned to Mexican waters. Yet they'd done it: they'd circled the globe. Or, rather, they'd *almost* done it. With Acapulco already behind them, they were 60 miles and 12 hours distant from a big celebratory welcome in Zihua. *Nereida* was happily motorsailing along in very little wind under a full moon and with a moderate swell running when Jeanne set her stopwatch for a 45-minute nap, as she'd done so many times before. With so little wind, *Nereida* was being steered not by the mechanical windvane self-steering device but by the electronic Raymarine autopilot. Jeanne had previously discovered a design quirk on this unit: that each time the battery discharged on the autopilot remote, the control head would switch into Standby mode. That is, the autopilot would silently disable itself—leaving the equivalent of a ship without a rudder. Knowing this, on the night of June 19, 2007, Jeanne plugged in the remote to keep it charged before she went to sleep. But the plug must have come loose. In the calm conditions and with the diesel's steady rumble, she never noticed the change in direction—until *Nereida* grounded on remote Playa Michigan.

"It was still dark with no lights on shore," she said. "No sign of anyone, in fact, for ages as I tried to set an anchor, which was difficult in the strong, swirling surf conditions. It was difficult to keep the chain taut enough to stop her from suddenly being heeled down the steep beach slope—and then she'd suddenly come back up the other way in the surge, often with a bang. I was worried the starboard side might begin to crack."

*Nereida*—whose birthday Jeanne had celebrated every July 4 since 1997—was doomed. At the time of her wreck, *Nereida* was for Socrates the perfect cruising sailboat. And more.

Many years later, speaking of that moment, Jeanne said, "When I lost that boat and I was busy salvaging stuff off it as it was sinking into the wet sand—it was horrible, because, you know, this is my teammate dying—I was saving the stuff I could get off her really for the next boat. There was no discontinuity in my mind. I just wanted to keep doing what I had been doing."

## Nonstop

*Nereida's* log entry. Sunday, January 6, 2013. Approaching Cape Horn:

I've had so many emails of support wishing me well as I try to round Cape Horn—especially after my last time here—it has been wonderful knowing that my journey is being followed by so many warm-hearted people… and makes this feel very special. Thank you all so much!

9am Bright sun—but wind dying…! Clear sky overhead but low cloud, ahead to port—to N and NE. Making only ~4.5 kt . Less than 110 miles to my 'Cape Horn waypoint' (103 miles S of Cape Horn itself)—my turning point into the S. Atlantic! Could become frustratingly slow going…

Waiting to get latest Ice report from the Vendée Globe management team to see where the two icebergs of concern to me have drifted to… (Later: The nearer one looks as though it's drifted out of my way a bit—although I'll still have to keep a good lookout when in that area. The further one looks to be getting nearer my course—all depends on winds over next few days, until I get closer). I'd mentioned, when sending a position report, that two bergs were possibly a problem for me—just got an email back from Guillaume in VG Paris HQ: *"Si jamais tu vois des Icebergs, merci de nous envoyer les photos!!"* ("If ever you see some icebergs, please send us the photos!") I replied, agreeing—but hope I don't get close enough to any!

Made use of calmer conditions to make some fresh coffee—lovely! Solar panels putting 4-6A into batteries, despite slight cloud. Warm in sun under canopy but air is cold. Cabin temperature: 10C; sea temperature: 8C—wearing lots of layers!

1pm. Struggling to make just 2.5 kt in light wind, about F2, from NW. Short rainshower mid-morning, otherwise sunshine with some cloud… Pair of magnificent Southern Royal albatross were circling around earlier for a long time before moving away into the distance… Then a (smaller, but still big) black-browed albatross and a small group of prions. Tiny white-rumped storm petrel nearly made me dizzy at one point—flew in circles around and around, close to sea surface! Sea is no longer rough but still easily 4m/12ft or more, at 8-12 second intervals—long, slow swell. Tried to take photos of the albatross, but not one came out showing the birds well…

Keep looking at grib (weather) files—the Low that was expected to form to E is now being shown there and very deep/intense—but is now expected to move away without causing me too much of a problem—fingers crossed the computer program has got that right!! Second Low to W is expected to diminish—so we might be about to have a lucky escape! (It's the two Lows either side so close to here that are causing our lack of wind with their opposing wind directions!)

6.30pm. We're down to almost zero boat speed but 1.5 kt SOG—a good thing there's a fair current that we're drifting East with! Just about making our course with the autopilot working hard… Still lovely bright sunshine, although the air feels cold. Finished off my stew—hot!

9.30pm. Took the wheel for a bit, despite the chilly air at sunset with a clear sky, and got us pointed in the right direction… A little more wind seemed to have come up (F2, 4-5 kt maybe?), so now we're back on course, making 2.4 kt again—feels fast compared with 0.3kt!

Sea is so much calmer, it feels weird—this is not the Southern Ocean I'm familiar with! The long rounded swell is down to just 3-4m.

24hr DMG at 7pm local time (Chile time!) (2300GMT ): 95 n.ml. (slow with dying wind today) Cape Horn 124 n.ml. away and my waypoint, off the continental shelf, well S of C. Horn, was 91 n.ml. away. The nearest island is now Isla Gonzalo, the S-most of Islas Diego Ramirez, 67 n.ml. away to NE . Land is now showing on my AIS screen—the islands around Cape Horn, just over 100 mls away.

In the summer of 2007 Jeanne Socrates—solo circumnavigator, almost—found herself suddenly, unexpectedly boatless. She was 65.

She had already recently sold the five-bedroom house in London in which she'd raised her family. And there was some insurance money after *Nereida's* loss. What next?

The one thing she knew was that she wanted another boat. "I came up to San Francisco with all my salvaged stuff," Jeanne said. "Because I was not too familiar with North American boats, I was saying to all my friends, 'Give me advice.' The Najad was a great boat. She sailed well *and* was comfortable at sea. And sturdy. So tell me what American boat would be a good one to get. And no one could actually come up with as good a boat as the one that I had lost—one that sailed well. The Taiwanese boats would be really lovely to live in, but they sailed like a tank."

The boat she chose? Another Najad—as much like the first as the builder would build.

"I went to look at a slightly bigger one. In fact, I was being told to get a 40-footer, and I tried one. But they all came with in-mast furling, which I did *not* want. And it was just a little too big for me. I felt that if I'm in rough conditions, I want to be easily able to grab hold of something, not have a dancefloor to cross

*With the new boat she set her sights on a*
*nonstop solo circumnavigation from the very beginning.*

from one side of the cabin to the other. I wanted to be safe in rough seas."

Jeanne ordered a new Najad 380, model year 2008, but with "a long, long, long list of changes and adaptations." When she bought her first cruising sailboat at age 55, she was green, yet her education and instincts had led her to a boat that never once held her back, even as her life and her goals evolved far beyond anything she could have reasonably imagined during the sailing courses of those English winters of a decade earlier. Now she was a seasoned sailor.

"I had spent 11 years making the previous boat better for cruising. She was all perfect to my mind. So I knew exactly what I wanted added to this boat to make her ready." That list included a staysail on a furler, slab reefing on the main with simple low-friction slides, and the ability to make sail changes from the cockpit or the mast. "I made sure that I could go right back to basics if anything happened to the single-line reefing that Seldén provided."

She named her new boat *Nereida.*

With the new boat she set her sights on a nonstop solo circumnavigation from the very beginning. As with so many other things in life, every voyage has had its share of starts and stops—and sudden, unexpected changes. Her first nonstop attempt was cut short due to rigging problems. The next was ended by a violent knockdown approaching Cape Horn.

Having arrived back at her starting point from one circumnavigation in August 2012 Jeanne Socrates, age 70, set off again that same October. "I felt cheated of my nonstop attempt. I was just unlucky to have got the knockdown and had the damage that I did. And obviously I'd learned a bit more about my passagemaking and where I should or should not have gone. And how to handle the boat. And so all the time, I'm learning. And gaining confidence."

Step by step, Jeanne kept sailing. Along the way she'd pushed not only her own boundaries but increasingly boundaries that none but a couple of dozen people on the planet had ever pushed before. She did it because that's what she likes to do.

On October 3, 2018, Socrates, age 76, embarked on what would become her fourth solo circumnavigation and her second successful nonstop solo unassisted circumnavigation, sailed by way of the five Great Capes.

What could have possessed her?

"I was kind of missing the ocean passages," she said. "I wanted to be in the

A justifiably proud—and relaxed—Jeanne Socrates in 2019, having just become the "oldest person to sail solo nonstop around the world via the Southern Ocean's Five Great Capes."

Southern Ocean again, because it's a very special place. You really feel privileged to be down there. And you are just at one with nature and the wilderness and the ocean and the birds and the sky. The sky is amazing, actually. Someone said, 'Well, you know, if you did go around again nonstop, you'd become the oldest person, as opposed to the oldest woman.' I thought, well, let's make that the reason for going around. It wasn't really. But let's see if I can raise some money in a good cause while I'm at it. So I was pleased to raise 4,000 pounds for the Royal National Lifeboat Institution."

*Nereida's* log entry. Monday, January 7, 2013. Approaching Cape Horn:

At 11:27:44 pm (local Chile time), we passed the longitude of the Cape Horn lighthouse and started changing course for the start of our Atlantic crossing…!!!!! I announced it to the Pacific Seafarers' Net, on the radio just then, who shared the excitement with me!! (Someone blew a trumpet!) In the south, a streak of clear sky showing daylight above the horizon, grey clouds everywhere else in the not-so-dark(!) sky, a big swell, but sea not as rough as earlier. With the wind from S-SSW, I eased the sheets for our new course of 076T—we made 6.5kt and rolled in the seas… Life felt good!

Wilson Fitt honed his boatbuilding skills early on an H-28, which, by trial and error, he learned to maintain and repair. Then he moved up to be the project manager for the restoration of the 160-foot schooner, *Bluenose II*.

# 18

# Wilson Fitt and the Nova Scotia Cruising Guide: Answering a Hundred-Year Call

*Finally we got down to the inevitable subject of boats and more particularly
to cruising boats, for, after all, what sort of a boat can hold a candle to a cruiser
for the great big gobs of enjoyment that it returns on the investment?*
—William Washburn Nutting, on building *Typhoon* (1920)

*You don't start out on a project like this without a well-developed capacity
for self-delusion about time, effort, and cost. I am no exception.*
—Wilson Fitt, on building *Christina Grant* (1999)

It was called Boulaceet.

Maskell's Harbour lies at 46°01.3'N, 60°47.1'W. You enter it by leaving
the green spar "GB23", the lighthouse, and Gillis Point to port, and leaving
the sand spit to starboard. But first you have to make your way to Nova
Scotia's Bras d'Or Lakes.

"This harbor was known to the older generation as 'Boulaceet.' In 1919,
anchored here aboard the yawl *Elsie*, Gilbert Grosvenor, William Washburn
Nutting, and Captain Morgan had a long conversation about forming a
North American partner to the Royal Cruising Club. This came to fruition in
1922 with the formation of the Cruising Club of America."

So reads the Maskell's Harbour entry in the 2020 edition of the *CCA
Cruising Guide to Nova Scotia,* published by Cruising Club of America
Nautical Publishers.

"Maskell's is one of the prettiest anchorages in the lakes, but it is also
within easy striking distance of Baddeck, so expect company. The surrounding
land (including the oysters found below the high-water mark) is privately
owned. The landowners are cruising folk and welcome yachts in the harbour.

A walk ashore to the lighthouse or a row down to the marine caves at the western end of the harbour is encouraged, but please remember to treat this property with the same respect that you would treat your own."

There's a lot to unpack in that entry. Who exactly sailed aboard *Elsie* on that seminal cruise a century ago? What did they discuss? By what spirit was their conversation propelled? And how on earth do you pronounce Boulaceet?

The keys to these questions lie with Bill Nutting, one of the parties to that conversation, and with the cruising guide's editor, Wilson Fitt of Chester, Nova Scotia.

## In Whom Fantasy Takes Over Real Life

Wilson came the long way round to his editor's role.

"My messing about with boats started at about 12 years of age, when a friend and I built a little plywood job that I don't think ever floated for more than a few minutes," he wrote in an unpublished manuscript about his own cruising origins and his subsequent building of an oceangoing sailboat. "My father had an L. Francis Herreshoff H-28, which I inherited at an unreasonably early age, and which by trial and error I learned to manage, maintain, and repair."

A self-described "paper-pusher," Wilson practiced law early in his career, then transitioned to construction project management. His portfolio went on to include the restoration of the iconic 160-foot schooner *Bluenose II,* owned by the Province of Nova Scotia.

But alongside Wilson's early career and family life ran another thread. Having sold the H-28, he read John Gardner's 1977 *Building Classic Small Craft* and built a 14-foot plank-on-frame Whitehall rowing boat of Eastern white cedar with mahogany seats and ash trim, a small craft that possessed enough of the fine entry, curved midsections, and stern tuck to occupy his soul for several seasons. A canoe of canvas-over-cedar soon followed.

"At some stage, before the canoe was finished," wrote Wilson, "my wife's suspicions were aroused when scrap lead started to appear in the back yard, to be joined by that most essential piece of boatbuilding equipment: a cast-iron tub in which to melt the lead."

With no yearslong apprenticeship in traditional wooden boatbuilding behind him but a shelf full of books, Wilson began to focus on *the big boat.* "The only book that seemed to make a big project doable was Bud MacIntosh's *How to Build a Wooden Boat.* With Sam Manning's drawings, MacIntosh cut through the mystique, dispensed with the fussiness of perfection, and made it all look like a straightforward piece of work that a normal person could accomplish. You don't start out on a project like this without a well-developed capacity for self-delusion

*Christina Grant* was launched in the summer of 1999.
She is the result of 7,500 labor hours
spread out over five and a half years by her owner, Wilson Fitt.

about time, effort, and cost. I am no exception, and MacIntosh's book was enough to push me over the edge."

When it came to a design, Wilson turned to William Atkin—the same source Nutting turned to after his consequential conversations at Boulaceet in 1919. The difference was that for Nutting, Atkin was an animated drinking-buddy, a daily colleague at the editorial offices of *MotorBoat* magazine in Manhattan. For Fitt, Atkin was a specter who'd crossed the bar and taken his place in the yacht designer's pantheon, gone some 30 years and more before the lofting began.

Wilson chose Atkin's 1939 design called *Jerry Colemore,* a 38-foot 6-inch knockabout (which Wilson, assisted by designer Jay Benford, modified into a cutter with a bowsprit to add half again to the boat's original sail area). Atkin had named his design for a young family friend, a lover of Friendship sloops, killed flying in World War I. "Here is a design worthy of the name," Atkin wrote. "She has all the earmarks of the yachty yacht: the homeliness and the shippyness of a Friendship sloop somewhat astern and to leeward. The lines show unusual thickness through the garboards, long flat buttock lines, firm bilges, generous flare in the forward and after sections, tumblehome in the mid-sections, rather full waterlines, and a wholesome bluffness in the contour of the deck. By the same token there is more headroom amidships with the lighter sheer."

*This is the point in the story where, as Wilson says,*
*"a desk jockey let his fantasy take over real life."*

A friend of Wilson's father had owned one of Atkin's *Jerry Colemore* designs, and Wilson "admired its robust unfussy look."

This is the point in the story where, as Wilson says, "a desk jockey let his fantasy take over real life." The boat's construction would be traditional carvel planking on steam-bent ribs with copper and bronze fastenings. Wilson found warehouse space in Halifax, then set up a lofting floor with ½-inch drywall sheets laid over rough plywood he salvaged from a construction site. "The drywall gave a smooth, clean surface, and the plywood held the nails around which battens were sprung." Later, he and his family moved their lives and the whole boatbuilding operation to an old fisherman's cottage in Indian Harbour near the famous Peggy's Cove that they renovated.

"I erected a 45-foot by 18-foot arch-roof plastic shed attached to the existing workshop on the property," he wrote. "The sight of this apparently massive empty structure made me realize what a big undertaking this was, and I thought seriously about whether this was just too much. However, having told too many people that I was building a boat, pride and stubbornness pushed me ahead. The neighbors, some of them old-time fishermen, were certain (so they later said) that the plastic shed would blow down with the first gale, but it stood with the strength of a reed for the next four winters."

The lead keel for this boat is not a simple slab-sided, flat-topped affair. Instead, it is all curves on the underside, with a short flat top and a long taper aft that matches the wedge-shaped deadwood. I made a wooden plug [the male form the keel would take], layer-cake style, from the same wood pile that made the moulds, fairing it with a variety of power tools and drywall crack-filling compound. The finished plug was about 14 feet long and needed several people just to move.

The next step was to build a big plywood box that looked like Frankenstein's coffin. The plug was suspended in the box, and concrete poured around it to create a female mould. In hindsight, it was grossly overbuilt, with almost a foot of concrete in places, and rebar throughout. I didn't fancy the idea of 10,000 pounds of molten lead running over my feet, so stuck with the "more is better" theory.

The design weight of the keel was 9,500 pounds, and I had about

11,000 pounds of miscellaneous scrap on hand, including old sewer pipe, roof flashing, wheel weights, and ballast pigs. I had intended to weigh and tally each piece as it went into the pot but forgot in the heat of the moment. So the best estimate of the final casting, based on what was left over, is 10,500 pounds.

I perched the fabled cast-iron bathtub on a 55-gallon drum, arranged a drain into the mould, and put two big propane space heaters on end, like rocket engines, under the tub. Three large handheld "tiger" torches completed the heat-generation equipment. A test run with a couple of hundred pounds of lead seemed to indicate that the rig would work, and the tub would not split asunder when the heat was applied. On the appointed day we loaded the tub with lead and fired up the torches.

My friends had divided themselves into two camps: those who wanted to see this happen, and those who wanted to be in a different county. Some of the former group, equipped with heavy gloves and face masks, helped to slog lead up the ramp to the tub, held torches, and watched as molten lead poured out in a clear silvery stream.

We burned about 400 pounds of propane but didn't generate quite enough heat to create a steady flow of hot lead. The melt was done in batches of 2,000 or 2,500 pounds each, resulting in a layer-cake casting with imperfect bonds between the layers. As the lead keel was to be held on with 14 one-inch-diameter bronze through-bolts, it seemed unlikely to fall apart.

The keel casting lasted until midafternoon and ended with large quantities of cold beer for the crew, laughter, and congratulations that no one was hurt.

The denouement, of course, was removing the keel from the mould. I rented a jackhammer and spent several days of hot, dirty, and noisy labour reducing the concrete mould to a pile of rubble and annoying our neighbours. I don't recall reading about this part of the process in the "romance of wooden boatbuilding" articles in *WoodenBoat* magazine. Perhaps I missed that issue.

In all, the build took 7,500 labor-hours—most of which was Wilson's own labor. He spent five years of evenings and weekends on the project, then quit his job and spent another six months of full-time work to finish the boat he would call *Christina Grant,* named for, and christened by his mother in her 80th year. That was in the summer of 1999. After six short shakedown weeks, he and his wife Thelma sailed her south.

"We did the whole sell-the-house, sell-the-cars, quit-the-job thing and went off to the Caribbean for a winter," Wilson said. They "dithered through the islands," he worked a stint in an Antigua boat shop, and they stayed long enough to enter the 2000 edition of the Antigua Classic Yacht Regatta in April—an event at which *Christina Grant* won the coveted first prize in the Concours d'Élégance.

Together with their oldest son, Wilson and Thelma came home to Canada in two hops by way of Bermuda. Of course, they returned to no house, no car, and no job. But they used the sabbatical to reinvent their careers and their home life.

## What They Said at Boulaceet

All of which brings us back to Nova Scotia and Nutting and the Maskell's Harbour conversation that launched first one voyage, then voyages and voyages beyond counting.

"We've been to Maskell's Harbour many times," said Wilson. "Boulaceet Farm"—it's a Mi'kmaq word, pronounced *BULL-uh-seet*—"was owned by three CCA members. I believe they have put it in a preservation trust. Maskell's is a lovely spot. It's within easy striking distance of Baddeck."

The 2020 edition of the Nova Scotia cruising guide takes it from there:

> Baddeck is most famous for its connection to Alexander Graham Bell. Nearby Beinn Bhreagh was his summer home, and his descendants still summer there. In 1956 the Canadian government opened the Alexander Graham Bell Museum in Baddeck. This striking building, in its beautiful landscape, overlooks Baddeck Bay in the direction of Bell's old summer home. One thinks of Bell only as the inventor of the telephone, but inside this museum are displays of Bell's many other interests, including devices to bring sound to the deaf and the kites and gliders he used on his many aeronautical experiments.

Once again, as we draw our focus from Wilson Fitt's Baddeck to Bill Nutting's Baddeck, we cross-fade from the kind of history that's preserved in museums into a living social circle of garrulous and energetic companions. Nutting first encountered this crowd in 1913 when he singlehanded his 28-foot cutter from New York into the Bras d'Or.

"Dr. Alexander Graham Bell, the grand old man of the scientific world, and Casey Baldwin, who smashes the aeroplanes when he's not racing yachts or playing cricket, entertained the crew of the *Nereis* at Beinn Bhreagh, and the chief engineer of my crew had a treat in looking through the shops and laboratories," wrote Nutting for an October 1913 edition of *MotorBoat*. "It's hardly necessary to state

*Christina Grant* evokes the self-reliant charms of cruising Nova Scotia. The Atkins-designed cutter hails from Baddeck, not far from Maskell's Harbour, beloved by many CCA members.

that Casey Baldwin lives at Baddeck. He's commodore of the yacht club and I'd heard a lot about him in Halifax. In fact, I was coming to think that Baldwin was giving the fogs a close run for first place as Nova Scotia's most prominent feature."

Late in that season of 1913 Nutting continued on from Baddeck to Newfoundland, then decommissioned *Nereis* at the French island outpost of St. Pierre. World War I interrupted his plans to return the next season, and it wasn't until 1919 that Nutting was able to rekindle his acquaintance with Casey Baldwin. Here the chronology becomes fuzzy, as Nutting introduced an error in his public record of what happened next, an error that subsequent writers (but not the Nova Scotia cruising guide editor) picked up. That said, Nutting's description of the scene at Boulaceet puts us right there with him and Casey in the saloon of a good boat:

> It would be hard to say just when the idea of the *Typhoon* had its beginning. Possibly it was one night in October, 1920, [sic] in the snug cabin of the *Elsie,* way down at the other end of Nova Scotia. Casey Baldwin and I, not to mention Johnnie Walker, had sailed up the Bras d'Or Lake after ducks and at nightfall had anchored in a little cove several miles from Baddeck. It had been a year since Baldwin had trod the gay white way and six since *Nereis* and I had plowed out the Great Bras d'Or Passage bound for Newfoundland.
>
> There were many things to talk about.
>
> Casey and I did most of the talking, while Johnnie, faithful fellow, just sort of stood by and furnished the inspiration.

Finally we got down to the inevitable subject of boats and more particularly to cruising boats, for, after all, what sort of boat can hold a candle to a cruiser for the great big gobs of enjoyment that it returns on the investment?

Many times before we had talked over the possibility of a cruise along the Labrador, or to Iceland, or even across the Atlantic, and so we kept at it until we had a pretty good idea of what a cruiser for this purpose should be. By this time Johnnie Walker was merely the empty shell of a departed spirit and we decided to call it a day.

In order to get to the subject of this story we'll have to skip the harrowing account of how two sleepy mariners, each afraid of the ridicule of the other, went overboard for a swim on the following cold, rainy, late October morning and how an accommodating duck made it possible for a bespectacled editor to rise several points in the estimation of a skeptical engineer. Suffice it to say that we spent the greater part of the following day in the drafting room of the Laboratory giving expression to our conclusions of the night before. Result: a 40-footer, fisherman style, ketch rigged with an auxiliary motor.

And the rest is the history of the founding of the Cruising Club of America, as related in chapters the early chapters of this book. Nutting and crew sailed transatlantic back and forth from North America to Europe, then returned to New York to start the conversations that would develop into the CCA.

Ten years after the club's founding and six years after Nutting's disappearance at sea between Greenland and Labrador, yachting historian W. P. Stephens reflected on the legacy of a man whom few cruising sailors in those days had ever heard of.

"The name of William Washburn Nutting means but little to them," wrote Stephens, "but they should realize the debt under which he has placed all Americans who are interested in the use and improvement of the cruising yacht. Would that he were with us tonight to enjoy the fruits of his labors."

## Extolling the Home Waters

From the CCA's earliest days, America meant more than the United States. Charter members included several of the cruising friends Nutting met on his visits to Baddeck, including Gilbert Grosvenor, Aemilius Jarvis, and of course Casey Baldwin. And though the founders deliberately avoided fixing themselves to a brick-and-mortar headquarters or clubhouse—"let us refuse stoutly to accumulate an on-shore contingent"—the cruising grounds of Nova Scotia have

*With that, Wise Wood turned to the club's two simple objectives: pleasure and service. "Among the services we render each other," he wrote, "we create a clearinghouse of nautical information, covering all of the factors involved in cruising. These include questions of geography, oceanography, meteorology, navigation, seamanship, hull type, sail plan, auxiliary power, commissariat, domestic and foreign social relations, cost, and safety."*

forever been among the group's spiritual homes.

"As those to the north of us are our intimate friends, of our own sea-loving stock" wrote Henry Wise Wood in a 1923 report on the CCA's plan and scope, "it would seem to be too narrow a view of our field did we rate ourselves only a national organization. As we are an off-shore club, composed of blue-water men whose playground lies well beyond the Volstead line, I suggest that we use in our title the word America in its geographical sense and not in its political sense. To do this should result in drawing into close relationship all of the deep-water amateur sailormen of our hemisphere."

With that, Wise Wood turned to the club's two simple objectives: pleasure and service. "Among the services we render each other," he wrote, "we create a clearinghouse of nautical information, covering all of the factors involved in cruising. These include questions of geography, oceanography, meteorology, navigation, seamanship, hull type, sail plan, auxiliary power, commissariat, domestic and foreign social relations, cost, and safety."

When Wilson Fitt became editor of the *CCA Cruising Guide to Nova Scotia* in 2018, he picked up a baton, relay-style, handed along by Nutting and his heirs for a hundred years and counting. But as we've said, Wilson came the long way round to that role.

A few years after *Christina Grant's* sabbatical season in the Caribbean, she again sailed away from the waters of the Canadian Maritimes for a spring cruise to Bermuda. "This is

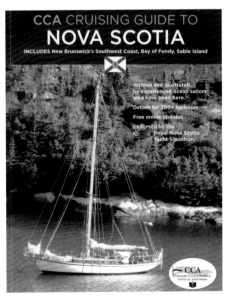

Wilson Fitt knows his native Nova Scotia well. Beginning in 2018, Fitt has edited the *CCA Cruising Guide to Nova Scotia*. He knows the yacht that graces the cover, too, like the back of his hands, because those same hands built her.

usually a weeklong voyage," Wilson told a reporter for his alumni magazine. "I had a crew of friends for the outbound trip and returned singlehanded in five and a half days—all part of the plan, not a mutiny! It was a personal challenge, not something that a person would often get an opportunity to do, and perhaps not something that most people would ever want to do."

In 2009, Wilson embarked on another singlehanded voyage, the kind that would have lit up Nutting's soul: transatlantic to the British Isles by the northern route.

My wife Thelma and I got underway from the home mooring in Chester, Nova Scotia, at suppertime on July 16th after a full day of business meetings in Halifax. We just went a few miles to a nearby cove and unwound over a bottle of wine, a nice meal, and a good sleep before the real voyage started.

The first leg was 550 miles to St. John's Newfoundland, course more or less due east magnetic. We started in a moderate southerly breeze with decent visibility, although both of us were feeling a bit "off our feed," which is usual at the beginning.

Second and third days were foggy, occasionally lifting to mere overcast, with generally moderate favouring breezes, but that night the wind came in at 25+ out of the southeast, putting us hard on the wind under staysail and double-reefed main in heavy rain. Rough and not much fun, but by then we had our sea legs and were doing fine.

The next morning on the Grand Banks brought a fine breeze and heavy fog that by afternoon cleared to a glorious day. At midnight the lighthouse at Cape Race, the southeastern tip of Newfoundland, was in sight and after dawn we had a beautiful view of the Avalon Peninsula as we coasted along to enter the narrows of St. John's, one of the great harbours of the world.

This was a stopover to visit my sister and top up on fuel and water. Thelma flew home, as arranged, and I was underway singlehanded by midafternoon on July 23rd bound for Scotland.

I know that some people think that singlehanded sailing is poor seamanship at best and possibly irresponsible. Near shore, where navigation is demanding and traffic is a constant issue, I think that may be the case. However, once clear of the land, my experience has been that traffic is sparse and there is little or nothing to see. I picked up five ships on the 16-mile AIS alarm on this trip, one of which altered course to pass within sight. Watch-keeping on small boats, even with someone on deck, is a hit-and-miss affair. Most of the time is spent huddled under the spray dodger looking aft or abeam, and the occasional look directly ahead is obscured by sails and gear. It's hard to see something as obvious as a big ship, let alone the much-feared half-submerged container waiting to sink you.

Irresponsible or not, in deep water I content myself with an hourly alarm that prompts me to take a look around, check the radar and AIS, and see that all is well on deck. Sometimes I oversleep.

The first week or so was generally fine with moderate northerly and westerly winds, clear skies, and moderate seas. It was marred only by my discovery that my satellite phone would not work, so I could not check in with home as promised. I did have a gadget called a SPOT that can send a canned message, lat/long, and Google map link by e-mail that worked very well, but I was in a funk at the notion that Thelma would be unnecessarily worried. I ended up speaking to two ships that relayed e-mail messages from me. The captain of the second ship, the *Jaeger Arrow,* seemed to be an enthusiast and altered course to take some pictures and e-mailed them, much to the delight of everyone at home.

Once offshore I always had three or four fulmars in sight. I don't know if they were the same birds all the way across or they worked a relay system. A couple of times a pod of pilot whales accompanied me for hours at a time, breaching and diving in a languid way and squeaking to each other so I could hear them from below. One afternoon a large group of dolphins joined, the acrobats of the sea, coming in from afar at high speed, leaping clear of the water, mingling with the pilot whales, playing under the bow, then disappearing again. The bird population always increased when whales and dolphins were nearby, picking up the table scraps, I suppose.

I played tag with a large low-pressure system for much of the second week. The wind went to the east and I could only fetch northeast on starboard tack. Finally, after getting tired of pounding along in gross discomfort in the general direction of the Faroes, I went over to port tack whereupon the wind blew harder than ever until I gave up and hove to under double-reefed main. By this point it was blowing 35, I suppose—I do not have an anemometer—but the boat and crew were quite comfortable, lying about 45 degrees to the wind and making around 2 knots with 15 degrees of leeway.

This lasted for a half a day, then the wind went light, and the sky cleared slightly. Encouraged, I got underway in a very confused sea, and sure enough the wind came in hard from the southwest as the centre of the low passed. This was good for a while, but it started to back again and by the next morning and before long I was back to pounding along in an easterly, hard on the wind, now making for Rockall. The wind increased, and I repeated the pattern, going about to port tack, getting fed up with going the wrong way and the violent motion, heaving to, and waiting it out.

I thought at the time that this was a new low, but apparently the first one stalled, and I caught up to it again. It blew harder than the first encounter—40 or more, I would say—but after the centre passed, I got underway in the southwesterly with storm jib and double-reefed main and made good time. Very rough with lots of water on the deck, but fast and in the right direction.

I sighted Malin Head at the northwestern tip of Ireland 13-and-a-half days and 1,750 miles out from St John's, as the wind finally eased. The tide was fair as far as Rathlin Island but against me around the Mull of Kintyre. Evening was approaching and, not wanting to continue through the night tired and alone in what seemed like congested waters (land fever), I stopped at Sanda Island for a good supper, a self-congratulatory drink, and a sleep. The next day was windy with rain squalls—typical Scottish weather, I think—as I sailed the remaining 60 miles or so up the Firth of Clyde to Rhu, near Helensburgh, a few miles downstream from Glasgow.

Thelma joined Wilson in Scotland "for a couple of weeks of tourism," then they decommissioned *Christina Grant* at a yard on the Firth of Clyde. The following season, they returned to join the Clyde Cruising Club for its 100th-anniversary cruise to the Hebrides and St. Kilda, and other outlying islands—"a marvelous time," he said of that cruise-in-company. And if you meet Fitt in some anchorage, you can ask him about his return trip home (attempted), *Christina Grant's* unplanned subsequent season in the British Isles, Thelma's prohibition of all future singlehanded passagemaking, and Wilson's double-handed voyage back to Chester with his son.

As Henry David Thoreau said of his own hometown—"I have traveled a good deal in Concord"— Fitt can say the same of his home waters. For the 2017 edition of the CCA's annual *Voyages* magazine he wrote of one particular cruise that deepened his love for and understanding of his own local cruising grounds. "Many years ago, when our three children were small," he wrote, "we spent an idyllic week on Cape Breton's Bras d'Or Lakes on our Herreshoff H-28 ketch, putting the bow up on the shore at Marble Mountain and pitching the tent on the beach. The kids swam, learned to row the dinghy, and messed around in boats to their hearts' content. They say you can't go back, but this summer we did just that, this time

*Christina Grant* welcomed visitors to her bright and tidy cabin, whether in Baddeck, Antigua, or Scotland.

Granddaughter, Olivia, sailing since 10, is happy to take the helm of *Christina Grant*, named for her grandmother.

with two of our grandchildren aboard our 38-foot traditional cutter."

If there was any single cause, perhaps it was this cruise that led to Wilson's taking on the editorship of the *CCA Cruising Guide to Nova Scotia*.

Gretchen McCurdy, her husband Kit of Mahone Bay, have had ties to the CCA's Bras d'Or Station going back decades. She remembers the progression of the Nova Scotia cruising guide back even longer. "The original cruising guides were done by people like Charlie Bartlett in the 1950s," she said. "Some of those folks who were up here in the early years would send them notes, and whenever any of us went out cruising, we all sent updates. The guides were in a loose-leaf multi-ring binder, and every winter we'd get this mailing, and you had to take the old page out and put in the new. Then the Royal Nova Scotia Yacht Squadron and

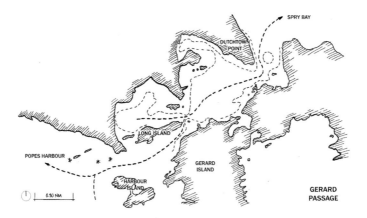

Working with Navionics, Wilson has adapted chartlets for the 2022 cruising guide that strip out extraneous detail and are simpler to use.

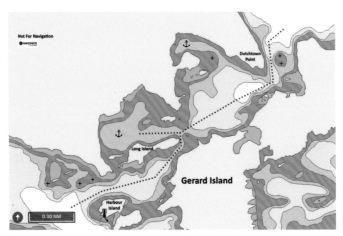

This chartlet is typical of the presentation in the 2020 cruising guide.

Old editions of the cruising guide presented hand-drawn chartlets that arguably included too much detail.

Wilson and Thelma Fitt preparing to welcome guests
in their home waters of Mahone Bay, Nova Scotia.

the CCA got together and published a book."

During that summer Wilson spent with his grandchildren on Nova Scotia's eastern shore, he paid close attention, and took good notes. "Wilson is a multi-talented man," said Gretchen. "As he moved into semi-retirement, he sent in a lot of detailed stuff for the guide. He did it for his own benefit, originally. Then he did it for our Station. Then it spread and was used more widely."

When the CCA envisioned a new modernized series of cruising guides under the umbrella of Cruising Club of America Nautical Publishers—a series that also includes volumes for Newfoundland, Labrador, and the Gulf of St. Lawrence—the brass recruited Wilson to lead the Nova Scotia guide.

"We have a lot of great people in our Station," said Gretchen. "But when you look at Wilson building this boat in his back yard, getting it into the water and spending a year on it, ultimately singlehanding it across the ocean, and then all this work he's done for the CCA—plus, he's open and friendly and generous with his time, willing to help anyone in any situation, a gentleman in every sense of the word—he is the kind of man that was envisioned as a member when they started this 100 years ago."

# PHOTO AND ART CREDITS

Cover, *Dorade* Anthony Blake, artist,
  adbblake@gmail.com
Back flap, photo of Tim, Lesley Davison
Back flap, photo of Sheila, Robbie Benjamin

4 Contents *Dorade* under sail Mystic Seaport,
  Rosenfeld Collection
12 Introduction David Thoreson
16 *Track of the Typhoon,* 1921
18 Mystic Seaport Museum
20-41 *Track of the Typhoon,* 1921
44 Mystic Seaport Museum
47-48 Atkin, William. *Of Yachts and Men.*
  New York: Sheridan House, 1949.
49 Bill Rowntree, PPL Media
55 Mystic Seaport Museum
57 Yachting Magazine
60 MIT Museum
61 Rudder Magazine
64 Kathleen L Kitto, with Creative Commons
  license
70 Tim Murphy
73-77 MIT Museum
80 Mystic Seaport, Rosenfeld Collection
81 Mystic Seaport Museum
82 Albert Pratt, courtesy of Harry Morgan
87 Mystic Seaport, Rosenfeld Collection
89 Mystic Seaport Museum
92 Kyle Dufur
93, 95 Carlo Borlenghi
96 Rolex/Daniel Forster
97 Sharon Green
98 Carlo Borlenghi
100, 105, 106, 107, 110, 111 Robert Johnson
113 Nantucket Historical Society
120 (inset) Queene Hooper Foster
120 Ross Sherbrooke

122 Concordia Company
123-129 Ross Sherbrooke
130, 132, 134 Queene Hooper Foster
137 Copyright Benjamin Mendlowitz
138, 140, 144, 146, 149, 151-155 Mystic
  Seaport Museum Carleton Mitchell
  Collection
155 "Finisterre 1956" Russ Kramer,
  www.russkramer.com
156, 159 Henry Fuller
160 Mystic Seaport Museum Carleton
  Mitchell Collection
161 Mystic Seaport Museum
165 Henry Fuller
173 Mystic Seaport Museum Carleton
  Mitchell Collection
174 Norman Fortier
176 McCurdy & Rhodes, Inc.
177, 179 Jonathan Nye
189 Courtesy of PLL Media
191, 193 Rives Sutherland
196, 198, 199, 202, 208-211
  Stan and Sally Honey
214, 216-217, 211, 229, 232, 236-237
  John Bockstoce
238, 239, 249, 251, 253, 254 Kuhner family
258, 260, 262, 266, David Thoreson
268 Rona House
271, 277 David Thoreson
278, 280, 283, 285, 290, 294, 295 Karen Fryer
296, 298-300, 304-305, 310 Rich Wilson
312, 315-316, 318, 322, 325, 327
  T. L. and Harriet Linskey
328, 330, 334, 340, 345 Kevin Light Photo
346, 349, 353, 355, 359, 360 Wilson Fitt
359 (Interior), 361 John Harries
359, 360 Wilson Fitt

# INDEX